From Setbacks to Success:
THE 1945 CLEVELAND BUCKEYES

EDITED BY VINCE GUERRIERI, THOMAS KERN, AND BILL NOWLIN
ASSOCIATE EDITORS LEN LEVIN AND CARL RIECHERS

Society for American Baseball Research, Inc.
Phoenix, AZ

From Setbacks to Success: The 1945 Cleveland Buckeyes
Edited by Vince Guerrieri, Thomas Kern, and Bill Nowlin
Associate editors Len Levin and Carl Riechers

Design: Rachael E Sullivan
Front cover artwork: Dominick Denaro
Back cover image: 1946 Negro Baseball Yearbook, National Museum of American History

ISBN 978-1-960819-44-4   ebook
ISBN 978-1-960819-45-1   paper

Library of Congress Control Number: 2025913460

Cronkite School at ASU
555 N. Central Ave. #406C
Phoenix, AZ 85004
Phone: (602) 496-1460
Web: www.sabr.org

Contents

Preface and Acknowledgments

This history of the 1945 Cleveland Buckeyes is the eighth in a series of Society for American Baseball Research books about the great Negro League teams of the first half of the twentieth century.

Until the emergence of the Buckeyes in 1942, no Negro League team formed in Cleveland survived more than a year. The timely combination of business manager Wilbur Hayes' business acumen and owner Ernie Wright's financial backing offered more than sufficient traction for the team to gain a foothold in the Forest City and establish its presence throughout the 1940s, even in the face of the challenges of the World War II years. The team would also gain some prominence with a couple of Negro American League pennants and its 1945 Negro League World Series triumph. However, things changed for the Buckeyes, as they did for all Negro League teams, after Jackie Robinson broke the White major-league color barrier in 1947 and the slow trickle of Black ballplayers into the American and National Leagues began. By 1949 Hayes, having bought out Wright, sought to mitigate the team's financial losses by moving it to Louisville. This effort failed, and the team moved back to Cleveland, only to still fail as fans shifted their allegiance to American and National League teams (and their minor-league affiliates), where the more promising Black ballplayers were now situated.

The high-water mark for the Buckeyes was undoubtedly 1945, when they won the Negro American League title and then, against all odds, defeated the perennial Negro National League champion Homestead Grays four games to none in the Negro League World Series.

This book provides a detailed account of the Buckeyes with essays about the players and the team officials who led the team to its World Series triumph. A complete season timeline, the story of League Park and Cleveland Stadium, where the Buckeyes played, the cultural context of the time, and articles about some standout games are also included. Biographies range from those for Wright and Hayes to Cleveland's standout players – Sam Jethroe, Archie Ware, Willie Grace, and Eugene Bremer – as well as player-manager Quincy Trouppe and the many position and role players the team employed. All offer an in-depth window into the makeup of the team and the journey each of these players was on, not only in 1945, but through their entire careers.

In addition to the players with biographies published in this book, a handful of players were identified in *The Negro Leagues Book* (1994), edited by Dick Clark and Larry Lester, as well as in James A. Riley's extensive work, *The Biographical Encyclopedia of The Negro Baseball Leagues*, or on Seamheads, as having appeared at some point with the Buckeyes in 1945. There are few if any details on most

of these players; the transient nature of players led to their ephemeral appearances on the roster or even just the occasional bench warming at best in any given year. As in prior books about the great Negro League teams, we note it is inevitable that we find players who cannot be identified or about whom we can find no evidence of their participation in the year on which the book is focused.

The following individuals have been omitted from this book for such reasons. That said, while they do not merit stand-alone essays, and their appearance in a 1945 Buckeyes game is in fact uncertain, we honor them by this listing and hope that a future researcher might unearth more details about their lives and baseball careers.

- **[First Name?] Breese.** No reference to a Breese appears in Riley's or Lester and Clark's books. However, Seamheads and Retrosheet show a "Breese" (first name and any other particulars unknown) having appeared as a pinch-hitter in a Buckeyes box score in 1945. Breese went 0-for-1. Retrosheet has him in a June 20, 1945, game

First Night Baseball Game of Season at Park Tonight

George Britt, catcher, Parnell Woods, third baseman, and Archie Ware, first baseman, above, for the board of strategy for the Cleveland Buckeyes, who face the Chicago American Giants, in the first night game of the season at 8:30 o'clock tonight at McCulloch Park.

Both teams are members of the Negro American League and present exceptionally strong lineups, including the two leading league hitters last season. Sam Jethroe of Cleveland topped the league's regulars with an average of .353 and collected the most hits, runs, total bases, doubles and stolen bases. Chicago's John Smith

hit .378, but played in only forty-six games after being discharged from the army.

The American Giants, first organized back in 1887, are owned by the president of the league, Dr. J. B. Martin, and play their home games in Comiskey Park in Chicago, home of the White Sox. "Candy Jim" Taylor is back at the helm of the Chicago team after two seasons of winning pennants with the Homestead Grays in the Negro National League.

Quincy Trouppe, star catcher, who has been a successful pilot in Mexico the last several years, is managing the Buckeyes.

Muncie Star-Press, May 14, 1945.

George Britt, Parnell Woods, and Archie Ware prepare for first night game of the 1945 Season.

against the Chicago American Giants played in Muncie, Indiana, a game won by Chicago 5-4.

- **Rayford Finch.** Finch shows up in Retrosheet as having pitched in four exhibition games, all in April. Riley notes his play for the Louisville Buckeyes in 1949 and the Cleveland Buckeyes in 1950 as well as appearances in the ManDak League with Elmwood in 1950 and 1951 and then Winnipeg in 1952. Riley also noted that Finch's "last season in organized baseball was with Danville in the Mississippi-Ohio Valley League in 1953, when he managed only a 1-2 ledger." He was born on July 12, 1924, in Glascock County, Georgia, and died on May 20, 1956, at the age of 31, place of death unknown.[1]

- **Jefferson Guiwn (or Guinn).** Guiwn may have appeared for the Buckeyes in 1945, as suggested by Clark and Lester, but neither Seamheads nor Retrosheet has a record of him in their database. Both Riley and Clark and Lester show him playing as a catcher in the 1943-1944 seasons, as a wartime reserve.[2] There is no information about his origins, birth, or death.

- **Nap Gulley.** A left-handed pitcher and outfielder, Gulley played throughout most of the 1940s. He was born on August 29, 1924, in Huttig, Arkansas. Riley wrote, "This lefthanded hurler had a good fastball, but his 'out pitch' was an overhand drop-curveball."[3] Seamheads does not show him as having played for the Buckeyes in 1945, but Clark and Lester and also Riley do.[4] Retrosheet identifies four games in which Gulley appeared, from mid-April to mid-May.

Napoleon Gulley.

Courtesy of the Negro Leagues Baseball Museum.

Gulley started an April 13 game against the New York Cubans in Fort Worth, Texas, giving up six runs in four innings. He appeared in three subsequent games, all against the Chicago American Giants. Seamheads captures his play in 1943 for the Buckeyes and then time with the Newark Eagles in 1947. He died on August 21, 1999, in Skokie, Illinois, at the age of 74.

- **Lovell Harden.** Lovell "Big Pitch" Harden was a right-handed pitcher born in Lauderdale, Mississippi, on December 17, 1917. Seamheads captures his limited play in 1944 and 1945 for a total of four games over both years. However, Retrosheet identifies 17 games in 1945 in which Harden appeared – eight exhibition games and nine regular-season games in which he either started or relieved. His only other season in the Negro Leagues was 1944, when he pitched in 18 games for the Buckeyes. He died in Erie, Pennsylvania, on November 15, 1996.

- **Phelbert Lawson.** Right-handed pitcher Lawson shows up in Seamheads as having started one game and thrown two-thirds of an inning for Cleveland in 1945. He was relieved by Satchel Davis, who finished the game on August 1, 1945, against the Baltimore Elite Giants in Harrisburg, Pennsylvania. The game ended in a 5-5 tie. He walked two, struck out one, and gave up two runs, both earned, with a home run. The math was not kind; it led to a 27.00 ERA. Lawson was born in Washington, Virginia, on October 22, 1919, and died in Canton, Ohio, on January 5, 2001. His one-game appearance for the Buckeyes is his only recorded time in the Negro Leagues.

- **Willie McCarey.** There is no record of McCarey in Seamheads for 1945, but he is captured in 1944 as having pitched in three games, one for the Buckeyes in which he picked up a win in relief despite giving up three runs in four innings. He also appeared in two games for the Cincinnati-Indianapolis Clowns. There is also no record of his birth or death. Riley wrote, "A wartime player, he appeared briefly with the Cleveland Buckeyes, but his playing time was severely restricted."[5]

- **George (or Al) Minor.** Minor had a good stint with the Buckeyes, first appearing with them in 1944 through 1948. Although Riley states that he played in 1945, Seamheads' depiction of his time with the team includes only 1944, 1946, 1947, and 1948. Box scores yet to be uncovered may find a 1945 connection. His career stats, primarily as a center fielder, show a batting average of .317 and an OPS of .773. Riley notes that Minor "stayed with the [Buckeyes] franchise when the ballclub relocated in Louisville in 1949, his last year in the Negro Leagues."[6]

- **Jesse S. Williams.** Jesse Sheron Williams was born in Meridian, Mississippi, on February 5,

1923, and came up through the ranks, primarily as a catcher. He also played shortstop and in the outfield. According to Riley, Williams "was signed off the Dayton, Ohio, sandlots in 1944 by the Cleveland Buckeyes. After being traded to the Chicago American Giants, he was released and signed again by the Buckeyes as a utility man for the next three years."[7] A switch-hitter, he appeared in five games, as referenced by Seamheads, and batted a paltry .133. However, Retrosheet identified 13 games in which Williams played, eight regular-season games (against Kansas City, Birmingham, Memphis, and Chicago) and five exhibitions. Williams died in Chicago on January 31, 1996.

- **Jesse F. Williams.** Not to be confused with Jesse Sheron Williams, Jesse F. also played for the Buckeyes, but records so far identify only his play (as a catcher) in 1944 and 1947 for certain. He may well have fit Riley's description as a "wartime reserve." He could have filled in when needed for the Buckeyes in 1945, but so far no records have been found. No other information on him is currently available.

Research has uncovered a very unusual item from 1945 – a 12-page booklet on that year's Cleveland Buckeyes team. We have reprinted six of those pages here, featuring team members and management. The remainder of the booklet is composed of advertisements for local businesses. The booklet can be seen in its entirety as part of the Cleveland Public Library Digital Gallery, housed at the library's Sports Research Center, located in the main branch downtown.

This book and those in the series that have preceded it have been made possible by over two dozen SABR members who have collaboratively and diligently researched and written each article. A difficult task in compiling a book like this continues to be the collection of photos of as many as possible of those portrayed in it. Some of the more obscure players pose challenges and we are grateful for the efforts of those who have been able to help in finding visual representations.

We express our thanks to the tireless efforts of our fact-checker, Carl Riechers, and copy editor, Len Levin. They have served in these capacities in earlier books in the series and are consummate professionals at what they do. And just to let everyone know, another book in this series is already in the works – the 1931 Homestead Grays, considered one of the greatest Negro League teams ever. We hope you enjoy yet another window on Black Baseball's past – the 1945 Cleveland Buckeyes.

—**Thomas Kern**

NOTES

1 James A. Riley, *Biographical Encyclopedia of the Negro Baseball Leagues* (New York: Carroll & Graf Publishers, Inc., 1994), 283.

2 Riley 342; Dick Clark and Larry Lester, eds., *The Negro Leagues Book* (Cleveland: Society for American Baseball Research, 1994), 137.

3 Riley, 343.

4 Riley, 342.

5 Riley, 527.

6 Riley, 554.

7 Riley, 852.

1945 Cleveland Buckeyes Timeline

By Vince Guerrieri

As 1945 dawned, World War II was winding down toward its conclusion – even if that wasn't apparent as the year began. After repelling the Nazis in the Battle of the Bulge, Allied troops were moving through Europe, making their way toward Berlin – and presenting the question of how to defeat the Japanese in the Pacific Theater after Germany's surrender.

Sports were in a precarious position as well. High-school, college, and minor-league teams suspended operations as men who would play or coach joined the service. Professional football teams merged, and although major-league baseball was deemed vital for morale in Franklin Roosevelt's "green light letter," a "work or fight" order – similar to the one that curtailed parts of two major-league seasons in World War I – was considered. Ultimately, the All-Star Game was canceled and travel was limited for the 1945 season.

Things were even more tenuous in the Negro leagues. If major-league baseball had a green light, the Negro leagues, formed as a place for Black ballplayers to play for largely Black crowds, had an "amber light," according to the *Call and Post*, the newspaper serving Cleveland's Black community.[1]

In the league's spring meetings, travel was cut 25 percent, and expansion was limited. But it still looked as though a good season was shaping up for Cleveland's entry into the Negro American League, the Buckeyes.

The Buckeyes had started three years earlier, and originally were scheduled to split their time between Cleveland and Cincinnati. But the team made League Park its full-time home – unlike the Indians, who were splitting time between League Park and Municipal Stadium, which had lights installed for night baseball – in 1943.

Prior to the 1945 season, the Buckeyes lured Quincy Trouppe from the Mexican League to become the team's player-manager. Trouppe, a catcher, drew favorable comparisons to Josh Gibson, regarded as the greatest player in the Negro leagues – and probably one of the greatest in any league. "He hits the ball hard and is a fine receiver, with a true fast-throwing arm and the ability to catch and throw with lightning like speed," said Buckeyes general manager Wilbur Hayes.[2]

Pittsburgh Courier sports editor Wendell Smith called the Buckeyes the American League's most balanced team and picked them to win the pennant, writing, "On paper, Cleveland has the best team in the Western circuit."[3]

The season was scheduled to begin on May 6, divided into two halves. The first half would begin with the Buckeyes playing the two-time defending NAL champions, the Birmingham Black Barons, and end on the Fourth of July, with the Buckeyes playing the Monarchs in Kansas City. The Monarchs had won four straight Negro League championships ending in 1942, and were expected to contend again, with their newest player, a former UCLA football star named Jackie Robinson, and Satchel Paige, regarded as one of the best pitchers of his day.

As the Buckeyes made their way through spring training in Oklahoma and Texas, including a doubleheader split against the New York Cubans in New Orleans on April 8, Jethroe was called to try out for the Boston Red Sox.[4] Could the Buckeyes lose their best player – but to the major leagues, which was all White under a "gentlemen's agreement"? As it turned out, the tryout was just to keep some Boston officials happy and allow the Red Sox to continue to use Fenway Park for Sunday baseball. Jethroe was never even informed by the team that he didn't make the cut.

The Buckeyes were ready to open the season against the Barons, who the *Call and Post* said were feeling cocky. But the Buckeyes were feeling optimistic too. "We put up a good fight and held our own," Hayes said after splitting a six-game preseason series in Texas with the Cuban All-Stars. "Trouppe's great catching is making all the difference with our pitching staff."[5]

Eugene Bremer (sometimes spelled Bremmer) got the nod in the first game of the season-opening twin bill at Birmingham. Closing in on age 30, the 5-foot-9 pitcher had 13 years' experience and three all-star appearances (he would add a fourth in 1945).

A native of New Orleans, Bremer started his pro career with his hometown Crescent Stars in 1932. Three years later, he latched on with the Shreveport Giants, followed by a stint with the Cincinnati Tigers, which found a home in the Negro American League when it was founded in 1937. A year later, Bremer ended up in Memphis, where he spent three years. He sat out 1941, but split 1942 between Memphis and the newly formed Ohio Buckeyes. By 1943, the Buckeyes made Cleveland their permanent home, and Bremer continued to pitch for them, as he was turned down from the service in World War II.[6]

Bremer threw a shutout to open the 1945 season, but the Buckeyes didn't fare so well in the nightcap, losing 9-3 to split. Willie Jefferson, who played for the Buckeyes with his brother George, took the loss.

The Buckeyes then made their way north, playing a doubleheader the following Sunday, May 13, against the Chicago American Giants – in two different states. Cleveland beat Chicago 9-8 in a game in Dayton, Ohio, behind home runs by Jethroe and Avelino Cañizares, then crossed the state line to win the nightcap 14-2 in Indianapolis, sparked by a nine-run fifth inning. General manager Wilbur Hayes said the team drew 2,500 in Dayton and 5,000 in Indianapolis.[7]

VASTLY IMPROVED BUCKEYES STRONG IN EVERY FIELD, MAY BRING OUT FANS 10,000 STRONG

Great Pitcher, New Catcher - Manager Plus Cuban Stars Will Supply Flash To Homecoming Team

Cleveland Call and Post, May 26, 1945

The Buckeyes then embarked on an arduous tour leading up to the May 27 home opener. They played a doubleheader against the Cincinnati-Indianapolis Clowns on May 20, met them again for an exhibition game at Red Bird Stadium (later known as Cooper Stadium) in Columbus two days later, and played the Fremont Green Sox at Swayne Field in Toledo two days after that.[8] The Buckeyes split the Sunday twin bill with the Clowns to roll into Cleveland tied for first place with Memphis, at 4-2.

Meanwhile, rumors were circulating about Black players in the White major leagues. Washington Senators owner Clark Griffith was accusing Branch Rickey of setting himself up as "the guiding light behind a new colored U.S. League," issuing an ultimatum to the Negro American and Negro National Leagues to join a new league or else. "Mr. Rickey is attempting to destroy two well organized leagues which have been in existence for some time and in which colored people of this country have faith and confidence," Griffith said.[9]

Nearly 10,000 fans crammed into League Park at East 66th Street and Lexington Avenue on May 27 for the home opener for the Buckeyes, to play the Memphis Red Sox in a doubleheader. The two teams were tied atop the standings of the Negro American League.

Led by player-manager Larry Brown, the Red Sox, like their major-league namesakes of the same time, were always regarded as long on talent but short on results. (They were also one of the few Negro League teams to have their own ballpark, Martin Park.)

Almost immediately, Buckeye fans were given excitement. Cañizares hit an inside-the-park home run, and Parnell Woods stole home for another run as the Buckeyes won the first game 3-1. George Jefferson started for the Buckeyes in the first game, but he gave way to brother Willie. The Buckeyes were able to turn a pair of double plays, a testament to the improved fundamentals player-manager Trouppe had been pushing since spring training dawned. The Buckeyes exploded for five runs in the fifth inning of the second game to gain a 6-2 win and a sweep of the doubleheader.

Three days later, the teams met for a Decoration Day doubleheader on Wednesday, May 30.[10] Again, the Buckeyes swept the Red Sox. The Buckeyes won the first game handily, 14-2, but were down two runs in the second game and down to their last out, when Avelino Cañizares laced a two-run single to tie the game. In the 10th, Woods tripled, and was singled home with the winning run by Archie Ware.

The Buckeyes had won four straight from the Red Sox, and were now sitting alone atop the standings, two games up in the loss column over the perpetual power Kansas City Monarchs.

As June dawned, *Call and Post* sports editor Bob Williams was completely sold on the Buckeyes. "They are quite a ball club, fortified in all departments," he said.[11]

Williams gave most of that credit to owner Ernie Wright, who was more than willing to spend for a championship, and one of Wright's key acquisitions, player-manager Quincy Trouppe. Williams's column in the June 2 edition of the weekly newspaper exhorted fans to support the team. "Cleveland fans will help get that championship team by their support and attendance at the home games," he wrote.[12]

Buckeyes Trounce Memphis Twice 3-1, 6-2; Play Clowns Here Sunday

Brilliant Opening Games Show Greatness As Buckeyes Prepare for Clowns Sunday

Cleveland Call and Post, June 2, 1945

The Clowns were scheduled to come to Cleveland the following weekend, but rain washed out the scheduled doubleheader on June 3. The Buckeyes then took to the road, with games in Texas, Oklahoma, and Arkansas. They won three of four from the Clowns, losing to them in Buffalo on June 10, and six of eight from the Red Sox, who were quickly becoming the team's punching bag. The Buckeyes also beat the Kansas City Monarchs 5-0 in Belleville, Illinois, on June 8, coming within one hit of a perfect game. The Buckeyes were up two games on the Monarchs in the loss column in the Negro American League when they returned to Cleveland for a doubleheader against the Chicago American Giants on June 17, "drunk with recent successes" with "blood in their collective eyes and a yen for bear," according to the *Call and Post*.[13] But the Buckeyes were only able to split the twin bill against the American Giants – and might not have even done that were it not for a controversial call.

The first game seemed interminable, locked in a tie going into the 13th inning. Cañizares walloped a double to lead off the home half of the inning. Ducky Davenport hit a comebacker to the pitcher, Gready McKinnis, who tried unsuccessfully to take Cañizares out at third. Davenport was safe at first, and the winning run was 90 feet away from home. An intentional walk loaded the bases, and Parnell Woods was up to bat.

With the infield pulled in, Woods hit a chopper to short. The shortstop threw home. It was a bang-bang play, and catcher Tommie Dukes missed the tag on Cañizares. Umpire Harry Walker called the runner safe, winning the game for the Buckeyes. Walker was immediately besieged by Chicago players and manager Candy Jim Taylor, who had come to Chicago after leading the Homestead Grays to back-to-back Negro World Series. Police had to separate the umpire from the American Giants.

Disputed Umpire's Decision Almost Disrupts Buckeyes--Giant Series

VISITORS WIN NIGHTCAP AFTER
BUCKEYES GAIN 2-1 VICTORY
IN CONTROVERSIAL DECISION
Players Mob Umpire Harry Walker For Ruling
In Thirteenth Inning Of Opener;
Police Restore Order

Cleveland Call and Post, June 23, 1945

Walker later said that Dukes missed the tag, and his foot was off home plate, so Cañizares was safe at home.

The second game started without incident, and the American Giants beat the Buckeyes 6-1. The two teams met for another doubleheader the following weekend – after games in Dayton, Indianapolis, Muncie, Indiana, and Toledo – as the end of the first half of the season drew near.

The Buckeyes chased Lefty McKinnis from the mound in the fourth inning, and then four innings later, battered Sug Cornelius. The Buckeyes batted around in the eighth inning, scoring eight runs on the way to a 17-2 win that saw every Buckeye player get a hit and score a run. George Jefferson got the win on the mound for Cleveland. There was still offense to come in the second game, a 10-1 win for the Buckeyes. Sam Jethroe went 7-for-9 at the plate in the doubleheader, 3-for-5 in the first game, and 4-for-4 in the nightcap, including an inside-the-park home run.

As June drew to a close, the Buckeyes were 27-9, with a three-game lead over the second-place Birmingham Black Barons and 11 games up on the Kansas City Monarchs. Jethroe was leading the league in hits, total bases, triples (with Trouppe), and home runs. Buckeyes teammates Archie Ware and Parnell Woods led the league in RBIs and stolen bases respectively.

The next stop was Ruppert Stadium in Kansas City, where the Buckeyes played the Monarchs – four games in as many days – a doubleheader on July 1, and another twin bill on Independence Day. The Buckeyes swept the first doubleheader, coming from behind in both games, and won the holiday doubleheader as well.

BUCKEYES LEADING, TOP AMERICAN CIRCUIT IN BATTING, FIELDING, CLINCH GRIP ON FIRST HALF HONOR

Cleveland Call and Post, July 7, 1945

The Buckeyes then swept the Cubans in a July 8 exhibition doubleheader, including a win over Luis Tiant Sr., and returned home as first-half champions, with a record of 31-9.

BUCKEYES, BLACK CRACKERS IN FINAL SERIES CLASSIC TONIGHT
Winner Of Series To Meet Homestead Grays

Atlanta Daily World, July 12, 1945

The Buckeyes beat the Atlanta Black Crackers, 9-1 in an exhibition July 12,[14] before opening the second half, like the first half, against the Birmingham Black Barons. They first played a doubleheader in Louisville on July 15, and then the next day returned to Cleveland, not to League Park on the city's east side, but 60 blocks west to Municipal Stadium, on the lakefront in downtown Cleveland, which had more than double the seating capacity – and lights. It was the first home night game of the season for the Buckeyes, who had a significant lead on the Barons, in part because the Barons played a fuller exhibition schedule on the East Coast.

The game was to benefit the Future Outlook League, an organization founded a decade earlier to get jobs for African Americans.[15] Combating the prejudice of the era with tactics like rent strikes and boycotts (one slogan was "Don't buy where you can't work"), the league was able to find work for many African Americans.[16] American entry into World War II led to increased employment opportunities for everyone, including African Americans, and the league was starting to refocus as the war drew to an end.

The game was part of a $150,000 fundraising campaign for a recreation center (ultimately, never built as the league's power continued to dissipate into the 1950s), and a crowd of more than 15,000 was anticipated – including, rumor had it, major-league scouts who were evaluating the Negro League talent, which the Buckeyes and Barons had in abundance.

For the Buckeyes, not only did George Jefferson have a record of 7-1 pitching, but he was batting .433, 31 points ahead of Ed Steele, the Birmingham outfielder in second place. Jefferson's teammate with the Buckeyes, Sam Jethroe, was hitting .394, and led the league with 31 runs, 56 hits, and 84 total bases. Parnell Woods led the league with 30 RBIs. Overall, the Buckeyes led the league with a .313 batting average, 213 runs scored, and 8 home runs. Defensively, they had a .965 fielding percentage, nine points over Kansas City, in second place. And as good as the Buckeyes were, they were getting better. They added Duro Davis from the Indianapolis Clowns.

The game was expected not just to be an event, but a pitched battle between two of the best teams in the Negro Leagues. And it was a battle – just not the kind that was envisioned.

In the bottom of the third, umpire James Thompson called the Buckeyes' Avelino Cañizares safe in a bang-bang play at first. Words were exchanged, and Thompson found himself in a confrontation with several Barons players. Home-plate umpire Harry Walker threw out the Barons' Lorenzo Davis, nicknamed Piper for his hometown in Alabama. Piper Davis, a foot taller and about 60 pounds heavier than Thompson, sucker-punched the umpire, who "fell over backwards like an obedient ten-pin, without even buckling in the knees."[17]

The crowd turned instantly. Fans were enraged, and "had the shameful incident occurred at League Park, where the fans are closer to the playing field, serious consequences might have developed."[18] Davis left under a police escort and Thompson swore out a complaint for assault and battery.[19] The Buckeyes won 6-2, almost as an afterthought.

After a game against the Barons the next day in Columbus, the Buckeyes' next opponent was the Clowns, the team that was trying to supplant the Buckeyes in Cincinnati. The Clowns began as an independent barnstorming team, the Ethiopian Clowns. They then split their time between Cincinnati and Indianapolis (ultimately making Indianapolis their full-time home starting in 1946). And after the debacle in the night game the previous week at Municipal Stadium between the Buckeyes and the Birmingham Black Barons, the Clowns lost to the Buckeyes in a game in St. Marys, Ohio, on July 21, and then played a doubleheader at League Park the following day.

It would be their first trip to Cleveland that season, and the Buckeyes took both games. The game was also notable for an appearance by James Thompson, who had been sucker-punched by the Barons' Piper Davis a week earlier. Davis, in addition to facing a criminal charge of assault and battery, had been suspended by Barons owner Abe Saperstein (who also owned the Harlem Globetrotters basketball team – which Davis played for as well).

Up next for the Buckeyes, on July 24, was probably the most famous Negro League team of all time: the Kansas City Monarchs. The big draw – and he would definitely take the mound against the Buckeyes – was ace pitcher Leroy "Satchel" Paige. Satch, who would find himself in front of Cleveland baseball fans again just three years later in an Indians uniform, was an ageless wonder who could seemingly pitch every day. He was already nearly 20 years into a career that saw him pitch across the Western Hemisphere, in the Negro Leagues (including, briefly in Cleveland for the 1931 Cleveland Cubs), on barnstorming tours, and in

Central and South America (occasionally, as he'd tell it, at the point of a gun).[20]

The Monarchs were a dynasty in the Negro Leagues in the early 1940s, thanks in no small part to Paige. But they also featured a fierce competitor and all-around athlete named Jack Roosevelt Robinson. Jackie Robinson was an Army veteran and lettered in four sports at UCLA. He had never played professional baseball and was coaching (and occasionally playing) college basketball at Samuel Houston College in Austin, Texas, when the Monarchs came calling.

And Robinson stepped into the batter's box against Eugene Bremer in the top of the ninth at League Park, with the Monarchs down 3-0. He hit a long fly ball more than 400 feet down the left-field line, and it cleared the fence – just inches outside the foul line, under the watchful eye of third-base umpire James Thompson, making his return to umpiring after his knockout at the hands of Piper Davis a little more than a week earlier at Municipal Stadium. Robinson then stepped back into the batter's box and hit another drive, not as long, but long enough down the right-field line to end the shutout with a solo home run.

John Scott then hit a comebacker to Bremer for the first out. Lee Moody singled to right, and then advanced to second on a groundout by pinch-hitter Hilton Smith. Chester Gray came in to pinch-run and scored on a double by Jack Matchett. It was now a one-run game with the tying run at second and two outs. Pinch-hitter Jim LaMarque flied out to end the game.

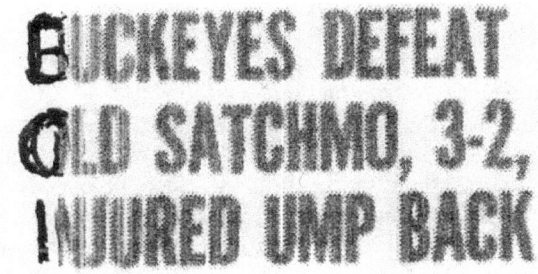

Cleveland Call and Post, July 28, 1945

The pennant was within reach for the Buckeyes, but first came the year's biggest showcase: the East-West Game, the Negro League all-star game.

The East-West All-Star Game started in the same year as the major-league-baseball All-Star Game, 1933. In fact, both were played at Comiskey Park in their first year.

The major league All-Star Game was originally conceived as a one-off by *Chicago Tribune* sports editor Arch Ward to coincide with the Century of Progress World's Fair of 1933, but became an annual tradition, for decades providing the only opportunity outside of exhibitions and the World Series where players from the National and American Leagues would meet.

The East-West Game was divided not by leagues but by geographic regions, with Pittsburgh serving as the westernmost point to be considered part of the "East." The game was created to be a moneymaker for owners of Negro League teams, who were subject not just to the Depression, but to the prejudices of the day – which could also take a toll on their pocketbooks.

By 1945, the game had become an event unto itself, even regularly outdrawing the mainstream All-Star Game – a trend that would continue by default that year, as wartime travel restrictions eliminated the All-Star Game, replacing it with a series of exhibitions.

While the White All-Star Game had become a moveable feast, traveling to different cities, the East-West Game stayed on the South Side of Chicago, and became a social event for African Americans, with celebrities like Louis Armstrong, Lena Horne, and Joe Louis in attendance. In fact, historian Larry Lester has written that the East-West Game was the biggest event in African American culture except for a fight by the Brown Bomber, Joe Louis.[21]

In 1945, four Cleveland Buckeye players were selected for the game: catcher-manager Quincy Trouppe, first baseman Archie Ware, pitcher Eugene Bremer, and outfielder Buddy Armour as a reserve. The East-West Game was more democratic than the All-Star Game. Although fans selected the lineups for the first two midsummer classics, for the following 11 years, teams were selected by the managers. The East-West Game lineup was voted on by fans, not at ballparks, but through African American newspapers like the *Pittsburgh Courier* and the *Chicago Defender*.

But two of the biggest Negro League stars were not at the game. Josh Gibson had been suspended by his team, the Homestead Grays, for violations of team rules. Satchel Paige refused to play because of a dispute with ownership over how much he'd get paid (as the most popular player in the Negro Leagues, Paige had the kind of leverage that eluded many players; in fact, it was only the year previous that players started receiving a stipend of $200 for playing in the game).[22]

The 1945 East-West Game, on July 29, was the poorest attended since 1939 – still drawing more than 31,000 fans – thanks in part to scalpers who were asking particularly outlandish prices. The West struck first in the second. The Memphis Red Sox' Neal Robinson legged out an infield hit. The Indianapolis Clowns' Alex Radcliffe hit a screamer to right field, ostensibly within reach of Wild Bill Wright of the Baltimore Elite Giants. But Wright didn't have his sunglasses, and lost the ball in the sun, letting Robinson take third. Robinson and Radcliffe both scored on Ware's hit into center field. Ware was then caught trying to steal second by Baltimore catcher Roy Campanella.

Trouppe was walked – the first of three free passes for the day – so pitcher Tom Glover could face pitcher Verdell Mathis of Memphis. He singled to left and Trouppe took third. Glover was then relieved by Bill Ricks of

Philadelphia, who faced the Monarchs' Jesse Williams. Williams hit a long drive to right, and Wright – still without his shades – lost what turned into a triple to score Mathis and Trouppe. The West added four more runs in the third for what turned out to be an insurmountable lead. The East put up five runs in the top of the ninth, but their comeback came up short in a 9-6 win for the West, their third triumph in a row.

Ware ended up with two hits and three RBIs. Trouppe got a hit in his only official at-bat. While Trouppe, Ware, Bremer, and Armour were in Chicago, the rest of the Buckeyes were playing the New York Cubans at the Polo Grounds on July 29, dropping both ends of a doubleheader.

There was little more than a month left in the regular season after the East-West All-Star Game, and the Buckeyes, already winners of the first half of the season, had designs on taking the second half as well – and a date in the Negro World Series.

The Buckeyes didn't have the star power of some other teams – the Homestead Grays had Josh Gibson, regarded as the best power hitter in the Negro leagues (and possibly all of baseball), and the Monarchs had Satchel Paige and Jackie Robinson – but they played well together and had more than their fair share of talent. The entire lineup was hitting over .300, led by Sam Jethroe, who had raised his batting average to a robust .409 and led the league with 16 stolen bases and eight triples. Buddy Armour was fourth in the league with a .360 average, and Archie Ware led the league with 36 RBIs.[23]

The Buckeyes then went to Detroit, making their first appearance at Briggs Stadium, with an August 5 doubleheader against the Chicago American Giants. The Buckeyes cruised to a win in the first game, 7-3, behind the solid pitching of George Jefferson, and were leading 3-2 after five innings of the second game when Detroit Tigers groundskeeper Neil Conway insisted that the game be called due to inclement weather. Conway was rushed by Chicago players and sought police protection. The next day, he protested to stadium management. "The question of whether to continue the use of the stadium to Negro ball clubs is now being studied," wrote the *Chicago Defender*.[24]

In exhibition on August 7 in South Bend, the Buckeyes clobbered the Hoosier Beers 13-0 on 21 hits.[25]

Controversy continued to follow the Buckeyes, who won an exhibition game by forfeit on August 8 in Harrisburg against the Elite Giants. Phelbert Lawson was brought on in relief for the Buckeyes in the bottom of the ninth in a game tied, 5-5. Lawson was accused of doctoring the ball, and Henry Kimbro refused to step into the batter's box unless a new ball was put in play, despite being ordered to do so by umpire Sonny Arp. Kimbro was called out, and further protestations led to Arp's awarding the game to the Buckeyes by forfeit.

The Buckeyes went to Newark to play an exhibition twin bill against the Eagles on August 12. In the first game, they faced a pitcher who within a few years became part of a major-league organization. Don Newcombe would be signed by the Dodgers the following year and was with the parent club in 1949. Newcombe shut out the Buckeyes in a 4-0 win.

And it appeared that the Buckeyes were going to be swept in the doubleheader, down 3-2 in the top of the seventh, when Cañizares – who'd booted a key grounder in the first game – smashed a triple to center field. He came around to score when Ware – who also allowed an unearned run in the first game with an error – singled, and the game was tied.

In the top of the ninth, Buddy Armour walked and took second on a sacrifice by Earl Ashby. Up stepped Cañizares, who lifted a single into left field, driving in what turned out to be the game-winning run.

The next stop was Birmingham, where the Buckeyes played a doubleheader against the Barons on August 19, beating them once and tying them in the nightcap.

The Buckeyes played the Barons throughout the South, as well as a weeklong series against the Red Sox, with five games in Memphis before returning to Cleveland for a four-game set with the Red Sox, including a twilight-night doubleheader at Municipal Stadium on August 30, to benefit the Future Outlook League. A huge crowd was expected, to celebrate the Buckeyes as well as the end of World War II – and the accompanying lifting of wartime travel restrictions.

The Buckeyes won the first game handily, 7-2, as George Jefferson got his 11th win of the year. Quincy Trouppe homered for the Buckeyes. George's brother Willie Jefferson pitched the second game, and Buddy Armour hit a home run to tie the game at 4-4. The game ended in a tie, called on account of darkness.

The second half of the season ended with a doubleheader at League Park on September 2 against the Chicago American Giants. Team general manager Wilbur Hayes was honored with a new car to replace the Chevrolet he had used to travel with the team – racking up more than 250,000 miles. The gift took on added significance since cars were hard to come by. (There were no new cars made for the 1943-45 model years, as auto companies had switched to wartime production.) The Buckeyes then swept Chicago and appeared to win the second-half crown as well to serve as the undisputed league champions, with a total record of 72-30, including a regular-season record of 53-15.[26]

Buckeyes Gain Undisputed Title As League Champions

Cleveland Call and Post, September 8, 1945

The Buckeyes would meet the Homestead Grays in the Negro World Series.

The Grays were a dynasty, the two-time defending World Series champs and winners of the last nine Negro National League pennants. The 1945 team had no fewer than five future Hall of Famers: Cool Papa Bell, Ray Brown, Josh Gibson, Buck Leonard, and Jud Wilson. But *Cleveland Call and Post* sports editor Bob Williams – who would serve as one of three commissioners for the World Series, with legendary *Pittsburgh Courier* sports editor Wendell Smith and Afro-American Newspapers sports editor Art Carter – liked the Buckeyes' chances.

"They have made every team in the league look like a bunch of amateurs this season," he wrote. "And if they fail to cop the title it will be the greatest upset imaginable."[27]

Playing baseball in the Negro Leagues was a nomadic existence. It wasn't uncommon for a team to play on multiple home fields in the same season. The Buckeyes started as a team dividing its time between Cleveland and Cincinnati. The Clowns divided their schedule between Cincinnati and Indianapolis, and the Homestead Grays – started in their eponymous city outside of Pittsburgh – played most of their home games at Griffith Stadium in Washington.

It also entailed numerous exhibitions (although in the days before a strong players' union, the same thing occurred in the White major leagues as well). So it wasn't too out of the ordinary to see the Buckeyes take on the Chattanooga Choo Choos in an exhibition on September 9, four days before they were slated to take on the Grays in the Negro World Series.

The Buckeyes beat the Choo Choos 14-5 in a perfect tune-up before more than 5,000 fans at League Park, which hadn't hosted a World Series game since the Indians beat the Brooklyn Robins in the 1920 fall classic. But while the Buckeyes hosted the first game of the World Series, it wasn't at League Park. It was under the lights at Municipal Stadium.

It was a long trip for the Buckeyes, who were likened to a team of scrubs just three years earlier. *Call and Post* sports editor Bob Williams said that Indians owner Alva Bradley, general manager Roger Peckinpaugh, and manager Lou Boudreau attended a game "and went away laughing because of the sloppy, untrained players who cavorted like second-rate sandlotters across the diamond."[28]

Willie Jefferson got the nod for the Buckeyes in the series opener on September 13, while Leroy "Lefty" Welmaker started for the Grays. The pitchers traded goose eggs for the first 6½ innings, but in the bottom of the seventh, Quincy Trouppe tripled to deep center, and after Buddy Armour struck out swinging, Johnnie Cowan hit a fly ball to left field that was deep enough to score Trouppe. The Buckeyes were on the board.

In the next inning, Archie Ware hit a screaming line-drive single to left field and advanced to second when Parnell Woods walked. Willie Grace hit a high fly ball to right field, which dropped in for a hit, giving Jefferson an insurance run – which he would need.

In the top of the ninth, Dave Hoskins singled to center with one out, took second on a walk to Buck Leonard and scored on Josh's Gibson single. Jefferson got Sammy

Bankhead to ground into a double play to end the game and give the Buckeyes their first World Series winning game ever.

The second game of the Negro World Series was played three days later, allowing the Buckeyes time to play an exhibition game in Dayton, Ohio, against the Kittyhawks, a team from Wright Field, home to a US Army Air Corps base. The Buckeyes blanked the Kittyhawks, 7-0, handing them their second defeat of the year. (The only other loss was to the Great Lakes Naval Training Station, a team populated with ringers from the White major leagues.)

Eugene Bremer got the nod to start for the Buckeyes, against the Grays' Johnny Wright. The Grays scratched across a run in the fourth and another in the fifth, but the Buckeyes tied the game in the bottom of the seventh when Willie Grace hit a home run over the towering right-field fence at League Park. Buddy Armour then doubled to right field and scored when Bremer's grounder to second was booted by Jelly Jackson.

In the bottom of the ninth of the tie game, Trouppe doubled to right and took third on a passed ball by Gibson (who by then was suffering from frequent headaches brought on by the brain tumor that would kill him within 18 months). Wright walked the next two batters to pitch to Bremer, who stroked the game-winning hit to right field.

The Buckeyes had a two-games-to-none lead in the World Series. The Grays won an exhibition in Dayton on September 14. Then the World Series headed to Forbes Field in Pittsburgh for Game Three.

"The 1945 World Series program should turn out to be a corker," Williams wrote in the *Call and Post* before the road trip started.[29]

The Buckeyes had taken that commanding lead with them into Pittsburgh, but the talent of the Grays, who fielded five future Hall of Famers, made no lead insurmountable. They had won the previous eight Negro National League pennants and two Negro League World Series. They hadn't been shut out in four years.

BUCKEYS AIM, TO DETHRONE HOMESTEAD GRAYS, CZARS OF ALL BASEBALL FOR SIX YEARS

Cleveland Call and Post, September 15, 1945

That changed with Game Three of the 1945 Negro World Series, on September 18, 1945. Rain forced the cancellation of the game in Pittsburgh at Forbes Field, so the teams traveled on to Washington. Griffith Stadium – the other "home field" for the Grays – was to host Game Four, but instead, it hosted Game Three. In fact, the field didn't get much of

a breather, hosting the Washington Senators and Detroit Tigers that day and the Buckeyes and Grays that night.

Before the game Buckeyes general manager Hayes got a telegram from Harold Burton, the former mayor of Cleveland, then serving as a Republican in the US Senate. (One of his former colleagues, Harry Truman, had just become president, and a day after Game Three, Truman would nominate Burton to the US Supreme Court as a bipartisan gesture. Burton was approved by voice vote – and would be one of the behind-the-scenes forces in 1954 for *Brown vs. Board of Education*, the Supreme Court decision striking down school segregation.)

George Jefferson got the nod for the Buckeyes, and he was firing bullets, giving up just three hits in his 17th win of the season. He was also the beneficiary of sparkling defense behind him. Second baseman Johnny Cowan did the baseball equivalent of standing on his head, with five fine fielding plays – including one throw from his knees in the third, and a leaping snare of a liner by Buck Leonard. A.B. "Happy" Chandler, the US senator from Kentucky recently appointed baseball commissioner, was said to have remarked to George Preston Marshall, "That was the best play I've ever seen in my life." (Chandler's presence at the game isn't surprising. Marshall's, on the other hand, was; the longtime owner of the NFL's Washington Redskins might have been the biggest racist in sports.[30]) Jefferson was staked to a 3-0 lead in the third inning. Willie Grace sacrificed home the first run of the game, and a bases-loaded single by Buddy Armour scored two more runs. The Buckeyes tacked on an insurance run in the ninth and won 4-0. They were one win away from toppling the Grays from atop the Negro Leagues.

Cleveland Has Grays Reeling and Rockin
Battling Bucks Win 2-1, 4-2, 4-0

Pittsburgh Courier, September 22, 1945

Game Four was at Shibe Park in Philadelphia on September 20. The Buckeyes got on the board in the top of the first thanks to a bases-loaded error by Jelly Jackson that scored two runs. It was all starting pitcher Frank Carswell would need.

Carswell picked up right where George Jefferson led off, piling up goose eggs. He got into a little jam in the third inning, hitting Jud Wilson with a pitch. Sam Bankhead erased the runner with a double play, but Ray Brown walked and then took third on a single by Jerry Benjamin. Carswell walked Cool Papa Bell to load the bases, then Dave Hoskins hit a chopper to second, forcing Bell out to end the inning.

The Buckeyes tacked on a run in the fourth on a fly ball by Johnnie Cowan, and two more in the seventh on a two-run single by Sam Jethroe. By then, the outcome of the game wasn't in doubt.

THE 1945 CLEVELAND BUCKEYES

Buckeyes Win World Championship

Chicago Defender, September 29, 1945

The Buckeyes won the game, 5-0, their second straight shutout of the Grays, to sweep the World Series. "A betting man with a mad crazy hunch could have gotten rich, literally rich off that series," wrote Bob Williams in the *Call and Post*. "Nobody with a grain of reason power would have conceded that Buckeyes four straight victories over the Grays."

Cleveland Rules Baseball World

Win Four
In Row to
Dethrone
Homestead

Pittsburgh Courier, September 29, 1945

Having followed the team all year, Williams knew they were special. But even he had no idea what they were capable of. "These fellows were great, and we hadn't really known them at all!"[31]

Bucks Beat Grays Four Straight To Win World Title

WINNERS BLANK
FADING CHAMPS
IN FINAL GAME

Michigan Chronicle, September 29, 1945

The Buckeyes' Negro League championship was a big deal – to the Black community. Although the team was covered regularly by the *Call and Post*, it received little notice in the mainstream press. But it wasn't long before Black baseball players were the toast of Cleveland – although not with the Buckeyes.

Integration was at hand. In its October 29 edition – while the paper was still running sports features on the Buckeyes' championship – the front page of the *Call and Post* proclaimed that Jackie Robinson had been signed by the Dodgers organization, and would play the following year for Montreal.

Meanwhile, Bill Veeck, son of the former Cubs executive, had gotten into baseball himself, buying the minor-league Milwaukee Brewers in 1942. After service in the war – where he'd lost part of a leg – he bought the Cleveland Indians in 1946.

In July 1947 Veeck signed Larry Doby, who had played against the Buckeyes with the Newark Eagles. By that time, the National League had already been integrated, by Jackie Robinson – another former Buckeye opponent, with the Kansas City Monarchs. After playing in Montreal in 1946, Robinson made his major-league debut with the Brooklyn Dodgers on April 15, 1947.

Also by 1947, the Buckeyes were alone as tenants of League Park. Veeck realized that he was leaving money on the table with every game played at East 66th and Lexington, and made Municipal Stadium the Indians' full-time home. League Park was also home to an NFL team, the Cleveland Rams, but they decamped for Los Angeles after their 1945 season – which also ended in a championship. The new football team in town, the Browns of the All-America Football Conference, practiced at League Park, but used Municipal Stadium for games.

After a lackluster 1946 season in which they finished third in the NAL, the Buckeyes won the pennant in 1947 but lost the World Series to the New York Cubans. By then, the writing was on the wall for them and for Negro League teams. The last Negro World Series was the following year, a win by the Homestead Grays. That same year, the Indians won the World Series – aided in large part by contributions from Black players Doby and Satchel Paige, whose signing was decried in some corners as a publicity stunt. (Paige went 6-1 for a team that was tied on the last day of the regular season, so every victory counted.)

By 1949, the Buckeyes had moved their home base to Louisville, limped through that season, and moved back to Cleveland for the 1950 season but then disbanded.

Although the White major leagues suddenly found themselves stocked with Negro leagues talent, only two of the players from the 1945 Buckeyes made it to the major leagues. Sam Jethroe was named National League Rookie of the Year in 1950 for the Boston Braves. (He remains the oldest player ever to win the honor, at 33.) Quincy Trouppe played for one year for the Indians as well. The title of his autobiography? *Twenty Years Too Soon.*

NOTES

1   "Negro American League Season Begins May 6," *Cleveland Call and Post*, March 17, 1945: 6B.

2   "Buckeyes Split Two with Cubans, Good Spring Games," *Cleveland Call and Post*, April 14, 1945: 19.

3   Wendell Smith, "The Sports Beat," *Pittsburgh Courier*, May 5, 1945: 16.

4   Jackie Robinson was also invited. Further reading: https://sabr.org/journal/article/jackie-robinson-in-1945-from-boston-tryout-to-a-negro-leagues-star/.

5   "Bucks Play Cubans, 'Rounding Out Nicely,'" *Cleveland Call and Post*, April 21, 1945: 18.

6   James A. Riley, *The Biographical Encyclopedia of the Negro Baseball Leagues* (New York: Carroll & Graf Publishers, 1994), 104. The book doesn't specify why Bremer was rejected for military service, but notes that he suffered a concussion and skull fracture in a 1942 car wreck near Geneva, Ohio, in which two of his teammates were killed.

7   "Bucks Set to Play in Cleveland May 27," *Cleveland Call and Post*, May 19, 1945: 6B.

8   These Green Sox appear to have been a local semipro team. Prior to US involvement in World War II, the Green Sox were a team in the Class-D Ohio State League. Managers included Luke Sewell and Slim Caldwell.

9   Art Flynn, "Griff Says B.R. Would Be Czar of Negro Loops," *The Sporting News*, May 24, 1945: 2.

10 Decoration Day, the forerunner to Memorial Day, was annually commemorated on that date; it wasn't until the 1968 passage of the Uniform Monday Holiday Act that it took its place as the last Monday in May.

11   Bob Williams, "Sports Rambler," *Cleveland Call and Post*, June 2, 1945: 6B.

12   "Sports Rambler," June 2, 1945.

13   Bob Williams, "Buckeyes Leading League; Play Chicago American Giants Here Sunday," *Cleveland Call and Post*, June 16, 1945: 6B.

14   Joel W. Smith, "Cleveland Buckeyes Top Black Crax, 9-1," *Atlanta Daily World*, July 13, 1945: 5.

15   "Future Outlook League Night Game to Feature League-Leading Bucks," *Cleveland Call and Post*, July 7, 1945: 7B.

16   https://case.edu/ech/articles/f/future-outlook-league.

17   Bob Williams, "Attack on Umpire Mars Ball Classic," *Cleveland Call and Post*, July 21, 1945: 1A.

18   "Attack on Umpire Mars Ball Classic."

19   Davis ended up being fined $250 by the league, and was on the hook for an additional $230 in court costs and medical bills.

20   https://nlbm.mlblogs.com/ciudad-trujillo-the-best-baseball-team-youve-never-heard-of-e548db6b98f9.

21   Larry Lester, *Black Baseball's National Showcase: The East-West All-Star Game, 1933-1953* (Lincoln: University of Nebraska Press, 2001), 1.

22   *Black Baseball's National Showcase*, 269.

23   "Jethroe Retains Am. League Batting Lead," *Atlanta Daily World*, August 16, 1945: 3.

24   "Bucks Defeat Chicago Twice; Calling of Second Creates Trouble," *Chicago Defender* (national edition), August 11, 1945: 7.

25   Bob Overaker, "Beers Lose; Host to Memphis Thursday," *South Bend Tribune*, August 8, 1945: 16.

26   Like many teams in the Negro Leagues, the Buckeyes played many games that didn't count in the standings.

27   Bob Williams, "Sports Rambler," *Cleveland Call and Post*, September 8, 1945: 6B.

28   "Sports Rambler," September 8, 1945.

29   Bob Williams, "Sports Rambler," *Cleveland Call and Post*, September 22, 1945: 6B.

30   Marshall famously owned the last team in the NFL to integrate, doing so reluctantly to play at the new D.C. Stadium, and when he died in 1969, his will established a charity, the Redskin Foundation, specifying that it "shall never use, contribute or apply any money or property for any purpose which supports or employs the principle of racial integration in any form."

31   Bob Williams, "Sports Rambler," *Cleveland Call and Post*, September 29, 1945: 6B.

Buddy Armour

By Jeff Findley

Although he didn't enjoy the prominence of many players of his era, Alfred Armour posted a solid professional baseball career, including three all-star appearances and a Negro League World Series championship in 1945. Because the peak years of his career predated talks of integrating the White major leagues, he never attained enduring fame on the scale of some of his peers, evidenced by a telling comment in 1941 when a preview article naming reserves for the Ninth Annual East-West All-Star Game in Chicago noted, "Alfred Armour, St. Louis (a sensational centerfielder who should be in the starting lineup ... can hit and throw: lack of publicity has kept this boy out of the headlines)."[1]

Armour was born on April 27, 1915, in Madison, Mississippi. The historical record of his youth has yet to be found. The family moved to Carbondale, Illinois, at some point before 1930, as that year's census shows him living there in the household of his grandparents, Alfred and Fannie. Alfred was a laborer at a tire factory, and Fannie was a laundress for a private family.[2] Armour's biological father, the son of his grandfather and also named Alfred, died in 1932, when Buddy was 17.[3]

The earliest mention of Alfred in the local press was in 1929, for his eighth-grade graduation from Crispus Attucks High School,[4] an African American school organized in 1920, which operated independently until its students were integrated into Carbondale Community High School in 1964.[5]

Attucks offered basketball and track and field as sports. The possibility of baseball is mentioned on the Illinois High School "Glory Days" website, but there is "no record of trophies or plaques won by Attucks in baseball or any other extracurricular activity at the state tournament level."[6] The record of past individual accomplishments fails to mention Armour.

In 1933 Armour appeared professionally as a reserve third baseman for the Indianapolis ABCs/Detroit Stars. His performance as an 18-year-old is modest: He played in nine games and went 4-for-25 (.160). However, he is not listed on a professional roster again until 1938, apparently toiling on semipro teams.

From 1934 to 1935, the trail of Armour's playing career goes cold. If he was a member of a professional organization, it's barely documented. More likely, he played for a barnstorming or semipro team, which wasn't uncommon for the time.

Two sources list Armour as reaching the Negro Leagues in 1936. All Mississippi Baseball, a blog self-described as highlighting Mississippi-connected players from preps to pros, past and present, notes that "Alfred Allen Armour reached the 'big leagues' of Black baseball in 1936, when he signed with the St. Louis Stars.[7]

A "bullpen" post on Baseball Reference asserts that "Armour got his start with the 1936 St. Louis Stars. After a couple years on the bench, he was the starting shortstop for the 1938 Indianapolis ABC's."[8]

Independent confirmation of this was elusive, as there is no statistical mention of Armour on either Baseball Reference or Retrosheet for the 1936 and 1937 seasons. But he appears in a photograph of the Mounds (Illinois) Blues, participants in the 1937 Illinois Semipro Baseball Championships in Elgin.[9]

Later, that team is mentioned as the predecessor to the Indianapolis ABC's, which became the Stars in 1939.[10]

Eliminated from play by the Elgin West Ends after winning two earlier contests,[11] the Blues returned to the St. Louis area and competed against area teams throughout the

Courtesy of Elgin Area History Society.

Buddy Armour.

remainder of 1937. Whenever a box score accompanies a summary of the game, Armour is generally listed at shortstop and batting second in the lineup.

Finally, in 1938, Armour secured a starting position, this one with the Indianapolis ABC's of the Negro American League. In the preview of an early series with the Atlanta Crackers, he is characterized as follows:

"Alfred Armour, short stop, throws right, hits life [left], is very fast, and a good hitter. He is rated by Manager [Big George] Mitchell to go to first base in 3 seconds."[12]

Indianapolis finished sixth with a 17-21 record with Armour mostly batting leadoff and again playing shortstop. Accounts differ regarding his offensive production, but Seamheads lists Armour as a .250 hitter in 17 games played. A Retrosheet download indicates 24 hits in 72 at-bats (.333 average). The discrepancy could be partially explained by the inclusion of three exhibition games.

With the franchise moving to St. Louis in 1939, the now St. Louis Stars fared no better than the ABC's, finishing sixth again in the Negro American League, but Armour, then 24, was hitting his stride as a player. Again, statistical sources differ slightly, but the Retrosheet log reports 29 hits in 94 at-bats for a .309 batting average. Generally batting in the middle of the order, he had 16 RBIs.

That season was also the first time Armour was referred to by his nickname. Early-season coverage of the Stars' 14-11 win over the Indianapolis ABC's stated that "'Buddy' Armour who was spiked Sunday night was still out of the lineup, [Marshall Riddle] playing short and Dan Wilson holding down second base."[13] No further explanation of the moniker was noted.

With ongoing financial difficulties, the club split its home games between St. Louis and New Orleans in 1940 and 1941, becoming the St. Louis-New Orleans Stars. Armour's emerging stardom was evident in an early-season preview of a series with the Atlanta All-Stars, in which he was characterized as a "shortstop who is exceptionally fast and a good fielder who carries the power of a 200-pounder although he weighs only 150."[14]

Armour put up impressive numbers in 1940, now as an outfielder, with John Lyles becoming the staple at shortstop. Armour's average was third among regular players with the Stars, .327 in 29 games, trailing only first baseman Ed Mayweather and second baseman Riddle in that category.

The Stars finished fourth in the Negro American League, well behind the Kansas City Monarchs, a team that included such greats as Buck O'Neil, Satchel Paige, and an aging Turkey Stearnes. But Armour's performance was garnering notice.

Back with the Stars in 1941, Armour's production waned, and he had yet to play for a first-division team in his professional career. The Stars were 21-27-3, with the Monarchs again winning the league. But despite the lack of team successes, 1941 saw Armour being selected as a reserve for the West team in the annual East-West All Star Game at Chicago's Comiskey Park.

In that game, Armour replaced Neil Robinson in center field in the fifth inning and singled in his first at-bat in the sixth but was stranded at second base. He struck out in the eighth, but a dropped third strike by East catcher Roy Campanella put him on first, and he ultimately scored the second run for the West in an 8-3 loss.

With ongoing financial struggles and a developing interest in the New York Black Yankees, Allen Johnson, a nightclub owner in Mounds, Illinois, and the Stars' financial backer, dissolved the Stars and attempted to move 10 players to the Black Yankees, then of the Negro National League. The other owners objected, but former Stars manager George Mitchell, serving as business manager for Johnson, cited a previous ruling by the league that "any owner could quit one league and join the other league taking at least 10 players with him."[15] The Black Yankees did field a team in 1941, and a comparison of rosters shows eight of the 1941 St. Louis-New Orleans Stars as members of the 1942 Black Yankees.

Professionally, 1942 was lost for Armour, as he was not among them.

The 1943 season was only marginally better. A member of the Negro National League II operating as the Harrisburg-St. Louis Stars with home games played on the Island Park diamond in Harrisburg, had a roster made up of former members of the St. Louis Stars, and "players recruited from the disbanded American circuit."[16] For Armour, that meant limited opportunity, as he wasn't part of the featured nine. The collective record of both teams was 12-32, again a second-class team performance that seemed to plague Armour's career.

The chronicling of his personal successes is hard to define, because many of his games were exhibitions or not formally reported. His official stats for 1943 show participation in 14 games, split between Harrisburg and the Black Yankees. But other new entries, including one in June 1944, note that "[the cleanup] hitter for Cleveland, Buddy Armour, plays left field and slugged the horsehide at a .330 clip in 1943."[17]

Armour's career break occurred when he joined the Cleveland Buckeyes early in the 1944 season. He was 29 years old. An early-season match with the New York Cubans introduced him:

"The Cleveland Buckeyes are confident that they have overcome the faults of their first week's practice, and with the addition of Alfred 'Buddy' Armour, former New Orleans-St. Louis Stars centerfielder, they believe they possess the punch and pitching to halt the Cubans."[18]

Finally playing for a contender, Armour was again selected to the East-West All Star Game. As a starter, he batted cleanup and got a hit, stole a base and scored two runs in the West All Stars' 7-4 victory.

THE 1945 CLEVELAND BUCKEYES

The Buckeyes finished second behind the Birmingham Black Barons, 15½ games back. For Armour, his season results showed a .296 batting average in 20 games, with 15 RBIs. Although considered by many as a left-handed power hitter, he failed to tally a home run.

On the cusp of greatness, Cleveland entered the 1945 season with a similar lineup and high expectations. Armour was again a fixture in the outfield, and the Buckeyes dominated the first and second halves of the season to win the Negro American League championship by a wide margin over the Kansas City Monarchs. At the end of league play, the Buckeyes lost only 17 times in 80 outings, qualifying them for a shot at the Homestead Grays, a Negro League dynasty and winners of the previous two World Series. Like the Buckeyes, the Grays had won both halves of their season.

Armour was positioned seventh in the batting order for the Series. His 3-for-3 performance in Game Three was a key element in the Buckeyes' 5-0 victory. The Buckeyes swept the Grays in four games, and after laboring with subpar teams for most of his career, Armour was a champion.

Armour returned to Cleveland in 1946. A new manager and multiple player changes to the core group found the Buckeyes less competitive, and they finished third behind Kansas City and Birmingham. But Armour regained his form, again batting over .300. (Seamheads lists his batting average as .333.) He was invited to and played for the North-South All Stars in a late-season clash against the Homestead Grays. But despite his production, Buckeyes general manager Wilbur Hayes traded him to the Chicago Giants for 24-year-old Clyde Nelson.[19]

Again saddled with a losing franchise (Chicago finished last in the 1947 Negro American League standings), Armour was still proficient on the field and was selected to the first 1947 East-West All-Star Game for the third time. (In 1946, 1947, and 1948, the Negro Leagues held two All-Star games a few days apart, one in Chicago and the other in New York or Washington.) As the starting right fielder in Chicago, he was 2-for-4 with two doubles and scored a run for the winning West team. He also played in the second game, starting in right field and going 0-for-1 before being replaced.

Armour stayed with the Giants in 1948 and again hit .300. But the team was once again a bottom-dweller, and with baseball being integrated and the Negro Leagues ultimately a casualty of that decision, his days in the spotlight were essentially over.

Reports of Armour playing in the Negro Southern League and the Canadian League are sporadically reported, but he did join the Homestead Grays, now an independent club, with a nod to his earlier accomplishments, in 1950.

"The signing of Buddy Armour was pleasing news to Manager Sam Bankhead, who immediately installed the former Cleveland Buckeye star in centerfield," wrote the *Washington Afro American*. "Armour, a capable defensive player, also will add to the Grays already power-laden batting attack. He was batting king in the Canadian League last year."[20]

It was the final year of the Grays, and the final year of Armour's baseball career.

When his baseball career ended, Armour settled back in Carbondale and worked as a custodian for the city. He was married with a daughter, according to the 1950 census.

After his career ended, occasional mentions in the local newspaper listed him as an instructor for the Carbondale Junior Baseball League.[21]

Armour died on April 15, 1974, after a two-year illness. He is buried in the Oakland Cemetery in Carbondale.

SOURCES

In addition to the sources cited in the Notes, the author accessed Retrosheet.org, Baseball-Reference.com, SABR.org, and Seamheads.com.

NOTES

1   Hayward Jackson, "Windy City All Agog Over Big Classic; Expect 40,000," *Atlanta Daily World*, July 15, 1941: 5.

2   1930 Census, *Ancestry.com*.

3   US, Deaths and Stillbirths Index, 1916-1947, *Ancestry.com*.

4   "Colored Pupils to Get Diplomas Tonight," *Carbondale* (Illinois) *Free Press*, May 29, 1929: 3.

5   Brad Pace, "The Spirit of Attucks Schools," https://carbondalespiritofattucks.weebly.com/the-spirit-of-attucks-schools.html.

6   https://illinoishighschoolglorydays.com/2022/03/01/carbondale-crispus-attucks-hs-bluebirds/.

7   www.allmississippibaseball.net/spotlight-on-4/ February 15, 2011, entry.

8   https://www.baseball-reference.com/bullpen/Buddy_Armour

9   "The Mounds Blues, With St. Louis Boys, Near the Illinois State Championship," *St. Louis Argus*, August 6, 1937: 6.

10   "Card Twin Bill," *Indianapolis Star*, July 23, 1938: 13. In 1937 a team from Mounds, Illinois (Blues) competed in the Illinois Semi Pro Tournament held in Elgin. A photograph of that team, with players identified, includes at least seven players who were on the roster of the Indianapolis ABCs of the Negro American League in 1938, including Armour. The ABCs moved to St. Louis in 1939 and became the St. Louis Stars.

11   "Elgin Defeats Colored Blues Last Night," *Dixon* (Illinois) *Evening Telegraph*, August 11, 1937: 6.

12   "Indianapolis ABC's Coming to Atlanta for Big Series," *Atlanta Daily World*, June 5, 1938: 5.

13   "Stars Show Power in Hot 19-10 Victory," *St. Louis Argus*, May 19, 1939: 11.

14   "Lucius 'Melancholy' Jones," "St. Louis Stars Play Atlanta Nine at Harper Field This Sunday," *Atlanta Daily World*, April 3, 1940: 5.

15   "Lucius 'Melancholy" Jones", "Sports Slants," *Atlanta Daily World*, March 11, 1942: 5.

16   "Enter Negro Nine in League Here," *Harrisburg* (Pennsylvania) *Evening News*, May 6, 1943: 21.

17   "Buckeyes Invade Twin City for Giant Twilight Game," *Hammond* (Indiana) *Times*, June 16, 1944: 21.

18   Hayward Jackson, "Bremmer's Pitching May Halt Cubans' Power in New Orleans," *Pittsburgh Courier*, April 22, 1944: 14.

19   "Buckeyes Get Nelson of Chicago in Trade for Armour," *Cleveland Plain Dealer*, December 31, 1946: 22.

20   "Grays Sign Buddy Armour," *Washington Afro American*, May 13, 1950: 30.

21   "Carbondale Boys Get More Lessons," *Southern Illinoisan* (Carbondale), May 23, 1958: 9.

Earl Ashby

By Mark Shirk

Earl Randolph Ashby Powbett led a fascinating baseball life. He was a backup catcher for the 1945 Negro champion Cleveland Buckeyes. He was given a chance to replace Josh Gibson as Homestead Grays catcher in 1947. He played in Canada, Mexico, Cuba, and the United States and perhaps other lands as well.

Earl Ashby.

From *1946 Negro League Baseball Yearbook.*

But he also never stayed in one place for very long. Ashby had a temper and a habit of finding trouble. He never seemed to produce as much as he was expected to. Little is known of Ashby's life outside of baseball. We do not even know when he died. What follows includes some speculation as Ashby played under multiple names throughout his career.

As the Negro Leagues disintegrated and Ashby and dozens of other players were left to find jobs playing baseball across North America, Ashby put together a career longer than a decade as a catcher, first baseman, and outfielder.

Very little is known of Ashby's early life, past his birthday of May 16, 1921, in Havana, Cuba. He was close to his 24th birthday when he first came to the United States to play for the Cleveland Buckeyes. Prior to a tilt against the then first-place Memphis Red Sox on May 26, 1945, sportswriter Bob Williams said, "Two Cuban stars, Avelino Cañizares and Earl Ashby, will be seen at shortstop, or possibly catch or outfield, for the first time in the Buckeyes Lineup."[1] The pair were "Aces in the Hole" for Cleveland and Ashby "stars as an extra catcher when he isn't strutting his stuff in and out field."[2]

Ashby did not play much for Cleveland, who had star catcher-manager Quincy Trouppe taking most of the time behind the plate as well as Jesse Williams. For this reason, Ashby became an option in the outfield but was not considered a starter there either. For the season he hit .269/.345/.346, a 101 OPS+. Ashby mostly played during exhibitions, though he did have one highlight. In the second game of a doubleheader on July 1, Ashby hit a late double and scored a run as part of a late comeback in a 5-3 win over the Kansas City Monarchs to give the Buckeyes a sweep.[3]

Ashby's and Jesse Williams's roles were celebrated by the *Cleveland Call and Post*, the city's African American newspaper: "[T]hese two boys have proven their worth both in the catching and hitting, and are to be given credit for aiding greatly in bringing the Buckeyes their new title."[4] In addition to winning the Negro American League pennant, the 1945 Buckeyes swept the Homestead Grays in four games in the Negro World Series. Ashby had a successful first season in the United States, even though he did not factor into the World Series victory.[5]

Ashby was not back with Cleveland after the 1945 season. It appears that he followed many other US-based players to Mexico in 1946, as Jorge Pasquel tried to build up the Mexican League. While there is no Earl Ashby listed in the records, there is an Edward Ashby who played with three teams: Mexico City, Veracruz, and Puebla.[6]

Ashby was back in the United States for the 1947 season. He began the year with the Birmingham Black Barons of the Negro American League but soon had the opportunity to replace the great Josh Gibson, who had died in January. Ashby had Gibson's imposing size and strong arm, so it was probably a chance worth taking. He had some moments with Homestead with multihit games against the New York Black Yankees, Philadelphia Stars, and New York Cubans.[7] Overall, Ashby hit .262 in 15 games for the Grays. Retrosheet shows 16 games, but none in which he appeared after July 20.[8]

That winter, a catcher named E. Randolph (who was likely Ashby though there is no definitive proof) played with Marianao of the Cuban Winter League, getting into one game and going 0-for-4.[9] Ashby came back to the United States for the 1948 season with the Newark Eagles. He made an early impression with a two-hit game and a home run in separate exhibitions against the Atlanta Black Crackers.[10] Reports were that Newark was excited to have Ashby as the starting catcher. One paper claimed, "Much is expected of Earl Ashby, who showed promise with the Grays last year"[11] and another reporting that Eagles manager William Bell was impressed[12] with the "hard working Cuban catcher."[13]

Ashby began the year as the starting catcher but played his last game for the Eagles on May 31. He would catch on with the defending champion New York Cubans, who had beaten the Buckeyes in the 1947 World Series, but according to Retrosheet he is known to have played in only one game for them, in August. For the season, Ashby hit .059 in 34 at-bats. His final line in the Negro major leagues was .196/.293/.284, a 61 OPS+.

From there, Ashby became one of numerous African American and Afro-Latino players who were baseball vagabonds. He spent 1949 playing for the Fulda (Minnesota) Giants of the semipro Centennial League.[14] Ashby joined a Giants squad with future Hall of Famer Hilton Smith, then 42. The locals deemed that Ashby "was the character of the two."[15] It is here that we begin to see evidence of Ashby's temper, which may explain his itinerant jumping around in the Negro leagues. Teammate Delly Koopman recalled, "Ashby could hit and he was a good catcher, but he had a temper. I stayed away from him. Sometimes, he would get mad at the pitcher, and he would take off the catcher's gear and say he was going to pitch."[16] During a game in Iona, the away fans were taunting Ashby and he responded with an obscene gesture that led to his arrest.[17] However, he had success in Fulda, with one source reporting that he hit .425.[18]

In 1978 columnist Patrick Reusse told the story of how Ashby caused a stir during a visit in Kinbrae, a hunting town near Fulda, when he showed up "dressed to the teeth." As one resident said, "We haven't seen a fellow that dressed up, before or since."[19] That a well-dressed Black man was

remembered in that town three decades later is a window into how hard it was for Black players (to fit in) in the early years after integration. It also provides some context for Ashby's disciplinary issues.

Ashby's baseball journey continued in 1950 with Drummondville of the Class-C Provincial League. Ashby was celebrated as a three-time Negro League champion who had hit .312 for the famed Homestead Grays. This was all untrue. Ashby's old manager and teammate Quincy Trouppe played for Drummondville the year before. Whether Trouppe recommended Ashby to Drummondville (or vice versa) is unclear but it appears that Drummondville thought they were getting Trouppe's protégé when Ashby arrived. Ashby acquitted himself well, hitting .292 with 3 doubles and 2 home runs in 22 games. However, he was sent on a trial to the Bridgeport Bees of the Class-C Colonial League in June, probably due to his temper. There is a May 17 report of his being thrown out of a game for yelling at an umpire.[20]

He did not impress with Bridgeport,[21] and Drummondville was forced to trade him to St. Jean for a player, Al Pajones, who did not play in the Provincial League that year. No statistics of his time in St. Jean have been found but there is a July 1 report that he was released after attacking teammate Rubén Gómez in a dispute that started over "unimportant stuff."[22]

After he left St. Jean, Ashby becomes hard to follow. It appears that he caught on with the Paris Lakers of the Mississippi-Ohio Valley League using the name Earl "Chico" Randolph.[23] However, he was suspended and released on August 3 for throwing his glove at an umpire in a disagreement on a catcher-interference call.[24] This was apparently not his first infraction with an umpire while playing with Paris. He also had a collision with Mount Vernon first baseman Pete Milinkov while running out a grounder.[25] It is unclear if the collision was anything out of the ordinary but given that he cannot have joined Paris until July, it was part of a pattern of ill-discipline and violence on the field.

Then on August 11, eight days after being released by Paris, Ashby was arrested and fined $15 in Fort Wayne, Indiana, for participating in a brawl and taking a swing at a police officer.[26] He was described as 27 years old (he was 29 at the time) and a suspended member of the Homestead Grays. It does not appear he was on the Homestead roster at the time, though it is also unclear why he was in Fort Wayne. Homestead was a nonleague barnstorming club by 1950 and it is possible, though unlikely, that Ashby did catch on with them again.

Ashby is listed as having played with the Duluth of the Northern League in June of 1951.[27] There is a report that he was assigned, on trial, to Mexican club Aguiles in 1952.[28] No statistics have been found for his time there. In 1953, it appears, he was back in Illinois. A Jimmy R. Powell played with Hannibal of the Mississippi-Ohio Valley League, hitting .382 in nine games. However, the manager of the Paris team, Tom Sunkel, protested a game that Paris played against Hannibal, claiming that Powell was in fact the suspended Chico Randolph.[29] Powell was released shortly after. This makes it possible that Randolph/Ashby's suspension was a permanent one. There is also a report of Powell spiking Mount Vernon first baseman Roger Werner, though it is unclear if this is the same incident reported above.

In 1954 Ashby appears to have played in Mexico (though it is unclear what team he played with), hitting a reported 19 home runs.[30] He was back in the United States in 1955, starting the season with the Port Arthur (Texas) Seahawks of the Big State League as a first baseman and utilityman. One report from this time said that he called New Orleans his home.[31]

However, his time in Port Arthur was short as *The Sporting News* reports that he was picked up by the Rochester Red Wings, the Triple-A club of the St. Louis Cardinals.[32] He was signed on an emergency contract as a backup catcher in case of an injury to catcher Bob Rand following an injury to catcher Charlie White. He was apparently signed in Toronto but not put on the roster.[33] Whether he was a free agent after his time in Port Arthur went sour or left directly from Port Arthur is unclear. It is also unclear why he was on the radar of the Rochester Red Wings, given his on-field demeanor.

Eventually Ashby was released on June 20 for disciplinary reasons. It appears that on the night of June 19, he was seen having drinks with a woman named Ive James. That night, James's boyfriend, Tom R. Blythers, was found stabbed to death. James was arrested on a charge of murder and Ashby was brought in as a material witness and held for 12 days. He had left town for New York after the incident and was found and brought back to Rochester by two detectives. However, it appears that Ashby was never a suspect, and he was paid $36 for his inconvenience. He also got medical attention during his time in Rochester after he claimed that James bit him on the finger the night of the incident. It turns out that the DA failed to indict James and Blythers' murder remains unsolved.[34]

After his release from Rochester, it was reported that Ashby's friend Sandy Amorós, a few months before making a World Series-saving catch for the Brooklyn Dodgers' only World Series title, got him a job playing in the Dominican League. The problem was that Ashby was still needed in Rochester so DA Harry L. Rosenthal called and vouched for him.[35] That said, there is no statistical record of Ashby playing in the Dominican Republic, which had switched to a winter league that season.[36] It is possible that if he did go down to the Dominican, he just did not get into any games. He was 34 at the time and was not playing in high-profile leagues.

This is where the trail on Earl Randolph Ashby Powbett runs cold. It is unclear what happened to him after he was released by the Rochester police. We do not even know when he may have died.

So what to think of Earl Ashby? First, he was a player with impressive physical traits who despite never putting it together as a star player kept getting chances based on those skills. Second, Ashby played at a time when many Black American and Latino players were given little choice but to be baseball nomads. The Negro leagues collapsed in the early 1950s and there were few opportunities in Organized Baseball as integration was slow and many teams, fearful of being "too Black," had unofficial quotas for the number of Black players they would employ and play at any one time. In fact, in many of his stops, like Fulda in 1949, Ashby appears to have been viewed as much as a sideshow as a baseball player. Ashby's ability to promote himself, use connections, and embellish his own credentials in the low-information environment of the times served him well. But it was still a challenging and entirely unnecessary situation.

This leads to the third story. Ashby had a temper and often found himself in trouble with umpires, players, and the authorities. It is nearly impossible to untangle this from the abuse he probably faced because of being a Black man in America in the late 1940s and early 1950s. This is no excuse for Ashby's actions but an explanation. So Ashby, a Negro League champion who reportedly hit .300 a few times, had a very unusual career in the context of baseball history, though perhaps not unusual for a Black man in his era.

SOURCES

All Negro League statistics are from Seamheads.com as of the close of 2024. All game-level data is from Retrosheet.org unless otherwise noted. The author would like to thank Adam Darowski, Bill Nowlin, Gary Ashwill, Gary Fink, Christian Trudeau, Ruben Sanchez, and Sean Lahman for their help with this research.

NOTES

1   Bob Williams, "Vastly Improved Buckeyes Strong in Every Field, May Bring Out Fans 10,000 Strong," *Cleveland Call and Post*, May 26, 1945: 7B.

2   "Aces in Hole Are Bucks' Cuban Stars," *Cleveland Call and Post*, June 2, 1945: 6B.

3   Retrosheet (https://www.retrosheet.org/NegroLeagues/boxesetc/1945/B07012KCM1945.htm).

4   "Here Is Buckeyes' Pitching Staff, Rated Peerless," *Cleveland Call and Post*, September 9, 1945: 7B.

5   RetroSheet (https://www.retrosheet.org/NegroLeagues/1945PS.html).

6   Baseball Reference: https://www.baseball-reference.com/register/player.fcgi?id=ashby-000edw. Negro League researcher Gary Ashwill told the author in an email exchange that he thinks Edward Ashby was Earl Ashby.

7   Retrosheet (https://www.retrosheet.org/NegroLeagues/boxesetc/1947/Bashbe1011947.htm).

8   That may be because no box scores have turned up. There is no record of his playing elsewhere that season.

9   Jorge S. Figueredo, *Cuban Baseball: A Statistical History: 1878-1961* (Jefferson, North Carolina: McFarland Publishing, 2003). Ashby's first two names were Earl Randolph and he was a Cuban catcher of the right age to be playing here. Ashby, as we will see later, had a habit of changing his name when it suited him as well.

10   Joel W. Smith, "Newark Eagles Sink Black Crackers By 19-2 Margin," *Atlanta Daily World*, April 22, 1948: 5; Joel W. Smith, "Newark Eagles Squeeze Out 8-5 Victory Over Atlanta Black Crax," *Atlanta Daily World*, April 27, 1948: 5.

11   "NNL Teams Begin Exhibition Contests," *Baltimore Afro-American*, April 3, 1948: 8.

12   "Newark Eagles Sign Max Manning, Ace Hurler, to Contract," *Philadelphia Tribune*, April 13, 1948: 10.

13   Joel W. Smith, "Newark Eagles, Black Crackers Clash Here Sunday," *Atlanta Daily World*, April 23, 1948: 5.

14   Armand Peterson and Tom Thomashek, *Townball: The Glory Days of Minnesota Amateur Baseball* (Duluth: University of Minnesota Press, 2006), 50-1.

15   Patrick Reusse, "Once Upon a Time in Fulda, Folks Were Tuned Into Baseball," *Minneapolis Star Tribune*, July 4, 1993 1C, 7C.

16   Reusse, 1993.

17   Reusse, 1993.

18   "Les Cubs Auront un Bon Receveur en Earl Ashby," *La Tribune* (Sherbrooke, Quebec), May 6, 1950: 18. Translated by Christian Trudeau. The source, a report from an interview with Ashby also claims that Ashby went 11-1 as a pitcher and led the team to the championship. However, it contains a lot of inaccuracies and may be an example of Ashby taking advantage of a low-information environment to embellish his résumé.

19   Patrick Reusse, "Reusse at Random: Frogs Destined to 'Croak,'" *St. Paul Dispatch*, August 24, 1978: 59.

20   "Les sportifs de Drummondville demandent la tête de Murphy," *La Tribune*, May 17, 1950: 20. Translated by Christian Trudeau.

21   "Bees Take Twin Bill From Kingston Colonial," *Bridgeport Post,* June 5, 1950: 26; "Bees Triumph Over Kingston Club 9-6," *Bridgeport Telegram*, June 7, 1950: 25.

22   Gerard Hebert, "Le Saint-Jean a perdu un excellent joueur avec R. Ste-Marie blessé," *Le Front Ouvrier* (Montreal), July 1, 1950: 14. Translated by Christian Trudeau.

23   Earl Randolph, The Sporting News Baseball Player Contract Cards, maintained by the LA84 Foundation and SABR.

24   "Paris Player Hits Ump," *Mt. Vernon* (Illinois) *Register-News*, August 2, 1950: 8; "Paris Lakers Release Fiery Cuban Catcher," *Terre Haute Tribune*, August 3, 1950: 20.

25   Email conversation between Gary Fink and Christian Trudeau handed to the author (and verified by both men) by Gary Ashwill. In the exchange Mr. Fink sources this from a Mount Vernon newspaper from July 24.

26   "Fined for Brawl," *Fort Worth Telegram*, August 11, 1950: Second Section.

27   Earl Ashby, The Sporting News Baseball Player Contract Cards, maintained by the LA84 Foundation and SABR.

28   "League Distributes Players of Pasquels' Two Teams," *The Sporting News*, March 12, 1952: 32.

29   Howard V. Millard, headline undecipherable, *Decatur* (Illinois) *Daily Review*, June 3, 1953:12.

30   "Les Cubs Auront un Bon Receveur en Earl Ashby." Ashby had a track record of polishing his credentials and never showed that type of power before.

31   "Hawks Brave Wind to Hold Workout," *Beaumont Enterprise*, March 28, 1955: 8.

32   "Deals of the Week," *The Sporting News*, June 22, 1955: 24.

33   "Dugout Diggins," *Rochester Democrat and Chronicle*, June 20, 1955: 19.

34   "Two Women Indicted on Murder Charges," *Rochester Democrat and Chronicle*, July 27, 1950: 22.

35   "DA Goes to Bat for Catcher," *Rochester Democrat and Chronicle*, July 6, 1955: 15.

36   Dominican League statistics can be found at: https://www.winterballdata.com/en.

Sam Bankhead

By Dave Wilkie

Hall of Famer and Negro League legend Judy Johnson called Sam Bankhead "one of the greatest outfielders we had."[1] Wilmer "Red" Fields, ace pitcher and 1948 World Series-winning Homestead Grays teammate, said, "He was the greatest team player I ever saw."[2] Blessed with a cannon for an arm, a penchant for clutch hitting, and the ability to play every position on the field, Sam enjoyed a 20-year-plus career playing with some of the most storied teams in baseball history. Left-handed slugger and All-Star Bob Harvey had this to say about Sam's throwing prowess: "He had a beautiful arm. Nobody tagged up at third and scored on a fly. He'd throw you out from the warning track."[3]

Samuel Howard Bankhead was most likely born on September 18, 1910, in Sulligent, Alabama.[4] His father, Garnett Bankhead Sr., labored in the coal mines and played first base in the Cotton Belt League, while his mother, Arie Armstrong, gave birth to five boys and two girls. Sam worked alongside his father loading coal until baseball led him to a better life.

All four of Bankhead's younger brothers played in the Negro Leagues. Fred was a slick-fielding second baseman from 1937 to 1948, making an All-Star appearance in 1942. Garnett played for three seasons from 1947 to 1949, including a short stint on the 1948 champion Homestead Grays with his brother Sam as manager. Joe had the shortest career, taking the mound a few times with the 1948 Birmingham Black Barons, and Dan became the first Black pitcher in major-league history when he took the mound on August 26, 1947, for the Brooklyn Dodgers.[5] Dan also hit a home run in his first major-league at-bat, but his success was short-lived; he was out of the majors by 1951.

Sam Bankhead punched his ticket out of the coal mines and into his Negro League career in 1929 with the Birmingham Black Barons, but he did not get much playing time as an 18-year-old rookie. From 1930 to 1932 he bounced around with Birmingham and the Louisville Black Caps until he finally found a home and a starting position with the Nashville Elite Giants.

In 1933 Negro League baseball introduced its inaugural East-West All-Star Game, which has been called "the pinnacle of any Negro League season," and described as "an All-Star game and a World Series all wrapped in one spectacle."[6] The annual games were so popular and star-studded that many observers, including Negro League historian Larry Lester, have credited them with helping to integrate Organized Baseball. Bankhead, as he often did in high-pressure situations, shined in these contests. A nine-time all-star at five different positions, Sam had 12 hits in 31 at-bats with 7 runs, 4 RBIs, and 2 stolen bases. He is also credited with scoring the first run in an East-West All-Star Game. Coincidentally, the National and American Leagues

SABR The Rucker Archive.

Sam Bankhead.

also debuted the major-league All-Star Game in 1933, but by the early 1940s it was often being outdrawn by its Negro League counterpart.[7]

After a solid season in 1934, his last with the Nashville Elite Giants, Bankhead moved on to one of the greatest teams in Negro League history, the Pittsburgh Crawfords. The 1935 Crawfords squad included future Hall of Famers Josh Gibson, Oscar Charleston, Judy Johnson, and Cool Papa Bell. Mark Koenig, shortstop for the 1927 New York Yankees, compared the '35 Crawfords favorably to his legendary World Series-winning team.[8] Bankhead made a seamless transition into this team of superstars, hitting .338 and playing a starring role as one of the Raindrop Rangers, a trio of speedy outfielders with Sam playing alongside Bell and Jimmie Crutchfield. Fanciful legend had it that the three players were so fast that they could keep a field dry by catching the raindrops before they hit the ground.[9] The Crawfords capped off their magical season with a hard-fought seven-game victory over the New York Cubans in the Negro League World Series. Bankhead had a solid Series with eight hits, including a clutch single and run scored that gave Pittsburgh the lead in the seventh inning of the seventh game.[10]

The Crawfords began a steady decline in 1936, but Bankhead remained reliable hitting .333. Though the Crawfords still ended up winning the Negro National League championship, no agreement could be reached with the Negro American League to play a World Series that year. After the season Gus Greenlee, owner of the Crawfords and creator of the East-West All-Star Game, was forced to cut payroll and players due to his involvement in racketeering. The Crawfords hung on through the 1938 season, but they were a mere shell of the team that dominated Negro League baseball from 1932 to 1936.

In 1937 Greenlee's misfortunes turned into a boon for Crawfords players Bankhead, Bell, Gibson, and Satchel Paige, as they were all recruited to play in the Dominican Republic for dictator Rafael Trujillo's Dragones team. Trujillo, a corrupt and violent leader, paid exorbitant salaries to these players in order to field a winning team to gain favor in the coming election. His two political opponents also fielded highly competitive teams made up largely of players raided from Negro League squads. The pressure on the Trujillo players was such that they felt that winning the championship was a life-or-death endeavor. The team would often be locked up at night to ensure that they would be in tip-top shape for the next day's game.[11]

Bankhead posted a .309 batting average with 21 hits in 68 at-bats, but it was Gibson's .453 average and Paige's 8-2 record that led the Dragones to the championship game against San Pedro de Macoris. In that game Bankhead had the most dramatic at-bat of his career. The Dragones were trailing 5-4 in the seventh inning against Negro League All-Star pitcher Chet Brewer when Bankhead strode to the plate with Bell on first base. Bell recalled:

"Brewer knew Bankhead was a great clutch hitter and tried to be careful with him. Too careful. The count went to three and one. Brewer came in with some smoke, but he got it high. I thought Bankhead would drive the pitch, but he had a big cut and fouled it back. Then he connected on the three-two pitch. He was a line-drive hitter, and this one went way over the left field fence. We were pretty happy."[12]

Paige retired the final six batters, five on strikeouts, to ensure the victory. "I guess we helped Trujillo stay in office," claimed Bell,[13] but the players could not get out of the Dominican Republic fast enough.

Bankhead, like many other Negro League players, treated baseball like a year-round job, and the winter of 1937 found him playing for the Santa Clara Leopards in Cuba. This turned out to be one of his finest seasons as he led the league in several categories, including a .366 batting average, 89 hits, 5 triples, and 47 runs scored.[14] The Leopards finished with a 44-18 record and stood in first place in the final league standings.[15]

The year 1937 proved to be a busy one for Bankhead as he also married Helen M. Hall on February 25. The two had a daughter, Brenda, in 1939, and a son, Anthony, in 1941. Anthony was diagnosed with colon cancer in 1970 and died at the age of 29. Brenda's fate is unknown, and Helen died on October 10, 1985 in Pittsburgh.

Bankhead was known as Hall of Famer Josh Gibson's best friend and confidant.[16] Josh Gibson Jr. had this to say about their friendship: "I know that as far back as I can remember, Sammy was a constant. I don't think they were inseparable, 'cause my father didn't get that close to nobody. But they clicked out of mutual respect."[17] Unfortunately the two were also known for their legendary drinking prowess. Stories of drinking contests that lasted long into the night, drinking on buses, between doubleheaders, and sometimes even during games, can be found in every Gibson biography and article where Bankhead is mentioned. In 1947 Bankhead was managing in Caracas, Venezuela, when he received a telegram announcing Gibson's death. All-Star catcher, Bill "Ready" Cash was there and had this to say: "Bankhead went out that night, got drunk, came in and tore up everything in his room. They had to send him home."[18]

Bankhead mended fences with Gus Greenlee in time to join the Pittsburgh Crawfords for the 1938 season. Greenlee had been upset that many of his star players had been lured to the Dominican Republic and had chosen money over loyalty. The Crawfords lacked star power that year as Gibson headed to the Homestead Grays while Bell and Paige played in the Mexican League. The Crawfords finished a pedestrian 25-23-1 in league play that placed them 12 games behind Gibson's first-place Grays.

The year 1939 marked the end of the great Pittsburgh Crawfords franchise, as Greenlee Field was demolished and replaced with housing projects.[19] Bankhead started the season with the relocated but short-lived Toledo Crawfords; however, he quickly jumped to the Homestead Grays to play second base with his old friend Josh Gibson. Bankhead hit a solid .292, as the Grays won the Negro National League pennant, but lost the Negro League World Series to future Hall of Fame catcher Roy Campanella and his Baltimore Elite Giants. Bankhead went 6-for-18 in the series for a .333 batting average.

Throughout the 1930s and 1940s, the integration of Black players into Organized Baseball was a hot topic for both Black and White sportswriters. Bankhead's name often came up in such discussions. In 1936 William G. Nunn, city editor for the *Pittsburgh Courier*, wrote, "We don't believe the majors can produce three outfielders with the all-around ability of 'Cool Papa,' Bill Wright or Bankhead."[20] Two years later White sportswriter Jimmy Powers of the *New York Daily News* wrote about seven Negro League players who would guarantee the New York Giants a pennant and included Bankhead as his starting center fielder.[21] Even White superstar players like Honus Wagner, Dizzy Dean, and Paul Waner went to bat for integration, but their cries fell on the deaf ears of antiquated thinkers like Washington Senators owner Calvin Griffith, Philadelphia Athletics owner Connie Mack, and Commissioner Kenesaw Mountain Landis.[22] Sadly, the window of time closed on Negro baseball legends like Gibson, (Buck) Leonard, Bell, Bankhead, and many others.

In the decade preceding Jackie Robinson's arrival in the major leagues, more than 100 players from the Negro Leagues played in Mexico.[23] Mexican business mogul and multimillionaire Jorge Pasquel was a big reason why. Pasquel, a strong and fearless leader,[24] wanted to turn the Mexican League into baseball's third major league. He lured dozens of Black players south of the border by offering them salaries that were two to four times greater than what they were making in the States.

In 1940 Bankhead signed with the Monterrey Carta Blanco, playing shortstop and leading the league in stolen bases with 32. He had 122 hits in 384 at-bats for a .318 average, but his team finished the year 10 games behind Pasquel's championship club, the Vera Cruz Azules.[25] The Azules fielded one of the most impressive lineups in baseball history with Bell, Gibson, Ray Dandridge, Leon Day, Martin Dihigo, and Willie Wells, each of whom eventually received enshrinement in Cooperstown.

Bankhead signed with Monterrey again in 1941, which turned out to be career year for him as he tore up the league with 142 hits in 405 at-bats for a stellar .351 average. He hit 8 home runs, scored 74 times, stole 19 bases, and drove home 85 runs.[26] In spite of Bankhead's batting prowess, the Monterrey team finished in last place with a 43-59 record, 24 games behind the repeating champion Azules.[27]

At the conclusion of the 1941 Mexican League season, All-Star catcher Quincy Trouppe formed a barnstorming team that played throughout the United States. The team was called the Mexican League All Stars and included the familiar names of Bell, Dandridge, Wells, Gibson, and

Bankhead. The team won all 10 of its games before disbanding for lack of financial support.[28] The well-traveled Bankhead then finished off the year by playing for the Ponce Leones in Puerto Rico.

Bankhead returned to the Negro Leagues with the Homestead Grays in 1942. Garnett Blair, pitcher for the Grays, said:

"Sam Bankhead to me was an outstanding player. He played shortstop and he would go behind third to get it and throw you out waist high across the diamond. He could not only play short, he could play second, third, he could play outfield, he could pitch, and he could catch. He was all around, so anytime I was pitching I said if that ball goes to Sam Bankhead, fine. There's nothing wrong with that, let it go there because if he got his glove on it, he was going to throw you out."[29]

Bankhead batted .283 while playing shortstop for the first-place Grays. On July 21, 1942, the *Mansfield* (Ohio) *News Journal* credited the Grays with a 79-4 record that included exhibition games.[30] The team reached the Negro League World Series but was quickly dismantled by Paige and the Kansas City Monarchs in five games.[31]

All the stars aligned for the Homestead Grays in 1943, but Bankhead uncharacteristically was the only regular player to hit under .300. The Grays finished the year with a 26-7-1 league record and won a hard-fought eight-game Negro League World Series against the Birmingham Black Barons.[32] With the scored tied 4-4 and two outs in the eighth inning, Bankhead delivered a clutch single to drive in what turned out to be the Series-winning runs.[33]

In what must have seemed like a foregone conclusion to the rest of the league, the Homestead Grays easily finished in first place in 1944 and 1945. Bankhead hit .253 in 1944 but rebounded to .341 in 1945. The 1944 team once again met the Black Barons in the World Series and easily dispatched them in five games this time. Bankhead went 7-for-20 (.350) in the Series. The 1945 Series was a different story for the Grays as they were swept by future major leaguer Sam Jethroe and the Cleveland Buckeyes. In contrast to his stellar 1945 season, Bankhead had an unexpectedly bad Series: 1-for-16 (.063).

The 1946 and 1947 seasons were both disappointments for the proud Homestead Grays. The 1946 team fell to fifth place with a losing record of 26-30-2, with Bankhead hitting .268. The 1947 squad finished in fourth place with a lowly 33-34-3 record and Bankhead's average dipped to an anemic .233. A Grays team composed of aging veterans, Jackie Robinson's integration of major-league baseball, and the tragic death of Josh Gibson on January 20, 1947, seemed to spell the beginning of the end for the Homestead Grays.

The 1948 season turned out to be a last hurrah for both the Homestead Grays and the NNL. The press was paying far less attention to the Negro Leagues by this point, but it is known that the Grays defeated the Baltimore Elite Giants in the NNL playoffs and met the Birmingham Black Barons in the Negro League World Series for the third time in six years. The Black Barons had knocked off a strong Kansas City Monarchs team in the NAL playoffs and featured a 17-year-old legend in the making, Willie Mays.

Bankhead helped lead the Grays to a five-game championship victory. After the series ended, the NNL disbanded, which meant that the 1948 Negro League World Series had been the last of its kind.

The Homestead Grays still fielded teams for the 1949 and 1950 seasons, with Bankhead staying on as player-manager. By all accounts these teams were highly competitive, with newspapers reporting records of 97-15 and 64-8 for the 1949 and 1950 seasons respectively.[34] In 11 box scores found from the 1950 season, an aging Bankhead banged out 18 hits in 45 at-bats.[35] The decline of the Negro Leagues continued apace, however, and the Grays folded after the 1950 season.

After Josh Gibson's death in 1947, Sam became a surrogate father for 16-year-old Josh Gibson Jr., who played second base and third base for Bankhead's 1949 and 1950 Grays teams; however, Josh Jr. could not escape his father's enormous shadow. In 1951 Sam took Josh Jr. with him north of the border to play in the Class-C Canadian Provincial League for the Pittsburgh Pirates-affiliated Farnham Pirates. Canada was where Bankhead attained one of baseball's most under-appreciated milestones by becoming the first black manager for a mostly White professional baseball team. Josh Jr. did not fare as well: While playing for Farnham, he broke his ankle sliding into second base, effectively ending his baseball career.

After spending the 1951 season in Canada, Sam and Josh Jr. returned home to the Hill District in Pittsburgh and took jobs working side by side for the Pittsburgh Sanitation Department. Josh Jr. had this to say about their experience together: "I worked with him. I listened to him still, like playin' baseball. He was one of the smartest guys 'cause he read all the time."[36]

Bankhead's post-baseball life has led to speculation, most notably by Negro League historian John Holway,[37] that the character Troy Maxson, from August Wilson's Pulitzer Prize-winning play *Fences* was based on Sam. Like Bankhead, Maxson was a bitter ex-Negro League star who worked on a garbage truck in Pittsburgh's Hill District. Bankhead was bitter that he never got the chance to play in baseball's major leagues,[38] and he refused to go to baseball games in his later years, even missing the chance to see his younger brother, Dan, pitch for the Brooklyn Dodgers. In a 1971 interview, Bankhead had this to say about major-league baseball: "After I quit, I never went to see a game again. I am not jealous, but I cannot be a fan."[39]

Sam preferred to stay close to home, playing cards with his buddies, endlessly talking about the old days, and – most of all – drinking. Bankhead's brother Fred died in 1972, and his youngest brother, Dan, died in 1976, events that made Sam lean on the bottle even more heavily than before. While the exact circumstances of Sam Bankhead's death are not known, it is known that he was shot in the head and killed on the night of July 24, 1976.[40] Whether he was shot by a friend after an argument in a downtown hotel, or shot in self-defense by a co-worker at the William Penn Hotel in downtown Pittsburgh, one thing is certain: Negro League legend Sam Bankhead's life came to an unceremonious end at the age of 65.

In 2005 the *Washington Post* honored Negro League legend Ted "Double Duty" Radcliffe upon the occasion of his 102nd birthday and asked him, "What player do you think of when you think of the Negro Leagues?" Radcliffe responded, "Bankhead. He was a great player."[41] Indeed, Bankhead had been picked as the first-team utility player as early as 1952 in a *Pittsburgh Courier* poll that named the all-time Negro League All-Stars.[42] He was universally respected as a player and manager and continually rose to the occasion when playing with and against the greatest players in Negro League history.

Bankhead would have made a tremendous major-leaguer. By all accounts he was an exceptional fielder, a speed demon on the basepaths, and a skilled batsman, as his lifetime .294 batting average attests. If non-league statistics are included, then his average shoots up to well above .300. Bankhead is also credited with a .375 average against White major leaguers in barnstorming games.[43]

As of 2025, there have been 351 people elected to baseball's Hall of Fame. Negro Leaguers have been grossly underrepresented, with only 44 players or executives honored with plaques thus far. When examining the scope of his entire career, it is not hard to envision a place for Sam Bankhead in the hallowed halls of Cooperstown.

This biography appears in Bittersweet Goodbye: The Black Barons, the Grays, and the 1948 Negro League World Series *(SABR, 2017) and* Pride of Smoketown: The 1935 Pittsbuirgh Crawfords *(SABR, 2020, both edited by Frederick C. Bush and Bill Nowlin.*

SOURCES

All statistics, unless otherwise noted, are from:

Seamheads.com

Holway, John B. *The Complete Book of Baseball's Negro Leagues: The Other Half of Baseball History* (Fern Park, Florida: Hastings House Publishers, 2001).

All statistics have been updated as of June 2025.

NOTES

1   John B. Holway, *Black Giants* (Springfield, Virginia: Lord Fairfax Press, 2010), 92.

2   Holway, *Black Giants,* 92.

3   Holway, *Black Giants,* 92.

4   Conflicting sources have Bankhead being born on September 18, 1905, in Empire, Alabama, but the 1910 birthdate shows up on both the US Social Security Death Index and on his gravestone in Sharpsburg, Pennsylvania.

5   Larry Lester and Wayne Stivers, *The Negro Leagues Book, Volume 2: The Players 1862-1960* (Kansas City, Missouri: Noir-Tech Research, 2020), 30.

6   Larry Lester, *Black Baseball's National Showcase* (Lincoln: University of Nebraska Press, 2001), 1.

7   Lester, 1.

8   Jim Bankes, *The Pittsburgh Crawfords* (Jefferson, North Carolina: McFarland & Company, Inc., Publishers, 2001), 148.

9   Lester, 88.

10   John B. Holway, *The Complete Book of Baseball's Negro Leagues: The Other Half of Baseball History* (Fern Park, Florida: Hastings House Publishers, 2001), 321.

11   John B. Holway, *Josh and Satch: The Life and Times of Josh Gibson and Satchel Paige* (New York: Meckler Publishing, 1991), 90.

12   Bankes, 110.

13   Bankes, 110.

14   Dr. Layton Revel and Luis Munoz, *Forgotten Heroes: Samuel "Sam" Bankhead* (Carrollton, Texas: Center for Negro League Research, 2011), 23.

15   Revel and Munoz, 23.

16   Brad Snyder, *Beyond the Shadow of the Senators* (New York: McGraw-Hill, 2003), 171, 274.

17   Mark Ribowsky, *The Power and the Darkness: The Life of Josh Gibson in the Shadows of the Game* (New York: Simon and Schuster, 1996), 164.

18   Brent Kelley, *Voices From the Negro Leagues: Conversations With 52 Baseball Standouts* (Jefferson, North Carolina: McFarland & Company, Inc., Publishers, 1998), 145.

19   Holway, *The Complete Book of Baseball's Negro Leagues,* 356.

20   Lester, 89.

21   Lester, 109-110.

22   Holway, *Josh and Satch,* 151-155.

23   John Virtue, *South of the Color Barrier* (Jefferson, North Carolina: McFarland & Company, Inc., Publishers, 2008), 11.

24   Virtue, 12.

25   Virtue, 85.

26   Revel and Munoz, 11.

27   Revel and Munoz, 11.

28   Revel and Munoz, 12.

29   Larry Lester and Sammy J. Miller, *Black Baseball in Pittsburgh* (Charleston, South Carolina: Arcadia Publishing, 2001), 75.

30   Revel and Munoz, 12.

31   Holway, *The Complete Book of Baseball's Negro Leagues,* 398-399.

32   Game Two ended in a tie.

33   Holway, *Josh and Satch,* 171.

34   Revel and Munoz, 19.

35   Revel and Munoz, 19.

36   Brent Kelley, *The Negro Leagues Revisited: Conversations With 66 More Baseball Heroes* (Jefferson, North Carolina: McFarland & Company, Inc., Publishers, 2000), 258.

37   Holway, *Black Giants,* 92.

38   August Wilson, *Fences* (New York: Plume, 1986).

39   Holway, *Black Giants,* 97.

40   Holway, *Black Giants,* 97.

41   "Ex-Washington Player Goes Back a Few Years," *Washington Post,* April 12, 2005. washingtonpost.com/archive/sports/2005/04/12/ex-washington-player-goes-back-a-few-years/4a2faf00-9223-4718-b46c-e1b8e0213a6b/?utm_term=.66be349249e0. Accessed December 31, 2016.

42   James A. Riley, *The Biographical Encyclopedia of the Negro Baseball Leagues* (New York: Carroll & Graff Publishers, Inc., 1994), 52.

43   Todd Peterson, *The Negro Leagues Were Major Leagues: Historians Reappraise Black Baseball* (Jefferson, North Carolina: McFarland & Company, Inc. Publishers, 2020), 228.

Eugene Bremer

By Leslie Heaphy

Eugene Joseph Bremer Sr., sometimes known as Gene, was born in New Orleans on July 18, 1916. He grew up in the city with his parents, three sisters, and grandmother. His father, Joseph, worked as a driver and his mother, Amanda, as a washerwoman. As a youngster he loved all sports and that led to his career as a pitcher from 1936 through 1948, in which he compiled a career record of 38-27 in 551 innings, with a 3.61 ERA in league competition.

Bremer's 90 starts included eight shutouts, but the highlight of his 12-year career was winning the Negro League World Series in 1945 as a mainstay of the staff for the Cleveland Buckeyes. Bremer's path to being a star was not always smooth, but he stuck it out and became a fan favorite in Cleveland, where he spent seven seasons of his career, and lived after his playing days were done.[1]

A right-hander who was listed at 5-feet-9 and 176 pounds, Bremer began his Negro Leagues pitching career in 1936 with the Cincinnati Tigers after pitching for the New Orleans Crescent Stars from 1932 to 1934 and the Shreveport Giants in 1935. After a second season with the Tigers, Bremer joined the Kansas City Monarchs and Memphis Red Sox in 1938 playing partial seasons with both clubs. After a second season with the Red Sox, Bremer spent 1940 bouncing around from team to team including a late summer stint with the Carta Blanca team in Mexico. He landed back in Cincinnati with the Buckeyes in 1942 as the team split its time between Cincinnati and Cleveland. He remained with the Cincinnati-Cleveland Buckeyes until he retired after the 1949 season when the Buckeyes moved out of Cleveland to Louisville. Bremer then remained in Cleveland until his death in 1971.[2]

One of Bremer's earliest shutouts came on July 11, 1937, for the Cincinnati Tigers against the Atlanta Black Crackers. The Tigers won 15-0 while Bremer gave up six hits and two walks. Bremer helped his own cause with one hit, one walk, and two runs scored. Four days later, Bremer pitched a 5-0 shutout over the Jacksonville Red Caps. A third shutout came that season on August 29, 7-0 against the Memphis Red Sox. Bremer was best known for his no-windup delivery, which often confused opposing batters and earned him the nickname Flash. Bremer also led the league that year with a 1.47 ERA. This impressive early work set a pattern for his Negro League career.

Bremer showed early on that he was not just a strong pitcher but also could be dangerous with the bat, hitting .279 in 233 at-bats in his career. In describing his performance in a 1942 game against the Birmingham Black Barons, a reporter wrote, "Eugene Bremmer [sic], pitcher who beat Satchell [sic] has been playing and pitching like a champion. In a recent game against the Barons he was at bat three times and hit three doubles."[3] Bremer had previously bested Satchel Paige and the Monarchs 2-1 on a five-hit complete game.[4]

Described by a reporter in 1944 as "one of the steadiest and most efficient hurlers in the game," Bremer made four appearances in the East-West Classic beginning in 1940 with additional appearances in the North-South Classic in 1944, 1945, and 1946.[5] The North -South classic was started because of the economic success of the East-West Classic and was planned to take place in early or late September each year. In his first appearance, in 1940, Bremer gave up two consecutive hits in his first inning of pitching. For the 1944 game Bremer was joined by five other Cleveland Buckeyes, giving them the largest contingent from a single team voted to play in the game.[6] In preparing the fans for the North-South Classic in September 1945, reporters talked about the "amazing Buckeyes" and the stars playing in the game. Bremer was described as "New Orleans' own sensational pitcher."[7]

Eugene Bremer.

As the push grew to integrate the White major leagues, a number of supposed tryouts were proposed for Negro League players in the early 1940s. One of them involved Bremer in 1942. Alva Bradley, owner of the Cleveland Indians at the time, had stated that he was open to the possibility of Black players playing with the Indians if they measured up. The sports editor of the *Cleveland Call and Post* proposed three players for Bradley to consider: Parnell Woods, Sam Jethroe, and Eugene Bremer. The tryout never actually took place. Bradley said the players did not measure up to the skill level he was looking for.[8] While a disappointment for all the players involved, this did not prevent Bremer from continuing to pitch successfully with the Buckeyes.

Bremer's career nearly ended in 1942 when he was involved in a car accident in September. The team's bus had broken down and so the players were traveling in multiple cars to get to their games. On September 7 Bremer suffered a concussion and fractured skull while two of his teammates, pitcher Joe Brown and catcher Smoky Owens, were killed near Geneva, Ohio. Alonzo Boone and Herman Watts were also injured in the accident. Bremer's career suffered a setback and he did not play again until the 1943 season. He later became a mainstay on the team that shut out the Homestead Grays in the 1945 Negro League World Series.[9]

Bremer came back in 1943 and won more games than all the Buckeyes pitchers except Theolic Smith who won five games to Bremer's four. The Buckeyes finished in second place behind the Kansas City Monarchs, who were the best overall team that season. Bremer's return to form shone in an 8-0 shutout over the Memphis Red Sox in July and another complete-game victory against the Cincinnati Clowns, winning 3-2 over Preacher Henry. In August, Bremer set a record with three straight shutouts over the Memphis Red Sox, 8-0, 4-0, and 4-0 in both league and exhibition contests.[10]

The 1944 season saw the Buckeyes again finish second, this time behind the Birmingham Black Barons. Bremer was able to return after being turned down by his draft board for military service because of the effects of the car accident. Bremer compiled a 4-2 record with a 2.63 ERA, second to teammate George Jefferson with a 1.78 ERA. The season got off to high expectations, resting on the prowess of the Buckeyes' highly touted "curveball artist" Eugene Bremer.[11]

The Buckeyes were the surprise in the 1945 World Series, being a young team still recovering from their 1942 tragedy. They had won the first and second halves of the Negro American League split season, but faced a dynasty in the two-time defending World Series champion Homestead Grays. The Grays were a veteran team, featuring five future Hall of Famers including catcher Josh Gibson. On paper the Grays looked like the odds-on favorite to win the series. Instead, the Buckeyes beat the Grays in four straight, including two shutouts. Newspapers wrote about the dominance of the "Big Four" on the mound and they

proved to be the difference in the series.[12] Willie Jefferson pitched the Buckeyes to a 2-1 victory in Game One while winning pitcher Bremer provided a bases-loaded walk-off double in Game Two for a 4-2 victory. Bremer gave up seven hits in nine innings while walking two and striking out five. He also committed a balk with Cool Papa Bell on third base, allowing him to score the tying run and setting the stage for Bremer's eventual game-winning hit. George Jefferson shut out the Grays 4-0 in Game Three and Frank Carswell pitched a 5-0 shutout in the deciding game.[13] The victory was largely credited to the "brilliant pitching" of the Buckeyes' "three aces" and the surprise outing by Carswell.[14]

Early in the 1946 season, manager Quincy Trouppe described his pitching staff as one of the best in baseball, led by the four who won the 1945 World Series. There were high expectations for the Buckeyes, but the club finished the season in third place behind the Kansas City Monarchs and the Birmingham Black Barons. The pitching staff did not live up to the hype and a few key hitters, like Sam Jethroe, saw their numbers drop from 1945. Bremer pitched only $33\frac{2}{3}$ innings, compiling a 3-0 record.[15]

Bremer had another chance to pitch in the World Series when the Buckeyes took on the New York Cubans in 1947. Bremer pitched in only $34\frac{2}{3}$ innings, mostly in relief, during the season, compiling a 2-2 record. A good example of his contributions came in a 8-6 win over Birmingham in June with Bremer pitching the final three innings for the win. After beating out the Monarchs for the league championship, the Buckeyes went on to lose the World Series 4-1-1 to the Cubans, who featured future Hall of Famer Minnie Miñoso. The Buckeyes tied the first game, 5-5, and won their only contest, 10-7, in the second game. Bremer lost the only game he pitched, starting Game Four against Dave Barnhill. Bremer gave up 12 hits in a complete-game loss, 9-4. As usual he did contribute at the plate, with two hits and one run scored.[16]

Bremer finished out his last full season with the Buckeyes in 1948 and left the team in early 1949 after the club moved to Louisville.[17] He appeared later in the year on the roster for the New Orleans Creoles, a team famous for its female second baseman, Toni Stone. Stone was 0-for-1 in an 11-9 loss to the Winona Chiefs where Bremer came on in relief.[18]

After his playing career was over, Bremer remained in Cleveland with his wife, Elizabeth, and their eight children. (He and Elizabeth Randolph had married in December 1937.) Bremer worked in the maintenance department for Hershaw Chemical Company in Cleveland. He died at the age of 54 in Cleveland on June 19, 1971.

Bremer's athletic legacy continued with his grandson J.R. Bremer, who played basketball with the Cleveland Cavaliers, Boston Celtics, and Golden State Warriors in the NBA from 2002 to 2004. The younger Bremer also played for many years in Europe before retiring and taking on the head coaching job at Cleveland Heights High School in 2019.[19]

SOURCES

In addition to the sources cited in the Notes, the author consulted Baseball-Reference.com and Retrosheet.org, and relied on Seamheads.com for all statistical information.

NOTES

1   Amanda Rumer, 1920 census, https://www.ancestry.com/search/collections/6061/records/57129539?tid=&pid=&queryId=cc76bc1e-18f8-4f3e-beac-edd62e8355f8&_phsrc=vkO32&_phstart=successSource; Joseph Rumer, 1920 census, https://www.ancestry.com/search/collections/6061/records/57129538?tid=&pid=&queryId=0e42a547-e6e2-4387-b6e3-7b33d87693b5&_phsrc=vkO30&_phstart=successSource.

2   "Mexico's Pros Clash Friday in Local Park," *Brownsville* (Texas) *Herald*, August 24, 1939: 22; https://agatetype.typepad.com/agate_type/2009/08/eugene-bremer.html.

3   "Am. Giants Vs. Buckeyes on Sunday," *Chicago Defender*, July 4, 1942: 19.

4   "Buckeyes in Split with Kansas City," *Chicago Defender*, June 20, 1942: 19.

5   "Negro Nines End Season Saturday," *Harrisburg* (Pennsylvania) *Evening News*, September 13, 1944: 13.

6   "Fans Warming up to Negro Classic," *Munster* (Indiana) *Times*, August 28. 1944: 9.

7   "Interest Soars in North-South Classic," *Pittsburgh Courier*, September 29, 1945: 12; "Ninth Inning Single Decides," *Pittsburgh Courier*, October 12, 1940: 18.

8   "Cleveland Indians to Tryout Three," *Norfolk* (Virginia) *New Journal and Guide*, September 12, 1942: A15; "Buckeye Player Profile – Eugene Bremer," http://www.clevelandbuckeyesbaseball.com/Bremer.html.

9   First String Battery of Negro League Team Killed," *Bowling Green* (Ohio) *Daily-Sentinel Tribune*, September 8, 1942: 3.

10   Eddie P. Jennings, "Say Forgotten Man of Buckeyes Is Bremmer," *Cleveland Call and Post*, March 11, 1944: 9B; "Buckeyes Split with Red Sox," *Cleveland Call and Post*, July 31, 1943: 11A; "Buckeyes' Jinx Lingers," *Cleveland Call and Post*, September 11, 1943: 11A; "Buckeyes Lead League," *Cleveland Call and Post*, August 14, 1943: 11A.

11   "Buckeyes of Baseball All Set," *Cleveland Call and Post*, January 22, 1944; "Bremer's Pitching May Halt Cubans' Power," *Pittsburgh Courier*, April 22, 1944.

12   "Negro Kings Play at Alcyon Tonight," *Camden* (New Jersey) *Courier-Post*, August 2, 1946: 21.

13   Dave O'Karma, "The Forgotten Championship," https://clevelandmagazine.com/in-the-cle/sports/articles/the-forgotten-championship; "Battling Bucks win 2-1, 4-2 in World Series," *Pittsburgh Courier*, September 22, 1945: 12.

14   "Win Four in Row to Dethrone Homestead," *Pittsburgh Courier*, September 29, 1945: 12.

15   "Negro Champs Boast Classy Pitching Staff," *Rochester* (New York) *Democrat and Chronicle*, June 4, 1946: 20.

16   "Buckeyes and Birmingham Split Two," *Pittsburgh Courier*, June 14, 1947: 15.

17   "Eugene Bremer, Vet Buckeye Hurler," *Cleveland Call and Post*, August 27, 1949: 6B.

18   "7 in 7th Give Chiefs 11-9 Win," *Winona* (Minnesota) *Republican Herald*, August 1, 1949: 12.

19   Bremer obituary, *Cleveland Plain Dealer*, June 22, 1971; Telephone conversation with Julius Bremer, January 7, 2025; "J.R. Bremer," https://www.nba.com/stats/player/2452/career.

John Wesley Brown

By Margaret M. Gripshover

John Wesley Brown came by his nicknames of "Lean Man" and "Slim Man" quite honestly. He stood 6-feet-1-inch tall and tipped the scales at less than 160 pounds. He was a right-handed pitcher who, despite missing part of the third finger on his pitching hand, posted an impressive 2.29 ERA over five seasons with the Cleveland Buckeyes. His career in the Negro American League began with Cleveland in 1944 and ended in 1949 with the Houston Eagles. Along the way, he had brief stints with the Chicago American Giants and the Louisville Buckeyes.

John Brown was born on October 23, 1918, in Hamburg, Arkansas, the Ashley County seat. Hamburg was also the birthplace of another pitcher, Harry Kane, who played for the St. Louis Browns, Detroit Tigers, and Philadelphia Phillies between 1902 and 1906; and of Naismith Memorial Basketball Hall of Fame inductee Scottie Pippen. Hamburg is located amid the pine forests of the Delta region of southeastern Arkansas, on the border with Louisiana, and not far from the Mississippi River. Brown's father, Henry Robson Brown, was born in Bastrop, Louisiana, but moved to

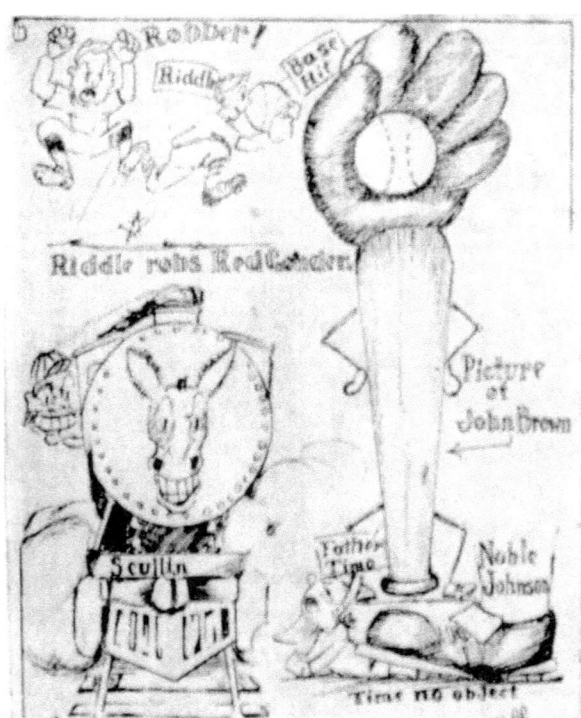

The only image of John Brown we could find is this cartoon from the July 10, 1942 St. Louis Argus.

Arkansas as a boy to live with his maternal aunt and uncle on a farm in Ashley County. John Brown's mother, Matilda Bethune Brown, who was also born in Ashley County, married Henry Robson Brown, who was 29 years her senior, in 1916. They had at least four children, John Wesley Brown being the second eldest. His father was a "decorator" who worked as a paperhanger. Both of his parents were literate, and they owned their home in Hamburg. Many of their neighbors were employed in the area's lumber yards and sawmills. By 1930, Henry Robson Brown moved his family about 15 miles southwest to Crossett, Arkansas, where John Brown and most of his family lived until his father's death in 1946.

Brown's athletic prowess was evident during his high-school years in Crossett. In 1936 he competed in a combined prep school-college track meet where he broke the Arkansas state record for the high jump, clearing the bar at a height of 5-feet-11½ inches.[1] After high school, Brown attended Arkansas Agricultural, Mechanical and Normal College (AAM&N) in Pine Bluff, known today as the University of Arkansas at Pine Bluff, the only historically Black college or university (HBCU) in the state. It is unknown if he played baseball for AAM&N. Brown did, however, play baseball during his summer breaks away from Pine Bluff. He was on the 1938 roster for the Greenville Black Bucks, a semipro team in Greenville, Mississippi.[2] On May 16 Brown and the Bucks defeated the Memphis African Clowns 10-5 in a twin-bill opener thanks to his "snaky slant[s]" and the fact that Memphis "clowned their way through both games."[3] The following year, the Greenville nine had a new skipper, "Prof. G.W. Brown," described as formerly with the Cuban Stars.[4] In April 1939 the Black Bucks, with "Manager Brown" at the helm, traveled to Crossett to tangle with the Crossett Stars.[5] Who was Professor Brown? Given that John W. Brown attended college, is it possible that "Prof. G.W. Brown" was in fact, "J.W. Brown"? Perhaps "G.W." was a typo? No one named "G.W. Brown" was found on the 1938 roster for the Cuban Stars. Professor Brown's identity is a mystery, but it is possible that he was John W. Brown, especially since, according to the Negro Southern League Museum, Brown did not play during the 1939 season.[6]

In April 1940, when the US Census was enumerated in Crossett, Arkansas, John Brown was working alongside his older brother Clarence Brown at a local sawmill. Both he and Clarence had one year of college to their credit, but neither was currently enrolled. Could John Brown's tenure at the sawmill account for the missing tip from one of his fingers, the injury he reported on his World War II draft card, dated October 16, 1940? When he registered for the draft, he was employed by the Crossett Lumber Company. The circumstances of losing the top of his "third finger" that was cut off at the "first joint" are unknown, but it did not prevent him from serving in the military during World War II or from pursuing a career in professional baseball.

Brown's baseball activities between 1940 and 1942 are difficult to document. Although at least one source claims he played for the Oklahoma Black Indians in 1940, the Bastrop (Louisiana) Blues in 1941, and the St. Louis Giants in 1942, the first published accounts of his professional baseball career appeared in 1942 when he played for teams in a St. Louis semipro industrial league.[7] The claim that he played for the "St. Louis Giants" is likely incorrect. The confusion is understandable. The St. Louis Giants aggregation played one season in 1924. Brown played for the "Curtiss-Wright Giants" of St. Louis in the 1940s.

Brown began his baseball career in earnest in 1942 in the competitive St. Louis segregated Colored Industrial League.[8] He saw action in the infield before migrating to the mound. Playing second base for the league-leading Scullin Steel Mules,[9] Brown was the team's "slugger" and by mid-season was hitting a blistering .421.[10] He was a local fan favorite, worthy of being featured in cartoon form in the *St. Louis Argus,* the city's African American newspaper, as an overly tall baseball bat, with a glove as his head.[11] Brown was one of the best in the league and was selected to play for the "West" in the annual St. Louis East-West game.[12] But his baseball career was thrown a curveball with the onset of World War II. He enlisted in the US Army and served as a private in Company F, 4th Quartermaster Regiment, at Fort Francis E. Warren in Cheyenne, Wyoming.[13] In March 1943 he wrote a letter to *Argus* sports columnist and Negro League historian Normal "Tweed" Webb, with this message for the fans back home.[14]

"Dear Tweed,

How's all the old gang in St. Louis? Tell them all hello and to keep 'em flying. This will be the first time in my career that I will miss training with the boys and will miss them! But tell them, for me that I will be in there pitching for a bigger and better cause. So they can continue to keep the ball rolling. Tell the youngsters to go out and take advantage of the greatest game in life – 'BASEBALL.' Tell 'em for me that they can't go wrong. Print my address so I can hear from some of the fellows. I will enjoy hearing from you and them. Write me all the news, Tweed. I will be here for about five weeks.

Your Buddy in sports,

John Brown

[Webb responded:] Well John, old top and all of my many friends in the armed service, we folks back home are praying for you all to return safely home soon. Oh yes – we had our second Blackout test last week. Since I am talking about war and what not, I wish the white papers and photo sections would play up our fighting race soldiers more. I hear they are raising sand.

Your Hot Stover."[15]

After his discharge from the Army, Brown returned to St. Louis and resumed his baseball career. In June 1943, Webb named Brown and few other players in the city's Municipal League as having "big league timber," and described Brown as a "human pinwheel when it comes to pitching baseball."[16] Webb also noted that William Brisker, a former sports reporter for the *Argus,* was now the business manager of the Cleveland Buckeyes and was in St. Louis fishing in the local talent pool.[17] At the time, Brown was pitching for the semipro Emerson Electrics of the Colored Industrial circuit, but Brisker didn't bite on Brown.[18] By August 1943, Brown left the Electrics and signed with the Curtiss-Wright Giants, joining a roster that included Luke Easter.[19] He pitched for the Giants in the Colored Industrial League playoffs with mixed results.[20] After he and the Giants were battered for three runs in the second inning by the Scullin Steel Mules, Brown was exiled to right field, where he made "two great running catches … and tripled to score the Giants' first run."[21] The Giants eventually kicked the Mules, 7-4, for the upset win.[22] It was his last season in the Colored Industrial League. Brisker and the Buckeyes finally decided that he was a keeper.

Brown signed with the Cleveland Buckeyes in the spring of 1944. In March he was one of eight St. Louis area players who were expected to board a bus headed for Clarksdale, Mississippi, to start spring training.[23] Two of the recruits had other plans. Theolic Smith opted to play in Mexico and Norman Young signed with the Kansas City Monarchs. Five others, Luke Easter, Charlie Hinson, Carl Whitney, Bob Palm, and Herman Purcell, did not play with any Negro League clubs in 1944. Of those from St. Louis who boarded the bus for Clarksdale, Brown was the only prospect to make Cleveland's 1944 roster.[24] Right out of the gate, on March 26, he proved his worth by leading the Bucks to a 4-3 preseason win over the Memphis Red Sox.[25] In July, with his "sinker ball working," he bested the Birmingham Black Barons, 6-2.[26] But Brown did not have a stellar rookie year in the NAL. In August he led the Bucks to a 12-2 victory over a local nine in Richmond, Indiana, but did little to help Cleveland's pennant hopes.[27] The Buckeyes finished the season a distant second behind the Black Barons. By the end of the 1944 season, Brown had a hefty 6.52 ERA in two official appearances in just 9⅔ innings pitched.

The Buckeyes' 1945 championship season began with spring training in Muskogee, Oklahoma, and with a new manager, Quincy Trouppe. Despite a sketchy rookie performance in 1944, Trouppe retained "lanky John Brown" on Cleveland's pitching staff.[28] Brown's previous year with the Buckeyes was so forgettable that some newspaper stories identified him as one of Cleveland's "newcomers," or simply as a pitcher formerly with a St. Louis club."[29] In

1945 he earned $450 a month plus travel expenses for his services.[30] He was primarily relegated to the bullpen but was not particularly effective as a reliever.[31] Brown enjoyed some success as a starter, especially against nonleague opponents, including his 7-3 win over the Twin Cities Independents.[32] On September 14, as the season was nearing its conclusion, he went the distance in a losing effort to the Homestead Grays, 3-1, in Dayton, Ohio.[33]

On September 20, with Frank Carswell on the mound, the Buckeyes clinched the Negro World Series for Cleveland by blanking the Homestead Grays, 5-0.[34] There was a pitcher named Brown on the mound during the series at Shibe Park, but it was Ray Brown of the Grays.[35] John Brown was not handed the ball in any of the Bucks' four World Series games thanks to all the starters going the distance. He did pitch for the Buckeyes after they claimed the crown, however, in a throwaway game against the Philadelphia Stars. He tallied a tidy 4-1 win to put a cherry on top of Cleveland's championship evening.[36] Three days after capturing the title, the Buckeyes faced off with the Grays for a doubleheader at Yankee Stadium, and this time the outcomes were quite different. The Grays exacted their revenge by sweeping the Buckeyes by the same score in each game – 7-1.[37] Brown was the losing pitcher in the nightcap before a crowd of 8,000.[38] According to official records, Brown finished the 1945 season with a 1-2 record and a stingy 1.73 ERA. In an interview in 1995, he recalled some different numbers and stated that his overall record for that championship year with the Bucks was 6-2 with a 3.46 ERA.[39]

Brown was with Cleveland when the Buckeyes headed to Birmingham in March 1946 to begin spring training.[40] With the 1945 World Series honors in hand, the Buckeyes had high hopes for a repeat. This was also the first year that Brown's nickname, "Lean Man," was seen in print on the sports pages.[41] His other sobriquet, "Slim Man," did not appear until 1949, and only after the Buckeyes temporarily relocated to Louisville.[42] No matter his name, the skinny on Brown in 1946 was that both he and Cleveland were headed for disappointment. In early June Brown was on the "sick list for several weeks" and was kept out of the rotation.[43] He made one appearance in an NAL game with the Bucks but lasted only four innings in a no-decision outing. By July, he was traded to the Chicago American Giants for Chet Brewer.[44]

Brown's impact on the Giants was minimal. Although he was on Chicago's roster, he does not appear to have been used in any official league games. In mid-August he did manage to bag a 4-3 victory for the Giants in an exhibition game against the Belleville Stags.[45] But Brown's lack of control was nearly his downfall against the local nine. All three of the Stags' runs resulted from the six walks issued by Brown.[46] In the end, the Buckeyes finished the 1946 season in third place in the NAL, while Brown and his Giants were the League's cellar dwellers. Some records indicate that John Brown appeared in the 1946 East-West All-Star Game

in Washington, DC, but he did not pitch.[47] He did have one at-bat as a pinch-hitter for the West All-Stars but did not make it to first base.

Brown's brief tenure with the American Giants came to end in 1946. In the spring of 1947, he was back on the mound for the Buckeyes for a swing through Florida.[48] He was one of three Cleveland hurlers used in an early April 6-2 win over the Jacksonville Eagles.[49] But it does not appear that he made an impact on the outcome of the Buckeyes' 1947 campaign. As the regular season was in full swing, newspaper coverage of Cleveland's results, and NAL games in general, became less frequent and with fewer details. Box scores and/or line scores were scarce, making it difficult to assess individual performances. Although Brown was touted as "the fastest pitcher in Negro baseball" and was "said to have developed an even faster delivery" after returning from Chicago to Cleveland, his name was nearly absent from published accounts of the Buckeyes' season.[50] When news of coming games was published, he was not mentioned among Cleveland's top hurlers.[51] Those honors were usually reserved for Alonzo Boone, Eugene Bremer, Chet Brewer, and Sammy Woods.[52] In 1947 the *Atlanta Tribune* was one of the few newspapers to publish NAL statistics. In early August, their list of the league's seven top pitchers did not include Brown.[53] The pitcher with the fewest games played and fewest wins on the list was the Indianapolis Clowns' Johnny Williams, with one win in six games.[54] Based on the *Tribune*'s accounting, as the 1947 season headed into its final lap, Brown played in less than six NAL games and had yet to notch a win. Brown's contributions to the Buckeyes' 1947 season were nearly invisible. According to official records, he made one appearance, tossed for three innings, and won one game. Brown did not spend much time on the mound that year, but at least his team enjoyed some success. Cleveland captured the NAL flag again, but lost the World Series crown to the New York Cubans.

In March 1948 Brown returned to the Buckeyes for spring training in Panama City, Florida.[55] The team had a new manager. Alonzo Boone replaced Trouppe, who was shifted to the Chicago American Giants.[56] Brown made his 1948 debut in the season opener against the Black Barons in Cleveland.[57] It was not pretty. He was one of three Buckeyes pitchers who collectively gave up 18 hits and ultimately a 15-2 loss in the first game of a doubleheader.[58] Chet Brewer, 38 years old, saved the day for Cleveland by capturing an eight-hit victory in the second game, 3-2.[59] The opener was a metaphor for the Buckeyes' mediocre season. They won just under half of their games and finished third out of six teams in the NAL. And although official records show Brown posting no wins or loses in NAL play in 1948, one published report credited him with an overall record of four wins against one loss.[60] Although little changed in his baseball fortunes, Brown did make one big move off the field. In 1948, he and his family relocated from Crossett to Detroit, where he lived for the remainder of his life.[61]

There were many changes in John Brown's baseball and personal life in 1949. As the NAL fortunes began to sag, his longtime employer, the Cleveland Buckeyes, morphed into the short-lived Louisville Buckeyes before reclaiming their Cleveland affiliation by the end of the season.[62] Brown continued to wear a Buckeyes uniform no matter which city claimed the team. He started the year by working as a reliever during a spring-training stop in Panama City, Florida.[63] In preseason play, Brown was touted as the "curve ball artist from the Ozarks."[64] By mid-April, "'Slim Man' Johnny Brown" had chalked up three wins.[65] By July, the Cleveland club, "who masqueraded for [a while] as the Louisville Buckeyes," were "reported broke and hope[d] to limp home until the finish of the season."[66] But before the geographically challenged Bucks began their summer campaign, Brown flew the coop for another nomadic nine, the Houston Eagles, formerly of Newark.[67] He saw action as a reliever for Houston and notched at least one win as a starter.[68] Records for the 1949 season are incomplete and Brown's accomplishments for the year are uncertain. But what is known is that after 1949, his Negro League baseball career was over. By the end of the season, his name no longer appeared in Houston's game reports. He retired from baseball in 1949 after what Brown described as a "bad bout of pneumonia."[69] After leaving the Houston Eagles and his baseball life behind, Brown returned to Detroit and started a new career as an appliance repairman for Detroit Edison, and later as a hardware distributor.[70]

John Brown's baseball life spanned over 13 years, the final six of which were in the NAL. He was a member of the Buckeyes' 1945 World Series championship team, and helped Cleveland claim the NAL flag in 1947. One of Brown's fondest memories of his baseball career was pitching to the Black Barons' rookie sensation, Willie Mays, during Mays' debut season with Birmingham in 1948.[71] Another was witnessing the greatness of Josh Gibson.[72] During a 1995 interview with a reporter for the *Detroit News*, he lamented the discrimination and barriers faced by African American ballplayers prior to Jackie Robinson breaking the color barrier.[73] He was circumspect and at peace upon reflecting on his six seasons in the NAL. Brown simply said, "I was just born too soon."[74]

John Wesley Brown died in Detroit on March 3, 1999, at the age of 80. He was survived by his wife, Naomi McCormick Brown. He was buried in Oak Ridge Cemetery in Woodhaven, Michigan.

SOURCES

Unless otherwise indicated, all Negro League statistics and records were sourced from Seamheads.com, baseball-reference.com, and retrosheet.org. Ancestry.com was used to access census, birth, death, marriage, military, immigration, and other genealogical and public records.

NOTES

1   Lynn Henning, "Negro League Player Has His Books, Memories," *Detroit News*, February 16, 1995: 65.

2   "Black Bucks Takes [*sic*] 1st. [*sic*] Tie 2nd," *Greenville* (Mississippi) *Delta Star*, May 17, 1938: 6.

3   "Black Bucks Takes [*sic*] 1st. [*sic*] Tie 2nd."

4   "Greenville, Miss.," *Pittsburgh Courier*, March 25, 1939: 22.

5   "Bucks Pry Lid Saturday," *Pittsburgh Courier*, April 15, 1939: 17.

6   "John W. Brown."

7   "John W. Brown."

8   Normal Webb, "Curtis-Wrights Almost Upset the Scullin Steel Co. 8-7," *St. Louis Argus*, May 15, 1942: 10, 11.

9   Normal Webb, "Curtis-Wrights Almost Upset the Scullin Steel Co. 8-7."

10   Normal Webb, "Hot Stove League," *St. Louis Argus*, July 3, 1942: 10; "Tandy Dope," *St. Louis Argus*, July 3, 1942: 10.

11   "Muny Music, *St. Louis Argus*, July 10, 1942: 11.

12   "East-West Game Sunday at Tandy Park," *St. Louis Argus*, August 7, 1942: 10.

13   Normal Webb, "Hot Stove League," *St. Louis Argus*, March 5, 1943: 10, 11.

14   Lorraine Kee, "'Tweed' Webb Helped Make Negro Leagues Fashionable," *St. Louis Dispatch*, April 29, 1995: 31.

15   Normal Webb, "Hot Stove League," *St. Louis Argus*, March 5, 1943: 10, 11.

16   Normal Webb, "Hot Stove League," *St. Louis Argus*, June 18, 1943: 10.

17   Normal Webb, "Hot Stove League," June 18, 1943: 10; "Kinloch Grays Get Top Rank Publicist," *St. Louis Argus*, April 9, 1948: 17.

18   Normal Webb, "Muny 1st Half to be Decided Next Sunday," *St. Louis Argus*, July 16, 1943: 10.

19   Normal Webb, "Giants Beat Scullins in Ninth with Bunt," *St. Louis Argus*, August 20, 1943: 10.

20   Normal Webb, "Giants Beat Scullins in Ninth with Bunt."

21   Normal Webb, "Giants Beat Scullins in Ninth with Bunt."

22   Normal Webb, "Giants Beat Scullins in Ninth with Bunt."

23   "Locals to Join Spring Training with Buckeyes," *St. Louis Argus*, March 17, 1944: 10.

24   "Four St. Louis Boys Making Grade with Cleveland Club," *St. Louis Argus*, April 14, 1944: 10.

25   "Four St. Louis Boys Making Grade with Cleveland Club."

26   "Cleveland Plays Chicago American Giants," *St. Louis Argus*, July 14, 1944: 10.

27   "Buckeyes Trounce Richmond, 12-2, in Twilight Contest," *Richmond* (Indiana) *Palladium Item and Sun-Telegram*, August 3, 1944: 8.

28   "Mgr. Troupe [*sic*] Will Begin New Job with Buckeyes in Spring Drill Mar. 24," *St. Louis Argus*, March 9, 1945: 10.

29   "Mgr. Troupe [*sic*] Will Begin New Job with Buckeyes in Spring Drill Mar. 24"; "Bucks Boast Veteran Club," *Oklahoma City Daily Oklahoman*, April 13, 1945: 18; Bob Overaker, "Beers and Buckeyes Clash Here Tonight," *South Bend* (Indiana) *Tribune*, May 18, 1945: 25.

30   Lynn Henning, "Negro League Player Has His Books, Memories."

31   "Clowns Split with Buckeyes," *Cincinnati Post*, May 21, 1945: 13; Gordon Graham, "Double Steal Gives Red Sox Thrilling Win Over Cleveland Buckeyes, 5-4," *Lafayette* (Indiana) *Journal and Courier*, September 6, 1945: 20.

32   "East Chicago Here Sunday, Memphis Red Sox Thursday," *Saint Joseph* (Michigan) *Herald-Press,* July 21, 1945: 7.

33   "Grays Top Buckeyes," *Dayton Journal,* September 15, 1945: 11.

34   "Buckeyes Blank Grays, Win Title," *Philadelphia Inquirer,* September 21, 1945: 24.

35   "Buckeyes Blank Grays, Win Title."

36   "Buckeyes Blank Grays, Win Title."

37   "Grays Win Two, but Too Late," *Pittsburgh Courier,* September 29, 1945: 12.

38   "Grays Win Two, but Too Late."

39   Lynn Henning, "Negro League Player Has His Books, Memories."

40   "Bucks to Train in Birmingham," *Chicago Defender,* March 16, 1946: 9.

41   "Negro Baseball Stars Will Be Seen in Game at Offerman [*sic*] Stadium," *Kenmore* (New York) *Press,* May 23, 1946: 4.

42   "Louisville and Memphis Split," *St. Louis Argus,* April 22, 1949: 20.

43   "Negro Champs Boast Classy Pitching Staff," *Rochester Democrat and Chronicle,* June 10, 1946: 20.

44   "Traded," *Chicago Defender,* July 13, 1946: 11.

45   "American Giants Defeat Stags, 4-3," *Belleville* (Illinois) *Daily Advocate,* August 14, 1946: 7.

46   "American Giants Defeat Stags, 4-3."

47   "Expect 30,000 to See East's Baseball Classic," *Chicago Defender,* August 10, 1946: 10.

48   "Start Training March 5," *Cleveland Plain Dealer,* January 13, 1947: 16.

49   "Atkins Helps Ohioans Defeat Jacksonville," *Pittsburgh Courier,* April 5, 1947: 14.

50   "Cleveland Buckeyes Play S.I. Oilers Under the Lights," *Staten Island* (New York) *Advance,* July 15, 1947: 12.

51   "Negro League Play to Open Here Tuesday," *Dayton Herald,* May 2, 1947.

52   "Negro League Play to Open Here Tuesday"; "Buckeyes Play Chicago Giants," *Dayton Herald,* May 28, 1947: 18.

53   "Negro American League," *Alabama Tribune* (Montgomery), August 8, 1947: 6.

54   "Negro American League."

55   Jimmie N. Jones, "Buckeyes Undergo Changes," *Ohio Daily-Express* (Dayton), February 26, 1948: 1, 4.

56   Jimmie N. Jones, "Buckeyes Undergo Changes."

57   "38-Year-Old Chet Brewer Is Still Hill Ace," *St. Louis Argus,* May 21, 1948: 17.

58   "38-Year-Old Chet Brewer Is Still Hill Ace."

59   "38-Year-Old Chet Brewer Is Still Hill Ace."

60   "Cleveland to Meet Creoles in Abbeville," *Lafayette* (Louisiana) *Daily Advertiser,* September 10, 1948: 17.

61   Lynn Henning.

62   James A. Riley, *The Biographical Encyclopedia of the Negro Baseball Leagues* (New York: Carroll & Graf Publishers, Inc., 1994), 495.

63   "Louisville Buckeye [*sic*] Win Spirited Game," *St. Louis Argus,* April 1, 1949: 16.

64   "Negro Nines Open a 2-Game Series Tonight," *Muskogee* (Oklahoma) *Times-Democrat,* April 12, 1949: 13.

65   "Louisville and Memphis Split," *St. Louis Argus,* April 22, 1949: 20.

66   Marion E. Jackson, "Sports of the World," *Atlanta Daily World,* July 20, 1949: 5.

67   "Houston Eagles Boast Highly Regarded Team," *Wichita Falls* (Texas) *Record News,* May 18, 1949: 11.

68   "Red Sox Lose, 7-5," *Memphis Commercial Appeal,* May 9, 1950: 20; "One Game for Monarchs," *Kansas City* (Missouri) *Times,* May 16, 1949: 15; "Collins Twirls No-Hitter as Kansas City Wins 14-0," *Pittsburgh Courier,* May 28, 1949: 24.

69   Lynn Henning.

70   Lynn Henning.

71   Lynn Henning.

72   Lynn Henning.

73   Lynn Henning.

74   Lynn Henning.

Avelino Cañizares

By Tony S. Oliver

Before Minnie Miñoso's cup of coffee with the Indians in 1949, another Black Cuban was the toast of Cleveland. Although Avelino Cañizares's story is not as well-known as the Cuban Comet's, Cañizares led the city to a coveted championship.

But then, in a flash, the "Cuban Wonder" was gone.

Avelino Cañizares Martínez was born on November 10, 1919, in Havana. Most of his biographical records are either lost or have not yet been found. His slight build (5-feet-7, 145 pounds), agility, sure hands, and speed made him the prototype shortstop in 1940s Cuba. He began his career with the Almendares Alacranes (Scorpions) in 1942-1943, though he was hitless in nine at-bats. He turned 24 years old during the 1943-1944 season and hit a robust .284.[1]

Since the Cuban season ran during the winter, Cañizares sought baseball opportunities outside the island during the summer months. He first played in Mexico in 1944 with the Tampico Alijadores (.305 average, 13 doubles and 4 triples in 73 games).[2]

Back in Cuba with, he tied for the league lead in runs scored in 1944-1945 (29) with Santos Amaro, Héctor Rodríguez, and Conrado Pérez, and was selected to the circuit's all-star game.[3] He hit .233 but provided stellar defense.[4]

Cañizares was coveted by Buckeyes manager Quincy Trouppe, who had scouted the infielder in the Mexican League when they played on opposing teams. According to James Riley, Trouppe's high opinion was warranted. Cañizares "studied hitters, positioned himself accordingly, and served as the 'glue' for the infield. That season he was compared to the Monarchs' Jackie Robinson and Birmingham's Artie Wilson."[5] The veteran Trouppe, himself an all-star catcher in the Negro Leagues, understood the value of defense. Contemporary records note that Cañizares was "known for his sensational fielding and solid hitting" and his "spark-plug play."[6] Cañizares duly signed with Cleveland and played in the Buckeyes' spring-training contests against the New York Cubans on April 8.[7]

Cañizares entrusted his bat and glove to do the talking from the club's home opener doubleheader: "The park resounded still louder when [Avelino Canizares, (sic)] a classy Cuban who can't even speak English, ripped around the bases for a home run within the park."[8] The press called him "the first player to capture the fans' attention without

the aid of ballyhoo."[9] The 10,000 fans in attendance cheered their Buckeyes as they swept the Memphis Red Sox, 3-1 and 6-2, on May 27.

By the end of May, the Buckeyes' .818 winning percentage led the league and Cañizares was hitting .400, third-best in the league.[10] His inside-the-park home run was still a newspaper topic a week later, with an article saying he had "sped around the bases at an unbelievable clip – so fast that fans didn't know he was making a home run of what looked like a double until he coasted over the plate."[11]

Local scribe Bob Williams noted that Cañizares had "crashed into the hearts of Cleveland fans for good with his stellar playing at shortstop, his pinch hitting, and that agile clip around the bases," as Cañizares tied the game with a two-out, two-run hit against the Memphis Red Sox.[12]

On the eve of a homestand, Williams noted, "Buckeye fans will come to League Park Sunday with special eyes for little Avelino Canizares, [the] flashy Cuban shortstop who has starred in all Cleveland appearances. While Cleveland leads the league in team standing the little Cuban-speaking [sic] shortstop leads the league in home runs, having clouted

A. CAÑIZARES

Avelino Cañizares.

out four circuit breakers this season while batting an average of .362."[13]

The hyperbole proved to be insufficient for the theatrics of June 17. Cañizares scored the winning run in the bottom of the 13th inning in the first game of a doubleheader against the Chicago American Giants. As the runner on third with the bases loaded and nobody out, he dashed for home on an infield groundball to shortstop. Although Cañizares appeared to be out, umpire Harry Walker "called him safe. ... After the call, three Chicago players grabbed and were about to strike the umpire when Cleveland's finest were able to intervene. It took a while but eventually peace was restored, and the second game was played."[14] Walker argued that "the catcher Dukes had his foot off the plate as Canizares arrived, otherwise he would have been out."[15]

Cañizares hit .344 in the first half (52-for-151), fourth best among the powerful Buckeyes batters.[16] Wendell Smith, *Pittsburgh Courier* reporter and doyen of Negro League baseball, considered Cañizares, Robinson, and Wilson to be "three young shortstops in Negro baseball who certainly should be given a chance to play in the major leagues."[17]

The July 16 contest against the Black Barons featured its own fireworks. Cañizares was again in the middle though he played no part in the hostilities. He beat out a throw to first base, but the Barons felt differently. After an argument with the umpire James "Jimmy" Thompson, "suddenly, without warning, (Piper) Davis uncorked a lightning-like swing from the waist, shoving his full weight directly into the little umpire's unguarded face."[18] The Buckeyes won the game, 6-1.

The Buckeyes swept a doubleheader against the Cincinnati-Indianapolis Clowns on July 22, though Cañizares is mentioned only as having advanced a runner with a sacrifice.[19]

Smith went further in his praise: "Probably at no time in the history of organized Negro baseball has there been three shortstops who were so near equal."[20] Newspapers debated the merits of worthy candidates and published the suggested batting orders for the East-West Game. The *Kansas City Call* advocated for its hometown hero: "Although three fine shortstops are running neck and neck for that position in the All-Star game Jackie Robinson of the Monarchs will probably win out since he is one of the most colorful players. ... The two other shortstops standing a good chance in the league are Canizares of Cleveland and Wilson of Birmingham."[21]

The July 26 *Chicago Defender* reported that Cañizares would start the game and Robinson would be on the bench. The weekly noted the embarrassment of riches for the Western's team middle infield in an article on the game's eve: "Avelino Canizares, Cuban shortstop with the Cleveland Buckeyes, wearing number 22 on his uniform, will start the game at shortstop. Considered one of the best in either league, Canizares gets the nod of Manager Welsh over Jackie Robinson, the UCLA all-around athlete who may see services before the game is over."[22]

The *Pittsburgh Courier*, in its July 28 edition, projected Cañizares to start at shortstop and Wilson at second base, but its non-alphabetic roster listed Wilson, Cañizares, and Robinson (as infielders) atop the potent West squad.[23]

The *Baltimore Afro-American*'s July 28 edition, however, named Robinson in the starting lineup but failed to mention Cañizares on the roster, even though other substitutes were listed.[24]

Cañizares did not play in the July 29 East-West Game; Robinson manned the position instead.[25] Other prospective starters, such as Josh Gibson and Art Wilson, did not see action either.[26] Though Robinson went 0-for-5 at the plate, he made a dazzling play in the field in the ninth inning to extinguish a West rally.

Cañizares made a costly error against the Newark Eagles in the first game of an August 18 doubleheader, a 4-0 Buckeyes loss, but atoned in the second game by scoring the tying run and driving in the winning tally in a hard-fought 4-3 contest.[27] The Buckeyes swept another doubleheader against Chicago on September 2, 1945. Cañizares belted an inside-the-park home run in the first game, a 6-2 victory.[28] His efforts were lauded by reporter Jimmy Jones, who noted, "Canizares was the shining light on the Buckeyes squad, displaying his stellar talents at bat and in the field, continuously, to earn the plaudits of the crowd."[29]

The 1945 Buckeyes are credited with 62 wins, 17 losses, and 1 tie in league competition (and 76-31-3 against Major League Black Teams).[30] Substantiated records credit Cañizares with 16 runs scored, 30 hits, 7 doubles, and a .375 average (30-for-80). On the field, he committed five errors in 164 innings for a .955 fielding average, 30 points above the league average. Modern metrics credit him with a 1.4 WAR, second-best in the team behind staff ace Eugene Bremer's 2.3.[31]

The Buckeyes and the Homestead Grays, winners of both season halves for their respective leagues, met in the Negro World Series. Cleveland was sanguine about its team prospects, though it warned caution against "the formidable array of batting and pitching talent [that] represents part of the championship Buckeye squad which has attained unprecedented honor within the brief span of four years."[32]

The *Cleveland Call and Post* noted that the "Buckeyes have more than an even chance to win the series from the Grays who have been steadily declining in the power and flash which highlighted some of their earlier title triumphs." It described Cañizares as "the flashy ... Cuban sensation who played shortstop and is a good clutch hitter."[33]

Cañizares went 3-for-15 in the championship series against the favored Grays. In the September 13 opener, Cleveland nipped the Grays 2-1, and Cañizares (0-for-3) was one of four Buckeyes held hitless by hard-luck loser Roy Welmaker.[34] However, Cañizares' defense was instrumental in preserving the victory in the ninth inning. After the Grays scored a run, they still threatened with runners on the corners, but Cañizares started a textbook 6-4-3 double play to quell the rally.[35]

Three days later, his two safeties helped Cleveland win another narrow game, 3-2.[36] He went 0-for-4 on September 18 in Giffith Stadium, Cleveland's third victory,[37] and collected one hit and one run in four plate appearances on September 20 as the Buckeyes won the title at Shibe Park, a neutral site.[38]

Despite his modest .200 average in the four-game sweep, he "gained uncontested right to the title 'Player of the year.' Canizares more than once caught the fancy and admiration of fans who marveled at his speed and perfection, and clutch hitting."[39]

Back in Cuba, Cañizares improved to .273 in 1945-1946 with a league-leading six stolen bases. The Buckeyes front office expected the shortstop to return in 1946, but he opted to play in the Mexican League. The contract was rumored to be less lucrative than Cleveland's offer, but a $3,000 bonus persuaded Cañizares to remain south of the border.[40] The Buckeyes turned to Billy Horne as their new shortstop while Cañizares was superb in 1946 with the Torreón Algodoneros de Unión Laguna (Cottonpickers). Under the tutelage of "el inmortal" Martín Dihigo, Cañizares produced a .298 batting average, stole 18 bases, and scored 72 runs in 90 games.[41] He was selected to the July 9 All-Star Game as the starting shortstop for the North team, led by another Cuban legend, Armando Marsans.[42]

Commissioner Happy Chandler and the major-league owners sought to persuade the Cuban League officials to bar players who had jumped to the Mexican League. While some light-skinned players were indeed under professional contracts with "Organized Baseball," the move smacked of hypocrisy as many dark-skinned Cubans were barred from the major and minor leagues. As the 1946 season neared, Cañizares and scores of others who had proven their mettle in the Negro Leagues returned to the Cuban clubs .[43]

Cañizares scored 46 runs in 1946-1947, and he was routinely among the top basestealers although his average dipped to .260.[44] On October 26, 1946, he was the first batter in the inaugural game of the Gran Estadio del Cerro (now known as "El Estadio Latinoamericano") in Havana, attended by 31,000 fans.[45] He led off for Almendares and was retired in the first inning, thus marking the first out of the stadium's history.[46] He nevertheless had a fine game (3-for-5) as his club defeated Cienfuegos, 9-1.[47] During offdays, he was among the many professional stars to make cameo paid appearances for the sugar-mill amateur teams, typically in the rural central provinces.[48]

The Buckeyes held hope that Cañizares would return in 1947, despite the Negro League's decree banning so-called deserters for five years.[49] However, Cañizares signed a reported $12,000 contract (a base figure of $8,400 and a hefty bonus) to play in Mexico in 1947, a figure thought to be twice his 1945 Buckeyes pay. The local press was

sympathetic to his choice, noting that the "contract calls for three days regular play per week, and $12,000 salary for the season. That is a first class pay in any man's baseball league."[50]

Cañizares played for the Tuneros (Tuna Fishermen) of San Luis Potosí in 1947 and appeared in a career-high 113 games as an offensive force: .281 average, 93 runs, 16 doubles, 6 triples, 24 stolen bases, and 72 walks. Among the contests was the first night game in Mexican League history; San Luis bested the Diablos Rojos (Red Devils), 10-7.[51]

Cañizares' best Cuban season was 1947-1948: a .310 batting average with a league-leading 114 hits and 53 runs.[52] He was again selected to the All-Star Game. However, he was not officially a member of Almendares but rather a doppelganger, the *Alacranes*. Cuban players formed the "independent league" to protest their working conditions. The circuit only lasted a year before the parties resolved their differences.

He split 1948 between San Luis and the Monterrey Sultanes (Sultans). His 14 stolen bases and .272 average helped the Sultanes to their second consecutive title.[53]

He was a key cog in the 1948-1949 Almendares team that won the first Caribbean Series, held in Havana. After hitting .251 in the regular season, he contributed four hits in 24 plate appearances as the hosts dominated the competition, winning all six of their games. However, the emergence of future big-leaguer Willy Miranda cut into his playing time. In a Lou Gehrig/Wally Pipp twist, Miranda cracked the lineup after "the Cuban star, Avelino Canizarez [sic] was sidelined with a Charley horse."[54] Despite playing with the club until 1952, he was no longer a regular and saw sporadic

Avelino Cañizares.

action, though he returned to the second Caribbean Series (this time held in San Juan, Puerto Rico).[55]

Cañizares finished his Cuban playing career with Cienfuegos in 1953-1954 and hit a mediocre .255. He batted .251 for his Cuban career (344-for-1371), scored 203 runs, and drove in 111.[56][57] Although he was featured in many baseball cards during his time, the backs were mostly used for advertising and thus lack any statistics or biographical tidbits.[58]

The fall of the color barrier opened doors in North America. In 1950 Cañizares played with the Sherbrooke Athletics of the Class-C Provincial League (98 games, .294 average, with 18 doubles). The team finished in second place (57-51) and lost the league title to the St. Jean Braves. Sherbrooke featured four other Cubans in its multi-ethnic roster: Silvio García, Armando Roche, (Andrés) Lauro Pascual, and Félix Zulueta.[59] In 1952 Cañizares played with the Keokuk Kernels of the Class-B Illinois/Indiana/Iowa League (.222 average in 65 games).

Cañizares split 1954 between the Diablos Rojos and Veracruz (.244 average, 10 stolen bases in 74 games).[60] He played two years in the Central Mexican League with Saltillo (1955) and Durango (98 games, .302 average in 1956).[61] He moved to the Méxicali Águilas (Eagles) of the Arizona-Mexico League in 1957 (.302/.384/.430 with 120 runs scored, 26 doubles, 8 triples, and 8 home runs in 123 games at 37 years of age) and 1958 (.359/.428/.454 27 doubles, 4 triples, 3 home runs). Both these circuits were Class C.[62]

In 1957, a dozen years after the Buckeyes' title, Cleveland media still regarded Cañizares highly enough to include him a list of great Negro players, alongside legends Josh Gibson, Satchel Paige, and Oscar Charleston.[63] While still active, he managed the Saltillo club of the Class-A Mexico Central League in 1964 but hit a meek .198 in 41 games.[64] He remained in the sport as both coach and pilot of other teams.

Cañizares married a Mexican woman and remained in Mexico after his playing career.[65] He died on December 13, 1993, in Mexico City at the age of 74. The Cuban Baseball Hall of Fame elected Cañizares to its ranks in 1997.[66] His Negro League Baseball Players Association profile is sadly barren: "Avelino played for the Cleveland Buckeyes in 1945. He spent most of his career playing in the Mexican Leagues and Cuba."[67]

SOURCES

In addition to the sources cited in the Notes, the author consulted baseball-reference.com and seamheads.com.

NOTES

1   Jorge S. Figueredo, *Who's Who in Cuban Baseball: 1878-1961*, McFarland and Company, 2003), 131-132.

2   Jesús Alberto Rubio, "Avelino Cañizares," *Beisbólicos* (Baseball-holics), April 5, 2009, https://www.beisbolicos.com/beis-bolicos.nsf/489cfd413995l594862570b20015c24f/12097eec908e6269 8625758f0081e8b9?opendocument (archived at https://web.archive.org/web/20200202071654/https://www.beisbolicos.com/beisbolicos.nsf/489cfd413995l594862570b20015c24f/12097eec908e62698625758f0081e-8b9?opendocument. Unless otherwise specified, All Mexican, US, and Canadian minor-league statistics mentioned in this biography stem from Rubio's insightful work.

3   "Carreras Anotadas," (Runs Scored Leaders), *Desde Mi Palco de Fanático: Memorias y Reflexiones del Béisbol Cubano,* https://desdemipalcodefanatico.wordpress.com/archivo/carreras-anotadas/.

4   Jorge S. Figueredo, *Who's Who in Cuban Baseball: 1878-1961.*

5   James Riley, *The Biographical Encyclopedia of the Negro Baseball Leagues* (New York: Carroll & Graf Publishers, 1994), 150.

6   Dave O'Karma, "The Forgotten Championship," *Cleveland Magazine,* https://clevelandmagazine.com/in-the-cle/sports/articles/the-forgotten-championship.

7   Cleveland Buckeyes Website, sponsored by Wayne Pearsall. https://www.clevelandbuckeyesbaseball.com/1945SPRINGTRAINING.htm

8   Dave O'Karma, "The Forgotten Championship." Most newspaper articles dropped the tilde (~) in Cañizares; occasionally spelled his last name as Canizarez; and sometimes misspelled his first name as "Avalino."

9   Stephanie M. Liscio, *Integrating Cleveland Baseball: Media Activism, the Integration of the Indians and the Demise of the Cleveland Buckeyes* (Jefferson, North Carolina: McFarland, 2014), 92.

10 Cleveland Buckeyes website, https://www.clevelandbuckeyesbaseball.com/1945openingDAY.html.

11 "Aces in Hole Are Bucks' Cuban Stars," *Cleveland Call and Post,* June 2, 1945: 6B.

12 Bob Williams, "Sports Rumbler," *Cleveland Call and Post,* June 9, 1945: 6B.

13 Bob Williams, "Buckeyes Leading League; Play Chicago American Giants Here Sunday," *Cleveland Call and Post,* June 16, 1945: 6B.

14 Cleveland Buckeyes website, https://www.clevelandbuckeyesbaseball.com/summer_in_the_city.htm.

15 "Disputed Umpire's Decision Almost Disrupts Buckeyes-Giant Series," *Cleveland Call and Post,* June 23, 1945: 18.

16 Cleveland Buckeyes website, https://www.clevelandbuckeyesbaseball.com/halfwaymark.html.

17 Wendell Smith, "The Sports Beat," *Pittsburgh Courier,* July 14, 1945: 12.

18 Cleveland Buckeyes Website, https://www.clevelandbuckeyesbaseball.com/SUMMER_IN_THE_CITY2.html.

19 "Buckeyes Take 2 Games From Clowns, Gird for Pennant," *Cleveland Call and Post,* July 28, 1945: 6B.

20 Gaylon H. White, *Singles and Smiles: How Artie Wilson Broke Baseball's Color Barrier* (Lanham, Maryland: Rowman & Littlefield, 2018), 30.

21 Willie Bea Harmon, "Sportorial," *Kansas City Call,* July 20, 1945: 6.

22 Fay Young, "Mathis to Start for West Against East on Sunday: Lefthander Will Make Bid to Halt East's Bats," *Chicago Defender,* July 20, 1945: 7.

23 "Expect 40,000 to Witness 'Dream Game' in Chicago," *Pittsburgh Courier,* July 28, 1945: 12.

24 "Afro Favors West Team in Annual All-Star Tilt," *Baltimore Afro-American,* July 28, 1945: 18.

25 Cleveland Buckeyes website, https://www.clevelandbuckeyesbaseball.com/AllStar.html.

26 "Mathis to Start for West Against East on Sunday," *Chicago Defender,* July 28, 1945: 7. The game's box score is available on Retrosheet: https://retrosheet.org/NegroLeagues/boxesetc/1945/B07290ASW1945.htm.

27   Jimmy Jones, "Buckeyes, Eagles Split Double-Header at Newark, 4-0, 4-3 in Thrillers; W. Jefferson Is Loser," *Cleveland Call and Post*, August 18, 1945: 6B.

28   Cleveland Buckeyes website, https://www.clevelandbuckeyesbaseball.com/September1945.html.

29   Jimmy Jones, "Buckeyes Gain Undisputed Title as League Champions," *Cleveland Call and Post,* September 8, 1945: 6B.

30   1945 Cleveland Buckeyes, Seamheads, https://www.seamheads.com/NegroLgs/team.php?yearID=1945&teamID=CBE&LGOrd=2&tab=metrics.

31   WAR as measured by Seamheads, https://www.seamheads.com/NegroLgs/team.php?yearID=1945&teamID=CBE&LGOrd=2&tab=bypos. Baseball Reference credits Cañizares with a 1.3 WAR and Bremer with a 2.6 WAR, https://www.baseball-reference.com/leagues/NAL/1945-other-leaders.shtml.

32   "Meet the Champs – Can They Dethrone Grays?" *Cleveland Call and Post,* September 15, 1945: 7B.

33   Jimmy Jones, "Buckeyes Aim, to Dethrone Homestead Grays, Czars of All Baseball for Six Years, " *Cleveland Call and Post,* September 15, 1945: 7B.

34   Cleveland Buckeyes website, https://www.clevelandbuckeyesbaseball.com/Game1.htm.

35   "Buckeyes Capture Three Straight From Wobbly Grays," *Michigan Chronicle* (Detroit), September 22, 1945: 15. A reconstructed play-by-play account of the game is available on Retrosheet: https://retrosheet.org/NegroLeagues/boxesetc/1945/B09130CVB1945.htm.

36   Cleveland Buckeyes website, https://www.clevelandbuckeyesbaseball.com/Game2.html.

37   Cleveland Buckeyes website, https://www.clevelandbuckeyesbaseball.com/Game3.html.

38   Cleveland Buckeyes website, https://www.clevelandbuckeyesbaseball.com/Game4WS.html.

39   "Key Personalities Who Sparked Amazing Championship of 'Cinderella' Team," *Cleveland Call and Post,* September 29, 1945: 6B.

40   Cleveland Jackson, "Mexican Baseball League Raids American Negro Teams," *Cleveland Call and Post*, February 23, 1946: 9B.

41   Jesús Alberto Rubio, "Avelino Cañizares," *Beisbólicos.*

42   "Gardella Emulates Ted, Hits Pair in Mex Classic," *The Sporting News*, July 17, 1946: 30.

43   "Cubans Name Ineligibles on Winter League Roster," *The Sporting News*, September 25, 1946: 24.

44   Jorge S. Figueredo, *Who's Who in Cuban Baseball: 1878-1961.*

45   Julio Pérez, "El estadio del Cerro, hoy Latinoamericano, cumple 70 años de existencia," *Radio Habana Cuba*, October 26, 2016, https://www.radiohc.cu/en/noticias/deportes/109959-el-estadio-del-cerro-hoy-latinoamericano-cumple-70-anos-de-existencia.

46   Roberto González Echevarría, *The Pride of Havana: A History of Cuban Baseball* (New York: Oxford University Press, 2001), 31.

47   Almendares-Cienfuegos box score, October 26, 1946, as reproduced in Angel Torres, *La Historia del Béisbol Cubano, 1878-1976,* self-published book.

48   Arquímedes Romo Pérez, "El béisbol en Morón III," March 23, 2023, https://www.radiomoron.icrt.cu/2023/03/23/el-beisbol-en-moron-iii/.

49   Stephanie M. Liscio, *Integrating Cleveland Baseball: Media Activism, the Integration of the Indians and the Demise of the Cleveland Buckeyes*, 105.

50   Cleveland Jackson, "Avelino Canizares Signs $8,400 Mexican Contract. Night Games Planned for League Park," *Cleveland Call and Post,* March 1, 1947: 8B.

51   Jesús Alberto Rubio, "Avelino Cañizares," *Beisbólicos.*

52   Jorge S. Figueredo, *Who's Who in Cuban Baseball: 1878-1961.*

53   Jesús Alberto Rubio, "Avelino Cañizares," *Beisbólicos.*

54   Pedro Galiana, "Miranda Sparks Almendares to 6 Wins," *The Sporting News,* January 26, 1949: 24.

55   William Pérez Villalba, *"Gloria del Beisbol Cubano,"* July 29, 2019, https://www.facebook.com/groups/222151257802610/permalink/3226464174037955/?paipv=0&eav=AfaLgISvyKH54FFO62guwMkjBRsTWOGSAqF3X0RLW-7ovD7HtueybQ1umOfFQMsNWco&_rdr.

56   Jorge S. Figueredo, *Who's Who in Cuban Baseball: 1878-1961,*

57   Other sources credit him with an additional run scored and run batted in, most notably Peter Bjarkman, *Baseball with a Latin Beat: A History of the Latin American Game* (Jefferson, North Carolina: McFarland, 2010), 189. Bjarkman credits *Béisbol Cubano, Récords y Estadísticas, 1878-1955,* as the original source.

58   Cañizares was featured in the 1945-1946 Caramelo Deportivo (considered the most important Cuban baseball card set) and the 1949-1950 Alerta Premium, a set of 8x11 black-and-white pictures of Cuban baseball players promoting "Antonio" (Antonio Prío Socarrás) for mayor of La Habana. Prío Socarrás was the brother of Cuban President Carlos Prío Socarrás, ousted by Fulgencio Batista in 1952.

59   Sherbrooke Athlétiques Team Photo, *Histoire de la ligue provinciale de baseball* (History of the Provincial Baseball League), https://www.lesfantomesdustade.ca/1950-1952/1950-sherbrooke-athl%C3%A9tiques.

60   Jesús Alberto Rubio, "Avelino Cañizares," *Beisbólicos.*

61   Jesús Alberto Rubio, "Avelino Cañizares," *Beisbólicos.*

62   Jesús Alberto Rubio, "Avelino Cañizares," *Beisbólicos.*

63   "Negro Baseball Contributed Plenty Players of Yesteryears Had Big Time Potential," *Cleveland Call and Post,* March 9, 1957: 4C.

64   Jesús Alberto Rubio, "Avelino Cañizares," *Beisbólicos.*

65   Roberto González Echevarría, 22.

66   The original Cuban Baseball Hall of Fame suspended inductions in 1961 after Castro's Revolution and restarted in 2015. The Cuban Baseball Hall of Fame in Miami elected players from 1962 to 1986 and sporadically since then. For more information, consult Rogerio Manzano, "Salón de la Fama del Béisbol Cubano," Desde mi palco de fanático, https://desdemipalcodefanatico.wordpress.com/archivo/salon-de-la-fama-del-beisbol-cubano/.

67   "Canizares, Avelino," Negro League Baseball Players Association (NLBPA) website, http://www.nlbpa.com/the-athletes/canizares-avelino.

Frank Carswell

By Margaret M. Gripshover

Frank Carswell was a right-handed pitcher whose career began in 1944 with the local Dan Montgomerys of Buffalo, New York; included stints in the Negro Leagues with the Cleveland Buckeyes, Harlem Colored Giants, Harlem Globetrotters, Chicago American Giants, and Indianapolis Clowns; and ended with a postseason barnstorming gig with Jackie Robinson's New York All-Stars in 1951. Although Carswell pitched only 11 official games in the Negro American League, one of those victories was a four-hit gem that clinched the 1945 Negro World Series for the Buckeyes.

Carswell was born in Jeffersonville, Georgia, near Macon in the central part of the state, on August 9, 1917. The identity of his father is uncertain. His mother died in 1930 when he was 13 years old, leaving him and his three siblings to live with relatives. Carswell left school after the eighth grade and went to work as a "chalk loader" in the kaolin mines in nearby McIntyre, Georgia. When he registered for the draft in 1940, he was working for the Edgar Brothers Company, at the time the owner of the largest kaolin mine in the United States.[1] Although Edgar Brothers sponsored a baseball team in the 1930s that competed against teams from area mills and mines, it appears that the league was for White players only.[2] Carswell's draft card in 1940 described him as 23 years old, standing 6-feet-2-inches tall,

CLOWN CHUCK CORPS— The Auscos hope every one of these Indianapolis Clown pitchers get into Wednesday night's game at Edgewater park. But whether they do or not, here they are from left: Percy Smith, Clarence Turner, Frank Carswell, Willie Gaines, Ray Maddix, Dioniso Amaro, Angel Garcia and Ted Richardson. Smith and Richardson threw here July 1 when the Auscos won out, 7-6.

Herald-Press (Indianapolis), August 25, 1953.

Frank Carswell with the 1953 Indianapolis Clowns.

and weighing 175 pounds. The only identifying mark on his body was a scar on the inside of his left wrist. Carswell signed his draft card with an "X," indicating that he was unable to sign his own name. With both of his parents deceased by 1940, Carswell named his aunt, Katherine Carswell of Jeffersonville, as his personal contact.

While Carswell was working at the kaolin mines, several members of his family left Georgia for Albion, Michigan, including his brother, Eugene Carswell and a paternal uncle, Otha Carswell. Both were employed as laborers at the Albion Malleable Iron Company, which actively recruited African Americans from the South to move to Michigan to work in the foundry as early as 1916.[3] While his brother and uncle answered Albion's call, it appears that Carswell did not.[4] He remained in Georgia, working in the mines until the early 1940s, when he moved to Buffalo, New York, the city he called home until his death in 1978.

It is curious that no record of Carswell in baseball has yet to be found prior to 1944, when he joined the Dan Montgomerys in Buffalo. At that time, he was 27 years old. It seems unlikely that he would pick up the game and develop into a talented hurler at that relatively advanced baseball age without any prior experience. If Carswell had any starts prior to 1944, they must have been under the radar, perhaps in leagues that received little or no attention from the predominantly White press in Georgia. But his arrival in Buffalo put him on the baseball map. Carswell's discovery as a pitching prospect was credited to Ralph "Square" Moore, who played for a variety of Negro League teams during the 1920s.[5] Moore arrived in Buffalo in the 1920s and pitched for the local Pete Hill's Colored All-Stars as well as for the Kansas City Monarchs and Cleveland Elites.[6] Moore continued to dabble in baseball into the early 1930s. In 1932 Moore picked up some broken pieces from the East-West Negro League and reconstituted them as the short-lived Buffalo Stars.[7]

The first published record of Carswell's baseball career came in the spring of 1944, when he pitched for the Dan Montgomerys of the AA Municipal League in Buffalo.[8] The team was named for a well-known local hotel, supper club, and Prohibition-era speakeasy owner, Dan Montgomery.[9] The Montgomerys were the only African American team in the "Muny" League and had some quality players. At least two of Carswell's teammates had prior experience in the Negro Leagues: Elton Gladney, who had a brief stint at shortstop with the Indianapolis ABCs of the Negro Southern

THE 1945 CLEVELAND BUCKEYES

League in 1932; and Pete McQueen, who in the 1930s had a few cups of coffee with the Little Rock Grays, Pittsburgh Crawfords, and Memphis Red Sox.

Despite Square Moore's faith in his pitching protégé, Carswell was off to a rough first season. In one of his early starts for the Montgomerys, he and his fellow hurlers were tagged for 19 hits in a 15-5 loss to the league-leading Black Rock Howells.[10] Carswell and his relievers were "unable to throw anything that the Howells couldn't hit."[11] Carswell didn't have much of a chance to get to know his fellow Montgomerys. In the summer of 1944, the Buckeyes were scouting for some new pitching talent. They gave George Provens of Canton, Ohio, a shot, but waited until 1945 to sign him.[12] In early July, Carswell inked his first contract with the Buckeyes.

Carswell made his debut as a starting pitcher with the Buckeyes on July 11, 1944, against the Memphis Red Sox in Hamilton, Ontario.[13] It was not pretty. Carswell was roughed up for five hits, three walks, and four runs in five innings in a 10-9 loss.[14] To his credit, Carswell struck out three, had one hit, stole a base, and scored a run, but it was not enough to make his first appearance as a Buckeye one for the books.[15]

Carswell redeemed himself a few days later when the Buckeyes defeated the Red Sox 6-3 in Dayton, Ohio.[16] The Bucks' errors helped give the Red Sox an early lead, but Carswell was not to blame. He was replaced on the mound by Lovell Harden, who benefited from a late Cleveland rally that sealed the come-from-behind victory. Carswell did not get much credit for the victory in the *Dayton Journal Herald's* coverage of the game. The newspaper misspelled his name as "Caldwell" in the line score.[17] This was not a one-off error. Carswell's surname sometimes appeared as "Cardwell" and his first name was mistakenly given as "William."[18]

The lowlight of Carswell's 1944 season was possibly the contest between the Buckeyes and the Simon Pures of Hamilton, Ontario, also known as the "Krustomen" for their manager, Matt Krusto.[19] Prior to the game, Cleveland's owner, Ernest Wright, commented that he "did not plan to start any second-rater," and that the Buckeyes "cannot afford a setback by an amateur club."[20] Wright was wrong about Carswell's abilities that day, but right about the potential embarrassment of losing to the amateurs, as discussed by a Hamilton journalist:

"Well, 1,733 of the faithful turned up for what the majority expected would be a landslide by the professionals. But such was not the case. Hamilton won 12 to 7, and don't let your best friend tell you that the Bucks pulled their punches. They tried from the drop of the hat, but it must be admitted that they did treat the Simon Pures cheaply at the outset by starting Carswell, a utility player, on the mound. Before Carswell reached the showers, and after only two men had been disposed of, the Krustomen had bounced his offerings off every fence in the park."[21]

Another account of the game noted that "the amateurs outhit the invaders by 15 to 13 and piled up a four-run lead in the initial stanza, when they drove Cardwell [sic], starting hurler for Cleveland, from the mound, to secure a lead they never relinquished."[22] Carswell lasted just two-thirds of an inning.[23]

Carswell's disastrous outing in Hamilton left him with nowhere to go but up. As the 1944 season entered its final lap, he redeemed himself with a 12-2 win over the Chicago American Giants.[24] "Tiny" Carswell, as he was described, struck out six, walked two, and limited Chicago to six hits.[25] He also "punctured three, his loss of control being in the early frames."[26] But a few weeks later, as the season drew to a close, Carswell was on the losing side of a 13-3 drubbing by the Baltimore Elite Giants, a game that drew just 700 spectators.[27]

The 1944 season ended with the Buckeyes a distant second place in the NAL behind the Birmingham Black Barons. Carswell finished the year with an abysmal 14.21 ERA. Only one other Cleveland pitcher had worse stats in that department – Willie McMeans, who ran up a catastrophic 27.00 ERA and did not return to the Buckeyes in 1945.

In the spring of 1945, Carswell was back as a member of the Buckeyes' pitching staff along with Eugene Bremer, Willie Jefferson, Lovell Harden, and John Brown.[28] And although Carswell played for Cleveland the previous season, he was sometimes described as a newcomer.[29] If his rookie year was largely forgotten by sportswriters and his name was often misreported, it may have been for the best because in 1945 Carswell was off to a good start. Even though his name appeared in the *South Bend* (Indiana) *Tribune* as "Jimmy Carswell," he was credited with having "breezed along in fine fettle," giving up six hits in a 9-4 victory over the local Hoosier Beers.[30] Carswell continued to find his groove at the end of May, when the Buckeyes battered the Memphis Red Sox, 16-7.[31]

In mid-June he was the "individual star of the game" and "chucked a beautiful ball" as Cleveland trounced the Chicago American Giants, 9-0.[32] In July Carswell downed another round of Hoosier Beers, defeating the South Bend nine, 7-3.[33] By early August, Carswell's record was 4-1.[34] He was not as fortunate a few weeks later when his teammates' errors contributed to his 8-4 loss to the Black Barons.[35] On the eve of the Negro League World Series, Carswell saved the day in the ninth inning when he came in with the bases loaded and sealed a 4-3 victory for the Buckeyes over the Glenwood All-Stars.[36] Carswell's regular season ended on an up-and-down note. In one of his last starts, he pitched a two-hit shutout gem to lead Cleveland to a 10-0 blowout over the American Giants.[37] But at Red Bird Stadium in Columbus, Ohio, he was under a cloud when a fog rolled in resulting in a 9-8 loss to the Homestead Grays.[38] Even with that gloomy outcome, Carswell's 1945 season was head and shoulders above his 1944 performance. But his biggest test was yet to come, when the NAL champion Buckeyes faced the Grays for something of greater consequence – the 1945 championship.

The first game of the 1945 Negro World Series, at Cleveland's Municipal Stadium, resulted in a 2-1 squeaker in favor of the Buckeyes, with Willie Jefferson on the mound.[39] The Buckeyes continued their winning ways by copping the next two games, 4-2 and 4-0.[40] Carswell kept the bench warm during the first three games but got the call for the Series finale on September 18. He sealed the deal for the Buckeyes with a sparkling four-hit, 5-0 shutout of the Grays at Shibe Park in Philadelphia to claim the Negro League crown.[41]

The Buckeyes didn't have much time to savor their championship victory and went right back to work against the Grays and others in a series of exhibition games. In Dayton, Ohio, Cleveland faced an all-White squad of major leaguers including Babe Dahlgren, Eddie Miller, and George Kell, among others.[42] The racial context of the tilt was noted by the *Dayton Herald,* which commented that the "argument as to the class of Negro ball was waged for years and this game tonight will give the Bucks a chance to prove it belongs with the elite."[43] This was not the first mention of race and equality after the season. When the Buckeyes and Grays faced off at Yankee Stadium, a mayoral candidate, Judge Jonah Goldstein, tossed out the first ball, upon which he had written, "Discrimination – swat it."[44] Despite Carswell's clutch performance that clinched the championship title, it does not appear that he pitched in any of Cleveland's post-Series tilts. Carswell was mentioned as a possible starter for the game in Dayton on October 1, but the contest was rained out and not rescheduled.[45]

In March 1946, when the Buckeyes announced their spring-training plans for Birmingham, Alabama, Carswell was among the pitchers who returned to the fold.[46] His spring flinging, however, did not get off to a great start. He was tagged with a 6-1 loss in a twin bill with the Barons.[47] On April 21 Carswell was the fourth hurler used by Cleveland in a 10-9 squeaker over Birmingham.[48] In early May, manager Quincy Trouppe trusted Carswell for their season opener in Dayton, a rematch against the Grays, with the assumption that Carswell held a "sign" over the Homestead nine.[49] But Dayton's weather gods were against him, just as they were the previous October, and the game was scrubbed.[50]

Carswell had to wait until May 5 for his 1946 debut, but the outcome in Cleveland was as grim as the weather in Dayton. He and the Buckeyes were felled by the Barons, 7-2, in a seven-inning ending to a doubleheader at League Park.[51] A week later, Carswell was the second of three hurlers employed by the Buckeyes in another loss to the Barons, this time at Rickwood Field in Birmingham.[52] On May 19 he gave up six hits in a 3-0 surrender to the Clowns at Victory Field in Indianapolis.[53] On Memorial Day Cleveland split a doubleheader with the Chicago American

Giants at Comiskey Park and Carswell's efforts in relief of Curtis "Lefty" Jones did nothing for the cause as the Giants clocked him for six runs to seal Chicago's 8-3 win.[54] His mood may have lightened on June 6 when he had his finest outing of the season, posting a 10-1 drubbing of the Atlanta Black Crackers of the Negro Southern League at Red Wing Stadium in Rochester, New York.[55] Carswell went the distance, fanned eight Black Crackers, issued two walks, and allowed just three hits.[56] Despite these few flashes of brilliance, Carswell was mainly used in relief. Such was the case on June 16 when he was the second of three hurlers used by Cleveland in a 9-6 loss to the Kansas City Monarchs, an error-strewn performance by the Buckeyes.[57] It was rinse and repeat for Carswell through most of summer of 1946. His only consistency was his inconsistency. He gave up at least four runs as a closer in a come-from-behind 7-6 loss to the Memphis Red Sox.[58]

At the end of July, Carswell broke his dry spell as a starter when he notched a "W" as the Bucks swept the Black Barons during a swing through New York.[59] He was the "hometown" hero when he vanquished Birmingham 8-6 at his old stamping grounds at Offermann Stadium in Buffalo, where he played with the Dan Montgomerys.[60] But as the summer dragged on, so did Carswell. On August 5, before a crowd of over 12,000, the Buckeyes and the Philadelphia Stars posted a curfew-induced 10-10 stalemate at Shibe Park.[61] The Buckeyes and Stars were part of a special twin bill with the Grays and Kansas City Monarchs. After the Grays copped the win, 3-2, in the opening game, the Buckeyes and Stars took the field.[62] Carswell pitched the final three innings in relief of Hosea Allen, and in the process gave up three runs that sealed the tie.[63] Three days later Carswell took the mound in a tilt against Memphis as part of a "three-team, two-night bargain bill" at Griffith Stadium in Washington that also featured the Grays.[64] Identified in game reports as "Bob Carswell," he was pummeled by the Red Sox' five hits and four runs in the fifth inning as the Buckeyes fell, 5-1.[65] At the end of August, he was dinged with a 5-2 loss to the Black Barons when he gave up four runs in the eighth and donated a comeback victory to Birmingham.[66] Carswell dropped another game for Cleveland on September 22 as a starter in a 7-2 defeat to the Red Sox at Russwood Park.[67] Casey Jones's two-out homer with two men on in the fourth sealed Carswell's fate.[68]

The 1946 Cleveland Buckeyes did not enjoy the same successes as they did in 1945, finishing a distant third to the Kansas City Monarchs. The 1946 season was one to forget for Carswell. His ERA ballooned to 10.00, echoing his dreadful rookie year in 1944 when he chalked up a ghastly 14.21 ERA. During his whole career with the Buckeyes, Carswell accumulated a 7.30 ERA. His last appearance in 1946 was likely in the North-South game in which Cleveland, in a bizarre twist of geographical logic, participated as a member of the South's squad. The game was slated for October 6 at Pelican Field in New Orleans and Carswell was mentioned among the stable of tossers for the South.[69] The South won, 1-0, but lacking a box score, it is unknown if Carswell pitched in the contest.[70] A second North-South game was slated to be played at Rickwood Field on October 13 and once again Carswell was listed as a possible starter.[71] But without further documentation, it is impossible to determine if he ever took the field.

In February 1947 the Cleveland Buckeyes were making plans for spring training in Florida, and Carswell's name was on the roster.[72] They were set to cross bats in Bradenton with the Dayton Royals, described as Cleveland's farm club.[73] Throughout the spring of 1947, newspaper coverage of the Buckeyes continued to name Carswell as a member of their pitching staff. It does not appear, however, that he saw much action, and when he did get the call, the outcome was rarely positive. On May 15 he was hammered by the Grays at Redbird Stadium in Columbus, Ohio, 10-3.[74] And then, on June 10, it was announced that Carswell was pegged to face the Black Barons in Buffalo.[75] How did he fare in front of his hometown crowd? That question remains unanswered due to the lack of published coverage of the game. What is known is that less than a month later, Carswell was no longer wearing a Buckeyes uniform. In early July he signed with the Buffalo Harlem Giants.[76] The Giants were a barnstorming team whose opponents were primarily local semipro outfits from western New York and Ontario. The Harlem Giants were known for recruiting former Negro League players and for their clowning and entertaining fans with their "amusing antics."[77]

What prompted Carswell to abandon the Buckeyes for the Buffalo Harlem Giants? Several reasons come to mind. First and foremost, it may not have been his decision. His pitching stats were not in his favor and the parting may have been at the behest of the Buckeyes' management. Another possibility is that he may have been recruited to join the Giants by a former Cleveland bullpen mate, Jeff Shelton, who had a brief stint with the Buckeyes in 1946. And finally, his move to the Harlem Giants may have been more for personal than professional reasons. His only son, Rudy Carswell, was born in Buffalo in 1947.

Carswell was slated to make his debut with the Harlem Giants on July 9 in Waterloo, Ontario.[78] Newspaper coverage of the Giants' games was sparse and the outcome of his first game with Buffalo is uncertain. That summer he did enjoy some success with his new mates. In mid-August, he held the Brantford (Ontario) Seniors to five hits in a 7-2 victory.[79] On August 20 he helped lead his new team to victory by shutting out the Koch-Wallace nine of Dunkirk, New York, 7-0.[80] Carswell gave up just two hits and was described as a pitcher "who also toils on the mound for the Cleveland Buckeyes of the Negro American league."[81] Carswell *toiled* for the Buckeyes earlier in the year but was no longer with the team, and it doesn't appear that he was on both rosters at the same time. After he signed with Buffalo, there are no records of Carswell playing for

Cleveland for the remainder of the 1947 season. Fortunately for Carswell, he did not burn his bridges with the Bucks. He was back in a Cleveland uniform by the spring of 1948.

Carswell kicked off spring training in April with Cleveland with a 10-4 win over the Memphis Red Sox in a doubleheader that drew 3,900 fans at Martin Stadium.[82] In early May Carswell demonstrated some "clever hurling" in a 15-3 drubbing of the Black Barons.[83] A week later, in Springfield, Ohio, Birmingham exacted its revenge by crushing Carswell and his team, 11-6.[84] The Buckeyes struggled throughout the summer to add games to the win column and keep their best players from being poached by White major-league teams. In July a teammate, outfielder Al Smith, was signed by the Cleveland Indians.[85] Carswell never got the call to "The Show." He remained with the Buckeyes through early June. The last mention of Carswell as a possible starter was a game between Cleveland and Memphis on June 8 in Dayton, Ohio.[86] That summer, he disappeared from the Buckeyes' roster and was not picked up by another Negro League team. In his final year with Cleveland, Carswell was credited with appearing in three games, had a 0-2 record, and rang up a 7.11 ERA. After the 1948 season ended, the NAL was in a financial and logistical tailspin. The league folded and Cleveland found itself as one of 10 teams in a new NAL.[87]

In the spring of 1949, Carswell discovered that he could go home again – back to the "Harlem Colored Giants," later repackaged as Abe Saperstein's Harlem Globetrotters.[88] In the spring of 1949, he found himself in familiar territory, barnstorming in the United States and Canada. He was named as one of the "fancy flingers" for the Trotters and started his season on a hot streak.[89] In late May, a "crafty" Carswell pitched a no-hitter for seven innings en route to a 6-0 win against the Studebakers in South Bend, Indiana.[90] That performance sparked rumors of interest from the Cleveland Indians and Saperstein was purported to have offered Carswell's services to a scout for an eye-popping $100,000.[91] The story made for good copy but one has to wonder how much of the report was serious journalism and how much was pure hucksterism by Saperstein. After all, the same columnist who wrote the story referred to Frank Carswell as "pitching sensation" "Lloyd Cardswell," a misspelling that appeared in various forms in the Trotters' press releases for the remainder of the season.[92]

Carswell's 1949 season with the Globetrotters was possibly one of his best. Although detailed newspaper accounts of the outcomes of the Trotters' games were far outnumbered by articles promoting coming games, when results were published, Carswell's wins outpaced reports of his losses – a definite improvement over his record with the Buckeyes. As Saperstein's nine traversed North America, Carswell's pitching prowess led his team to impressive wins in Canada, California, Oregon, Nebraska, and Montana, before the team headed back east.[93]

In 1950 Carswell left his home in Buffalo and hit the road once more with the Globetrotters. With 100 wins and just 19 losses to their credit during the 1949 season, the Trotters were on a roll. Carswell's name still occasionally appeared in newspapers as "Lloyd Cardswell," especially early in the season, including some of their first games with the Brooklyn Cuban Giants in Kentucky.[94] It is difficult to determine his record for the 1950 season. Only a handful of his appearances were mentioned in newspapers and included wins over the Cuban Giants in Davenport, Iowa, in June, and Decatur, Illinois, in September.[95] Carswell's tenure with the Globetrotters ended with the 1950 season.

By the spring of 1951, Carswell, now nearly 34, reported to the Chicago American Giants' spring training in Meridian, Mississippi.[96] He was counted among the "eight pitching prospects to make the Giants a contender in the Negro American League pennant."[97] But he didn't have much of a chance to dirty his Giants uniform. By June he had been sold to Syd Pollock's Indianapolis-Buffalo Clowns for the reported hefty price of $7,500.[98] Carswell quickly proved his worth with a five-hit win over the Philadelphia Stars.[99] But the summer of 1951 wasn't all fun and games for the Clowns. In July, their bullpen was decimated when two pitchers, Harry Butts and Pedro Naranjo, were "bribed" to defect to the "Canadian Manitoba-Dakota Circuit" (presumably the Mandak League), and a third hurler, Whit Graves, was induced to jump to the Dominican Republic's summer leagues.[100] Other players, including outfielder Nat Peeples and Honey Lott, were sold to the Brooklyn Dodgers and the Chicago White Sox respectively.[101] Pollock was apoplectic. From his perspective, the players received fair salaries, the turnstiles were humming, and their chances of making it to the majors were high if they remained with the team.[102] Pollock was quoted as saying that the jumpers "cut their noses off to spite their faces." But Carswell did not take the leap, remaining with the Clowns for the remainder of the season. It was another up-and-down year for Carswell. In early July he dropped a game to the Monarchs in front of his hometown crowd in Buffalo, 9-4.[103] And then, on July 20, he pitched a two-hit shutout against the Baltimore Elite Giants at Sulphur Dell in Nashville to win 2-0.[104] He finished the season with a 4-4 record.[105]

In September 1951 the Clowns and the Monarchs staged a "month-long series, which has been branded as the World Series of the Negro American League."[106] That series morphed into a barnstorming tour with Jackie Robinson's All-Stars that continued through the end of October. During that time, the Clowns were repackaged as the "New York All-Stars," and "Negro American League All-Stars" as fodder for Robinson's traveling nine. Carswell was on the roster for all three iterations. His postseason record is uncertain, but based on published accounts of the contests, he enjoyed no success on the mound against Robinson's team, although the crowds loved it. In Knoxville, Tennessee, 7,500 enthusiastic fans roared as Robinson rocketed one of Carswell's

offerings over the left-field fence.[107] On October 22, over 3,000 turned out to see Carswell defeated by Robinson's All-Stars in Asheville, North Carolina, 6-3.[108] It was noted that the Asheville crowd was composed of roughly 1,000 White fans and the "remainder were Negroes, turning out to watch members of their race perform who have made good in the higher brackets of baseball."[109] The last report of Carswell starting for his squad against Robinson's All-Stars was on October 29 in New Orleans, when he was on the losing end, falling 10-6 before a crowd of 4,000.[110]

In the early 1950s Carswell crossed paths with two of the greatest baseball players of all time –Jackie Robinson and Hank Aaron. In the 1951 postseason, he barnstormed with the teams that faced Robinson's All-Stars. In 1952 he was Aaron's teammate on the Indianapolis Clowns. Carswell re-upped with the Clowns in April 1952 and wore number 38.[111] He was primarily used in relief in the spring, but by mid-season he notched a pair of good wins as a starter against the Philadelphia Stars and the Chicago American Giants.[112] As the season drew to a close, Carswell, aided by Aaron's "brilliant fielding and hefty slugging," battled the Black Barons for a 16-10 win in Knoxville.[113] That partnership worked well in the postseason when the Clowns captured the Negro League World Series by winning seven of 12 games from the Black Barons.[114] Carswell "led the Clowns' hurlers in the series with two wins and no losses," while Aaron blasted five homers and hit .402 during the championship run.[115] It was one of the better seasons of Carswell's career. The Clowns toured in style in a "$30,000 motor coach" and on at least one occasion drew over 22,000 fans, no doubt thanks to their teenage rookie, Hank Aaron.[116] Over the thousands of miles racked up that summer, Carswell got to know Aaron. He observed his daily habits, including one in particular that earned the youngster his nickname, Pork Chop.[117] According to Carswell, "The man ate pork chops three meals a day, two for breakfast, two for lunch, three for dinner, and a spare [from] time to time for a snack."[118] Carswell continued, "We all called him Pork Chop," and added that thanks to Aaron, other players started "thinking about strict pork chop diets so's they could hit like he could."[119]

The 1953 season was Carswell's final year in baseball. He returned to Pollock's Indianapolis Clowns, but Aaron did not; he signed with the Boston Braves and was on his way to a Hall of Fame career. But in April the Clowns added a new player to the roster, Toni Stone, a female second baseman who was sure to capture headlines and bring curious fans through the turnstiles.[120] The Clowns were managed by Albert "Buster" Haywood in his final year with the team. Haywood used Carswell primarily as a reliever in the spring and as a starter later in the season, just as he had the previous year.[121] In late May Carswell pulled out a 9-4 win over the Monarchs before a sparse crowd of less than 2,000 at Muny Stadium in Omaha, Nebraska.[122] In mid-July he had a bad night against the Black Barons in Asheville, giving up nine hits and losing 3-0.[123] The Barons roughed him up again during the last week in July, this time at Sulphur Dell by a score of 14-1.[124]

Carswell's summer continued on a downhill slide when he and the Clowns were dethroned by the Monarchs in mid-August in Kansas City, 4-1. The regular season ended with a thud for Carswell, but he had one last role to play before ending his career. In the 1953 postseason, the Clowns barnstormed against the "Negro Western All-Stars," essentially a junior-varsity squad formed by a subset of Indianapolis players.[125] Haywood was in charge of the Clowns' "A Team," while Carswell was tapped to wrangle the "All-Stars."[126] In late October, Carswell took over the reins for the Clowns when they played a two-game series against Robinson's All-Stars at Pelican Stadium in New Orleans.[127] Robinson's squad included the Cleveland Indians' Luke Easter and the Brooklyn Dodgers' Gil Hodges.[128] Nine thousand fans filled the stands to watch Robinson's nine capture the first game, 4-3.[129] Carswell's final game likely came in an exhibition on November 5 in Miami against Robinson's All-Stars – a 15-5 loss to end his career.[130] Carswell's career as a manager was brief but he made a positive impression on his team. According to Clowns infielder Gordon Hopkins, "Carswell was a good manager. I liked him. He was one of the Clowns' old pitchers and he was taking care of managerial things for the All-Stars. He was a wonderful manager; he wasn't too hard on the guys. He gave us a lot of flexibility, but he just wanted to see what everybody could do."[131]

After the 1953 Clowns' season ended, Carswell hung up his uniform for good and headed back home to Buffalo, where he took a job at the Chevrolet metal-casting plant in Tonawanda, a suburb on the north side of Buffalo.[132] He retired from Chevrolet in 1972 "due to illness."[133] At the age of 61, Frank Carswell, known to his family as "Spark," died in Buffalo on October 23, 1978, and was buried in Ridge Lawn Cemetery in Cheektowaga, New York.[134] He was survived by his wife, Carrie Hunley Carswell, and his son, Rudy Carswell.

SOURCES

Unless otherwise indicated, all Negro League statistics and records were sourced from Seamheads.com and baseball-reference.com. Ancestry.com was used to access census, birth, death, marriage, military, immigration, and other genealogical and public records.

NOTES

1   John W. Hammond, "Around the Circle," *Macon* (Georgia) *Telegraph*, March 25, 1934: 10. Kaolin is a soft white mineral widely used in manufacturing.

2   "Industrial League May Be Organized, *Macon Telegraph*, April 17, 1935: 2.

3   Isaac D. Kremer, "Albion Interactive History," Website, *Isaac D. Kremer, Main Street America*, http://isaackremer.com/albion/business/b_albion_malleable/.

4   James A. Riley, *The Biographical Encyclopedia of the Negro Baseball Leagues* (New York: Carroll & Graf Publishers, 1994), 155. Riley incorrectly identified Atlanta as Carswell's birthplace and erroneously placed his boyhood years in Albion, Michigan.

5   Riley, 155, 565.

6   "Hill's Stars Win Over Silver Creek," *Buffalo Times*, August 13, 1926: 17; Riley, 565.

7   "Buffalo Stars Organize," *Buffalo Times*, August 9, 1932: 6.

8   "Rock Howells Go Big Time, Set for Stadium Party," *International Gazette* (Buffalo), June 10, 1944: 1.

9   David Montgomery, "Legends of the Lost City," *Buffalo News*, August 5, 1990: E1, E2.

10 "Black Rocks Trounce Montgomerys, 15-5, Retain Muny Lead," *Buffalo Courier-Express*, June 5, 1944: 13.

11 "Rock Howells Go Big Time, Set for Stadium Party."

12 "Buckeyes to Give Proven a Tryout," *New Philadelphia* (Ohio) *Daily Times*, June 22, 1944: 9.

13 "Buckeyes Unable to Retain Lead," *Hamilton* (Ontario) *Spectator*, July 11, 1944: 18.

14 "Buckeyes Unable to Retain Lead."

15 "Buckeyes Unable to Retain Lead."

16 "Series Taken by Cleveland," *Dayton* (Ohio) *Journal Herald*, July 14, 1944: 6.

17 "Series Taken by Cleveland."

18 "Simon Pures Provide Upset Exhibition with Pros," *Hamilton Spectator*, August 11, 1944: 24; "Negro Nines End Season Saturday," *Harrisburg* (Pennsylvania) *Evening News*, September 13, 1944: 13.

19 Tommy Moore, "Krustomen Get Two Tests from Now Until Weekend," *Hamilton Spectator*, August 10, 1944: 21.

20 "Krustomen Get Two Tests from Now Until Weekend."

21 Tommy Moore, "Navy May Not Have Team to Start O.R.F.U. Race," *Hamilton Spectator*, August 11, 1944: 25.

22 "Simon Pures Provide Upset Exhibition with Pros," *Hamilton Spectator*, August 11, 1944: 24.

23 Tommy Moore, "Navy May Not Have Team to Start O.R.F.U. Race."

24 "Buckeyes Beat League Foe, 12-2," *South Bend* (Indiana) *Tribune*, August 26, 1944: 8.

25 "Buckeyes Beat League Foe, 12-2."

26 "Buckeyes Beat League Foe, 12-2."

27 "Baltimore Routs Buckeyes, 13-3," *Harrisburg Evening News*, September 18, 1944: 11.

28 "American Giants Meet Buckeyes on Saturday Evening," *Waco* (Texas) *Tribune-Herald*, April 15, 1945: 8.

29 Bob Overaker, "Beers and Buckeyes Clash Here Tonight," *South Bend Tribune*, May 18, 1945: 25.

30 "Hoosier Beer Defeated, 9-4, by Buckeyes, *South Bend Tribune*, May 19, 1945: 8.

31 "Buckeyes Win Third Straight," *Dayton Daily News*, May 29, 1945: 12.

32 "Buckeyes Rout Giants 9 to 0," *Dayton Daily News*, June 19, 1945: 16.

33 Bob Overaker, "Beers Shine Afield, but Buckeyes Win, 7-3," *South Bend Tribune*, July 20, 1945: 21.

34 "Two Games on Island Field," *Harrisburg Patriot*, August 1, 1945: 11.

35 "Black Barons Defeat Cleveland Club," *Montgomery* (Alabama) *Advertiser*, August 21, 1945: 6.

36 "Peg Parsons, "Armour's Homer Paces Buckeyes to 4-3 Victory Over All-Stars," *Erie* (Pennsylvania) *Daily Times*, September 12, 1945: 12.

37 "Buckeyes Make It a Banner 'Hayes Day,'" *Cleveland Plain Dealer*, September 3, 1945: 31.

38 "Grays Edge Buckeyes in Abbreviated Battle," *Columbus* (Ohio) *Dispatch*, September 13, 1945: 16.

39 "Buckeyes Win," *Akron* (Ohio) *Beacon Journal*, September 14, 1945: 28; John Holway, *The Complete Book of Baseball's Negro Leagues: The Other Half of Baseball History* (Fern Park, Florida: Hastings House Publishers, 2001), 426.

40 Holway, 426.

41 "Cleveland Buckeyes Hold Negro Baseball World's Championship," *Monongahela* (Pennsylvania) *Daily Republican*, September 21, 1945: 2.

42 "Major All-Stars Here Tonight," *Dayton Herald*, October 1, 1945: 9.

43 "Major All-Stars Here Tonight."

44 "The Sports Note Pad," *Baltimore Afro-American*, September 29, 1945: 30.

45 "Major All-Stars Here Tonight"; "Game Called," *Dayton Daily News*, October 2, 1945: 20.

46 Jimmie N. Jones, "Cleveland Buckeyes, World Champions to Open Spring Training at Birmingham, Ala.," *Atlanta Daily World*, March 20, 1946: 5.

47 "Buckeyes, Barons Split," *Pittsburgh Courier*, March 30, 1946: 26.

48 "Cleveland Buckeyes Shade B'ham Black Barons, 10-9," *Atlanta Daily World*, April 23, 1946: 5.

49 "Rains Blocking Negro Opener," *Dayton Herald*, May 2, 1946: 22.

50 "Buckeyes and Barons Clash Here Tuesday, *Dayton Daily News*, May 5, 1946: 21.

51 "Buckeyes Divide Pair with Barons," *Cleveland Plain Dealer*, May 6, 1946: 18.

52 "Black Barons Break Even," *Birmingham Post*, May 13, 1946: 11.

53 "Clowns Blank Cleveland on Garcia's Two-Hitter," *Indianapolis Star*, May 20, 1946: 18.

54 "Bucks, Chicago Divide Holiday Doubleheader," *Chicago Defender*, June 8, 1946: 11.

55 "Cleveland Nine Routs Atlanta, 10-1," *Rochester Democrat and Chronicle*, June 8, 1946: 19; William J. Plott, *The Negro Southern League: A Baseball History, 1920-1951* (Jefferson, North Carolina: McFarland & Co., 2015), 157.

56 "Cleveland Nine Routs Atlanta, 10-1."

57 "Monarchs Take Two from Cleveland," *Chicago Defender*, June 22, 1946: 11.

58 "Memphis and Bucks Divide," *Chicago Defender*, July 13, 1946: 11.

59 "Buckeyes Win Three from Barons," *Chicago Defender*, August 3, 1946: 11.

60 "Buckeyes Triumph, 8-6," *Buffalo Courier-Express*, July 28, 1946: 16.

61 William J. Scheffer, "12,435 Watch as Grays Win; Stars Tied," *Philadelphia Inquirer*, August 6, 1946: 25.

62 "12,435 Watch as Grays Win; Stars Tied."

63 "12,435 Watch as Grays Win; Stars Tied."

64 "Red Sox Trip Bucks, 5-1; Then Bow to Grays, 4-2," *Atlanta Daily World*, August 9, 1946: 5.

65 "Red Sox Trip Bucks, 5-1; Then Bow to Grays, 4-2"; "Homestead Grays Tops in Capital 3-Team Bill," *Dayton Daily Bulletin*, August 9, 1946: 4.

66 "Birmingham Swipes Pair," *Chicago Defender*, August 31, 1946: 11.

67 "Red Sox in Victory," *Memphis Commercial Appeal*, September 23, 1946: 13.

68 "Red Sox in Victory."

69 "North-South Game Sunday," *Chicago Defender*, October 5, 1946: 11.

70 "Negro Leagues Stage Single Game Today," *Birmingham News*, October 13, 1946: 37.

71 "Negro Leagues Stage Single Game Today."

72 "New Shortstop for Cleveland," *Chicago Defender*, February 8, 1947: 20.

73 "New Shortstop for Cleveland."

74 "Homestead Grays in Win Over Cleveland," *Columbus* (Ohio) *Dispatch*, May 16, 1947: 25.

75 "Buffalo's Carswell to Hurl Negro Game Opener," *Buffalo News*, June 10, 1947: 29.

76 "Carswell with Harlem Giants," *Buffalo News*, July 9, 1947: 5.

77 "Clarence Center Fire Co. Ball Team to Play Harlem," *Amherst Bee* (Williamsville, New York), June 20, 1946: 6.

78 "Harlem Giants Nine Plays at Clarence Tonight," *Buffalo News*, July 9, 1947: 5.

79 "Buffalo Giants Win," *Buffalo Courier-Express*, August 18, 1947: 14.

80 "2,000 Watch Koch-Wallace Nine Lose, 7-0, to Giants," *Dunkirk* (New York) *Evening Observer*, August 21, 1947: 18.

81 "2,000 Watch Koch-Wallace Nine Lose, 7-0, to Giants."

82 "Red Sox Gain Split," *Memphis Commercial Appeal*, April 12, 1948: 18.

83 "Cleveland Buckeyes Defeat Black Barons," *Atlanta Daily World*, May 7, 1948: 8.

84 "Birmingham Barons Outslug Cleveland Buckeyes, 11-6," *Springfield* (Ohio) *Daily News*, May 11, 1948: 13.

85 "Indians Sign Alonzo Smith," *Atlanta Daily World*, July 15, 1948: 5.

86 "Memphis Lineup Revamped for Game Tonight," *Dayton Herald*, June 8, 1948: 22.

87 "Grays Quit League; New Circuit Formed," *Baltimore Afro-American*, December 11, 1948: 7.

88 "New Tigers to Be Seen at Home Game Tomorrow," *Kitchener-Waterloo* (Ontario) *Record*, May 6, 1949: 23.

89 "New Tigers to Be Seen at Home Game Tomorrow."

90 Bob Towner, "Globetrotters Defeat Studebaker Baseball Team," 6-0," *South Bend Tribune*, May 24, 1949: 17.

91 Ken McConnell, "Before and After," *Daily Province* (Vancouver, British Columbia), May 21, 1949: 7.

92 Ken McConnell, "Before and After"; "Globetrotters Defeat Local All-Star Team," *Eugene* (Oregon) *Guard*, July 24, 1949: 14; "Trotters Boast Negro Ball Stars for Game Wednesday at Hudson," *Albany* (Oregon) *Democrat-Herald*, July 25, 1949: 7; "Stars Fill Globetrotters Ranks," *Chadron* (Nebraska) *Record*, August 12, 1949: 8.

93 "Airlifters Bow to Trotters in Thrill-Packed Cambell Benefit Game," *Great Falls* (Montana) *Tribune*, July 4, 1949: 9; "Harlem Nine Sweeps Pair From Davids," *Oakland Post-Inquirer*, July 18, 1949: 14; "Globetrotters Defeat Local All-Star Team"; "Trotters Boast Negro Ball Stars for Game Wednesday at Hudson"; "Stars Fill Globetrotters Ranks"; "Globetrotters Tag 11 to 2 Loss on Miles City Club," *Miles City* (Montana) *Star*, August 17, 1949: 7.

94 "Negro Nines Play Twin-Bill Next Sunday," *Louisville Courier-Journal*, May 14, 1950: 32; "Globetrotters Meet Cubans at Hoptown," *Madisonville* (Kentucky) *Messenger*, May 17, 1950: 14.

95 Jerry Jurgens, "Trotters Sock 22 Hits; Slam Cubans, 13-5," *Davenport* (Iowa) *Daily Times*, June 10, 1950: 6; "Globetrotters Top Brooklyn Cubans, 9 to 1," *Decatur* (Illinois) *Herald and Review*, September 4, 1950: 13.

96 "Ame. Giants Open Spring Training," *St. Louis Argus*, March 2, 1951: 20.

97 "Ame. Giants Open Spring Training."

98 "Clowns' Manager Purchases Player," *Macon* (Georgia) *News*, June 7, 1951: 21.

99 Les Matthews, "Sports Train," *New York Age*, June 9, 1951: 14.

100 "Indianapolis Clowns Baseball News," *Macon News*, July 3, 1951: 13.

101 "Indianapolis Clowns Baseball News"; Alan J. Pollock, *Barnstorming to Heaven: Syd Pollock and His Great Black Teams* (James A. Riley, ed.), (Tuscaloosa, Alabama: University of Alabama Press, 2006), 222.

102 "Indianapolis Clowns Baseball News."

103 "Clowns, Monarchs Divide Twin Bill," *Buffalo Courier-Express*, July 9, 1951: 14.

104 "Carswell Shuts Out Giants in Dell Tilt," *Nashville Tennessean*, July 21, 1951: 10.

105 "Veteran Ball Stars Return Signed Contracts to Clowns," *Alabama Tribune* (Montgomery), April 4, 1952: 7.

106 "Clowns Engaged in Month Long Series," *Macon News*, September 12, 1951: 25.

107 Frank Weirich, "Jackie Robinson Mobbed as Stars Win Game, 9-6," *Knoxville* (Tennessee) *News-Sentinel*, October 17, 1951: 16.

108 "Robinson's All-Stars Defeat AL Nine, 6 to 3," *Asheville* (North Carolina) *Times*, October 23, 1951: 15.

109 "Robinson's All-Stars Defeat AL Nine, 6 to 3."

110 "Robinson's All-Stars Win," *Washington Evening Star*, October 30, 1951: 16.

111 "Clowns Ink 4 Including Sub for King Tut," *Chicago Defender*, April 5, 1952: 17; "Negro Teams Meet Today," *Baltimore Sun*, May 18, 1952: 7D.

112 "Clowns Capture Round Robin in Negro Loop Ball," *Buffalo Evening News*, July 21, 1952; "Clowns Overcome Giants in 'Straight' Ball Game," *Elmira* (New York) *Star-Gazette*, August 1, 1952: 12.

113 "Rookie Leads Clown Victory," *Knoxville News-Sentinel*, September 20, 1952: 6.

114 "Clowns Baseball Champions," *Macon Telegraph*, October 13, 1952: 2.

115 "Clowns Defeat Barons to Win NAL Playoff, 7-5," *Chicago Defender*, October 18, 1952: 18.

116 "Hall Drug Battles Famed Indianapolis Clowns Tuesday Night," *Battle Creek* (Michigan) *Enquirer*, August 10, 1952: 16; "First in Sports, *Buffalo Courier-Express*, August 13, 1952: 18.

117 Pollock, 228.

118 Pollock, 228.

119 Pollock, 228.

120 "Clowns and Baseball Notes," *Macon Telegraph*, April 2, 1953: 26.

121 "Birmingham Nine Blanks Clowns Before 3,563," *Asheville Citizen*, July 14, 1953: 15.

122 "Game Won by Clowns," *Omaha Morning World-Herald*, May 27, 1953: 28.

123 "Birmingham Nine Blanks Clowns Before 3,563."

124 "Black Barons Rout Indianapolis, 14-1," *Nashville Tennessean*, July 25, 1953: 11.

125 "Clowns, Western All-Stars Schedule Game Here Sept. 13," *Winston-Salem* (North Carolina) *Journal*, September 6, 1953: 20; Brent Kelley, *The Negro Leagues Revisited: Conversations with 66 More Baseball Heroes* (Jefferson, North Carolina: McFarland & Co., 2010), 291.

126 "Clowns, Western All-Stars Schedule Game Here Sept. 13."

127 "9,000 See Big Leaguers; 2nd Game Tonight," *New Orleans Item*, October 26, 1953: 20.

128 "Robinson's All-Stars Win at Little Rock," *Shreveport Journal*, October 23, 1953: 29.

129 "9,000 See Big Leaguers; 2nd Game Tonight."

130 "All-Stars Beat Clowns 15-5," *Miami Times*, November 7, 1953: 1.

131 Kelley, 294.

132 "Frank Carswell, Ex-Pitcher," *Buffalo News*, October 27, 1978: 36.

133 "Frank Carswell, Ex-Pitcher."

134 "In Memoriam," *Buffalo News*, October 27, 1978: 36.

Johnnie Cowan

By Darren Gibson

*"That was the best play I've
ever seen in my life."*
Happy Chandler, soon-to-be commissioner of
baseball, September 18, 1945, reportedly com-
menting on a sparkling play by Cowan in the
1945 Negro World Series[1]

From his Stockham Valves and Fittings industrial league
team in Birmingham, Johnnie Cowan moved in 1940 to the
Birmingham Black Barons of the Negro Southern League.
Later, in the midst of World War II, he earned a shot in
1944 with the Cleveland Buckeyes of the Negro American
League. Cowan made the most of his opportunity, starting
at second base a year later when the Buckeyes won the 1945
Negro World Series.

Cowan and the Buckeyes returned to the championship
two years later, losing this time to the New York Cubans.
After stints with the Memphis Red Sox and again with the
Black Barons, Cowan returned to Stockham, eventually becoming their manager in the 1950s, before finally receiving
recognition, well after retiring, as a Negro Living Legend.

Johnnie Wart Cowan was born on May 31, 1913,
in Pleasant Hill, Alabama, about 110 miles south of
Birmingham. He was the fourth of eight children born to
Henry Cowan, a farmer, and Lena (Butler) Cowan.

Not much information has been unearthed about
Cowan's younger years, or how he and his family migrated
north to Birmingham. However, by 1932, the 19-year-old
Cowan had begun a long history of playing ball (and working) for Stockham Valves and Fittings, which played in the
Negro Industrial League run by the YMCA. The next year,
1933, Cowan played for an airport semipro team in the

newly formed New Deal League in Birmingham. In one
May tilt, the right-hander "hit well for the losing team" and
even relieved on the mound.[2]

In early 1934 Cowan (at times cited as Johnny Cowans)
tried out for the Black Barons (also sometimes referred
to that year as the Black Giants) of the Negro Southern
League, a team organized by Frank Purdue and Ludie
Keys.[3] The rookie Cowan was usually penciled in by manager Bill Perkins (a Pittsburgh Crawfords catcher who was
holding out) playing third base and batting in the eighth
spot.[4] Cowan's three-run home run helped Birmingham
sweep the Atlanta Black Crackers on June 3.[5]

It's unclear what became of Cowan in 1935, but he returned to the Black Barons for 1936 and became the "new
Black Baron second sacker."[6] Cowan collected four hits,
including a triple and double, in a doubleheader sweep
of the Montgomery Gray Sox on June 14,[7] which ran
Birmingham's record to 25-6.[8] Cowan would later reminisce
about playing at Rickwood Field, saying "I loved playing at
Rickwood. The field was so beautiful and it was a regulation
field. They kept it up, unlike many black ballfields."[9]

Johnnie married Daisy Sands, a South Carolina-born
schoolteacher, in April 1937. They would have a son,
Charles, and a daughter, Evelyn. Cowan returned to play
for his work squad at Stockham. His extra-inning double
in August gave Stockham a win against its archrivals, the
American Cast Iron Pipe Co.("Acipco").[10] It seems Cowan
spent 1938 and 1939 in Birmingham playing in various local
leagues.

Cowan did play in three games with the Black Barons
in 1940, going 1-for-11 at the plate. His October 1940 draft
registration listed him as married, brown-eyed, 5-feet-10
and 160 pounds, working as a chucker and machine operator
at Stockham. Cowan was invited to play for a Birmingham
all-star squad in September against Satchel Paige's All Stars
while second baseman Tommy Sampson was recovering
from being hit by a bat.[11]

Back with Stockham in 1941, Cowan, playing second
base, "showed the fans some sensational fielding" in a
July game against Acipco.[12] He earned a tryout with the
revamped Black Barons and manager Winfield Welch in
September 1941, along with other stars of the local industrial
league including first baseman Jim Canada, outfielders Piper
Davis and Ed Sickle, and catcher Bill Perkins.[13] Apparently,
in Cowan's case, it did not pan out, as in October, Cowan,
playing for Stockham, was with the City Negro Industrial

Johnnie Cowan.

Courtesy Cleveland History Museum.

League All-Stars in a five-game series against the Black Barons.

Playing in a benefit game in August 1942 for Stockham and manager Joe Borden, Cowan "executed the fielding gem of the game" in a loss to undefeated Acipco, which had Piper Davis and, later, Sam Hairston.[14] The next day, Cowan, possibly pressed into service, debuted with the Cleveland Buckeyes, going 2-for-5 while playing third base, then second, on August 21 in a doubleheader defeat at the hands of the Black Barons in Birmingham.[15] Less than a week later, Cowan "led the explosives for Stockham" in a 13-1 drubbing of US Pipe of Bessemer, Alabama.[16] He returned to play for Stockham in 1943. He also played second base with a Birmingham all-star team managed by Ed Steele in a series against the Atlanta Black Crackers in August 1943.[17]

In April 1944 Cowan signed with the Buckeyes and reported to spring training in Clarksdale, Mississippi. Buckeyes manager-third baseman Parnell Woods had been summoned by his draft board for a pre-induction examination. Cowan competed with Herman Purcell (who eventually became a pitcher) for the Buckeyes infielder opening.[18] He was described by a sportswriter as "a fast baserunner and a good hitter."[19] After Cowan won a job, one newspaper report held that "Johnnie Cown [sic], a 31-year-old veteran from Pleasant Hill, Alabama, is doing a remarkably good job at the hot corner";[20] another that "Johnny Cowan of Birmingham … will make you sit up and take notice."[21] However, Woods was rejected by the draft board and quickly returned, although two other Buckeyes infielders, second baseman Marshall Riddle and shortstop Billy Horne, reportedly were drafted.[22] So Norman Young moved to shortstop, and Cowan to second base, although Horne returned from the Army by mid-May and Young was traded to the Kansas City Monarchs.[23] Cowan was soon labeled "the season's find of the rookie crop," and part of a Cleveland infield quartet "judged to be the best all-around inner defense in Negro baseball."[24]

The Buckeyes split with the Indianapolis Clowns in Cleveland on May 14 with Cowan batting second. He belted a three-run home run in a win on July 7 over the Memphis Red Sox.[25] By August, Cowan was labeled a "brilliant performer in his first year" with Cleveland.[26] He went 4-for-5 with a double and triple in a 12-6 victory over the Outwin (Wisconsin) Zephyrs on August 17.[27] The new Buckeye just over a week later had two triples, two singles, and a walk for a perfect night in a 12-2 drubbing of the Chicago American Giants.[28] The Buckeyes finished just behind the Birmingham Black Barons for the NAL pennant. Seamheads shows Cowan hit .237 over 17 league games. He also led NAL second basemen in fielding percentage (.947)[29] Cowan earned the nickname "J-Hands" for his large and deft hands around the infield.

Returning to the Buckeyes for the 1945 campaign, and under their new manager, catcher Quincy Trouppe, Cowan knocked in the go-ahead run with a double in a 9-8 win over the Chicago American Giants of Chicago at Katy Field in Waco, Texas, on April 26. By late May, Cowan had replaced second baseman Billy Horne, who was now in the Navy.[30] Cowan was "playing great ball," a sportswriter commented.[31] The Buckeyes won the first half in the Negro American League.

Before a July 29 doubleheader loss to the Cuban Stars in front of 6,000 at the Polo Grounds (the same day as East-West Game attended by Buckeyes Lloyd Davenport, Archie Ware, Trouppe, and Eugene Bremer), Cowan was labeled a "midway guardian and double play artist" alongside shortstop Avelino Cañizares.[32] Cowan led off, going 0-for-5, in a 4-3 loss again to the Cubans on July 30 at Dexter Park in Brooklyn. On August 10 Cowan "started the prettiest double play ever seen here," with a "remarkable stop and throw" in a win over the Lloyd (Pennsylvania) Athletic Club.[33]

The Buckeyes won both halves of the NAL season, and thus faced the Homestead Grays in the 1945 Negro World Series. Cowan notched the first hit and RBI of the Series.[34] His sacrifice fly scored manager Trouppe (who had tripled) with Cleveland's first run on September 13 at Cleveland Stadium in Game One, which the Buckeyes won, 2-1. The Buckeyes won three days later, 4-2, at League Park to take a 2-0 Series lead.[35] Cowan was identified as part of an "airtight" Cleveland infield, which included Woods at third, Cañizares at shortstop, and Ware (also from Birmingham) at first.[36]

The Buckeyes defeated the Grays 4-0 on September 18 at Griffith Stadium in Washington to go up three games to none. Cowan's defensive prowess caught the attention of many a spectator. He made an incredible snag of a mid-game liner of the bat of the Grays' Buck Leonard. A reporter overheard US Sen. Albert "Happy" Chandler, in attendance and just over a month away from becoming the new commissioner of baseball, state, "That was the best play I've ever seen in my life."[37] Later accounts claim Chandler hailed Cowan as "the best infielder I've ever seen."[38] Cowan's son Charles, after his father had died, relayed the quote as "Johnny Cowan is one of the best groundball men I've ever seen."[39] After another Cowan defensive gem, The Cleveland Call and Post reported, "The Washington fans almost jumped out of their seats when Cowan threw a ball on one knee to retire the side."[40] Regardless of the superlatives, Cowan's heroics greatly impressed the attendees.

Capping the historic run, Cleveland beat the Grays 5-0 at Shibe Park in Philadelphia on September 20 to win the Series.[41] Cowan, Trouppe, and Cañizares were singled out for their "brilliant playing and strategy." Cowan, it was said, "really found his place in the sun as he fielded strategic balls which spelled the difference between win and lose for the opposing Grays."[42]

Statistics from Seamheads show Cowan as a light hitter, not accumulating a single extra-base hit in over 100 plate appearances in 1945. He ended the year on the diamond by going 1-for-4 as the starting second baseman for the South

Courtesy Baseball History Museum.

L to R: Parnell Woods, Avelino Canizares, Johnnie Cowan, Archie Ware.

All-Stars (with five Buckeyes as starters) on October 7 in New Orleans as they fell to the North All-Stars, 7-1.[43]

Cowan experienced his best offensive season for the Buckeyes in 1946, hitting .313 over 17 official contests. A newspaper called him a "timely-hitting second sacker."[44] Another proclaimed him as "just about as fine a ballplayer as you'll find any place. ... He really covers territory."[45] The "fleet" Cowan was nonetheless rated "a shade" slower than Indianapolis Clowns second sacker Ray Neil in August 1946, although the Erie fans "marveled at (Cowan's) play."[46] Cowan was also described as "one of the best defensive second basemen."[47]

Cowan returned in 1947 for his last of four seasons with the Buckeyes. He was in the running at second base for the West squad at the Negro League All-Star Game, along with Birmingham's Piper Davis (who was selected) and the Clowns' Ray Neil. Cowan belted a two-run homer off Martin Crue in a 9-7 defeat of the New York Cubans on August 31 at the Polo Grounds.[48] Still under manager Trouppe, the Buckeyes won the Negro American League pennant but fell in the Negro World Series to the New York Cubans, four games to one (with one tie). Cowan hit a three-run homer in the Game One opener, which ended 5-5.[49] The Buckeyes were described as a little long in the tooth with manager-catcher Troupe, pitcher Chet Brewer, outfielder Sammy Jethroe, and Cowan all in their 30s or older.[50]

After the 1947 season, the Buckeyes made wholesale changes. Alonzo Boone replaced Troupe as manager, with Troupe being sold to the Chicago American Giants, where he became the manager. They traded Clyde "Lefty" Williams to the Indianapolis Clowns for catcher Buster Haywood.[51] Sam Jethroe and Al Smith went to play in Puerto Rico, Archie Ware went to Venezuela. Chet Brewer went to Mexico for $600 per month.[52] In February 1948 Cowan was sold to the Memphis Red Sox (at the same time Ed Steele was traded to Memphis for Red Longley,[53]) with Leon Kellman replacing Cowan at second for Cleveland. Memphis appointed catcher Larry Brown

as the new manager.[54] Before shipping off for Memphis, Cowan manned third base for former Black Barons manager Tommy Sampson's Birmingham All-Stars in Atlanta against the Black Crackers.[55] Cowan would form a solid double-play combo with player-coach Willie Wells Jr., formerly of the New York Black Yankees. Cowan hit only .175 in 11 league games (40 at-bats). Memphis finished fourth in the NAL in 1948. In mid-October, after the regular season, Memphis, with Cowan, as the "flashy fielding second baseman," faced an all-star team coordinated by Jackie Robinson and Roy Campenella at least twice.[56]

Cowan returned to Memphis for 1949, playing for new manager Goose Curry.[57] Cowan homered on April 10 in a 6-5 win against the league's new entry, the Houston Eagles.[58] However, by September, Cowan was back with Birmingham in a three-game series against the Buckeyes. He was placed on Memphis's reserve list at the end of the season.

Back with Birmingham in April 1950, Cowan "clouted a 360-foot homer for the Black Barons" in their opener.[59] He and young center fielder Willie Mays were a part of manager Vic Harris's lineup through April and May. However, by June, Cowan had moved to the Elmwood (Winnipeg, Manitoba) Giants of the independent Manitoba-Dakota (Mandak) League. Ray Finch pitched for them and Cowan Hyde, a 1948 Memphis teammate of Cowan's, also was a teammate. Fellow Birminghamian Lyman Bostock Sr. competed for the crosstown Winnipeg Buffaloes and played in the Mandak for four seasons. Cowan tallied two doubles in a mid-July contest against the Minot (North Dakota) Mallards.[60] Cowan hit .249 in 45 games. Elmwood finished in last place. By the end of September, Cowan was seen once again patrolling second base for the Birmingham Black Barons against one of his former teams, the Memphis Red Sox.[61]

With the Black Barons and new manager Ed Steele committing to a youth movement for 1951, Cowan was not retained, so he returned to his Stockham Valves and Fittings team, which he represented in an August Negro YMCA Industrial League all-star game at Rickwood Field.

Not done playing competitive ball just yet, Cowan suited up in the summer of 1952 for a "Canadian Stars" team of players previously from the Negro American and Negro National Leagues who migrated to play in Canada and who were embarked on a US tour.[62] It was managed by Freddie Shepard, formerly of the Black Barons, and also included catcher Harry Barnes. They played the Havana Cuban Red Sox on July 18 at Legion Field in Montgomery, then the Zulu Giants from Louisville in a doubleheader on July 27 at Rickwood.

Cowan began managing the Stockham squad in 1953. His son Charles played with him, then later against him in the industrial league for rival Acipco. After his active playing days were over, Cowan got heavily involved with the 45th Street Baptist Church. He was a co-chairman of a

Men's Day event at the church.[63] He also was as an usher, deacon, and singer.

In April 1987 the retired Johnnie and Daisy celebrated their 50th wedding anniversary with their two children (Charles and Evelyn), eight grandchildren, and seven great-grandchildren.[64] They lived in the East Lake community. In 1989 Cowan was invited to a three-day celebration of the Negro Leagues in Atlanta.[65] In August 1991 Cowan attended a Black Legends of Baseball reunion in Cooperstown, New York, with fellow Alabamians Bostock, Piper Davis, and others.[66] In July 1993 he was invited to the major leagues' All-Star Game in Baltimore and recognized as one of 25 Negro League Living Legends. He was quoted as saying, "We need more managers and higher-ups now. Baseball is such a business now, if you don't get some kind of accountability, you don't know where (minority hiring) is going to go."[67] During this time, his son, Charles, was member of the Friends of Rickwood, a group tasked with the old Birmingham field's restoration.

Johnnie Cowan died on October 24, 1993, at the age of 80 in Birmingham and is buried at Shadow Lawn Memorial Gardens in Birmingham. He was survived by his wife; Daisy; his son, Charles; his daughter, Evelyn; his brother, James; a niece, Harriette Williams; eight grandchildren; and nine great-grandchildren, all of Birmingham.[68]

SOURCES

In addition to the sources shown in the Notes, the author consulted Johnny Cowans' Baseball Hall of Fame file, Seamheads.com, Baseball-Reference.com, and MyHeritage.com.

Wayne Pearsall, Cleveland Buckeyes Baseball website, accessed December 26, 2024: https://clevelandbuckeyesbaseball.com.

NOTES

1   Dave O'Karma, "The Forgotten Championship," *Cleveland Magazine,* April 28, 2006. Accessed online December 26, 2024. (https://clevelandmagazine.com/in-the-cle/sports/articles/the-forgotten-championship).

2   "Gross Drug Takes Airport Team, 17-2," *Birmingham Post-Herald,* May 22, 1933: 8.

3   Wilson L. Driver, "Birmingham to Show They Do Come Back in Baseball," *Chicago Defender,* March 24, 1934: A5.

4   Cowan's last name was occasionally misspelled as "Cowans" or even "Cowas" during this time.

5   "Black Giants Annex Couple Over Atlanta," *Birmingham Post-Herald,* June 4, 1934: 8.

6   "Black Barons Play Gray Sox in Night Game," *Birmingham News,* June 15, 1936: 12.

7   "Gray Sox Beaten in Double-Header by Black Barons," *Birmingham Post-Herald,* June 15, 1936: 10.

8   "Bruton Brothers Get Mound Posts for Sunday Tilts," *Birmingham News,* June 12, 1936: 14.

9   Anne Ruisl, "Rickwood Remains More Than Field of Dreams for Black Barons," *Birmingham News,* July 14, 1993: 102.

10   "Stockham Wins 2nd Straight Victory from Acipco; Fist Fight Figures in Seventh," *Atlanta Daily World,* August 20, 1937: 5.

11   "'Satchel' Paige Comes to Town with Stars to Play Black Barons," *Birmingham News,* September 27, 1940: 16.

12   "Acipco Ends Stockham's Clean Slate," *Atlanta Daily World,* July 29, 1941: 5.

13   "Black Barons Play Black Yanks Double Header Sunday 2 PM," *Birmingham Weekly Review,* September 26, 1941: 7.

14   Jimmy Couey, "Acipco Beats Stockham in Benefit Game," *Birmingham News,* August 21, 1942: 44.

15   "Black Barons Win Twin Bill from the Buckeyes, 5-2 and 3-0," *Birmingham Weekly Review,* August 22, 1942: 7.

16   "Stockham Blasts U.S. Pipe 13-1; Near Title," *Atlanta Daily World,* August 26, 1941: 5.

17   "Birmingham All-Stars Rout Black Crax, 6-4, in 'Rubber Game' of Heated Series," *Atlanta Daily World,* August 10, 1943: 5.

18   "Four St. Louis Boys Make Grade with Cleveland Club," *St. Louis Argus,* April 14, 1944: 10.

19   "Cleveland Buckeyes Lose Parnell Woods," *Chicago Defender,* April 8, 1944: 9.

20   Russ J. Cowans, "Buckeyes Face Loss of Pilot to the Army," *Michigan Chronicle* (Detroit), April 15, 1944: 16.

21   "Ware Acting Manager as Bucks Lose Woods to U.S." *Cleveland Call and Post,* April 15, 1944: 10B.

22   "Buckeyes Open Arc Season at Ducks Tuesday," *Journal Herald,* April 29, 1944: 8.

23   "Buckeyes are Strengthened for Game Here Tomorrow," *Buffalo Evening News,* May 17, 1944: 15.

24   "Black Barons Will Meet Buckeyes Here Friday," *Dayton Journal Herald,* May 21, 1944: 14.

25   "Buckeyes Pound Ball and Win," *Dayton Herald,* July 8, 1944: 5.

26   "Leading Sluggers of Negro League Will Accompany Cleveland Buckeyes Thursday," *Muskegon* (Michigan) *Chronicle,* August 16, 1944: 12.

27   "Great Lakes Colored Team Next for Outwin Zephyrs," *Muskegon Chronicle,* August 18, 1944: 14.

28   "Buckeyes Beat League Foe, 12-2," *South Bend* (Indiana) *Tribune,* August 26, 1944: 8.

29   "Bucks Lead in Batting, Fielding; Jethroe Is League Champ," *Cleveland Call and Post,* October 14, 1944: 6B.

30   "Buckeyes, Memphis in League Game Here," *Dayton Daily Bulletin,* May 24, 1945: 3.

31   Wendell Smith, "The Sports Beat," *New Pittsburgh Courier,* June 2, 1945: 12.

32   "Cleveland Buckeyes Here for Twin Bill With Cubans," *People's Voice* (New York City), July 28, 1945: 29.

33   "Buckeyes Beat Lloyd; Negro GI '9' Here Monday," *Delaware County Daily Times* (Chester, Pennsylvania), August 11, 1945: 10.

34   Jimmy Jones, "Buckeyes Beat Grays First Two Games of Series, 2-1, 3-2," *Cleveland Call and Post,* September 22, 1945: 6B.

35   Wendell Smith, "Battling Bucks Win 2 to 1, 4 to 2 in World Series," *New Pittsburgh Courier,* September 22, 1945: 12.

36   Wendell Smith, "The Sports Beat," *New Pittsburgh Courier,* September 22, 1945: 12.

37   Dave O'Karma, "The Forgotten Championship," *Cleveland Magazine,* April 28, 2006. Accessed online December 26, 2024. (https://clevelandmagazine.com/in-the-cle/sports/articles/the-forgotten-championship).

38   American Loop Negro Teams Clash Here Tomorrow Night," *Montgomery Advertiser*, May 26, 1946: 11.

39   Jimmy Bryan, "Glove Man Johnnie Cowan Remembered Fondly by Peers," *Birmingham News*, October 28, 1993: 21.

40   Harry Walker, "World Series – Dots and Dashes," *Cleveland Call and Post*, September 29, 1945: 6B.

41   William J. Scheffer, "Buckeyes Blank Grays, Win Title," *Philadelphia Inquirer*, September 21, 1945: 24.

42   "Key Personalities Who Sparked Amazing Championship of 'Cinderella' Team," *Cleveland Call and Post*, September 29, 1945: 6B.

43   Retrosheet.org. (Retrosheet Boxscore: North All Stars(N) (NAS) 7 South All Stars(S) (SAS) 1).

44   "Buckeyes Face Ex-Manager Here," *Flint* (Michigan) *Journal*, August 2, 1945: 28.

45   Peg Parsons, "Realm of Sports," *Erie Daily Times*, July 4, 1946: 15.

46   "Indianapolis Clowns Play Crescents Here Tonight," *Erie Daily Times*, August 20, 1946: 15.

47   "Cleveland Nine to Play G.E. Club Here Tonight," *Fort Wayne* (Indiana) *News-Sentinel*, September 21, 1946: 24.

48   Haskell Cole, Cleveland Homers Beat Cubans, 9-7," *New Pittsburgh Courier*, September 6, 1947: 13.

49   "Buckeyes Take 1st World Series Tilt," *Baltimore Afro-American*, September 27, 1947: 14.

50   Russ J. Cowans, "Sports Chatter," *Michigan Chronicle,* September 27, 1947: 14.

51   Jimmie N. Jones, "Buckeyes Undergo Changes," *Ohio Daily Express* (Dayton), February 26, 1948: 2.

52   Jimmie N. Jones, "Along the Sports Trail," *Ohio Daily Express*, February 27, 1948: 2.

53   "Memphis Strengthens Lineup; Gets Ed Steele," *Chicago Defender*, February 28, 1948: 11.

54   "Brown to Pilot Memphis Red Sox," *New Pittsburgh Courier*, February 21, 1948: 17.

55   Joel W. Smith, "Ellison, Barnes to Share Spotlight Here Sunday," *Atlanta Daily World*, April 9, 1948: 5.

56   "Top Negro Stars in Game With Robinson Here Monday Night," *Houston Post*, October 14, 1948: 29.

57   Sam Brown, "Memphis Red Sox Gunning for 1949 Pennant; Team Looks Good," *Kansas City* (Kansas) *Plain Dealer,* April 29, 1949: 6.

58   "Red Sox Trip Eagles, 6-5," *Memphis Commercial Appeal,* April 11, 1949: 17.

59   "Black Barons Win Two from Clowns, 6-4, 4-0," *Birmingham Herald*, April 17, 1950: 12.

60   "Danielson Hurls Mallards to Win," *Regina* (Saskatchewan) *Leader-Post,* July 17, 1950: 14. Was called Joe Cowan.

61   "Fine Crowd Sees First Game at GHA Park," *Hattiesburg* (Mississippi) *American*, October 2, 1950: 9.

62   "Visitors Sub for Black Barons Here Sunday," *Birmingham News*, July 27, 1952: 41.

63   "Church to Hold Men's Day Observance," *Birmingham News*, June 15, 1952: 26.

64   "Golden Weddings," *Birmingham News*, April 12, 1987: 23E. The obituary incorrectly identified niece Harriette Williams as a third child of the Cowans.

65   Malcolm Moran, "Former Negro League Stars Take Sentimental Journey," *Wilmington* (North Carolina) *Morning Star*, June 7, 1989: 12.

66   Ron Ingram, "Baseball Opens Its Doors," *Birmingham News*, August 18, 1991: 37.

67   Lisa Farbstein, "Negro League Stars Back Jesse Jackson," *Carroll County Times* (Westminster, Maryland), July 11, 1993: 13.

68   "Cowan, Johnnie," *Birmingham Post-Herald*, October 27, 1993: 41.

Lloyd Davenport

By Bill Johnson

In many ways, the baseball career of Lloyd Davenport was quite similar to those of many of his fellow Negro League players. Rising from athletic obscurity in New Orleans, he eventually played for and managed an array of Negro National and American League squads, spent seasons in Mexico, and occasionally wintered in Cuba and Venezuela. He ended his career in the never-segregated Manitoba-Dakota (ManDak) League, and is credited with two games on the roster of the 1953 Danville [Illinois] Dans in the previously segregated Mississippi-Ohio Valley League.

Davenport, known variously as Ducky or Bear Man, proved to be a special talent. He was one of the faster outfielders of his time and was selected for five East-West All-Star Games over his career. He was considered by some "to be almost as heavy a hitter as the peerless Jud Wilson."[1] One of the stars for the 1938 Negro American League champion Memphis Red Sox, he was part of a second championship team – albeit in a reserve role – with the 1945 Cleveland Buckeyes. At 5-feet-6 in height, and weighing 155 pounds, Davenport displayed as much "pop for the pound" as any player in the game's history.[2]

Lloyd Benjamon Davenport was born in New Orleans on October 28, 1911, to Walter (a janitor) and Rody Davenport. What follows is speculative, as precise records do not exist (or have not yet been discovered), yet reasonable. One of the larger slave-holding families in western Mississippi, the Davenport family, occupied much of Claiborne County.[3] After the Civil War and Emancipation, many of the former Davenport enslaved people remained in the area out of sheer familiarity with the land, at least through the early years of Reconstruction.[4] Lloyd's paternal grandfather, George W. Davenport, born in 1855 in Mississippi, had married Lloyd's grandmother in Vicksburg, Mississippi, less than 10 miles from the Davenport grounds. It is quite possible that this was the origin of the Lloyd Davenport surname. The entire clan migrated to New Orleans in the latter years of the nineteenth century, and it was there that Walter and Rodd [notably, there are two different spellings among various records] started their family.

The youngest of three boys in the family, Lloyd lived a relatively anonymous life until 1934, when he signed to play with a local Negro team, the independent New Orleans Crescent Stars. His speed and overall ability were obviously enough to earn him a contract offer from the Philadelphia Stars, and Davenport grabbed the opportunity.[5]

The fairy-tale beginning quickly turned into near-tragedy. In the first inning of a season-opening May doubleheader against the Grays, Davenport fractured an ankle while trying to beat out an infield hit.[6] He was out of action for two months. But he made his way back to the action by the Fourth of July. The hype resumed, with one local writer noting, "Lloyd 'Bearman' Davenport, of whom great things are expected, is back in uniform and in a few weeks the fans may look for him in the regular lineup. … Davenport is said to be up with the leaders."[7] Still, Davenport failed to live up to the billing in Philadelphia. He played in only 34 league games over the 1935 and 1936 campaigns, getting only 120 plate appearances and batting .176. Not surprisingly, when an opportunity arose with the Cincinnati Tigers for the 1937 season, a team led by the colorful Ted "Double-Duty" Radcliffe, Davenport made the move.

This decision proved to be a good one. Davenport was batting over .300 in early May, and his bat stayed hot for

Lloyd Davenport.

the first half of the season.[8] The 1937 season marked the first time Davenport was selected to play in the East-West All Star Game. Starting in the outfield for the West squad, he doubled and scored a run in four at-bats in the loss to the East.[9] For the season, he slashed .382/.463/.844, and his OPS+ of 139 would eventually prove the second-highest mark in his career. His wagon appears to have been tied to that of manager Radcliffe, and when the latter left Cincinnati for the Memphis Red Sox, Davenport followed.

If 1937 had been a good choice for the outfielder as a player, 1938 brought him his first Negro American League championship. Davenport's OPS+ of 138 was ninth in the league, and in large part contributed to Memphis's Negro American League title. However, following a drastic falloff in his batting the next season, Davenport and former Tiger teammate Jesse Houston, among others, answered the call "South of the Border," and relocated to Mexico to both work and play baseball in a much more racially permissive setting.

Working for the Fleishman Company, owner of the largest Coca-Cola bottling plant in Mexico, Davenport revived his baseball career with the Aliajadores [Lightermen] de Tampico, batting .356, delivering a slash line of .356/.405/.493. He returned to the United States with the Birmingham Black Barons as well as the Red Sox for the 1941 season. As reported in May 1942, "TH Hayes, Jr., owner of the Birmingham Black Barons baseball club of the Negro American League has been fined $25 by Dr. J.B. Martin, president of the league, for allowing Lloyd Davenport to participate in the opening game, Sunday, May 10, at Birmingham, when Birmingham was host to the Jacksonville Red Caps on the ground that Davenport is the property of the Memphis Red Sox who protested the game."[10] This was the first genuine harbinger of possible future issues with Davenport, who – in addition to displaying tremendous baseball skills – had a penchant for taking the path most advantageous to him. Coming out of the Great Depression and in the midst of a world war, it is tough to fault Davenport for simply doing his best to survive. Still, in the eyes of some of the baseball writers, he was displaying little loyalty to teams that had previously signed him.

Despite the occasional controversy, Davenport played often and well. In 1943 he was traded to the Chicago American Giants for James "Cool Papa" Bell,[11] and that summer was again selected to the West squad in the East-West All Star Game. Davenport went hitless in that game, but the West still prevailed 2-1 on a ninth-inning homer by Buck Leonard. For the year, the now-31-year-old logged an OPS+ of 141, the highest in his career. The American Giants finished fourth in the league, albeit with a winning record (37-33-1 in the NAL and 45-38-1 overall), and may have marked one of the best managerial efforts of Ted Radcliffe's career.

Bingo DeMoss replaced Radcliffe as manager for the 1944 campaign, but the American Giants' managerial

slot proved to be more a carousel than a podium. In July DeMoss was sacked after an argument with a team executive and was replaced by Lloyd Davenport. DeMoss, who had been in the game since 1905, had played for Rube Foster and teamed with the great Pete Hill back in the 1920s, and had a strong sense of his own version of right and wrong in baseball. He did not care about ruffling figurative feathers among club secretaries and writers, and accepted the termination without a squeak. He was back at the helm of another club, the Brooklyn Brown Dodgers, the next year.[12]

In 1944 Davenport played well the first half of the season and genuinely used his entire range of baseball skill, from manager to pitcher to outfielder to slugger. The American Giants owned "a pitcher who is leading the league," a newspaper exclaimed. "His name is Lloyd 'Ducky' Davenport, regular centerfielder for the Giants and manager for the team. Davenport, who went in to relieve Gerd McKinnis when the Giants met the Memphis Red Sox here on July 2, has won three and lost none. In the 21 innings Davenport has pitched he has yielded 19 hits, 13 runs, six bases on balls, struck out six and hit two batsmen.[13] He has appeared in seven games. … Furthermore this same Davenport is staggering around under a batting average of .328, 17 points higher than Serrell, leading hitter for the Monarchs."[14] Given his successes that year, Davenport was again selected to play in the East-West Game in 1944. He also continued to attract more than his fair share of attention, both positive and negative, and both on and off the diamond. In mid-1944, Pittsburgh Crawfords owner Gus Greenlee conducted an economic raid on Chicago and its talented roster. Greenlee signed four of their players.[15]

As player-manager, Ducky Davenport lasted only a month before being shown the door as well after covertly trying to negotiate a better deal with Gus Greenlee and his attempted resuscitation of the Pittsburgh Crawfords. Davenport was not alone in that foray, as Pennington and all-star pitcher Gready McKinnis were also looking for bigger slices of the money pie. Giants owner J.B. Martin acted quickly to quell the rebellion. He traded Davenport to the Cleveland Buckeyes, replaced him as manager with John Bissant, and suspended the other two conspirators.

In early September, the *Pittsburgh Courier* noted, "The Chicago American Giants announced Sunday that Manager Lloyd (Ducky) Davenport, brilliant centerfielder, had been sold to the Cleveland Buckeyes. Although the purchase price was not announced, it was reliably reported that Owner Ernie Wright of Cleveland paid $4,000 for the ex-Chicago star, one of the largest sums ever paid for a player in Negro baseball. Meantime, trouble loomed over the deal. Davenport has been playing with Gus Greenlee's Pittsburgh Crawfords, now touring the Northwest. It is not known whether Cleveland will be able to lure the speedy outfielder away from the Crawfords. Wright said he has ordered Davenport to report."[16]

The series of moves, by both Davenport and several team owners, ultimately irritated at least one prominent member of the press. Russ Cowans, at one time known in Michigan at the "Black Dean of Sportswriters,"[17] scalded Davenport in one specific 1945 column:

Lloyd (Ducky) Davenport is another bright example of the type of ball player who needs to be barred from baseball. While under contract with the Chicago American Giants in 1944, Davenport accepted $600 from Gus Greenlee to join the Pittsburgh Crawfords. He was already indebted in advance money to the Chicago team up and above $300. He didn't report in [sic] the Crawfords, neither did he return the money Greenlee had advanced him. Before that Davenport was one of the principal factors in organizing a clique to dispose of Elwood (Bingo) DeMoss as manager of the Chicago team. Davenport was later named manager of the team, but repaid Owner Martin by refusing to repay the advanced money. Traded to Cleveland last year, Davenport jumped to Mexico two weeks ago, carrying with him some of Owner Ernest Wright's Money. It's an even bet that he was advanced some money by the Mexican owners. It's also an even bet that he'll be back before the season is over. Yep Davenport is a bad egg and shouldn't be placed in any owner's basket."

Such direct criticism was rare, even at that time, but Cowans was convinced that Davenport had played fast and loose with baseball's organization. Davenport did join several other Negro American League stars in jumping to the Mexican Leagues. The promises of more money and more freedom were simply too great a temptation. By this time he was married, and was likely looking for any and all baseball opportunities to increase his net income.[19]

Still, his 1945 campaign – or, at least, the first half of the season – was another terrific showcase for Davenport. With Cleveland, he was again selected to play in the East-West Game, hit a double in four at-bats, and scored a run. It proved to be his final contribution to the Buckeyes' championship season. At the end of August, Davenport joined with several other Negro American League players, including Art "Superman" Pennington and Gready McKinnis, teammates from his Chicago American Giants days, in moving south, to Mexico.

The summer of 1945 quickly morphed into a figurative springtime in America. World War II was concluding and, along with the attendant attenuation of the economic depression of the 1930s, provided the United States with an unfamiliar sense of security. But there was still discrimination in the game, and the disparity of pay between players in the two Negro Leagues and players in White baseball was stark. Players with Davenport's ability in the segregated American and National Leagues were making almost $20,000 per year, a staggering disparity.

Into this breach marched Bernardo and Jorge Pasquel, Mexican millionaires who owned a team in the Mexican League and who shared a vision of that league reaching parity with, perhaps even superiority to, professional baseball in the United States. Jorge served as president of their league, and the brothers began raiding talent, both White and Black, from throughout their Northern neighbor. The Pasquels were not timid, offering baseball commissioner A.B. "Happy" Chandler a five-year contract that included $50,000 in annual salary, plus an expense stipend, to move to Mexico and become commissioner of their league.[20] They tried to seduce Boston slugger – and World War II Marine Corps pilot – Ted Williams with a three-year contract that would have paid the star $500,000,[21] and were looking to make a similar offer to pitcher Bob Feller.[22] The Pasquels ultimately persuaded 26 players to jump the border, most notably Mickey Owen, Max Lanier, and Sal Maglie.[23]

Their efforts were not limited to the White leagues. The Pasquels were just as interested in Negro League players, especially since they could obtain the Black players for much less money than the White counterparts. It was a full-on, albeit legal, grift. The Black players saw $5,000 per season as a fortune, but they were still making only about 20 cents on the dollar in comparison to the White players. Still, $5,000 was $5,000.

Davenport hit .352 in 30 games with Nuevo Laredo in 1945, and .293 with the same team in 1946.[24] He remained in Mexico, with the Azules de Vera Cruz, in 1947 and 1948, but age was beginning to take its toll, and his average slipped to .265 in his final season. While playing with Almendares in Cuba in the winter of 1946, along with Buck O'Neil and Gentry Jessup among others,[25] he had again been selected for an all-star team to tour the United States. This time, however, this was a barnstorming squad playing a series against a Bob Feller-led team of major leaguers.[26]

By 1949, with the color barrier finally broken in baseball, Davenport returned to the United States and tried to catch on with the American Giants, the Pittsburgh Crawfords, and even the [now] Louisville Buckeyes, but to no avail. He wintered in Venezuela with the Navegantes del Magallanes, but he and Margie again returned to the United States in early 1950 and he took a job as a janitor with the city of Chicago.[27]

In 1951 Davenport reportedly signed with the Chicago American Giants, but there are no available statistical records to confirm this. He did, however, head north to join the ManDak League, signing with the Elmwood Giants for the '51 season.[28] In what was his most productive game of the year, playing with fellow Negro Leaguers Cowan Hyde, Jesse Douglas, and the ageless Double Duty Radcliffe,[29] Davenport went 4-for-4 in a 12-3 Elmwood win over the Winnipeg Buffalos on July 31.[30]

Out of Organized Baseball in 1952, Davenport returned to the game, this time in a desegregated minor league, with the Danville Dans of the Class-D Mississippi-Ohio Valley League. Baseball-reference.com reports that he appeared in two games, but there are few details about his performance. Notably, Davenport's final documented game came on May 27, 1953. Playing in right field, he went 0-1 in a 6-5 loss to the Mt. Vernon Kings.

There is little available about Davenport's post-baseball life. In September 1985 he died and was buried in the Holt Cemetery in his hometown of New Orleans. Unlike the quasi-mythical careers of Negro stars like Josh Gibson and Satchel Paige, Lloyd Davenport's life was highlighted by two decades of moving from team to team, winning championships and enduring the unforgiving failures that only baseball can impose, of playing baseball throughout the Western Hemisphere and then falling back into professional anonymity as a Black man in pre-Civil Rights Act America. His life, in many ways, illustrates the real life of most baseball players who were born too soon to reap the benefit and reward of athletic celebrity, the kind of life explored by August Wilson in his play *Fences*. Lloyd Davenport was not Troy Maxson, but his life was, and is, a tile of the American mosaic, and one worth knowing.

SOURCES

This biography was constructed using a number of sources. All statistical information referred to in the text was derived from the Negro League database available at www.seamheads.com.

NOTES

1   "Philadelphia Stars Lose Lloyd Davenport Account Injuries" *Norfolk (Virginia) New Journal and Guide*, May 18, 1935: 14.

2   Height and weight information taken from the Seamheads Negro League Database (online). There are other reports and documents listing slightly different height/weight combinations, but the Seamheads data is the closest to a true average.

3   Tom Blake, *Claiborne County, Mississippi Largest Slaveholders from 1860 Slave Census Schedules*, Online: https://freepages.rootsweb.com/~ajac/genealogy/msclaiborne.htm.

4   Emilye Crosby, *A Little Taste of Freedom: The Black Freedom Struggle in Claiborne County* (Durham: University of North Carolina Press, 2005), 3.

5   "Philadelphia Stars Open Against Grays, May 4th" *New Journal and Guide*, April 13, 1935: 14.

6   "Philadelphia Stars Lose Lloyd Davenport Account Injuries."

7   "Stars Acquire New Catcher in Shake-up," *Philadelphia Tribune*, July 4, 1935: 12.

8   "Cincinnati 9 Is Host To Detroit: Probable Lineup," *Chicago Defender*, May 8, 1937: 13.

9   "Baseball Classic Goes to Eastern All-Stars," *Kansas City* (Missouri) *Call*, August 13, 1937: 7.

10   R.S. Simmons, In general remarks in the *Atlanta Daily World*, May 19, 1942: 5.

11   "Notes," *Kansas City Call*, April 2, 1943: B16.

12   http://www.nlbemuseum.com/history/players/demoss.html.

13   The Seamheads website has calculated Davenport's statistics and corrected various inaccuracies that have been reported in newspaper articles over the years.

14   "American Giants Have Strong Pitching Staff," *Michigan Chronicle* (Detroit), July 29, 1944: 15.

15   "McKinnis, Chi Hurler, and Davenport Among Quartet with Craws," *New York Amsterdam News*, August 26, 1944: 6B.

16   "Cleveland Buys Chicago Manager," *Pittsburgh Courier*, September 2, 1944: 12.

17   Terry Cabell, "Friends Remember Russ ... and the Way It Was," *Michigan Chronicle*, October 21, 1978: A1, A4.

18   Russ Cowans, "Russ Cowans' Sport Chatter," *Michigan Chronicle*, August 18, 1945: 15.

19   There are several passenger lists noting that Lloyd and Margie Davenport sailed to and from Cuba in 1945. Margie was only 22 at the time, and the formal record of their marriage is unlocated, but a later picture in the news, including Margie with some of the other wives, show a young, happy, Mrs. Davenport acting quite at home with the lifestyle.

20   Associated Press, "Chandler Is Offered Mexican Job," *Boston Globe* April 7, 1946: 34.

21   Roger Birtwell, "Cronin Tries to Stall Mexican's $500,000 Pitch to Ted Williams," *Boston Globe*, March 9, 1946: 1.

22   Associated Press, "Pasquel to Raid Every Major League Club Except Cards," *Boston Globe*, September 10, 1946: 9.

23   "Mexican League Banned Players," Baseball Almanac. Online: http://www.baseball-almanac.com/legendary/Mexican_League.shtml. Accessed February 24, 2019. This was based on various reports including the *1950 Reach Baseball Guide and Record Book*, as well as editions of the *New York Times* from August 7, 1946, and March 7-June 6, 1940.

24   Statistics taken from Pedro Treto Cisneros' *The Mexican League: Comprehensive Player Statistics 1937-2001* (Jefferson, North Carolina: McFarland & Co., 2011), 123.

25   Online: Almendares (Liga Profesional Cubana 1946-47) | Desde Mi Palco De Fanático (wordpress.com), located at https://desdemipalcodefanatico.wordpress.com/numeros/almendares-liga-profesional-cubana-1946-47/.

26   "Davenport Slated for All-Star Nine Duty," *Afro-American*, July 20, 1946: 16. ???? Baltimore? Washington?

27   1950 US Federal Census, https://www.ancestry.com/discoveryui-content/view/227012936:62308.

28   Western Canada Baseball 1951 ManDak League Game reports. Online: https://attheplate.com/wcbl/1951_20i.html.

29   Barry Swanton, *The ManDak League: Haven for Former Negro League Ballplayers, 1950-1957* (Jefferson, North Carolina: McFarland & Company, 2006), 22.

30   https://attheplate.com/wcbl/1951_20i.html.

Roosevelt Davis

By Jay Hurd

The June 6, 1945, headline in *The Dispatch* (Moline, Illinois) read, "Cincinnati Clowns to Play at Davenport Friday Night." The piece to follow reported, "Some of the greatest names in Negro baseball appear in the Clowns' lineup, among them being Roosevelt 'Duro' Davis, second only to 'Satchel' Paige in Negro pitching circles."

Hyperbole or not, Davis, 41 years old at the time of this article, had played baseball for nearly 30 years – a veteran of the Negro National League (I and II), the Negro American League, the Mexican League, and multiple independent leagues.

While records of Roosevelt Davis and his family are, at best, minimal and inconsistent, it appears certain that he was born in Bartlesville, Oklahoma, on November 19, 1904. His father, Will, was born on April 10, 1880, possibly in Bartlesville. Roosevelt's mother has been identified as Anna; however, records indicate that Will did not wed until 1909 when he married, in nearby Arkansas, Octavia Campbell of the Cherokee Tribe, Foreman, Sequoyah, Oklahoma. It is unclear when Octavia died, but by 1935 Will lived in Peoria, Illinois, where he remained until his death in 1960. A brief obituary states that Will had been widowed for a number of years and left a son, Roosevelt; a daughter, Oleander; and a sister, Bertha.[1] While his earlier employments may have varied (including California vineyard worker)[2], during the final 26 years of his life in Illinois Will Davis had been employed as a janitor by the U.S. Barge Lines.

Roosevelt may have attended the Douglass School, which was founded in 1907 for Bartlesville's Black students.[3] The 1920 US Census shows Roosevelt, age 15, living in Bartlesville, not with his father and/or mother, but with his aunt Bertha Mackey and her two sons, Eddie and Robert.

There is also uncertainty in regard to exactly when Roosevelt began to play, but his name appears in Bartlesville newspapers in the early 1920s, including one game summary in which he is identified as a pitcher for the Coffeyville, Kansas, baseball team.[4] At this time, and perhaps already in years prior, his baseball talent became evident and he played on other teams including the Wichita (Kansas) Monrovians[5] and an integrated team in Tekamah, Nebraska.[6]

The St. Louis Stars, members of the newly organized Negro National League, added him to their roster as a starting pitcher in 1924. He was listed as 5-feet-9 and 168 pounds, and he batted and threw right-handed. He appeared in 25 games that season, compiled a 7-4 record, pitched 121⅔ innings, and held a 4.29 ERA. The Stars' squad, managed by 40-year-old James Allen "Candy Jim" Taylor, included James "Cool Papa" Bell and Willie "El Diablo" Wells. After the season Davis married Lillian Turner of Omaha, Nebraska, on December 5, 1924. How long they remained married is unknown, and it appears that they had no children.

Davis again was a starting pitcher for the 1925 Stars, and his 17-7 record helped the team to reach the Negro National League Championship Series against the Kansas City Monarchs. Although the Stars lost the series, Davis had secured his spot in the starting rotation. For the season, he started 21games, completed nine, and struck out 54 batters.

Roosevelt Davis.

In 1926 Candy Jim Taylor left the St. Louis Stars to manage the Detroit Stars; St. Louis's new manager, Dizzy Dismukes, led his team to a third-place finish, and Davis compiled a 8-5 record, with only one complete game, in 18 starts. In 1927 Taylor managed St. Louis to a 62-37 record and a second-place finish. Davis pitched to an 11-8 record that year. Davis appeared in 23 games during the 1928 NNL season, although he made only eight starts, and achieved a perfect 8-0 record; however, he made only a brief one-inning appearance in one game of the championship series. The team, again managed by Taylor, did very well, posting a 61-26 record in league play, and won the Negro National League pennant in the championship series against the Chicago American Giants.

In 1929 Davis split the season between the St. Louis Stars, with Taylor in his final season as the manager, and the Chicago American Giants, managed by Jim Brown. Davis compiled a 6-7 record for St. Louis, but he was with Chicago by the time the team played a seven-game series versus a team of American Leaguers that included Wally Schang, Charlie Gehringer, and Harry Heilmann. The American Giants won the series, five games to two. Davis pitched in two games, one complete-game start and one relief appearance, and struck out six while pitching to a 1.69 ERA in 10⅔ innings.

By then Davis resided in St. Louis. The 1930 U.S. Census listed him as a single lodger who was employed in "League" industry as a ballplayer. The 1930 season again saw Davis play with two teams: the Stars, now managed by John Reese, and the Kansas City Monarchs, managed by Charles Wilber "Bullet Joe" Rogan. He was 1-0 in two appearances for the Monarchs but posted a stellar 10-3 regular-season mark for the Stars and won his only start against the Detroit Stars in the NNL Championship Series, which St. Louis won in seven games.

Davis led a peripatetic existence in 1931 as he pitched for three teams. He was 1-0 with the St. Louis Stars before he joined the Indianapolis ABCs, also of the Negro National League, and played again for manager Candy Jim Taylor; Davis won only one of five decisions for the ABCs. He moved on to the Pittsburgh Crawford Giants, a member team of the Independent Clubs League that was managed by Bobby Williams. In Pittsburgh, he posted a 2-2 record that included a shutout and 20 strikeouts in 27⅓ innings pitched.

With the 1932 season came yet more change for Davis. With the Cuban Stars West, also known as [Syd] Pollock's Cuban Stars of the East-West League, he pitched in two games. He also pitched in four games with the Cleveland Stars, another squad that was part of the East-West League. His composite record was 1-3 and he had a cumulative 3.61 ERA.

Davis again played a minor role in the 1933 season, this time for the Columbus (Ohio) Blue Birds of the Negro National League, who were managed by another familiar name, Dizzy Dismukes. Davis had a 2-2 record in eight

appearances (four starts), but he had a sparkling 2.66 ERA in 44 innings pitched. The 1933 campaign was also when Davis taught Bill Byrd how to throw the spitball. Once Byrd became known for the spitball, he often faked throwing that pitch "for psychological reasons" to confuse batters.[7] Indeed, Davis himself was a master of the spitball and, "legal or not, he was deemed one of the best spitball and emery-ball pitchers in black baseball."[8] Davis's prowess in applying "slippery elm juice" to the ball would create interesting moments later in his career.

The most notable event for Davis in 1933 occurred when Neil Churchill, who owned an integrated team in Bismarck, North Dakota, recruited him after consulting with Chicago's Abe Saperstein.[9] The Bismarck Tribune's account of Davis's debut noted, "Davis caught the fancy of local diamond enthusiasts in his first game here Sunday when he blanked Fort Lincoln 16-0, allowing only three hits, striking out 16 (four in one inning), getting three hits and driving in five runs."[10] He was later joined in Bismarck by other Negro Leaguers who included, most notably, Satchel Paige.[11]

In 1934 Davis joined forces with Paige, Josh Gibson, James "Cool Papa" Bell, and player-manager Oscar Charleston on the NNL's Pittsburgh Crawfords. He pitched in only five games, starting two and compiling a 1-0 record. He soon made a return trip to North Dakota, along with Quincy Trouppe and Satchel Paige. This time, Davis played for the New Rockford club while Paige and Trouppe again provided Bismarck with a formidable battery. The Bismarck Tribune remained complimentary to Davis even as he pitched for a rival team, and wrote about his loss to Bismarck, "Roosevelt Davis, a former teammate … turned in a good pitching exhibition but his erratic support gave him little chance against the Capital City team."[12]

At 30 years old, Davis returned to the Crawfords for their 1935 championship season. After finishing the first half of the season with a record of 26-6, the Crawfords defeated the winners of the second-half pennant, the New York Cubans, in a hotly contested seven-game series. Davis fashioned a 5-1 record in 13 appearances (eight starts) during the regular season, but he was a key cog for the team in the championship series. He made two complete-game starts and one relief appearance against the Cubans and put up a 2-1 record pitching 23⅔ innings against the Cubans. Had it not been for Davis's tough-as-nails pitching efforts, the New Yorkers might have prevailed against the team that many consider to be the finest Negro League squad in history, the 1935 Pittsburgh Crawfords.

On the heels of his great performance in the 1935 championship, Davis moved to New York, where he joined the Black Yankees for the 1936 season. Manager Bob Clarke led the team to a 21-16-1 record in NNL play; Davis put up a 2-4 record. The following season, Davis made one appearance for the Black Yankees before he rejoined the Crawfords, who were still being managed by Oscar Charleston. Davis pitched to the same 2-4 record (all for the Crawfords) he had accumulated the previous season and saw his ERA balloon to 5.04 over 44⅔ innings with the Steel City team.

By 1938 it appeared as though Davis's career might be nearing its end. He once again split time between two teams, playing for the Black Yankees, managed by Walter Cannady, and the Newark Eagles of Abe Manley and Dick Lundy. His cumulative statistics included a 0-1 record in three appearances (one start) and a 6.75 ERA in only eight innings of work.

Perhaps in the hope that a change of scenery might help, Davis moved south to join the Memphis Red Sox of the Negro American League in 1939. On this team, managed by Ted "Double Duty" Radcliffe, Davis started four games, completed three and, while striking out 16, compiled a 1-3 record and brought his ERA down to 3.82. That same year, Davis made his only venture outside the United States to play for the Monterrey team in the Mexican League. He was one of "the stars of the first year" of the Monterrey Sultanes, who were later renamed the Industriales.[13] During his stint south of the border, Davis was 3-6 in 11 starts, struck out 49 batters, and had a 3.76 ERA in 67 innings.[14]

While baseball had become Davis's main source of income, he still needed to supplement his finances with employment in the winter months. His October 16, 1940, draft registration form indicates that he lived in Chicago and that he was employed by the Palmer House hotel (likely as a waiter).[15] Keenly aware of the limitations of baseball income, Davis noted that "off season employment should have been 'tackled and solved long ago. Baseball players have to eat and sleep and see the laundry man in December as well as June."[16]

It also happened that, during the 1939 season, Satchel Paige's ailing arm miraculously healed, and Paige returned to J.L. Wilkinson's "B" team in Kansas City.[17] To prove that Paige could indeed pitch again, Wilkinson and Abe Saperstein scheduled a game with the Palmer House Stars. Paige later recounted, "Abe says, 'If Satch is great again let's let his arm speak for us. The hottest arm in Negro baseball is Roosevelt Davis: How about putting Satch up against him?'" However, Paige knew Davis and he said "Now wait. That Roosevelt Davis throws a cut ball. I don't like to throw no cut ball. … Davis scratches the ball with his nails and his belt buckle. That makes the ball sail and Davis knows how to control it."[18] Paige continued, "So Abe books a game in late September with the Palmer House Indians, the team Roosevelt Davis was pitchin' for. … They got three hits and we win, 1-0."[19] Lost in Paige's account is whether he actually faced off against Davis that day, or whether a different pitcher took the mound for the Palmer House team.

Davis returned to the Memphis Red Sox in 1940 as a pitcher and occasional left fielder, but he mostly pitched for the Palmer House Stars in independent baseball. As the Stars traveled north from spring training in Texas, they stopped to play the Kansas City Monarchs in a seven-game series:

"[T]he Palmer House team was credited with downing the Monarchs six times before finally losing, 2-1, to Satchel Paige. Roosevelt Davis took the loss in that game even though he struck out 10 Monarchs (besting Paige's eight strikeouts). Davis was accused of scuffing the ball, though nothing came of the accusation."[20] He continued to pitch for the Palmer House nine, with success and controversy. "In 1940 they came in fifth in the Wichita National Semi-Pro Tournament, relying on the solid pitching of Roosevelt Davis."[21] His reputation as a creative pitcher preceded him: "Roosevelt Davis 38 year old Palmer House pitcher, who was ejected from the game in the ninth inning by Umpire Virgil Blueitt [sic] when he refused to surrender what Kansas City players charged was a tampered ball, struck out ten, yielded seven hits, and gave two walks. … Umpire Bluett chased Davis from the field amusing the crowd by putting on a wrestling act with the Palmer House coaches."[22]

Davis now settled in Chicago and, in addition to playing for the Palmer House squad, also anchored the Chicago Brown Bombers' pitching staff in 1942. In 1943, at the age of 38, Davis pitched in nine games for the Cincinnati Clowns of the Negro American League. He made six starts and completed them all, hurled one shutout, and posted a 2.35 ERA over 61⅓ innings. Davis had brief stints with the same team – now known as the Cincinnati-Indianapolis Clowns – in 1944 and 1945 before his professional pitching career came to an end. In 1944 he finished the year at 3-1, and in 1945 he had no wins and no losses in one start.

Roosevelt Davis played 20 seasons in the Negro Leagues. During that time, he played for 12 teams in four leagues while also competing in multiple independent leagues, where he played alongside many of baseball's greatest players, both Black and White. He compiled a 98-63 record, with a .609 winning percentage, and a 4.11 ERA in Negro League play. Despite a well-founded reputation for using the spitball, cut ball, and emery ball, he had remarkable control of his pitches.

On January 22, 1950, the Chicago Chapter of the Baseball Writers Association of America held its annual meeting at the Palmer House. During the occasion, "Some observant sports writers … spotted vaguely familiar faces" among the waiters. Five waiters in starched shirts and ties turned out to be veterans of the Negro Leagues and among them Roosevelt Davis, the first black player brought to Bismarck by Neil Churchill in 1933, the scuffed-ball maestro … in his Mid-forties (and balding), he carried serving trays for a living."[23]

Roosevelt Davis died on December 28, 1968, in Chicago at the age of 64. He was buried in the Burr Oak Cemetery in Alsip, Illinois. Through the efforts of the SABR Negro Leagues Committee and its Grave Marker Project, a marker noting his career in Negro League baseball was dedicated and placed at his gravesite in 2005.

SOURCES

Unless otherwise indicated, all Negro League statistics were taken from Seamheads.com. Additional sources of content include Baseball-Reference.com, Ancestry.com, Newspapers.com, the Oklahoma and Kansas Historical Societies, and a statistical bio prepared by SABR member Kevin Larkin.

NOTES

1 Find a Grave, Will Davis, April 10, 1880-November 11, 1960, findagrave.com/memorial/187482031.

2 Alan J. Pollock, *Barnstorming to Heaven: Syd Pollock and His Great Black Teams* (Tuscaloosa, Alabama: University of Alabama Press, 2006), 125-126.

3 Bartlesville, Oklahoma, segregated Black students from the rest of the student population until 1956. Bartlesville, Oklahoma Public School site, bps-ok.org/home/district/history/douglass.

4 "Black Oilers Down Hotshots, Score 4-3," *Bartlesville* (Oklahoma) *Morning Examiner*, June 30, 1922.

5 "Panthers Open with Wichita Monrovians," *Daily Oklahoman* (Oklahoma City), April 29, 1923.

6 Pollock, 125.

7 Negro Leagues Baseball Museum, *"William Byrd,"* nlbemuseum.com/history/players/byrd.html.

8 Mark Schremmer, "Negro League Greats Started in Topeka," *Topeka* (Kansas) *Capital-Journal*, August 6, 2011. cjonline.com/article/20110806/SPORTS/308069876.

9 Donald Spivey, *If You Were Only White: The Life of Leroy "Satchel" Paige* (Columbia, Missouri: University of Missouri Press, 2012), 102.

10 "Bismarck Nine Will Play Gray Ghosts of St. Louis Here Tonight; Expect Roosevelt and Mates Will 'Pack 'Em In,'" *Bismarck* (North Dakota) *Tribune*, June 28, 1933.

11 Spivey, 102-103.

12 "Bismarck Hammers Roosevelt Davis; Wins from Rockford, 13-3," *Bismarck Tribune,* June 18, 1934.

13 Martha Cedillo, "Sultanes de Monterrey, el Iceberg de Beisbol," milenio.com/especiales/sultanes-el-iceberg-del-beisbol

14 Pedro Treto Cisneros, *The Mexican League: Comprehensive Player Statistics, 1937-2001* (Jefferson, North Carolina: McFarland & Company, Inc., 2002), 469.

15 Of note: Roosevelt identifies his father, Will, as next of kin on his draft registration form. Will Davis, at the age of 61, registered for the draft on April 27, 1942.

16 Neil Lanctot, *Negro League Baseball: The Rise and Ruin of a Black Institution* (Philadelphia: University of Pennsylvania Press, 2004), 163.

17 "Satchel Paige," National Baseball Hall of Fame, baseballhall.org/hall-of-famers/paige-satchel.

18 Satchel Paige, as told to Hal Lebovitz, *Pitchin' Man: Satchel Paige's Own Story* (New York: Ishi Press International, 2015), 60.

19 *Pitchin' Man*, 61.

20 Leslie Heaphy, "Palmer House Stars," *The National Pastime*, 2015, https://sabr.org/research/palmer-house-stars.

21 Leslie Heaphy, ed. "Chicago Teams in the Negro League Era," *Black Baseball and Chicago: Essays on the Players and Teams* (Jefferson, North Carolina: McFarland & Company, Inc. 2006), 34.

22 James Segreti, "Satchel Paige Pitches, Grins, and Conquers," *Chicago Tribune*, September 23, 1940.

23 Tom Dunkel, *Color Blind: The Forgotten Team That Broke Baseball's Color Lines* (New York: Grove Press, 2004), 267. According to the Center for Negro League Baseball Research, Davis also pitched in 1945 for the Philadelphia Stars and the Cleveland Buckeyes. He may also have played at one point during his career for the Brooklyn Royal Giants.

William "Willie" Grace

By Kelly Boyer Sagert

Baseball fans everywhere can picture the scene. In 1945, the Cleveland Buckeyes stood in first place after the first half of the season with fans hoping that the momentum would continue in the second half. Then their leading hitter—Lloyd "Ducky" Davenport who was batting .264—left the team to play in Mexico. Just the fans' rotten luck! Would the season falter? Who would step up to fill his shoes?

Fortunately for the fans, plenty of players contributed to finishing the season with a 72-31 record and a .699 winning percentage, including William "Willie" Grace, a switch-hitting outfielder and occasional pitcher. In the World Series, Grace batted .313—chipping in with a "rare home run"[1] and three RBIs—in a four-game World Series sweep over the Homestead Grays, the defending champions.

Perhaps it's a bit of a miracle that Grace ended up playing professional ball in the first place. He was born on June 30, 1917 to Nathan and Jittie Lang Grace in Meridian, Mississippi. His father worked as a fireman while his mother took in laundry at home.

Grace was a toddler during the heart of the Spanish flu pandemic. Between the spring of 1918 and the early summer of 1919, this disease killed between 10 million and 21 million people worldwide.[2] In the United States, this flu affected more than one in four Americans with infants and young children being especially vulnerable.[3]

Homing in more closely to Grace's circumstances, in Mississippi, Black residents died at significantly higher rates than White ones.[4] After all, Black communities at that time were "already beset by many public health, medical, and social problems," according to the National Library of Medicine, "including racist theories of black biological inferiority, racial barriers in medicine and public health, and poor health status."[5]

Yet, young Willie survived.

Willie grew up with siblings named Ruby, Fred, Minnie, Walter, and Mallie.[6] He started playing baseball when he was 13 or 14 years old[7] and graduated from Harris High School in Meridian. He later recalled watching teams of White players in Memphis during those years, thinking about how they didn't do anything that Black teams couldn't.[8]

In 1942, Grace was managing a Mississippi ball club. He enlisted in the Army fight at Camp Shelby in World War II. Before reporting, he and one of his best friends went to a club they frequented—with his friend wearing a white shirt

that Grace had loaned him. His friend began arguing with a female in the club, and Grace tried to stop him. When his friend wouldn't stop, Grace "kinda hit him—knocked him down." Grace suggested that they finish the fight outside but then "heard the people fallin' off stools." He looked up to see that his friend had pulled a gun on him. The so-called friend shot Grace in the leg and the hand. People carried Grace to the hospital, and the military deferred his service, saying they'd be in touch later.[9]

Grace recovered and headed to Erie, Pennsylvania to play ball. The military, once again, deferred his service. He was finally cleared as fit for military service in 1945. By then, both World War II and the record-setting season with the Cleveland Buckeyes had ended—and, after all this back-and-forth, the military never actually called him up.[10]

In the interim, Dizzy Dismukes, the traveling secretary of the Kansas City Monarchs, and a guy described as "Uncle Jim Taylor" had come to see Grace and another player, James Bell, in the South play ball.[11] This likely happened in Laurel, Mississippi.

Bell, however, was already in the service. Through this process, Grace ended up talking to Ernie Wright, the Buckeyes' owner and, in spring 1942, signed with the team.[12]

By this time, Grace had survived both the Spanish flu epidemic and gunshot wounds in the leg and hand, avoiding a bloody war because of deferments. He joined with the team shortly after Buckeyes catcher Ulysses Brown and pitcher Raymond Owens died in a tragic automobile

Willie Grace.

accident[13] during the year that the team was the Cleveland-Cincinnati Buckeyes.[14]

Grace was 6 feet tall and weighed 170 pounds. He was a switch-hitter and threw left-handed. Known primarily for his strong arm, he was noted for also having good bat control. His batting power, speed, and defensive skills fell closer to the middle of the pack.[15] During his time playing ball, he gained the nickname of "Fireman"—perhaps because of his powerful throwing arm.[16]

Grace largely played in the outfield but did pitch (although how often isn't clear; perhaps that took place during exhibition games). In a 1995 interview, he recalled the end of his pitching career. The team was "shaggin' fly balls and I was just gonna roll the ball back to the infield." After he picked up a ball, another player jokingly said that the batter was running to second, so Grace "hauled off and threw the ball," falling to the ground, injured. He pitched a couple of games after that, including one in 1944 that he recalled as a no-hitter through the seventh before the manager took him out. After that, he became a full-time outfielder, usually in right field.[17]

In 1944, Grace batted .228. In 1945: .321. That year, out of 82 plate appearances, Grace had 25 hits, including a triple and a home run, and he scored 7 runs with 11 RBIs. He had an on-base percentage of .346 and a slugging percentage of .397.

The Buckeyes ended the 1945 Negro American League season with a .699 winning percentage, —and, while it's true that baseball rosters, overall, were depleted because of the war, in a 2006 interview, Grace noted that their World Series opponent—the Homestead Grays—still had an incredibly powerful team with Josh Gibson catching, Buck Leonard at first, and Cool Papa Bell in the outfield. He was quoted as adding Judy Johnson to the list; either he or the writer made a mistake, almost certainly meaning Jud Wilson.[18]

Beating the Grays, Grace told the interviewer, was the "greatest thing that ever happened to me as a ballplayer."[19] He recalled hitting his home run in game one (although it happened in game two), not expecting that to happen at all because the fence at League Park went all the way to the top of the grandstand. After he hit the ball and began to run the bases, he still didn't realize what he'd accomplished until someone told him it was over the fence. He'd tried to hit a home run there many times in batting practice but "it all happened," he said, "when it had to happen."[20]

With minor errors, Grace shared other memories of his role. He said that, out of the five or six runs scored in this four-game sweep (the Buckeyes actually scored 15), he drove in three of them. He accomplished one of them, he remembered, through an unexpected bunt to the right, scoring Archie Ware, although newspaper reporting stated that Grace "rallied to the occasion and the cause with a looping single" in right.[21]

In the seventh, when all wasn't looking good for the Buckeyes, Grace allowed fans to breathe a collective sigh of relief. "Sammy Bankhead was forced to fly out to Willie Grace for the final out and the end of the suspense period."[22]

In game two, Grace enjoyed his moment in the sun. The game story in the *Cleveland Call and Post* said: "Grace Socks Homer. The game ended like a lurid story-book account, or a made-to-order movie baseball thriller, for the more than 10,000 fans who forgot to shiver under overcast skies as Willie Grace, Buckeye outfielder, opened the seventh inning with a bang. With a resounding crack that brought the dejected Buckeye fans to their feet Grace smacked the ball neatly over the right field Gem Safety Razor ad and strutted around the sacks in that fateful seventh."[23] This home run accounted for his second RBI in the Series. In Game Three, he hit a sacrifice to bring home the first run.[24]

In his 2006 interview, Grace shared details about what players got paid, saying that there was the official salary and what you got paid under the table. Official league salaries when Grace played, he said, could average between $5,000 and $7,000 a year. He got paid $600 a month. He also worked at Hammermill Paper on unlimited "victory shifts" for 65 cents an hour—a job that he continued through 1980, long after he'd finished playing baseball. Players like Buck Leonard and Josh Gibson, he said, could make more than $900 a month. Later, when Grace played in the Washington Senators farm system in 1951, his official salary was $327 monthly but, in actuality, he received $675 each month.[25]

During 1946-1948, Grace experienced better batting seasons than in previous years. In 1946, he hit for .368 and, in June, was listed as the 10th best batter in the league, percentage wise, at .303. In September, he ranked number eight at .325.

In one game, the headline reads, in part, "Willie Grace Stars at Bat" with text calling him the "big noise" in the game. The article added that the "fleet footed gardener" got a hit at all four at-bats. "His 2 singles, a double and a triple was good for a thousand percent in the hitting averages."[26]

Grace also played in both of the Negro Leagues' two All-Star games in 1946.[27] [28] He started in both, getting four hits in eight at-bats: a .500 average and earning the headline reading "Willie Grace Shines at Plate."[29] That year, he was named as the Buckeyes' most valuable player.[30] Grateful fans awarded players with gifts. Grace received a gold keychain from Shaw Jewelers.[31]

That year, the Buckeyes ranked first in the league for on-base plus slugging, batting average, on-base percentage, and slugging percentage.

In 1947, Grace batted .326 and, in July, his average of .321 placed him as the third highest on the team.[32] On a windy day in May, the player who got the most hits won a radio from Boyd's Furniture Store—and "Hustling Willie Grace showed that he is a real money player . . . It's Willie's radio, now."[33] He also won the Louis B. Selzer Trophy as the Outstanding Buckeye Player, voted in by his teammates.[34] [35]

In a doubleheader against the Memphis Red Sox, Grace hit an RBI double against the right-center-field wall in the first game and went to third on a single. The pitcher tried to pick him off. Grace, "quick to see what had happened, streaked for home to break the 2-2 deadlock" for the team's 40th win of the season. In the second game, Grace doubled to the right-field wall, moved to third on a single, and stole home, helping to secure win number 41.[36]

This was the year that the Buckeyes lost the World Series to the New York Cubans in six games. Grace said he believed the Buckeyes were a better team than in 1945, but the Cubans were just too good.[37] In the game they did win (one game was a tie), Grace stood out (the headline "Joe Atkins, Willie Grace Flash Power at Plate" reflected), with a "trio of clean singles."[38]

In 1948, he batted .313 and played in the second of two East-West matchups of the league stars.[39]

After Jackie Robinson had broken the color barrier in the White major leagues, it was natural for newspapers to speculate on who might be next. In July, the *Indianapolis Recorder* noted how five Buckeyes were batting above .300, including Grace, and that "one or more it is reported are being watched by Big League scouts."[40]

Grace never made it to the White big leagues, and 1948 actually ended what could be considered his peak years. In 1949, he followed the team to Louisville, batting .221[41] and serving as one of only three veterans from the 1945 championship team alongside Archie Ware and George Jefferson.[42] By season's end, though, Grace was part of the team's reserve list.[43] He finished his Negro Leagues career with the Houston Eagles in 1950, batting .273.[44]

Then aged 34, he played a season with the Erie Sailors of the Class-C Middle Atlantic League, a farm team for the Washington Senators.[45]

The *Altoona Mirror* welcomed him, saying that "Erie has one of the outstanding Negro players of the last decade in outfielder Willie Grace."[46] In May, Grace stole four bases in one game, also hitting a triple.[47]

Grace told a reporter in 2006 that the Sailors set a minor-league record that year, beating the Niagara Falls team 13 times in the season; but, in the playoffs, Erie lost to Niagara Falls. That year, Grace batted .293 and stole 12 bases. Grace told an interviewer that he and two other Black players were on the farm team so that the Senators could claim they had Black players in their system without having to have one on their major-league team.[48]

Grace was released in February 1952.[49] He said that he had an opportunity to play in Texas. He decided, however, that, after playing for a couple of decades—and having married a woman in the area—it was time for him to settle down. He married Shirley Jefferson, a registered nurse.[50]

Records are contradictory near the end of Grace's baseball career with one source showing he played for the Houston Eagles in the Negro Leagues in 1951[51] and another showing that he played in Texas before playing for Erie.[52] Because Negro League records are incomplete and often contradictory, Grace's career can't be statistically summed up the way in which we're accustomed to with players in what was termed major-league baseball. But, from what we do know of Grace, it's clear that he contributed a key role to a team that had reached the highest levels of success available to them.

Grace continued to work at the Hammermill Paper Company until his retirement in 1980. He and his wife, Shirley, had two sons, Darryl and Greg, and four grandchildren: Darryl, Jr., Sydney, Monica, and Stephen. At some point, Grace and his wife divorced.[53]

Later summing up his career, Grace said "Winning the 1945 Negro Leagues World Series and being voted MVP in 1948 by a Cleveland newspaper were very rewarding to me."[54] Asked who were the greatest baseball players, he mentioned Stan Musial, Mickey Mantle, and Joe DiMaggio but ultimately settled upon Willie Mays. As far as pitchers, he went with Satchel Paige and Martin Dihigo.[55]

In November 1996, Grace was inducted into the Ohio Baseball Hall of Fame along with Herb Score.[56]

Grace's positive attitude clearly shines through in his interviews. In one with *Cleveland Magazine*, quotes include Grace saying "I tell myself I was lucky" and remembering how "[a] lot of players would come and go, but it was fun. You were having so much fun."[57]

Willie Grace funeral booklet.

In his later years, Grace suffered from glaucoma and a tired memory, living in the Presque Isle Rehabilitation and Nursing Center. On his dresser, he kept cigars, family photos—and a group photo of the 1945 Buckeyes.[58]

William Grace died on November 18, 2006 in Erie, at the age of 89. The funeral home laid out a baseball memorabilia display for his services; Grace was the last of Erie's "prominent group of Negro League players." As one attendee noted, "It's not only the passing of a generation, but to a certain extent the end of an era."[59]

His son Darryl remarked how "Dad had a full life. He just lived and ate baseball all the time."[60]

When, in 2020, segregated teams received major-league status, Darryl noted how pleased his father would have been. Darryl remembered "several baseball-related trips" he made with his father after his career ended. "He'd be so tickled when we'd go to card shows and people would want his autograph. He wasn't a resentful man." And, now, "Everybody will know how great those players were."[61]

SOURCES

In addition to the sources cited in the Notes, the author consulted Seamheads.org.

NOTES

1   "Willie Grace," Negro League Baseball Museum. https://nlbemuseum.com/history/players/grace.html

2   Alice Reid, "The Effects of the 1918–1919 Influenza Pandemic on Infant and Child Health in Derbyshire," *International Journal for the History of Medicine and Related Sciences*. National Library of Sciences. January 1, 2005: 49 (1):29-54. https://pmc.ncbi.nlm.nih.gov/articles/PMC1088249/

3   "The Deadly Virus: The Influenza Epidemic of 1918," National Archives and Records Administration. https://www.archives.gov/exhibits/influenza-epidemic/

4   Ashton Pittman, "In Mississippi, COVID-19 Exceeds Great Influenza's 1918 Death Toll," *Mississippi Free Press*. February 4, 2021. https://www.mississippifreepress.org/in-mississippi-covid-19-exceeds-great-influenzas-1918-death-toll/

5   Vanessa Northington Gamble, "'There Wasn't a Lot of Comforts in Those Days:' African Americans, Public Health, and the 1918 Influenza Epidemic," Public Health Records. National Library of Medicine. 2010: 125(Suppl3):114-122. https://pmc.ncbi.nlm.nih.gov/articles/PMC2862340/

6   Willie Grace Obituary, *Erie Times-News*, November 20-21, 2006. https://www.legacy.com/us/obituaries/erietimesnews/name/willie-grace-obituary?id=25844460

7   Brent Kelley, "Willie Grace was part of the best team in Cleveland history . . . in 1945!" *Sports Collectors Digest*, November 10, 1995.

8   Kelley.

9   Kelley.

10   Kelley.

11   Kelley.

12   Kelley.

13   "Willie Grace," Negro League Baseball Museum.

14   "Cleveland Buckeyes," Encyclopedia of Cleveland History. https://case.edu/ech/articles/c/cleveland-buckeyes

15   "Cleveland Buckeyes," Negro League Baseball Museum.

16   "Willie Grace," MLB.com, https://www.mlb.com/player/willie-grace-819311

17   Kelley.

18   Kelley.

19   Kelley.

20   Kelley.

21   Jimmy Jones, "Buckeyes Beat Grays First Two Games of Series, 2-1, 3-2," *Cleveland Call and Post*, September 22, 1945: 17. *https://newspaperarchive.com/call-and-post-sep-22-1945-p-17/*

22   Jones.

23   Jones.

24   Jones,

25   Kelley.

26   Cleveland Jackson, "Buckeyes, Monarchs Divide Twin Bill, 4-1, 1-5; Willie Gracey Stars at Bat," *Cleveland Call and Post*, June 15, 1946: 22. HTTPS://NEWSPAPERARCHIVE.COM/CALL-AND-POST-JUN-15-1946-P-22/

27   "Big League Scouts to Eye Negro Stars at Diamond Classic," *Cleveland Call and Post*, August 10, 1946: 23. https://newspaperarchive.com/call-and-post-aug-10-1946-p-23/; "Willie Grace." Negro League Baseball Museum.

28   "Willie Grace." Negro League Baseball Museum.

29   George Lyle, Jr., "NAL Mound Stars Fail to Check NNL Batsmiths as East Nine Wins at Wash.," *Cleveland Call and Post*, August 24, 1946: 20. https://newspaperarchive.com/call-and-post-aug-24-1946-p-20/

30   Cleveland Jackson. "Carnizares, Woods, W. Jefferson May Return to Buckeyes; Travel Troubles Kept Stars in S.A.," *Call and Post*. February 22, 1947: 22. https://newspaperarchive.com/call-and-post-feb-22-1947-p-22/

31   "Cleveland Fans Honor Buckeye Players with Gifts," *Cleveland Call and Post*, August 31, 1946: 19. https://newspaperarchive.com/call-and-post-aug-31-1946-p-19/

32   "Bitter Rivals Renew Feud Started in 1945; Johnny Wright Will Hurl," *Cleveland Call and Post*, July 26, 1947: 22. https://newspaperarchive.com/call-and-post-jul-26-1947-p-22/

33   Cleveland Jackson, "Headline Action: Fly Balls Have Holiday," *Cleveland Call and Post*, May 10, 1947: 23. https://newspaperarchive.com/call-and-post-may-10-1947-p-23/

34   "Remember September," *Call and Post*, January 4, 1957: 21. https://newspaperarchive.com/call-and-post-jan-04-1947-p-21/

35   Photo caption, *Call and Post*. September 7, 1946: 20. https://newspaperarchive.com/call-and-post-sep-07-1946-p-20/

36   "Jethroe Runs Wild on Sacks as Brilliant Pitching by Clarke, Smith Squelch Rivals," *Cleveland Call and Post*. August 9, 1947: 22. https://newspaperarchive.com/call-and-post-aug-09-1947-p-22/

37   Kelley.

38   Cleveland Jackson, "Joe Atkins, Willie Grace Flash Power at Plate; Rapid Fans Brave Inclement Weather to See Fray," *Cleveland Call and Post*, May 10, 1947: 22. https://newspaperarchive.com/call-and-post-may-10-1947-p-22/

39   A.S. "Doc" Young, "Buckeyes Beat Blues; Steppers Win; Three In East-West," *Cleveland Call and Post*, August 21, 1948: 18. https://newspaperarchive.com/call-and-post-aug-21-1948-p-18/

40   "Buckeyes Play Clowns Friday Night, July 30," *Indianapolis Recorder*, July 31, 1948: 11. https://newspaperarchive.com/indianapolis-recorder-jul-31-1948-p-11/

41   "Cleveland Buckeyes," Negro League Baseball Museum.

42   "Brings Roster of Young, Hustling Players Back Home for Karamu Benefit with Indianapolis Clowns," *Cleveland Call and Post*, July 23, 1949: 18. HTTPS://NEWSPAPERARCHIVE.COM/CALL-AND-POST-JUL-23-1949-P-18/

43   Chart provided by the National Baseball Hall of Fame

44   "Cleveland Buckeyes," Negro League Baseball Museum.

45   Kelley.

46   Rudy Cernkovic. "Middle Atlantic Baseball League Starts Tonight," *Altoona Mirror*, May 3, 1951: 29. https://newspaperarchive.com/altoona-mirror-may-03-1951-p-29/

47   Associated Press, "New Castle Atop Middle-Atlantic," *Indiana* (Pennsylvania) *Evening Gazette*, May 14, 1951: 11. https://newspaperarchive.com/indiana-evening-gazette-may-14-1951-p-11/

48   Kelley.

49   "Player Transactions," *The Sporting News*, February 27, 1952: 29. https://newspaperarchive.com/st-louis-sporting-news-feb-27-1952-p-29/

50   Shirley A. Grace Obituary, *Observer-Reporter* (Washington, Pennsylvania), September 17, 2014. https://www.legacy.com/us/obituaries/observer-reporter/name/shirley-grace-obituary?id=18398405

51   Chart provided by the National Baseball Hall of Fame

52   "Cleveland Buckeyes," Negro League Baseball Museum.

53   Willie Grace Obituary.

54   "Cleveland Buckeyes," Negro League Baseball Museum.

55   Kelley.

56   "Baseball Day," *Times-Reporter* (Philadelphia), October 27, 1996: 13. https://newspaperarchive.com/dover-new-philadelphia-times-reporter-oct-27-1996-p-13/

57   Dave O'Karma, "The Forgotten Championship," *Cleveland Magazine*, April 28, 2006. https://clevelandmagazine.com/in-the-cle/sports/articles/the-forgotten-championship

58   O'Karma.

59   "Willie Grace RIP," Baseball Fever, November 23, 2006. https://www.baseball-fever.com/forum/general-baseball/the-negro-leagues/18163-willie-grace-rip

60   "Willie Grace RIP."

61   Josh Reilly, "MLB's Recognition of Negro League records includes Jethroe, others with Erie ties," *Erie Times-News*, December 29, 2020. https://www.goerie.com/story/sports/2020/12/29/mlbs-recognition-negro-league-records-includes-eries-jethroe-others/4037179001/

Billy Horne

By Jeb Stewart

Billy Horne was a Negro League second baseman and shortstop who played for several clubs in his 15-season career, from 1935 to 1949. He was a left-handed hitter, threw right-handed, stood 5-feet-5 and weighed 152 pounds. Nicknamed Little Grumbler and Aussa, Horne was regarded as a fine defender and appeared in several all-star games.[1]

William Joseph Horne was born on February 20, 1916, in New Orleans. A 1920 census record listed his race as "mulatto,"[2] identified his mother as Anna "Horn," and noted that he had an older sister named May.[3] They lived in a rooming house in New Orleans' Third Ward, and his mother, a widow, found work as a servant for a family.[4] Nothing is known about his father.

Horne dropped out of high school after his junior year,[5] but not much else is known about his education, upbringing, or interest in baseball. Negro league player-manager Winfield Welch, who managed Horne for parts of three seasons with the Acme Colored Giants from 1935 to 1937,[6] was regularly credited for his early development as a player.[7] The Colored Giants were "an unofficial minor league team for the Kansas City Monarchs" and future hall of Famer Buck O'Neil played for them in 1936.[8] Acme's home city was billed as Shreveport, Louisiana, and the team occasionally hosted games in the city.[9] However, the Colored Giants

Billy Horne.

spent most of the time on the road, barnstorming across the United States and into Canada.

During this period, Horne may have briefly served as a batboy for the Pittsburgh Crawfords. A photograph of the Negro National League All-Stars, who won the 1936 Denver Post Tournament, appeared in the *Kansas City Call*.[10] A young man in a "Pittsburgh" jersey, identified by the newspaper only as "Horne," appears kneeling in the front row next to Josh Gibson, who was wearing a Crawfords uniform. A significantly clearer copy of this picture appears in Phil S. Dixon's *The Negro Baseball Leagues: A Photographic History*.[11] Dixon concluded that Horne was a batboy.[12] While 20 would have been old for a batboy, a comparison of the young man in this photo with Billy Horne's picture on the Seamhead's website reveals a remarkable physical resemblance.[13] However, his name did not appear in any news stories about the Crawfords in 1936, so the question will remain unanswered unless additional information is uncovered.

In mid-April of 1937, the Shreveport Tigers signed Horne to a contract and the news story noted that he was a *former* member of the Acme Giants.[14] The details of Horne leaving the Colored Giants are lost to history. A few days after the signing, the mayor of Shreveport announced that the Tigers would not be allowed to play games at Dixie Field due to complaints "of the use of the grounds by negroes," which forced them to play home games on the road.[15] Horne's name never appeared in a game story or box score for the Tigers. By Memorial Day, he had returned to the Colored Giants.[16]

Baseball historians Dick Clark and Larry Lester concluded that sometime in 1938, Horne joined the Monroe (Louisiana) Monarchs,[17] but no contemporary newspaper articles have been found to confirm this. Another source claimed (in 1941) that Horne "came from the [Ethiopian] Clowns to the [Chicago American] Giants in 1939."[18] No article or box score has been found to confirm that Horne ever played for the Clowns from 1937 to 1939. Questions will persist regarding how he spent the 1938 campaign until additional resources are uncovered, but it is undisputed that at some point in 1938, he joined Candy Jim Taylor's Chicago American Giants of the Negro American League. But the details of the signing are lost to history.

His name was initially spelled "Horn" and first appeared in a box score as a shortstop for the American Giants in a 9-8 comeback win over the Madison Blues in July.[19] He went hitless in four at-bats, recorded five assists in the field, and made no errors.[20] His first single memorialized in a box score came two weeks later in a 4-2 loss to the Kansas City Monarchs, although Horne probably had hits in other games that went unreported.[21] He followed up that performance with two hits, including a home run, against the Kansas City Monarchs in an 11-4 win in late July.[22]

The American Giants finished with a 41-37-3 record and a third-place finish in the NAL but missed the playoffs. For his part, Horne batted .278 in 16 games and posted a 128 OPS+.

By 1939 Horne was on the verge of becoming a star. In a game against the Madison Blues, he led the American Giants with two hits, a stolen base, a run scored, and five assists.[23] Fans began noticing his rangy defense, even when it was sometimes uneven. In a game in June, a report noted that "Billy Horn was the busiest man in either infield outside of the first baseman. He had four putouts, five assists, and two errors."[24] He received the highest vote total among all second basemen for the West in East-West All-Star voting with 401,286 and finished ahead of Curtis Henderson (387,333) and Newt Allen (206,120).[25]

The first of the two scheduled East-West All-Star games was played at Comiskey Park on August 6, 1939. Horne did not get into the game until the fifth inning with the West trailing, 2-0. He singled to right field in his first at-bat but got no farther as East pitcher Roy Partlow pitched out of trouble.[26] In the eighth inning, the West squad rallied to take a 3-2 lead. Horne then drove in an insurance run in the West's 4-2 victory:

"The game was held up until the groundskeepers could clear the field of straw hats and paper. The fans had staged a story book scene. What pent-up enthusiasm had been left in the crowd was turned loose. Manager George Scales of the East waved Partlow to the shower and Scales' New York Black Yankees' teammate, Bill Holland, went to the mound. Alex Radcliffe dumped a single into center field and [Mule] Suttles then proceeded to lose Neal Robinson's fly in the sun and it went for a two-base hit, putting A. Radcliffe on third. Strong was purposely walked and the bases were full. Billy Horne, Chicago American Giants' second sacker, put into the game at second in the fourth when A. Radcliffe had been shifted to shortstop and [Ted] Strong on first to relieve Jelly Taylor, was up. Horne and A. Radcliffe worked a squeeze play. Horne pushed the ball to [Buck] Leonard and A. Radcliffe getting home with the fourth and last run for the West. Leonard had no chance to get A. Radcliffe at the plate, therefore all he could do was to tag Horne out."[27]

In the second East-West All-Star Game, at Yankee Stadium, the East got revenge, winning 10-2.[28] Horne was hitless in two at-bats.[29]

The American Giants did not live up to lofty expectations in 1939.[30] While they improved to a second-place finish, Chicago finished with a slightly worse NAL record of 41-38-0. They missed the playoffs again as the Monarchs won the league's first-half title and met the second-half champion St. Louis Stars in the playoffs. Horne's batting average reportedly sank to .232, although all Negro League statistics remain incomplete.

That winter, Taylor left Chicago to manage the Birmingham Black Barons, an NAL rival.[31] Wilson Redus replaced him at the helm. Under his leadership, the American Giants fell to a disappointing 24-30-2 record and finished fifth in the NAL. Horne, now 24, should have returned as an established player on the American Giants. However, in *Black Baseball and Chicago: Essays on the Players, Teams and Games*, baseball historians determined that "Billy Horne jumped his contract and then was welcomed back by H.G. Hall without any penalty at all."[32] No news reports explained the reasons for Horne's absence and return.

Although he played professionally in Chicago, Horne continued to reside in New Orleans. A 1940 Census record noted that he lived in the city's Second Ward.[33] He was single, identified his occupation as "ball player," and reported earning $1,273.[34] During the season, "he was presented with a Gold Trophy by the Cross Roads Athletic Club of New Orleans during a doubleheader that involved the American Giants and the Birmingham Black Barons. Xavier Student Jesse Russell presented Horne with the trophy as a former member of the club."[35] Based on the limited box scores, Horne's batting average reportedly slipped to just .186.

In August, the *Chicago Tribune* reported that he had been elected as a starter for the West in the East-West All-Star Game.[36] There is no record of Horne on the West's roster. Baseball historian Larry Lester later determined that he finished fifth in the voting for second base.[37] However, he did appear for the South in one of the North-South All-Star Games, played at Pelican Park in New Orleans. Per Seamheads, Horne hit a triple, walked, and drove in a run in three plate appearances for the South. He was also involved in turning two double plays at shortstop and committed no errors in the field.[38]

The stands in American Giants Park burned that winter and the team relocated to Comiskey Park for the 1941 campaign.[39] The American Giants were favored to win the NAL.[40] The *Chicago Sunday Bee* gushed with enthusiasm over their prospects:

"With many old favorites back in the fold, lured by the attractive program being pursued by the south side club in its efforts to regain the glory of past years, and the new players among the best ever recruited, it's no wonder that the pennant bee is starting to hum among the [Giants]."

. . .

'Candy Jim' Taylor is back as manager after a season of piloting the Birmingham Black Barons. The wily Taylor, one of the top-ranking Negro managers, is tickled pink with his squad and has gone on record as saying it's the team to beat for the Negro American League crown.

Further cause for rejoicing is the return of such old favorites as Willie Cornelius, the great pitcher; 'Pepper' Bassett sensational young catcher; Billy Horne, top second baseman, and others after being away awhile."[41]

Despite the positive predictions, Chicago finished last in the NAL with a terrible record of 18-36-2. While Horne batted .211, based on the available box scores, he had some bright moments. In late May he collected four hits in five at-bats, including a double, in an exhibition game against Council Bluffs.[42] The fans chose him as the West's second baseman in the East-West All-Star Game.[43] He appeared in the game as a shortstop and did not get a hit in two at-bats, but was flawless in the field with three putouts, three assists, and no errors.[44]

In November 1941, Horne married Bertha Williams in New Orleans;[45] any details about their life together, including any children they may have had, have been lost to history.[46]

In 1942 Horne, now 26, joined the expansion Cincinnati-Cleveland Buckeyes, although the reason for his departure from Chicago is unknown.[47] In previews, he was repeatedly cited as a pivotal player:

• The *Muskogee* (Oklahoma) *Daily Phoenix and Times-Democrat* observed that "[o]utstanding players for the Cincinnati team are Billy Horne, considered the best second baseman in negro baseball. ..."[48]

• The *Atlanta Daily World* reported that "Billy Horne, second baseman, is rated with the best in the league and does a neat piece of fielding as well as hitting. ..."[49]

• The *Cleveland Call and Post* called him "the nucleus" of the Buckeyes' infield.[50]

Once the season got underway, reports frequently cited Horne's smooth glove work as the reason for the success of the Buckeyes' defense. The *Pittsburgh Courier* reported that "[t]he Buckeyes were hailed as the best Negro team ever to play in this city [Columbus, Ohio]. First baseman [Archie] Ware and Second baseman Billy Horn also showed plenty of class in their fielding and several times had the crowd on their feet with spectacular playing."[51] The *Cleveland Call and Post* had an even more descriptive writeup of Horne's defensive prowess:

"Fans who saw Billy Horne, Archie Ware, and center-fielder [Sonny] Harris do their stuff at League

Park last Sunday, when the Bucks split a double-header with the Jacksonville Red Caps agree that a close approach to major league ball-handling is achieved by this trio. Harris tries hard at the plate, going out with each cut at the ball. Horne hit the dust five times as he dived for balls which barely escaped him. His play to retire the side after Jacksonville had scored two runs in the first inning of the second game last Sunday, was a pip. He went to his left, and to the edge of the grass where he fielded a hard-hit ball perfectly and without lost motion threw to first, beating the runner by a split step."[52]

Horne's contribution to the Buckeyes was not limited to defense. In late July, the club split a doubleheader with the Homestead Grays.[53] He contributed three hits, including a double, in the first-game loss. In the second game, he came to bat with the game tied in the bottom of the ninth and a runner on third. "Billy Horne put all [his] five-foot one-inch frame into a swat which sent the ball sizzling out into right center. [Eugene] Bremer trotted home ... the game was over ... 4449 of the fans made bedlam of League Park."[54]

The Buckeyes finished with an enviable record of 50-27-2, which was remarkable for an expansion franchise. However, they finished second, one game behind the first-place and NAL pennant winner Kansas City Monarchs. So good was the Buckeyes' performance that, in his Sportlight column, John Fuster reckoned that any contest between the Cleveland Indians and the Buckeyes "would be a fairly even game."[55] He cited Horne as part of an infield that matched the Indians;[56] in another article, Fuster argued that he should have made the West's all-star squad.[57]

Ernest Wright, the president of the Buckeyes, cited him as a prospect who could make the White major leagues immediately.[58] Based on the available box scores, Horne played well, batting .275 with an OPS+ of 106. He led the Buckeyes with 7 stolen bases and 13 walks, and finished second on the squad with 27 runs scored.

Desiring a better contract, the 27-year-old Horne initially refused to report to the Buckeyes' spring-training camp in 1943.[59] He soon ended the holdout.[60] On May 2 he appeared in a spring-training game for the Harrisburg-St. Louis Stars against the Buckeyes. He got an infield hit and scored the Stars' only run in a 1-1 extra-innings tie.[61] Whether this was during his contract dispute is unknown; he was presumably loaned to the Stars because this was the only game he appeared in for them.

By mid-May, Horne was the Buckeyes' permanent fixture at shortstop and helped turn six double plays against the Memphis Red Sox.[62] Another report noted that "Horne is the spark plug of the infield, and he and [Marshall] Riddles [sic] form a great double play combination. They have completed as many as eight double plays in one game."[63]

Once again, Horne was also a solid hitter in the Buckeyes lineup and led the attack with four hits against

THE 1945 CLEVELAND BUCKEYES

the Cincinnati Clowns in an 11-0 win.[64] Cleveland got off to a fast 6-1 start,[65] and the *Pittsburgh Courier* reported that "they are well out in front in the league race and are being hailed the most sensational team in sepia baseball."[66] However, both Horne and the Buckeyes soon cooled off.

Cleveland was swept in a doubleheader at Chicago in mid-June with Horne making a critical error in the first game when he missed a groundball.[67] He made up for the mistake with a spectacular over-the-shoulder running catch into short left field in the second game, but the Buckeyes still lost.[68] A week later, Chicago traveled to Cleveland and swept another twin bill from the Buckeyes as Horne went hitless in the first game.[69] On the return trip to the Windy City, the American Giants again defeated Cleveland in the first game of a double bill in a brutal 14-inning affair, 6-5.[70] After playing so poorly in Sunday doubleheaders against Chicago, the Buckeyes were fortunate that the second game was rained out.[71]

While Cleveland soon began winning games again, including a doubleheader sweep of the Clowns[72] and another win over the Monarchs,[73] they could not catch the second-half NAL champion American Giants. Chicago played the first-half champion Black Barons in the NAL playoffs. The Buckeyes finished with an overall NAL record of 39-27-2, second-best in the league, but missed the postseason again.

Seamheads.com reports that Horne's performance in 1943 was good enough for him to be named as a second baseman to the South's All-Star squad, where he went 0-for-4 at the plate, but recorded two putouts and had two assists in his five innings of play.

Before spring training got underway in Clarksdale, Mississippi, in 1944, Wilbur Hayes, the general manager of the Buckeyes, reviewed his roster and remarked confidently, "I am sure that I will give the Cleveland fans a championship club."[74] Columnist Eddie P. Jennings agreed, and wrote that "[e]ven now, I dare to predict that they will cop the pennant for '44."[75] Horne was expected to move back to second base, but he again spent most of the year at shortstop."[76]

On March 11 Jennings informed his readers that he would write a profile the following week on "Billy Horne, the best second baseman in the league,"[77] but the story never surfaced. Even so, sportswriters recognized the veteran leadership Horne contributed:

"Although the Buckeye club is one of the youngest in the fast Negro American League, it is distinguished in having on its roster some of the better known Negro baseball stars. In this category are Billy Horne, shortstop, and Jimmy Crutchfield, right fielder. Each has rocketed his name high in Negro baseball circles as members of other clubs and joined up under Manager [Parnell] Woods when Cleveland entered the league."[78]

During spring training, a controversy arose, as Hayes accused owners in the Mexican League of trying to lure players to jump their contracts.[79] He claimed that "the Mexican interests have tried to take Billy Horne, sensational shortstop, and Willie Jefferson, a dependable pitcher of Cleveland."[80] While Horne honored his contract, he missed the end of spring training after being drafted into the US Army.[81] However, he was able to return to the lineup by Opening Day;[82] another report clarified that he had been "recently discharged from the Army."[83]

In late May, Horne was credited with contributing a key single in the second game of a doubleheader sweep of the Black Barons in front of 8,000 fans at League Park.[84] He played well enough during the first half of the schedule to be mentioned as one of the Buckeyes who might make the East-West All-Star Game.[85] He was later named as a reserve to the West squad,[86] but did not appear in the game.[87] Remarkably, the Buckeyes sent six players to the All-Star Game including Horne, Bremer, Woods, Ware, Sam Jethroe, and Buddy Armour, while a "sadly depleted Buckeyes squad" continued to play league games in their absence.[88]

The frequent travel and all the games may have begun to take a toll on Horne's body. In July he suffered an injury against the American Giants while sliding into third, but did not miss much time.[89] Late in the season, he suffered an undisclosed injury that was part of a rash of injuries on Cleveland's roster.[90] The injury was serious enough to sideline him for at least two weeks.[91] Despite the injuries, he posted a .963 fielding percentage, which led all NAL shortstops.[92]

Cleveland finished in second place, albeit a distant 15½ games behind the NAL champion Black Barons. They had a winning record for the third straight season (45-42), but again missed the playoffs. Their fortunes would change in 1945.

With an overall three-year winning percentage of .583, the Buckeyes were recognized by sportswriters during the early spring as "a powerhouse in the Negro American League" and "a well-balanced ball club that promise[s] to make their presence felt in the Negro American League Championship race."[93]

Before the schedule got underway, a Texas newspaper previewing a game between the Buckeyes and the American Giants reported that "Flashy Billy Horne has been moved over to second base from shortstop to make room for a highly touted newcomer, Avelino Cañizares."[94] GM Hayes explained the move:

"I have never seen a smoother shortstop than our new Cuban Avelino Canizarez, who is a wizard at getting the ball away from him fielding. He throws well from any position. ... I have practically my same squad of last year with one change in the infield, that at shortstop. Thus, Billy Horne and

Johnny Cowan can fight it out for second base, and you know they are good."[95]

When the Buckeyes met the Birmingham Black Barons at Rickwood Field on Opening Day, Cleveland's new manager, Quincy Trouppe – after apparently having been forgiven for trying to lure players to Mexico the year before – recalled that Birmingham had won the last two NAL flags and avoided a playoff by winning both halves in 1944. He asserted that the Buckeyes were finally ready to claim the pennant.[96] However, they would have to do so without Horne, as he was set "to face induction into the armed forces within the next 10 days."[97]

Throughout 1945, series previews regularly mentioned Horne as the starting second baseman.[98] However, when a rare box score appeared, Cowan's name appeared at the position.[99] Seamheads.com determined that Horne only appeared in two games the entire season.

With Horne's replacement at shortstop, Cañizares, leading Cleveland with a .375 batting average, the Buckeyes romped to a title with a 62-17-1 record, winning both halves of the NAL season just as Birmingham had the year before, and then swept the Homestead Grays in the Negro World Series.[100] For Horne, the title must have been bittersweet. Cleveland won the championship, but his military commitment caused him to miss the Series. Bob Williams of the *Cleveland Call and Post* observed that Cañizares' presence at shortstop helped ease Horne's absence.[101] He added, "Losing Horne and finally, Duckey Davenport, certainly a most valuable player, Trouppe's squad still stayed on top of the heap, closing the gaps as if they never existed."[102]

Before spring training in 1946, Horne, now 30 years old, was released from his military commitment and was free to return to the Buckeyes.[103] Although some sources claim that Horne was in the Army,[104] several stories clarified that he served in the Navy.[105] He was initially penciled in as the starting shortstop after Cañizares reportedly signed with the Algodoneros (Cottonpickers) de Unión Laguna of Torreon in Mexico.[106] Reports soon appeared suggesting that Cañizares' return was imminent and that Horne was shifting back to second base.[107] These rumors proved to be incorrect and Horne remained at shortstop throughout the spring.[108]

On April 21 Horne doubled in Cleveland's 10-9 win over the Black Barons;[109] in June, he had three hits, including "two towering three baggers," as the Buckeyes crushed the Atlanta Black Crackers, 10-1,[110] but it was one of his final highlights with the club.

A news story in late July reported that Horne had been traded to the Chicago American Giants for shortstop Ralph Wyatt.[111] Other stories confirmed that Horne was a member of the American Giants,[112] and his photo appeared in an advertisement for a game between Chicago and the Stag Beers in August.[113] No game stories or box scores have been found showing Horne as having played in a game for Chicago in 1946.[114] Other reports suggested that he represented the Buckeyes in the North-South All-Star contests; these games

were played as a series in New Orleans, Baton Rouge, and at Rickwood Field in Birmingham in October.[115] Horne's fly ball plated the only run in the South's 1-0 win at Pelican Stadium.[116] Whether he finished 1946 as a member of the American Giants or the Buckeyes, his career in the NAL had come to an end.

In 1947 Horne returned home and played shortstop for the New Orleans Creoles, a new entry in the Negro Southern League.[117] The Creoles were managed by "Harry Williams, former all-around star for the New York Black Yankees."[118] Horne was hailed as "a former star with the Cleveland Buckeyes."[119] In a preview for a game against the Staten Island Oilers at New York's Polo Grounds, a story misinterpreted the reasons for Horne's presence in the minors:

> "At shortstop for the Creoles will be one of the
> most promising Negro players in the business,
> Bill Horne, who has had trials with the Chicago
> American Giants and Cleveland Buckeyes. Horne,
> only a youngster, was sent down for further season-
> ing, but next year he is expected to make the grade
> in the Negro National League."[120]

At age 31, and with nine years in the NAL behind him, Horne may have had designs on returning to the big leagues, but he was neither a youngster nor a prospect.

Early in 1947 the Creoles earned an unusual split in a doubleheader against the Atlanta Black Crackers. Atlanta had won the first game, 3-1, and led a back-and-forth second game, 6-5, when the Black Crackers began stalling for darkness.[121] The umpires called the game and declared a forfeit, with the Creoles winning the contest, 9-0.[122]

The Creoles reportedly finished in third place in the first half of the NSL,[123] but won the second-half crown.[124] They eventually fell to the Asheville Blues, who had won the first half, in the NSL playoffs.[125] That October, Horne played for the South All-Stars, who were managed by Harry Williams and included numerous players from the NAL, in a Blue-Gray classic against veterans of the NNL.[126]

Drastic changes came to New Orleans in 1948. A preview noted that "[t]he Creoles, sporting an almost entirely new lineup, have only Billy Horne and Oliver Andry back from a strong 1947 club, and are traveling under a new manager, Tommy Brown, formerly of the Memphis Red Sox and the New York Black Yankees."[127] Horne occasionally played second base,[128] but most often played shortstop and regularly charged the offense with his hitting.[129]

New Orleans made news in the sports world with the addition of female players. "On the Fourth of July, the Creoles played the Nashville Cubs in a doubleheader in Louisville, Kentucky. Two women, Fabiola Wilson and Lovie Dymond, 'played three innings and were a hit with the crowd.'"[130] Later that month, they signed another woman, right fielder Wilson MacDonald, who was reportedly a student at Xavier University in New Orleans.[131]

By midsummer, the Creoles reportedly had a 24-6 record and eventually won the NSL pennant.[132] Once again, Horne appeared in an all-star game, this time as a shortstop for the American-Southern Aces, a combined group of stars from the NAL and NSL, against the NNL All-Stars.[133]

During the offseason, New Orleans left the NSL and became a member of the Negro Texas League.[134] Horne left the Creoles and became the player-manager of the league's Shreveport Tigers.[135]

Throughout the spring of 1949, the Tigers chased the first-place Creoles and trailed by only a half-game on June 2.[136] When they met the next day, Shreveport won, 5-1, and briefly moved into first place.[137] However, New Orleans rebounded to win the next game, 6-4, and retook the lead.[138] In early July the Tigers trailed the Creoles by just 1½ games.[139] New Orleans was in first place until the end of July, when the league folded due to "financial wrangles and inferior type ball clubs."[140]

By the time news of the league's collapse had been announced, Horne had already rejoined the Creoles as a shortstop.[141] He formed a part-time double-play combination with second baseman Toni Stone, another female player, who split time with Joe Wiley.[142] The Creoles, who were backed by Abe Saperstein, survived by barnstorming after the NTL collapsed.[143]

Late in the fall, the Creoles formed an "all-star" team with other Negro Leaguers and faced off against Jackie Robinson's Major League All-Stars at Ponce de Leon Park in Atlanta. The Creoles' lineup included pitcher Jimmie Newberry and players Piper Davis, Pepper Bassett, T.J. Brown, Lyman Bostock Sr., and Horne.[144] Robinson's All-Stars won, 15-5.[145] In probably his final appearance in a Negro League box score, Horne had one hit in five at-bats.[146]

Research has not uncovered whether Horne continued to play baseball in 1950, but he did not appear in the Negro Leagues. He briefly played in Canada in 1951. "Halfway through the 1951 ManDak schedule, Horne answered an appeal from the Carman Cardinals to join their lineup. He hit just .207 in twenty-one games."[147]

Horne's post-baseball life is a complete mystery. How he made a living during the 18 years after he left professional baseball is unknown. He died in New Orleans in November of 1969, but the exact date, cause of death, and burial site are not known either. No obituary has been uncovered, and no surviving family members have been identified.

Horne was frequently cited in news stories for his solid play, but none of the articles ever included any direct quotes from him, and no feature stories about him while he was playing have been unearthed. (If only Eddie P. Jennings had written Horne's profile in 1944!). His name fell away from the sports pages as soon as he left the game. He was never mentioned in any retrospective articles either. This is probably because he died before most baseball researchers discovered the Negro Leagues and finally gave attention to many long-forgotten stories. Information about Horne's

career is incomplete in most books about the Negro Leagues if he is mentioned at all. He does not have a player file with the National Baseball Hall of Fame Library either.[148]

As a result, any biography of Billy Horne will always be one-dimensional unless more information is uncovered. What can be remembered about Horne are the many colorful descriptions of him as a player that often appeared in print. He was "small but speedy," a "top second baseman," "a bright performer at second base," a "crack infielder," a "Colored Star," a "tough little second sacker and pivot man on those Cleveland couple-killings," "flashy," "an outstanding shortstop," "the mighty mite of the infield," a player who played his position "with baseball greatness," and "the nucleus" of his clubs.[149] Even if he did not give interviews to sportswriters, they always respected "the hustle Horne displayed."[150] He did his job on the field and the box scores tell the story of a player who nearly always contributed something positive to his teams.

In 2020, Major League Baseball announced that seven professional Negro Leagues, including the Negro American League, had been accorded major-league status.[151] Horne has finally been recognized as a major leaguer for eight of his summers in the Negro American League.

ACKNOWLEDGMENTS

The author wishes to thank Phil S. Dixon for taking the time to answer questions regarding the photo of the Negro National League All-Stars, and whether the batboy was Billy Horne. The photo in Phil's book certainly looks like him. The author greatly appreciates Gary Ashwill of Seamheads for clearing up a mystery regarding the identity of Dan Henderson in the 1939 East-West All-Star voting, In addition, the author thanks Cassidy Lent for searching for a clip file for Horne. Finally, it is sometimes difficult to have a full-time career and still find time to research and write a biography. Accordingly, the author appreciates his wife Stephanie's enduring patience.

SOURCES

In addition to the sources cited in the Notes, the author relied on Seamheads.com for statistical information, except where otherwise indicated.

NOTES

1   James A. Riley, *The Biographical Encyclopedia of the Negro Baseball Leagues* (New York: Carroll & Graf Publishers, 1994), 293; https://www. seamheads.com/NegroLgs/player.php?playerID=horne01bil.

2   This is an archaic and offensive term that was discontinued by the census after 1920.

3   Louisiana. New Orleans City. 1920 US Census. A later census record identified Horne's race as "Negro." Louisiana. New Orleans City. 1940 US Census.

4   Louisiana. New Orleans City. 1920 US Census.

5   Louisiana. New Orleans City. 1940 US Census.

6   "Colored Hurlers Fan 28 Men In Tie Game," *Regina* (Saskatchewan) *Leader-Post*, August 23, 1935: 21; "Acme Giants Win Over All-Stars by Score of 14-2," *Davenport* (Iowa) *Daily Times*, September 11, 1935: 15." Local Seniors Lose To Visitors 7-0 and 10-4," *Rock Island* (Illinois) *Argus*, May 13, 1936: 18; "Acme Giants Beat East Siders, 7-1," *Grand Forks* (North Dakota) *Herald*, May 27, 1936: 10; "Local Seniors Lose To Visitors 7-0 and

10-4," *Saskatoon* (Saskatchewan) *Star-Phoenix*, July 9, 1936: 10; "Colored Giants Split Two Here" *Spokane* (Washington) *Chronicle*, July 27, 1936: 11; "Giants Wallop Texas Spiders," *Mason City* (Iowa) *Globe Gazette*, September 10, 1936: 16; "Dunseith Colored Nine Clinches Win With Three Run Attack in Eighth," *Bismarck* (North Dakota) *Tribune*, June 1, 1937: 8.

7   "Buckeyes Here Next Thursday," *Kellogg* (Idaho) *Evening News*, July 12, 1940: 2; "Welch Signed as Barons' Manager," *Michigan Chronicle* (Detroit), February 13, 1943: 19; "Black Barons Coming Home For July 25th," *Birmingham Weekly Review*, July 24, 1943: 7.

8   https://sabr.org/bioproj/person/buck-oneil/.

9   "Shreveport Giants Will Play Dallas," *Shreveport* (Louisiana) *Journal*, June 6, 1935: 9.

10   "Champions of Denver Post Tournament," *Kansas City Call*, August 21, 1936: 7. 6

11   Phil S. Dixon with Patrick J. Hannigan. *The Negro Baseball Leagues: A Photographic History* (Mattituck, New York: Amereon, 1992), 220.

12   Dixon, 220.

13   For his part, Dixon does not have additional information or photos of the batboy. Facebook message from Phil S. Dixon, January 9, 2025.

14   "Tigers to Stage Double Header at Dixie Field," *Shreveport Times*, April 16, 1937: 24.

15   "Negro Teams Will Not Use Dixie League Park," *Shreveport Times*, April 20, 1937: 13.

16   "Acme Giants Rout Bismarck Nine 8 to 4 In First Start Of Season," *Bismarck Tribune*, June 1, 1937: 8.

17   Dick Clark and Larry Lester, eds., *The Negro Leagues Book* (Cleveland: SABR, 1994), 196.

18   "Clowns Star with Giants," *Cincinnati Post*, July 14, 1941: 11.

19   "American Giants Blast Wallie Zuehls, Blatz, Win Rubber Game, 9-8," *Capital Times* (Madison, Wisconsin), July 8, 1938: 15.

20   "American Giants Blast Wallie Zuehls, Blatz, Win Rubber Game, 9-8."

21   "Monarchs Win From Chicago," *Fargo Forum, Daily Republican, and Moorhead Daily News* (Fargo, North Dakota), July 26, 1938: 9.

22   "Fancy Slugging – Giants Beat Monarchs, 11-4," *Des Moines Register*, July 29, 1938: 9.

23   "Error Beats Negro Club in Ninth Inning," *Capital Times*, August 10, 1939: 15.

24   "Zuehls Has an Edge in Slab Duel," *Wisconsin State Journal* (Madison), June 16, 1939: 19.

25   Larry Lester, *Black Baseball's National Showcase, The East-West All-Star Game, 1933-1953* (Lincoln: University of Nebraska Press, 2001), 139. Lester identified "Henderson" as "Dan Henderson," but Curtis Henderson was the only player with that surname to play in the NAL in 1939. Baseball historian Gary Ashwill confirmed that the player in question was Curtis Henderson, not Dan Henderson, who played for the Toledo Crawfords that season. Email from Gary Ashwill, February 3, 2025. He also referred the author to a newspaper article, which also referred to Curtis Henderson as "Dan" that year. "Cleveland Bears Clash With Orlando Crawfords Sunday, " *Kansas City Call*, July 14, 1939: 37.

26   Lester, 125.

27   Lester, 126.

28   Lester, 138.

29   Lester, 138.

30   "Chi Team Stamped as One of Best in American League," *Pittsburgh Courier*, April 15, 1939: 16.

31   "Jim Taylor in Tenn.," *Atlanta Daily World*, January 10, 1940: 5.

32   Leslie A. Heaphy, ed., *Black Baseball and Chicago: Essays on the Players, Teams and Games* (Jefferson, North Carolina: McFarland & Company, Inc., 2006), 51.

33   Louisiana. New Orleans City. 1940 US Census. The census corrected the spelling of his surname, "Horne," which was incorrect in the 1920 census.

34   Louisiana. New Orleans City. 1940 US Census.

35   Heaphy, 85.

36   "West's Negro Team Named in All-Star Poll," *Chicago Tribune*, August 11, 1940: 25.

37   Lester, 152.

38   https://www.seamheads.com/NegroLgs/year.php?yearID=1940&lgID=NSA&tab=fld.

39   "American Giants to Start the Season With a Stronger Team Than in 1949," *Chicago Tribune*, May 10, 1941: 8.

40   "American Giants to Start the Season With a Stronger Team Than in 1949."

41   "Giants Plan Opener for Sunday, May 8," *Chicago Sunday Bee*, May 4, 1941: 10.

42   "Scott Smashes Three-bagger With Bases Loaded to Give Bluff's Team 9-8 Decision Over Giants," *Council Bluffs* (Iowa) *Daily Nonpareil*, May 31, 1941: 6.

43   "Rival Teams Tied With 4 Games Each," *Baltimore Afro-American*, July 26, 1941: 19.

44   "50,000 See East Defeat West in Classic, 8-3," *New Journal and Guide* (Norfolk, Virginia), August 2, 1941: 12.

45   New Orleans, Louisiana, US, Marriage Records Index, 1831-1964.

46   No information was found regarding Horne in the 1950 US Census.

47   Riley, 393; "Bucks Pound Out Victory Over Paige, 12-9," *Cleveland Call and Post*, April 11, 1942: 11.

48   "Cincinnati, Birmingham Negro Nines Mix Tonight," *Muskogee* (Oklahoma) *Daily Phoenix and Times-Democrat*, April 28, 1942: 7.

49   "Cincy Buckeyes Ready to Pry 1942 Lid," *Atlanta Daily World*, May 12, 1942: 5.

50   "Morgan Gets Annual Track Championships," *Cleveland Call and Post*, May 2, 1942: 11.

51   "Cincy Bucks Sweep Bill," *Pittsburgh Courier*, May 16, 1942: 17.

52   "'Cool Papa' to Appear Here Sunday," *Cleveland Call and Post*, June 6, 1942: 10.

53   Clarence L. Simmons, "Grays Shellack Jefferson in First Game, but Bow to Mister Brewer in Second," *Cleveland Call and Post*, July 25, 1942: 11.

54   "Grays Shellack Jefferson in First Game, but Bow to Mister Brewer in Second." Despite the height reference in this article, we earlier used the 5-foot-5 height listed by Seamheads.

55   "John Fuster's Sportlight," *Cleveland Call and Post*, June 27, 1942: 10. In 1942 the Indians went 75-79-2, finishing fourth in the American League.

56   "John Fuster's Sportlight."

57   John Fuster, "A Pat on the Back for the Bucks and a Few Suggestions for the Negro American League," *Cleveland Call and Post*, June 27, 1942: 11. Horne finished third with 83,829 votes behind Tommy Sampson (124,506) and Fred Bankhead (92,672). Lester, 206.

58   "Cleveland Agrees to Give Tryouts to Negro Players," *Cleveland Call and Post*, August 1, 1942: 21.

59   "Cleveland Appears League Title Threat," *St. Louis Argus*, May 7, 1943: 10.

60   "Buckeye Leadoff Man Ill," *Cleveland Call and Post*, May 22, 1943: 10.

61   "Cleveland Comes From Behind to Tie Up the Old Score at 1-1, *Cleveland Call and Post*, May 8, 1943: 10A.

62   "Two New Infielders Play for Buckeyes," *Cleveland Plain Dealer*, May 22, 1943: 16; "Fans Interest Intense Over Games Sunday," *Cleveland Call and Post*, May 29, 1943: 10A.

63   "Coloured Teams Will Show Here Thursday, June 17," *Hamilton* (Ontario) *Spectator*, June 11, 1943: 29.

64   "Buckeyes' Smith Shuts Out Clowns With One Hit, 11-0," *Buffalo News*, June 3, 1943: 20.

65   "Standings," *Pittsburgh Courier*, June 5, 1943: 18.

66   "The Cleveland Buckeyes … Most Sensational Team in Sepia Majors," *Pittsburgh Courier*, June 5, 1943: 18.

67   "Clevelanders Lose Twin Bill to Chicago Giants," *Cleveland Call and Post*, June 19, 1943: 10A.

68   "American Giants Knock Cleveland Out of Lead," *Michigan Chronicle* (Detroit), June 19, 1943: 20.

69   "Chicago Giants Stop Bucs Winning Streak," *Kansas City Call*, June 25, 1943: 47. There was no box score for the second game.

70   "Chicago Giants Stop Bucs 6-5 in 14-Inning Game," *Kansas City Call*, July 2, 1943: 10.

71   "Chicago Giants Stop Bucs 6-5 in 14-Inning Game."

72   "Bucs Take Two From Clowns," *Kansas City Call*, July 9, 1943: 41.

73   "Cleveland's Ace Tames Monarchs," *Pittsburgh Courier*, June 10, 1943: 18.

74   Bob Williams, "Cleveland Buckeyes Eye Coming Baseball Season," *Kansas City Call*, February 4, 1944: 8.

75   Eddie P. Jennings, "Buckeyes Should Be 1944 Champs," *Cleveland Call and Post*, February 19, 1944: 10A.

76   "Buckeyes Leave Friday for Miss.," *Cleveland Call and Post*, March 8, 1944: 9B.

77   Eddie P. Jennings, "Says Forgotten Man of Buckeyes Is Bremer," *Cleveland Call and Post*, March 11, 1944: 9B.

78   "Bears and Bucks Battle Here Tonight," *South Bend Tribune*, July 26, 1944: 14.

79   "Cleveland Official Says Mexicans Are 'Stealing' Players," *Pittsburgh Courier*, March 25, 1944: 12.

80   "Cleveland Official Says Mexicans Are 'Stealing' Players."

81   "New Keystone Pair for Cleveland Team," *Dayton Daily News*, April 29, 1944: 5.

82   "Clowns, Bucks Open League Play Today," *Louisville Courier-Journal*, May 7, 1944: 52.

83   "Buckeyes Are Strengthened for Game Here Tomorrow," *Buffalo News*, May 17, 1944: 15.

84   Wendell Smith, "Good Hurling Beats Barons," *Pittsburgh Courier*, May 27, 1944: 11.

85   "All-League Stars Show in Negro Game Today," *Knoxville Journal*, June 12, 1944: 8.

86   "West Favored to Win Annual Classic Tilt," *Michigan Chronicle*, August 12, 1944: 15.

87   Lester, 238.

88   "Victorious East-West Players Rejoin Bucs to Play Clowns Sunday," *Cleveland Call and Post*, August 9, 1944: 6B.

89   Bob Williams, "Memphis Team Will Test Mettle of Buckeyes Who Lost One to Champs, 9-0," *Cleveland Call and Post*, July 8, 1944: 6B.

90   "Buckeyes vs. Chicago Giants in 2 Games Here This Week," *Dayton Daily News*, August 27, 1944: 5.

91   Bob Williams, "Buckeyes Win Two; Play Homestead Grays Here, Sunday: Beat Chicago 15-9, 4-2; Buck's Big Bats to Clash With Grays Here at League Park, Sunday," *Cleveland Call and Post*, September 9, 1944: 6B.

92   Stephanie M. Liscio, *Integrating Cleveland Baseball: Media Activism, the Integration of the Indians and the Demise of the Negro League Buckeyes* (Jefferson, North Carolina: McFarland & Company, Inc., 2010), 211.

93   "Buckeyes to Begin Workouts Today," *Muskogee Daily Phoenix and Times-Democrat*, March 25, 1945: 3; "American Giants Meet Buckeyes on Saturday Evening," *Waco* (Texas) *Tribune-Herald*, April 15, 1945: 8.

94   "American Giants Meet Buckeyes on Saturday Evening." Lest anyone forget that the indignity of segregation still ruled in the Deep South, the same story reminded readers that "[a] special section of the Katy park stand will be roped off for the white fans."

95   "Buckeyes Split Two Games With Cubans, Good Spring Games," *Cleveland Call and Post*, April 14, 1944: 19.

96   "Black Barons in Two Tilts Sunday," *Birmingham News*, May 5, 1945: 5.

97   "Bucks Defeat Chicago Twice," *Michigan Chronicle*, May 5, 1945: 15.

98   "Clowns Oppose Veteran Team," *Cincinnati Post*, May 18, 1945: 25; "Beers And Buckeyes Clash Here Tonight," *South Bend Tribune*: May 18, 1945: 25; "Cleveland Negroes Here Tonight – 8:15," *Lafayette* (Indiana) *Journal and Courier*, June 6, 1945: 10; "All 3 Clubs Loaded With Star Diamond Performers," *St. Louis Argus*, June 8: 1945: 10; "Stars Meet Negro Team Here, 8:30," *Belleville* (Illinois) *Daily Advocate*, June 29, 1945: 7; "Buckeyes Play Black Crackers Tonight," *Alabama Journal* (Montgomery), July 13, 1945: 9.

99   "Union City Red in High Gear, Battle Dexters," *Brooklyn Eagle*, July 31, 1945: 14.

100   https://www.seamheads.com/NegroLgs/year.php?yearID=1945&lgID=NAL; Bob Williams, "Manager Quincy Trouppe, Man Behind the Scenes, Was the Deciding Factor," *Cleveland Call and Post*, October 27: 1945: 6B.

101   "Manager Quincy Trouppe, Man Behind the Scenes, Was the Deciding Factor."

102   "Manager Quincy Trouppe, Man Behind the Scenes, Was the Deciding Factor."

103   "Billy Horne to Join Buckeyes," *Chicago Defender*, January 26, 1946: 9.

104   "Buckeyes Are Strengthened for Game Here Tomorrow"; David Finoli, *For the Good of the Country: World War II Baseball in the Major and Minor Leagues* (Jefferson, North Carolina: McFarland & Company, Inc., 2002), 297.

105   "Billy Horne to Join Buckeyes"; "Cleveland's Champion Buckeyes Open Spring Training," *Dayton Daily Bulletin*, March 21, 1946: 1; "Bucks to Play Crackers On April 7," *Atlanta Daily World*, March 20, 1946: 5; "World Champion Buckeyes Oppose Birmingham Sunday," *St. Louis Argus*, March 22, 2017: 17.

106   "World Champion Buckeyes Oppose Birmingham Sunday"; Jimmie Jones, "Buckeyes Start Spring Training With Strong Squad; List 15 Games," *Cleveland Call and Post*, March 30, 1946: 8B.

107   "Skipper Troupe Out to Maintain Record," *Atlanta Daily World*, April 4, 1946: 5; "Cleveland Faces Black Yankees in 8:30 Contest," *Florence* (South Carolina) *Morning News*, April 17, 1946: 8.

108   "Cleveland Buckeyes to Play Chicago Giants Here Sunday," *Dayton Daily News*, April 28, 1946: 21.

109   "Cleveland Buckeyes Shade B'ham Black Barons, 10-9," *Atlanta Daily World*, April 23, 1946: 8.

110   "Cleveland Nine Routs Atlanta, 10-1," *Rochester Democrat and Chronicle*, June 8, 1946: 19.

111 "Gen. Beightler to See Benefit Game For V.F.W. Tomorrow," *Plain Dealer*, July 16, 1946: 14. As to Chicago's motivation for the deal, according to baseball historian Paul Debono, "[Ralph] Wyatt was criticized by the *Chicago Defender* for not running out a ground ball, which resulted in a double play in a situation where the Giants might have been able to score, costing a game to the Birmingham Black Barons. A month later Wyatt refused to accompany the team on a road trip and was subsequently sold to the Cleveland Buckeyes." Paul Debono, *The Chicago American Giants* (Jefferson, North Carolina: McFarland & Company, Inc., 2007), 170.

112 Red Sox to Play Giants," *Memphis Commercial Appeal*, July 26, 1946: 24; "Memphis Meets Chicago Giants Tomorrow Night," *Belleville Daily Advocate*, July 29, 1946: 6.

113 "Baseball Tuesday Night," *Belleville News-Democrat*, August 12, 1946: 6.

114 Horne was not listed in the only box scores the author could locate. "Bunt and Triple in Eighth Shoved in Winning Run," *Belleville Daily Advocate*, August 14, 1946: 7; "American Giants Defeat Clowns, 6-4, With Rally In Eighth," *Decatur Herald and Review*, August 30, 1946: 13. Seamheads.com does not show Horne on Chicago's roster in 1946 either. https://www.seamheads.com/NegroLgs/team.php?yearID=1946&teamID=CAG&LGOrd=2.

115 Lucius "Melancholy" Jones, "North-South Classic Rickwood Sunday," *Weekly Review* (Birmingham), October 12, 1946: 7; "Negro Leagues Stage Single Game Today," *Birmingham News*, October 13, 1946: 37.

116 "Negro Leagues Stage Single Game Today."

117 William J. Plott, *The Negro Southern League: A Baseball History, 1920-1951* (Jefferson, North Carolina: McFarland Publishing, 2014), 234, 236.

118 "Black Crax Will Be Out to Sweep Series," *Atlanta Daily World*, May 21, 1947: 5.

119 "Fans Look Forward to Sensational Thriller," *Atlanta Daily World*, June 10, 1947: 5.

120 "Negro Team From Southern Circuit Under the Lights," *Staten Island* (New York) *Advance*, July 8, 1947: 14.

121 "Crax Win Opener; Forfeit Nightcap" *Alabama Tribune* (Montgomery), June 20, 1947: 7.

122 "Crax Win Opener; Forfeit Nightcap."

123 Plott, 175.

124 "Negro Southern Loop Teams Book Playoff Game Here," *Shreveport Times*, September 14, 1947: 34.

125 Plott, 176-77.

126 "Blue and Gray Meet Thursday," *Waco Times-Herald*, October 8, 1947: 12.

127 "Nashville, New Orleans Negro Teams at Clarks," *Monroe* (Louisiana) *Morning World*, April 23, 1948: 11.

128 "Southern Loop Rivals Set for Crucial Tilt," *Atlanta Daily World*, June 5, 1948: 5.

129 "Studebakers Beat Creoles; Play Tonight," *South Bend Tribune*, July 8, 1948: 23 (2-for-4 with a run scored); "Oliver Nine Splits With New Orleans," *Battle Creek* (Michigan) *Enquirer*, July 12, 1948: 9 (1-for-4 with a stolen base); "New Orleans Beats Autos By 7-6 Count," *South Bend Tribune*, July 8, 1948: 23 (1-for-5 with a run scored).

130 Plott, 185.

131 "Creoles Feature Girl Outfielder," *Greensboro* (North Carolina) *News and Record*, July 25, 1948: 43.

132 Plott, 185, 188.

133 "All-Star Negro Battle Tonight," *Monroe Morning World*, September 29, 1948: 10.

134 Plott, 191.

135 "Famous Negro Baseball Team Here Tomorrow," *Shreveport Journal*, April 16, 1949: 6; "Tigers Meet Giants Today," *Shreveport Times*, April 17, 1949: 38; Shreveport Tigers Will Make Debut," *Shreveport Times*, May 11, 1949: 21; "Tigers Beat San Antonio in Twin Bill," *Shreveport Times*, June 2, 1949: 17; "New Orleans Creoles Play City Circuit All-Stars Friday," *La Crosse* (Wisconsin) *Tribune*, July 26, 1949: 12.

136 "Shreveport Tigers Will Make Debut"; "Tigers Beat San Antonio in Twin Bill."

137 "Tigers Topple New Orleans; Cop TL Lead," *Shreveport Times*, June 4, 1949: 6.

138 "Creoles Retake Negro Loop Lead," *Shreveport Journal*, June 4, 1949: 6.

139 "Tigers to Meet Eagles Friday," *Shreveport Times*, July 6, 1949: 17.

140 "Texas Loop Folds," *Pittsburgh Courier*, July 30, 1949: 10.

141 "New Orleans Creoles Play City Circuit All-Stars Friday."

142 "New Orleans Creoles Play City Circuit All-Stars Friday."

143 "New Orleans Creoles Play City Circuit All-Stars Friday"; "Creoles Survive as Texas League Folds," *Atlanta Daily World*, August 4, 1949: 5.

144 "Jackie Robinson's All-Stars in Tilt With Creole All-Stars Here," *Atlanta Daily World*, October 15, 1949: 6.

145 "Jackie Robinson All-Stars Beat Creoles Before 7,500," *Atlanta Daily World*, October 18, 1949: 5.

146 "Jackie Robinson All-Stars Beat Creoles Before 7,500."

147 Barry Swanton and Jay-Dell Mah, *Black Baseball Players in Canada: A Biographical Dictionary, 1881-1960* (Jefferson, North Carolina: McFarland & Company, Inc., 2009), 85; Barry Swanton, *The ManDak League: Haven for Former Negro League Ballplayers, 1950-1957* (Jefferson, North Carolina: McFarland & Company, Inc., 2006), 114.

148 Cassidy Lent of the Baseball Hall of Fame library, email correspondence with author, February 27, 2024.

149 "Signs Sherbath. Paugh; Freck Is Benched," *Capital Times* , June 14, 1939: 17; "Giants Plan Opener for Sunday, May 8," *Chicago Sunday Bee*, May 4, 1941: 10; "Buckeye Club Strong Entry," *Waco Times-Herald*, April 17, 1945: 6; "Fans to See Strongest American Giants Team," *Chicago Daily Calumet*, July 8, 1941: 6; "Colored Star," *The Life* (Berwyn, Illinois), July 9, 1941: 9; "Standalone Photo," *Cleveland Call and Post*, June 20, 1942: 10; "Buckeyes Rated Tops Among Negro League Clubs," *South Bend Tribune*, July 25, 1944: 12; "Leading Sluggers of Negro League Will Accompany Cleveland Buckeyes Thursday," *Muskegon* (Michigan) *Chronicle*: August 16, 1944: 12; "Erickson of Mosox to Face Creoles' Nine Here Thursday," *Fargo* (North Dakota) *Forum*, August 17, 1949: 16; "New Orleans Creoles Play City Circuit All-Stars Friday"; "Morgan Gets Annual Track Championships," *Cleveland Call and Post*, May 2, 1942: 11.

150 "Strong Negro Clubs to Vie in Lippincott," *South Bend Tribune*, September 12, 1941: 33.

151 https://www.mlb.com/news/negro-leagues-given-major-league-status-for-baseball-records-stats.

George Jefferson

By John V. Haynes II

George "Jeff" Jefferson's meteoric rise and fall differed greatly from the trajectory of his older brother Willie's late-blooming career. At just 22 years old, George was pitching in the Negro World Series for the Cleveland Buckeyes, and by his 30th birthday he was out of professional baseball.

George Leo Jefferson was born 18 years after Willie, on August 8, 1922, in Boley, Oklahoma, to farm workers Douglass and Lula Jefferson. At the time, Boley was a unique place in America – a wealthy all-Black town with two banks, two colleges, a power plant, and a railroad depot.[1] According to the Dawes Rolls that documented Native Americans in the region, Douglass Jefferson was listed as a member of the Creek Freedmen, mixed-race individuals who were descended from slaves and the native Creek tribe. In addition, Douglass was a World War I veteran who returned from service in France three years before George was born. Besides Willie, census data notes, George had at least three additional older siblings: sisters Tamor and Dorthea, and brother Lucky, who like Willie had moved out before George was born.

Growing up, George was a well-rounded young man and prolific athlete. In 1937 his Boley grade-school basketball team won the Okfuskee County championship.[2] When he wasn't on the hardwood or baseball diamond, George was active in both the Negro Boy Scouts and the Civilian Conservation Corps through high school.[3] The Boley branch of the CCC had a baseball team called the Boley Wonders, though it is unknown if George played.

Historian James A. Riley notes that George was discovered while pitching in the Denver Post Tournament as a teenager, though what year and team are unknown.[4] In 1938, at just 16 years old, George spent the summer with the Oklahoma City Black Indians, playing right field when he wasn't on the mound.[5] He remained with the team through July of the following year.[6] George remained active in sports throughout high school, receiving a varsity letter before graduating in 1941.[7]

From the Black Indians, Jefferson moved to the semipro Stillwater, Oklahoma, Tigers. In 1941 he had his breakout season and became the Tigers' leading pitcher; by July he racked up seven wins, including three shutouts against all competition. Two of the shutouts occurred in a four-day stretch. With what was described as a "dazzling in-curve" in his repertoire, "the Tigers have another Satchel Paige in 'Cannon Ball' Jefferson," the *O'Collegian,* the campus newspaper at Oklahoma A&M University commented.[8]

After the fast start to the 1941 season, details of George's whereabouts become hazy. According to his draft card, in 1942 he was employed on his brother Lucky's farm in Oklahoma. However, the local newspaper's draft lottery announcement places his actual address in Erie, Pennsylvania, where older brother Willie resided with several of his Cleveland Buckeyes teammates in the offseason.[9] No records have been found of any military service by George. Riley asserts that Jefferson was known to have a "mean-streak" and killed a White man in Kansas, forcing him to go on the run.[10] However, 1942-1943 may have been the period during which George was enrolled in Langston University in Langston, Oklahoma, where he was a member of the baseball, basketball, and track teams.[11]

Other records list George Jefferson on the Jacksonville Red Caps for the 1942 and 1943 seasons, though it is unclear if he truly played on the team.[12] In addition, Okmulgee, Oklahoma, native Frazier Robinson wrote in his memoir that George and his brother Willie also pitched for a team

George Jefferson, with the American All-Stars in Caracas, Venezuela, 1945.

in Clearview, Oklahoma, at the same time, though what year is unknown.[13]

In March 1944 George joined his brother on the Buckeyes. Willie had been playing for the Buckeyes since their inception in 1942 and likely recruited him to the team. George made an immediate impact, reportedly striking out 15 in his first two appearances.[14] Currently attributed statistics credit George with a 2-3 record and a 1.78 ERA in 60⅔ innings.

The next season, 1945, was a breakout year for the Jefferson brothers as the Buckeyes rode their arms all the way to the pennant. Including postseason play, George is officially credited with a 4-2 record, a 3.48 ERA, and five complete games; however various sources including a 1946 yearbook list an 11-1 record and a 1.75 ERA.[15]

George was passed over for the East-West All-Star Game. He recounted years later that he was told by West manager Winfield Welch that at the age of 22, he was too young to be selected.[16] The snub would mean little as he earned a chance to shine in the postseason.

The Buckeyes were up two games to none over the perennial juggernaut Homestead Grays in the Negro World Series when George Jefferson got the call to start in the third game at Griffith Stadium in Washington. Yielding only three hits, Jefferson and the Buckeyes stunned the Grays, 4-0. It was the first time the Grays had been held scoreless since 1942.[17] Two days later, the Buckeyes beat the Grays again to win the championship. After the Series, Jefferson remained with the Buckeyes and pitched in the same game as his brother in at least one exhibition, a 7-1 loss to the Grays at Yankee Stadium on September 23.[18]

After the 1945 season and with integration on the horizon, George joined the American All-Stars, an all-Black team that included Sam Jethroe, Roy Campanella, and Jackie Robinson. The team was organized by Newark Eagles owner Effa Manley and first played a five-game series at Ebbets Field in Brooklyn against a White team assembled by Chuck Dressen. Jefferson did not play in the series. The team then traveled to Venezuela, where it played in the Serie Monumental (Monumental Series) against three other teams. Brother Willie played for both the Estrellas del Caribe (Caribbean All-Stars) and Estrellas Zulianas (Zulia Stars). The Estrellas Negras, as the locals called them, finished the Caracas leg of the tour with a 7-2 record.[19]

Years later, Jefferson recalled his relationship with teammate Jackie Robinson during the tour:

"Jackie and I never could get along. ... He would say hard things to me all the time; he [later] said that the reason he did that was there was something he saw in me that he was trying to get out of me. He said that someday, I would have the chance to go to the majors, and he wanted me to be prepared so that I'd be able to take it."[20]

Around Christmas Day, Robinson left the team for Panama, and on New Year's Day 1946 Jefferson followed.[21] Riley writes that Jefferson's early exit had less to do with

opportunity elsewhere and more to do with a contract dispute that ended in George choking a promoter.[22] It was in Panama that George's hopes of making it to the major leagues were dashed by a devastating injury. He recalled years later that a hard landing after making an off-balance throw from the third-base line resulted in a fractured clavicle.[23] On March 28 George returned to the US unaccompanied via passenger ship. His was the only name on the manifest with "baseball player" listed as an occupation.

In an illustration of the inaccuracies of news reports based on team-issued press releases, the *Cleveland Call and Post* reported in April that George was reportedly in "fine shape" when he returned to Buckeyes camp from Panama with teammates Sam Jethroe, Quincy Trouppe, and Willie Grace. News of the injury was further buried as he was named the starting pitcher for the first exhibition game of the season against Ival Goodman's semipro Cincinnati Aces in Dayton, Ohio, on May 20. Results of the game were never reported.[24] He was also billed as the starter for matchups against the Atlanta Black Crackers and Memphis Red Sox in late May and early June, but it is likely that he was scratched. Just a day after Jefferson was unable to record an out against the Clowns in his first appearance of the season, the June 8 edition of the *Call and Post* revealed that he had a "sore arm" that was "not responding to treatment."[25] By July 20, he had reportedly logged only three relief appearances.[26] None of these or subsequent appearances in 1946 appear in George's statistical record. Without George, Eugene Bremer (who was also injured), and Willie (who remained in Venezuela) in the rotation, the Buckeyes struggled mightily, finishing with a 37-35-3 record and 17½ games behind the first-place Kansas City Monarchs.

In the offseason, George was listed on the roster of the "Negro All-Stars" for a September 15 matchup against the Seattle Steelheads in Indianapolis.[27] It is unclear if Jefferson played in the game, however, as the results were not reported.

In February 1947 the Buckeyes announced that George would take part in spring training, having "recovered fully" following surgery.[28] A month later, George ran into legal trouble in Erie when he was arrested for pointing a gun at police raiding an illegal speakeasy he was in.[29] The trouble with the law evidently did not prevent George from traveling; he was captured in multiple photographs published in the *Call and Post* depicting several Buckeyes players leaving for Florida on March 8.[30]

Several days later Jefferson arrived in Panama to join an all-Black team sponsored by General Electric. In their first matchup, against the Brooklyn Dodgers on March 11, Jefferson pitched in relief during an 8-1 loss.[31] The trend continued for much of the Dodgers and their Montreal farm team's trip, with the exception of a 7-6 General Electric triumph on March 13.[32] On March 18 Jefferson "did a brilliant job" in four innings of work but ran out of gas and lost to Jackie Robinson and the Montreal Royals, 8-5. Jefferson gave up five runs and nine hits in the series finale on March 21, a 5-0 loss to the Dodgers.[33]

After returning to the United States, George returned to the Buckeyes but saw little action on a pitching-heavy roster, logging only a single recorded appearance on the mound in 1947 and again in 1948. No longer able to throw a fastball, George was clearly never the same pitcher after the injury. Instead, he relied on a variety of off-speed and junk pitches, but he could throw effectively for only a few innings at a time.[34] Always a decent hitter, he remained an asset to the Buckeyes as he transitioned to manning first base or pinch-hitting when he wasn't on the mound, though most of these appearances likely occurred in exhibition games. Perhaps another reason for George's limited action in 1948 was additional legal trouble; in June he was found guilty of firearm possession and fined $50.[35]

When the Buckeyes moved to Louisville for the 1949 season, Jefferson followed. His steep decline was evident when he gave up 11 hits in a 7-0 loss to the Birmingham Black Barons on May 28.[36]

Sometime before spring training in 1950, Jefferson was named the Buckeyes' road secretary as the club abandoned Louisville and returned to Cleveland.[37] As Buckeyes general manager and part-owner Wilbur Hayes touted the club's shift toward a "youth movement," Jefferson's role was that of a veteran presence and one of the few players left from the 1945 championship team. During spring training, he coached the Buckeyes second-string team during at least one intrasquad game.[38]

According to teammate Willie Grace, it was during the 1950 season that he and Jefferson were invited to dinner with a Brooklyn Dodgers scout. The scout was not interested in the pair but in their opponent, Baltimore Elite Giants infielder Jim Gilliam. Partly based on Jefferson's recommendation, the Dodgers signed Gilliam a short time later.[39]

In June Jefferson accompanied the Buckeyes on a road trip to New York. With an abysmal 3-33 record, the team never returned home and folded by mid-July. George remained in upstate New York and was signed by the Olean Oilers of the Class-A PONY league. Also on the team was Chuck Harmon, who went on to integrate the Cincinnati Reds in 1954. In his Oilers debut on July 27, Jefferson, playing first base, went 3-for-5 at the plate with an RBI in an 11-3 victory over the Batavia Clippers.[40] His tenure with the team lasted less than two weeks and on August 4 he was released.[41]

In 1951 George joined the Youngstown A's of the Class-C Middle Atlantic League. His Opening Day debut with the A's, a pinch-hit single in an 8-3 loss to the Erie Sailors, was overshadowed by two other notable events, former Buckeyes teammate Willie Grace's three hits and three RBIs for the Sailors, and the pomp and circumstance of a ceremonial first pitch by Cy Young, who lived in nearby Peoli, Ohio.[42] Much like his tenure with Olean, his time with

Youngstown was also short; on May 17 he asked for and was granted his release.[43] He moved back to Erie and joined the Erie Pontiacs of the local semipro Glenwood League. Among his teammates on the Pontiacs was Willie Grace.[44] In 1953 he moved to the independent semipro Erie Lakers, joining former Buckeyes teammates Grace and Walter Crosby.[45] Primarily playing in the outfield, his playing time was limited as he battled a pulled back muscle.[46]

In 1954 George took a job with the Hammermill Paper Company, where he would eventually retire. On July 13, 1954, he narrowly escaped with minor injuries when he was hit by a train while walking to work.[47] Two weeks later, he was back in right field for the Pontiacs,[48] for whom he continued to play through at least 1956. In the winter months, he played basketball in the Erie city recreational league, ranking third in scoring in 1955.[49]

In 1958 George married Lillian Manus of Erie; the couple had been together since his playing days.[50] Lillian was the younger sister of Jemilu Franklin, who married his brother Willie sometime between 1941 and 1943. George remained somewhat active in his later years, appearing in local old-timers' games in 1962,[51] 1973,[52] and 1975.[53] The 1962 appearance listed George among "the old-time Hammermill players," indicating that he may have played for a company-sponsored semipro team at one point.

George spent his days off volunteering his time at the Booker T. Washington Community Center in Erie, coaching youth baseball and basketball. In 1960 his basketball team won the city's recreation league championship,[54] and in 1963, he accompanied the team to Canada, where it played in the International Blackball Basketball Invitational Tournament.[55]

Legal troubles continued to plague George for years, including arrests for assault and battery and disorderly conduct in 1954,[56] unpaid parking violations in 1957, and assault and battery in 1962.[57] In 1971 his wife, Lillian, died. George medically retired from Hammermill shortly after.[58] On April 28, 1981, he collapsed in the Vernon Township courthouse while giving witness testimony in a case against a state trooper accused of violating state liquor and gambling laws. The *Erie Daily Times* reported that George suffered a "mild heart attack" and was hospitalized.[59]

As interest in the Negro Leagues renewed in the 1980s, George was a regular attendee at reunions and was interviewed about his experiences in 1981 for the University of Kentucky's A.B. "Happy" Chandler Oral History Project. On September 21, 1985, Jefferson died at Hamot Medical Center in Erie. Preceded in death by his wife and brothers, he was survived by four daughters, three sons, two stepsons, and three sisters.[60] He was buried back home in Boley, Oklahoma. In reporting his passing, *Erie Daily Times* columnist Ed Mathews called Jefferson "one of the greatest athletes to ever live in Erie."[61]

SOURCES

In addition to the sources cited in the Notes, the author used Ancestry.com to gather biographical data including birth, death, marriage, family, and military-service information. Except where otherwise indicated, all Negro League player statistics and team records were taken from Seamheads.com.

NOTES

1. "Boley," The Encyclopedia of Oklahoma History and Culture, https://www.okhistory.org/publications/enc/entry?entry=BO008, accessed December 30, 2024.

2. "IXL Wins Events for Negro Group," *Okfuskee County News* (Okemah, Oklahoma), April 22, 1937: 5.

3. "Boley Camp Boys at Silver Springs," *Okemah Semi-Weekly Herald*, August 7, 1932: 7.

4. James A. Riley, *The Biographical Encyclopedia of the Negro Baseball Leagues* (New York: Carroll and Graf Publishing, 1994), 420.

5. "Negro Teams to Play at El Reno," *El Reno* (Oklahoma) *Daily Tribune*, June 30, 1938: 8.

6. "Boley," *Oklahoma City Black Dispatch*, July 1, 1939: 8.

7. "Boley," *Oklahoma City Black Dispatch*, May 3, 1941: 11.

8. Tom Steph, "Translations," *O'Collegian*, July 22, 1941: 3.

9. "Ninety Called to Service On Sept. 11," *Weleetka* (Oklahoma) *American*, September 8, 1943: 1.

10. Riley, 420.

11. "Interview with George L. Jefferson, May 23, 1981," University of Kentucky Libraries Louie B. Nunn Center for Oral History, https://kentuckyoralhistory.org/ark:/16417/xt7pnv997v43, accessed December 30, 2024.

12. Riley notes that Jefferson had a 15-8 record in 1942 and 6-3 record in 1943, but he does not appear in Seamheads data and no corresponding newspaper accounts have been found.

13. Frazier Robinson, *Catching Dreams: My Life in the Negro Baseball Leagues* (Syracuse, New York: Syracuse University Press, 2000), 7-8.

14. "Eight Hurlers Unbeaten," *New Pittsburgh* (Pennsylvania) *Courier*, May 27, 1944: 11.

15. "1945 All-America Team," *Negro Baseball 1946 Yearbook*, 1946.

16. Jefferson interview, 1981.

17. "Buckeyes Threaten Rout of Long-Time Champions," *Washington Afro American*, September 22, 1945: 30.

18. "Retrosheet Boxscore: Homestead Grays (HOM) 7 Cleveland Buckeyes (CVB) 1," https://www.retrosheet.org/NegroLeagues/boxesetc/1945/B09231HOM1945.htm, accessed December 30, 2024.

19. "Forgotten Heroes: Marvin 'Tex' Williams," Center for Negro League Baseball Research, https://irp.cdn-website.com/33d0c3d0/files/uploaded/Marvin_Williams%202019-10.pdf, accessed December 30, 2024.

20. Jefferson interview, 1981.

21. Jefferson interview, 1981.

22. Riley, *The Biographical Encyclopedia of the Negro Baseball Leagues*, 420.

23. Jefferson interview, 1981.

24. "Ival Goodman to Play With Buckeye Foes," *Dayton* (Ohio) *Journal Herald*, May 17, 1946: 17.

25. Cleveland Jackson, "Headline Action," *Cleveland Call and Post*, June 8, 1946: 9.

26. Cleveland Jackson, "Headline Action," *Cleveland Call and Post*, July 20, 1946: 21.

27. "Jefferson, Wyatt Play With Negro All-Stars," *Indianapolis Star*, September 12, 1946: 24.

28. "Jefferson's Arm Recovers: Buckeye Mound Star Undergoes Successful Arm Operation," *Cleveland Call and Post*, February 1, 1947: 8.

29. "Police Arrest 34 Persons in Gambling Raid," *Erie* (Pennsylvania) *Daily Times*, February 15, 1947: 3.

30. "Buckeyes Depart for Spring Training," *Cleveland Call and Post*, March 8, 1947: 15.

31. "Dodgers Win," *Binghamton Press and Sun-Bulletin*, March 11, 1947: 17.

32. "Paepke Fifth Dodger to Bid for 1st Base," *Brooklyn Eagle*, March 13, 1947: 21.

33. "Dodgers End Panama Series with 5-0 Victory," *Detroit Free Press*, March 22, 1947: 10.

34. Jefferson interview, 1981.

35. "Firearms Violator Found Guilty," *Erie Daily Times*, May 11, 1948: 13.

36. "Barons Blank Buckeyes 7-0," *Louisville Courier-Journal*, May 28, 1949: 153.

37. "Hayes Expects to Burn Opposition in Negro Loop With Flaming Youth," *Cleveland Call and Post*, March 25, 1950: 15.

38. "Buckeye Bats Boom as Training Grind Starts," *Cleveland Call and Post*, April 1, 1950: 15.

39. Brent Kelley, *Voices from the Negro Leagues: Conversations with 52 Baseball Standouts of the Period 1924-1960* (Jefferson, North Carolina: McFarland Publishers), 141.

40. "Oilers, Dodgers Win, Remain Within Points of Each Other," *Olean* (New York) *Times-Herald*, July 28, 1950: 13.

41. "Oiler Odds 'n Ends," *Olean Times-Herald*, August 4, 1950: 15.

42. "Cy Young Still Perfect, Throws Three Strikes," *Erie Daily Times*, May 5, 1951: 11.

43. Dick Stone, "The Hot Corner," *Erie Sunday Times*, May 20, 1951: 13.

44. "Fultons Bow to Millcreek," *Erie Daily Times*, June 25, 1951: 13.

45. "Jefferson Signs With Erie Lakers," *Erie Daily Times*, May 13, 1953: 23.

46. "Lakers Host Tonight to Titusville Black Ash," *Erie Daily Times*, July 15, 1953.

47. "Hit By Train, 2 Escape Death," *Erie Daily Times*, July 13, 1954: 1.

48. "Pontiacs Tip Merchants at Bayview," *Erie Daily Times*, July 28, 1954: 19.

49. "Bus Brandon Top Scorer," *Erie Daily Times*, January 5, 1955: 42.

50. Jefferson interview, 1981.

51. Gene Cuneo, "Hammermill Night," *Erie Daily Times*, June 21, 1962: 21.

52. "Muny Star Nines Vie at Ainsworth," *Erie Daily Times*, August 12, 1973: 7.

53. Fred Miller, "Glenwood League Star Game Carded June 29," *Erie Times-News*, June 22, 1975: 22.

54. "City Rec Cage Champs," *Erie Times-News*, April 3, 1960: 34.

55. "Play in Canada," *Erie Times-News*, February 24, 1963: 5.

56. "Arrest Two for Assaults," *Erie Daily Times*, October 25, 1954: 15.

57. "Man Denies Argument, Assault," *Erie Morning News*, October 16, 1962: 20.

58. Jefferson interview, 1981.

59. "Witness Hospitalized," *Erie Daily Times*, April 29, 1981: 9.

60. "George L. Jefferson" (obituary), *Erie Daily Times*, September 23, 1985: 12.

61. Ed Mathews, "Odds and Ends," *Erie Daily Times*, September 24, 1985: 6.

Willie Jefferson

By John V. Haynes II

Of the Jefferson brothers who briefly constituted one of the most formidable one-two punches in any Negro League pitching rotation, Willie "Bill" Jefferson was the more accomplished. Yet unlike his brother, Willie was a late bloomer, not reaching his prime until he was approaching his 40s. Also unlike his brother, who had a well-documented and checkered personal life, little is known of Willie's adult life outside of baseball.

William Jefferson was born 18 years before his brother George Jefferson, on January 27, 1904, in Clearview, Oklahoma (then known as Indian Territory). According to census data, his father, Douglass, who was living and working on a farm with the Cushingberry family, was only about 22 years old at the time. Just two years earlier, he fathered Willie's older brother, Lucky, in 1902 with Fannie Jones. It is likely that Willie and George had different mothers.[1] Clearview, like several towns in Okfuskee County, including nearby Boley, where younger brother George was later born, was one of more than 50 all-Black towns in the state. Clearview boasted its own post office, general store, and two-story hotel. By 1914, educator and activist Booker T. Washington, who advocated for Black economic self-reliance, owned more than 5,800 acres of land in the county.[2] Douglass is listed on the Dawes Rolls (the federal government's attempt at documenting Native Americans at the turn of the century) as a member of the Creek Freedmen, a term that described mixed-race individuals with both Native and Black ancestry.

By 1920, 16-year-old Willie was living with the Lovett family, a move that likely occurred when his father served in France with the US Army in 1918-1919. The 1920 census lists him as Bilan and Delia Lovett's "step-nephew." Though he doesn't appear in subsequent census data in Oklahoma after 1920, he listed his father's wife, Lula, as his next of kin on his World War II draft card in 1942.

Although "grammar school" is listed on his draft card as his highest level of education, the *Pittsburgh Courier* noted in 1936 that Willie was "once the best twirler on Langston University's team," though it is unclear when he was there.[3] Langston University, in Langston, Oklahoma, is the state's only Historically Black university, producing several Negro Leaguers including teammate and Monarchs pitcher Zack Foreman and his brother George.

At the beginning of his career, Willie stayed somewhat close to home. From 1928 through 1935, he played with independent outfits in Oklahoma, Arkansas, Kansas, and Iowa including the Arkansas City Oilers,[4] Arkansas City Beavers,[5] Ponca Hot Shots,[6] and Sioux City Ghosts. It was with the Ghosts that he first faced major-league-caliber competition. At the age of 30, in a 1934 tournament in Wichita, Kansas, that featured 54 teams from across the country, Jefferson led the Ghosts to a fourth-place finish. A few days later, on August 30, he took a no-hitter into the seventh inning against the Monroe Monarchs in a tournament game that the Ghosts eventually won, 7-4. The *Omaha World-Herald* called the victory over the 1932 Negro Southern League champions "a little surprise."[7]

In 1936 Willie joined the Claybrook Tigers, an independent team in Arkansas that broke away from the crumbling Negro Southern League. Jefferson's signing with the team may have occurred under dubious circumstances. According to historian Phil Dixon, a Coca-Cola salesman tipped Claybrook manager Ted Radcliffe about a player who

Willie Jefferson.

was doing time in prison for theft in Cleveland, Mississippi. Radcliffe then persuaded club owner John Claybrook to pay $300 to the warden in exchange for Willie Jefferson's release.[8]

In 1937 Radcliffe was named manager of the Cincinnati Tigers of the new Negro American League. Radcliffe was quickly reunited with Jefferson when the Tigers reportedly acquired Willie from the Kansas City Monarchs before the season began.[9] Jefferson immediately made headlines in the Black national press when he hurled a 4-0 shutout over the Middle-Atlantic League's Dayton Ducks, a Class-C affiliate of the Chicago White Sox. In the recap of his performance, the Chicago Defender noted that Jefferson was a native of Greenwood, Mississippi.[10] His recorded league stats for the season were less impressive: a 1-2 record and a 5.72 ERA in eight appearances totaling 39⅓ innings. He may have had other things on his mind – on July 4, his father, Douglass, died in Red Oak, Oklahoma. By the fall, it appears, he was relegated to bullpen duty on a crowded pitching staff, closing out a 9-2 victory against the Detroit Stars in South Bend, Indiana, on August 6.[11] When he wasn't pitching, he made at least three recorded appearances in left field for the Tigers.[12]

After the Cincinnati Tigers folded in the offseason, Jefferson followed Radcliffe and nearly a dozen other Tigers players to the Memphis Red Sox in 1938. With the sudden infusion of talent, the Red Sox flattened Negro American League competition and won the first-half title, their only pennant in franchise history. Willie was flexible for the Red Sox, starting and throwing five complete games and closing out five games in 13 appearances, good for a 3-5 record and a 3.67 ERA. He did not appear in the postseason series with the Atlanta Black Crackers that ended in controversy due to a dispute over venues. (No series between the Negro American League and Negro National League champions was played.) On October 2 he struck out eight and gave up one unearned run for the South All-Stars in a 3-1 victory over the North All-Stars in Memphis.[13] After the season Jefferson moved West and joined Red Sox teammate Porter Moss on the Philadelphia Royal Giants of the California Winter League. With the Royal Giants, Jefferson pitched two complete games, including a 3-1 victory over the Joe Pirrone All-Stars on Christmas Day.[14]

Jefferson returned to Memphis again in 1939, registering only 35 recorded innings but throwing three complete games and a shutout. He then became part of the steady stream of Black players who were lured south of the border for more pay and better working conditions, joining Monterrey Carta Blanca of the Mexican League. In 1940 he shattered Martin Dihigo's single-season league record of 18 wins, logging a 22-9 record along with a 2.65 ERA. His work in 1941 was less stellar as he fell to a 9-16 record.

Despite previous threats of lifetime bans, in 1942 all but two of the "prodigal sons" including Jefferson, Josh Gibson, Willie Wells, and Ray Dandridge returned to the Negro Leagues. Jefferson joined former Cincinnati Tigers teammate Eugene Bremer on the newly formed Cincinnati-Cleveland Buckeyes of the Negro American League.[15] At the all-star break in July, he was reportedly voted the league's most valuable player,[16] though curiously he was not selected for the East-West Game.

On August 15, 1942, Willie was purchased by the Philadelphia Stars for an undisclosed sum.[17] In his first Stars appearance, he pitched a shutout and gave up only three hits in a 5-0 victory over the Chicago American Giants. On September 4 Jefferson went 3-for-4 at the plate in an 8-5 Stars defeat by the New York Black Yankees.[18] Just three days later, a car accident in Geneva, Ohio, killed two Buckeyes players and injured five more. The Cincinnati Enquirer reported that Jefferson returned to the Buckeyes as one of only two available pitchers on the roster for a September 10 matchup against the Black Yankees in Cincinnati.[19] Devastated, the Buckeyes lost the remainder of their schedule, including a doubleheader at home. It is unknown if Jefferson appeared in any of those games; box scores from the games have yet to be found.

After the season, Willie moved to Erie, Pennsylvania, along with several Buckeyes teammates. Buckeyes owner Ernest Wright provided housing, maintained steady employment, and kept a close watch on his players in Erie. Erie was listed as his home of record when he enlisted in the Army on November 9, 1942. Little is known of his military service aside from his discharge a short time later.

After his discharge, Willie returned to the Buckeyes for the 1943 season, headlining a revamped pitching staff that featured Ross "Satchel" Davis and Theolic Smith. On June 2 Willie threw a shutout in a 4-0 victory over the Cincinnati Clowns in Buffalo. Four days later, he pitched 12 grueling innings and scored the winning run in a 4-3 walk-off win over the Monarchs in Buffalo.[20] On August 25 in Erie, he struck out 11 in a 4-3 victory over the Homestead Grays.[21] Currently listed statistics show a 3-6 record and a 4.41 ERA in 65⅓ innings of work.

After the season, Willie returned to Erie and obtained a job at the General Electric plant in support of the war effort during the winter months. Sometime between 1941 and 1943, he married Jemilu Myrtle Franklin of Erie, a widow and a waitress at Ernest Wright's Pope Hotel.[22] (Jemilu's younger sister, Lillian Manus, would marry George in 1958.)

In March 1944 the Pittsburgh Courier reported that Jefferson and Bremer were offered contracts in Mexico.[23] Jefferson remained with the Buckeyes through the first months of the season, posting a 4-5 record and a 4.13 ERA in 10 recorded appearances. Eventually he reported to Mexico, posting a 3-4 record and a 4.07 ERA in 55⅓ innings with Puebla.[24]

For the Jefferson brothers, 1945 was a banner year as they led the Buckeyes to the Negro American League pennant. According to the team's yearbook and unofficial records, George boasted a 16-1 record while Willie maintained a 14-2 record. Willie was named to the West's pitching staff in the East-West Game, but he did not appear.[25] Currently available statistics are more sparse and show only six appearances including the World Series. This discrepancy likely exists as the team's recorded statistics may have been against all levels of competition, and box scores for the 1945 season have not been found.

In the World Series, Willie drew the Game One starting nod at Cleveland Stadium. Jefferson and Grays starter Roy Welmaker each threw shutout ball through six innings before the Buckeyes rallied for one run each in the seventh and eighth innings. With the tying and go-ahead runs on base in the top of the ninth, Jefferson induced a game-ending double play by Sam Bankhead. The 2-1 Buckeyes victory "was a storybook ball game that ended like a movie thriller … the likes of which has not been seen here in many a moon," Wendell Smith of the *Pittsburgh Courier* wrote.[26] The Buckeyes went on to sweep the Grays for their first and only title. Willie appeared in only the Series opener, but the brothers remained with the team and appeared together in least one exhibition, a 7-1 loss to the Grays at Yankee Stadium.[27]

In the offseason, the Jefferson brothers took their talents to Venezuela. While George joined the American All-Stars, Willie played for both the Estrellas del Caribe (Caribbean All-Stars) and Estrellas Zulianas (Zulia Stars). In the finale of the Serie Monumental (Monumental Series), Willie pitched 13 innings and stole home for Zulia in a 7-6 victory over the American All-Stars.[28] Presumably before this performance, Willie provided some insight into how he was viewing his time in South America when he remarked to the *Pittsburgh Courier*'s Wendell Smith in December that "things here aren't as interesting as they were when I saw you in Mexico."[29]

The Buckeyes were unable to replicate their previous year's success with the brothers in 1946. While George nursed injuries that kept him sidelined for most of the season, Willie remained in Venezuela with the Sabios del Vargas (Vargas Wisemen) of the new Liga Venezolana de Béisbol Profesional. The *Cleveland Call and Post* noted in May that Jefferson was due to return after the season ended in the summer,[30] but a follow-up story on June 8 stated that he "indicated by his silence to Manager [Wilbur] Hayes' correspondence that he would not return to the states." Jefferson and teammate Parnell Woods were promptly suspended for five years. Statistics show that he was able to sneak in a single recorded appearance with the Buckeyes in 1946 – a third of an inning in which he gave up six runs and four hits. Behind the arms of Jefferson and his former rival Roy Welmaker, Vargas would go on to win the LVBP's championship while Jefferson was named a league all-star. Remaining in Venezuela, Jefferson and Woods continued playing for local teams in the Zulia region throughout the summer.[31]

A joint session of the Negro American and National League owners before the 1947 season affirmed the five-year ban on Jefferson, Woods, and Avelino Cañizares. Buckeyes ownership argued without success that Jefferson and Woods wound up stranded due to their passports being held by Venezuelan officials.[32] Jefferson moved to Cuba and joined the pitching staff of the Habana Leones in the only season of the Cuban Players League, recording a 1-0 record in eight appearances.[33]

Back stateside and likely evading the ban by playing outside of the confines of the Negro National and American Leagues, Willie split 1948 with the independent Cincinnati Crescents,[34] San Francisco Sea Lions,[35] and the Negro Southern League's New Orleans Creoles.[36] In May 1949 he signed with the New Castle Nats of the Middle Atlantic League, an affiliate of the Washington Senators, and was expected to pitch out of the bullpen.[37] It is unclear if he made any appearances with the team.[38] By June, he reportedly returned to the Creoles,[39] though his second stint in New Orleans appeared to be brief as the ban was presumably lifted for him to rejoin the Buckeyes for a doubleheader against the Indianapolis Clowns in July.[40] Willie remained in Cleveland for the 1950 season, giving up six runs in a 6-1 loss to the Memphis Red Sox on July 2.[41] By the end of the month, the Buckeyes folded for good in the wake of a disastrous 3-33 start.[42]

At the age of 47 in 1951, Willie moved to Canada and joined several Negro League veterans including former Cincinnati teammates Lloyd Davenport and Ted Radcliffe on the Elmwood Giants of the integrated Manitoba-Dakota (Mandak) League, registering a 5-7 record in 17 appearances.[43] On July 12 Jefferson led the Giants to the finals of the $1,500 Brandon Invitational tournament with a one-hit 3-0 victory over the Carman Cardinals.[44] Giants general manager Curly Haas name-dropped Jefferson directly as the Mandak League sought to move up to Class-B classification in 1952. He noted that Jefferson was "good enough to win games," but that there would be "no place for old men like him in our new league."[45]

Willie instead joined the independent Baton Rouge Hardwood Sports, leading the all-Black team to the finals of the $6,000 Indian Head Invitational Tournament.[46] On July 26 he returned to old form and threw a shutout in a 2-0 victory over the Moose Jaw Maples.[47]

Now 49, Jefferson returned for one last season in 1953 with the Regina Caps, an all-Black team managed by Jim Williams. On July 6 he yielded 13 hits in a 12-3 loss to Moose Jaw.[48] Less than two weeks later, on July 17, he was released.[49] He was also listed in some accounts as a member of the semipro Erie Lakers throughout the year, though he may have been confused for George, who was Erie's starting right fielder.[50]

Sometime before 1948, Willie and Jemilu separated,[51] and on July 16, 1964, she died. Willie's brother George is named in her obituary as her brother.[52] Willie's whereabouts at the time of her death is unknown. The couple had no children.

Willie was residing in Houston when he died of unspecified causes on May 31, 1972. He was interred close to home at Prairie Springs Cemetery in Okemah, Oklahoma. His brother George died a decade later and was buried near him.[53] No obituary has been found.

SOURCES

In addition to the sources cited in the Notes, the author used Ancestry.com to gather biographical data including birth, death, marriage, family, and military service information. Except where otherwise indicated, all Negro League player statistics and team records were taken from the Seamheads Negro Leagues database.

NOTES

1   Public records available on Ancestry.com attribute Douglass and Lula's marriage to 1924. No information regarding Willie's mother has been found.

2   "Clearview," The Encyclopedia of Oklahoma History and Culture, https://www.okhistory.org/publications/enc/entry?entry=CL009, accessed January 1, 2025.

3   Chester Washington, "Chez Says," New Pittsburgh (Pennsylvania) Courier, September 26, 1936: 14.

4   "Ashton shut out by A.C. Negroes," Blackwell (Oklahoma) Journal-Tribune, August 13, 1930: 7.

5   "Ark City Beavers Meet Milford in Skirmish Tonight," Wichita Beacon, August 16, 1933: 6.

6   "Hot Shots Will Play Double-Header Sunday," Ponca City (Oklahoma) News, September 18, 1931: 11.

7   "Ghosts Whip the Monarchs," Omaha World-Herald, August 30, 1934: 20.

8   Phil Dixon and Patrick Hannigan, The Negro Baseball Leagues, 1867-1955: A Photographic History (Mattituck, New York: Amereon House, 1992), 211.

9   No statistics or proof of Willie Jefferson's time on the Monarchs exists. He may have been traded before playing a game for the team, or the newspaper account may have been incorrect. "Hoosiers Are Rivals of Tiger Nine Today," Cincinnati Enquirer, May 29, 1937: 13.

10 "Cincy Team Nips Dayton in Thriller," Chicago Defender, May 8, 1937: 15.

11 "Tigers Rout Detroit Club at Lippincott," South Bend (Indiana) Tribune, August 7, 1937: 6.

12 "1937 Cincinnati Tigers," Seamheads Negro Leagues Database, https://www.seamheads.com/NegroLgs/team.php?yearID=1937&teamID=CT&LGOrd=2&tab=fld, accessed December 18, 2024.

13 "Retrosheet Boxscore: South All Stars(S) (SAS) 3 North All Stars(N) (NAS) 1," Retrosheet, https://www.retrosheet.org/NegroLeagues/boxesetc/1938/B10020SAS1938.htm.

14 William McNeil, The California Winter League (Jefferson, North Carolina: McFarland Publishing, 2002), 194-195.

15 "Good Staff Boasted," Cincinnati Enquirer, May 3, 1942: 34.

16 "Buckeyes Oppose Giants Tomorrow," Akron Beacon-Journal, July 6, 1942: 12.

17 "Ches Buchanan Blanks Potent Bushwicks, 6-0," Philadelphia Tribune, August 15, 1942: 14.

18 "Black Yankees Defeat Stars, 8-5," Philadelphia Inquirer, September 4, 1942: 32.

19 "Buckeye Club Plays Black Yankees," Cincinnati Enquirer, September 9, 1942: 18.

20 "Buckeyes Split Two With Monarchs, Hold Lead," Cleveland Call and Post, June 12, 1943: 11.

21 "Sports," Paterson (New Jersey) Morning Call, August 26, 1943: 18.

22 Jemilu is listed in the Erie city directory as a widow in 1941 and Willie's wife in 1943.

23 "Cleveland Official Says Mexicans Are 'Stealing' Players," New Pittsburgh Courier, May 25, 1944: 12.

24 "1944 Pericos de Puebla," Seamheads Negro Leagues Database, https://www.seamheads.com/NegroLgs/team.php?yearID=1944&teamID=PUE&LGOrd=7, accessed December 9, 2024.

25 "All-Star Tilt Scheduled for Comiskey Park," Michigan Chronicle (Detroit), July 21, 1945: 14.

26 Wendell Smith, "Battling Bucks Win 2 to 1, 4 to 2 in World Series," New Pittsburgh Courier, September 22, 1945: 12.

27 "Retrosheet Boxscore: Homestead Grays (HOM) 7 Cleveland Buckeyes (CVB) 1," https://www.retrosheet.org/NegroLeagues/boxesetc/1945/B09231HOM1945.htm, accessed December 30, 2024.

28 Javier Gonzalez and Carlos Figueroa Ruiz, Campos de Gloria: El beisbol en Venezuela, 127 años de historia 1895-2022 (Biblioteca Digital Banesco), 389-391.

29 Wendell Smith, "The Sports Beat," New Pittsburgh Courier, December 22, 1945: 16.

30 Cleveland Jackson, "Ohio Lads Stave Off Disaster as Injuries Riddle Buch's Staff," Cleveland Call and Post, May 25, 1946: 22.

31 Carlos Figueroa, "Sabios de Vargas premiered LVBP titles," Ultimas Noticias, https://en.ultimasnoticias.ve/noticias/deportes/sabios-de-vargas-estrenaron-titulos-de-la-lvbp/, accessed December 17, 2024.

32 "Saperstein Turned Down; Ban on Jumpers Stays," Los Angeles Tribune, March 8, 1947: 14.

33 Jorge S. Figueredo, Who's Who in Cuban Baseball, 1878-1961 (Jefferson, North Carolina: McFarland Publishing, 2015), 390.

34 "Auscos Meet Tough Cincinnati Crescents Tonight," St. Joseph (Michigan) Herald-Press, June 15, 1948: 8.

35 Bob Towner, "Hanyzewski Pitches Studebakers to Win," South Bend Tribune, July 14, 1948: 25.

36 William Plott, The Negro Southern League: A Baseball History, 1920-1951 (Jefferson, North Carolina: McFarland Publishing, 2015), 236.

37 "Nats Will Play Vandergrift Pioneers Twin Bill Here Tonight," New Castle (Pennsylvania) News, May 25, 1949: 20.

38 Though he was listed on the roster according to newspaper accounts, Jefferson does not appear in statistical records for the team. "1949 New Castle Nats Statistics," Baseball Reference, https://www.baseball-reference.com/register/team.cgi?id=165e2aao, accessed December 9, 2024.

39 "New Orleans Creoles Meet Cubans at League Park," Cleveland Plain Dealer, June 26, 1949: 42.

40 "Clownmen Held Even by Bucks," Baltimore Afro-American, July 16, 1949: 15.

41 "Listless Buckeyes Drop Two," New Pittsburgh Courier, July 8, 1950: 24.

42 "Cleveland Buckeyes Fold Up," Kansas City (Missouri) Call, July 28, 1950: 8.

43 "1951 Statistics," Western Canada Baseball, https://attheplate.com/wcbl/1951_2.html, accessed December 9, 2024.

44 "1951 Tournaments," Western Canada Baseball, https://www.attheplate.com/wcbl/1951_1k.html, accessed December 9, 2024.

45   "Mandak Loop to Continue," *Regina* (Saskatchewan) *Leader-Post,* October 17, 1951: 23.

46   "1952 Baton Rouge," Western Canada Baseball, https://www.attheplate.com/wcbl/1952_1g11.html, accessed December 9, 2024.

47   "Tourists Nip Maples in Quickie," *Regina Leader-Post,* July 28, 1952: 19.

48   "Double Win for Maples," *Saskatoon* (Saskatchewan) *Star-Phoenix,* July 7, 1953: 12.

49   "1953 Game Reports," Western Canada Baseball, https://attheplate.com/wcbl/1953_1i.html, accessed December 9, 2024.

50   "Lakers Top Jamestown, 3-1," *Erie Sunday Times,* May 3, 1953: 44.

51   The 1948 Erie city directory lists Jemilu, George, and Lillian but makes no mention of Willie. Willie is listed as Jemilu's husband in 1946.

52   "Mrs. J. Jefferson" (obituary), *Erie Daily Times,* July 17, 1964: 21.

53   "William Jefferson (1904-1972)," Find a Grave Memorial, https://www.findagrave.com/memorial/70370257/william-jefferson, accessed December 28, 2024.

Sam Jethroe

By Bill Nowlin

Sam Jethroe was the National League Rookie of the Year in 1950, playing for the Boston Braves, and the first African American to play major-league baseball in Boston. Five years earlier, he'd tried out for the Boston Red Sox at Fenway Park, along with Jackie Robinson and Marvin Williams, but the Red Sox pursued none of them. Robinson went on to break the major-league color barrier and won Rookie of the Year in 1947.

Near the end of his life, Jethroe struggled financially because he was denied a major-league pension for lack of sufficient service time.

At 6-feet-1 and 178 pounds in his prime, the switch-hitting Jethroe (who threw right-handed) was known as the "Jet" – and many considered him the fastest man in baseball in his day. He was a better than average batter, although not nearly as accomplished on defense.

Sam Jethroe with the Boston Braves.

After his playing career ended, when asked which year was his first in professional baseball, Jethroe told the Hall of Fame it was 1948. That was the year he first played in the minor leagues – in the outfield for the Montreal Royals, the Brooklyn Dodgers' top farm team. He played in 76 games and hit for a .322 average, with just one homer and 25 RBIs. He wasn't as much for driving in runs, but he got on base a lot and scored 52 runs. In Montreal again in 1949, he played a full 153 games and hit for a .326 average, with 83 RBIs and a league-leading 154 runs scored. He set a league record with 89 stolen bases. His 207 base hits and 19 triples also led the International League, and he was one of the three outfielders named to the league all-star team. Under manager Clay Hopper, Montreal won league flags in 1946, with Jackie Robinson, and in 1948 with Jethroe.

Jethroe's speed on the base paths earned him the sobriquet "Jet Propelled Jethroe," later shortened to "The Jet." He was also dubbed "Larceny Legs" and "Mercury Man" and "The Colored Comet."[1]

Jethroe was ready for the major leagues. And for Branch Rickey, this was a chance to cash in on his outfielder's talent.

But 1948 was not truly Jethroe's first year of professional baseball. That came a full decade earlier, when Jethroe played for the Indianapolis Clowns in the Negro American League. The *Boston Chronicle* reported he hadn't played baseball at Lincoln High School but had been a star at softball.[2] As was not uncommon in those days, he did not graduate from high school until he was 23, in 1940. While still in high school, he played for the Indianapolis Clowns in the Negro American League, in 1938; in 1940 and 1941 he played semipro ball, declining several offers from "Negro professional teams" in order to care for his mother, who was quite ill. She died on New Year's Eve in 1941.[3] Jethroe returned to pro ball in earnest in 1942 to play for the Cleveland Buckeyes, for whom he played into early 1948.[4] It was a Buckeyes uniform Jethroe wore when he took part in the 1945 tryout at Fenway Park.

Negro Leagues statistics aren't as complete as we would like; but that Jethroe was brought back year after year speaks to good performance, and that he was signed to Montreal and fared well there also testifies to his talents as a ballplayer. Four times he was selected to the Negro Leagues' East-West All-Star Game, playing in seven games—two games apiece in 1942, 1946, 1947, and one in 1944.

Samuel Jethroe came from a farming family in Old Zion, Lowndes County, Mississippi. His parents moved to East St. Louis, Illinois at some point, perhaps very shortly after Samuel was born. His parents were Albert "Chip" Jethroe, who at the time of the 1930 census had his own farm at East St. Louis, and Janie Jethroe, who worked as a sheller in a nut factory. She also worked some as a domestic, according to news stories contemporary to Sam's career. Sam had a sister, Rachel, who was about a year older, and a brother, Jessie, about four years younger. According to census records, Janie had been born Mary Jannie Spruil. Sam's notarized birth certificate said his mother's name was Jannie Adams.[5]

We believe that Sam was born on January 23, 1917 in Lowndes County, though both he himself and the Social Security Death Index gave his birthplace as East St. Louis. He gave his year of birth as 1922, and a number of contemporary accounts indicate years ranging from 1918 to 1922; however, his reported age at the time of the 1930 census was 13 years old. We assume that those later years reflected a fictional "baseball age"; they were there to make him appear younger and thus to offer longer future potential for a team that might sign him. "I was born in 1917," he later confirmed to Rich Marazzi.[6] When he came to the big leagues, it was with the Boston Braves in 1950. Fortunately, age wasn't an issue to his manager, Billy Southworth. "I don't care if he's 50, just as long as he can do the job."[7]

Jethroe played semipro ball while growing up, playing for both the East St. Louis Colts and St. Louis Giants. He would hitchhike to Sportsman's Park in St. Louis and peek through a knothole to watch Dizzy Dean and the Cardinals.[8] And he grew up almost next door to Hank Bauer. "His backyard touched my backyard, and we'd play games, Hank Bauer's team and my team," Sam said.[9] Of course, Bauer's team was all White and he went on to the major leagues, while Jethroe "would play doubleheaders for the East St. Louis Colts, then head over to St. Louis for a night game… those teams were all black…and I made hardly nothing."

Marazzi writes that Jethroe, while with the Buckeyes in 1942, led the Negro American League in numerous categories – batting average, base hits, runs scored, doubles, triples, and stolen bases.[10] In 1944, his .353 average led the league.

It was in early 1945 that Jethroe took part in the tryout at Fenway Park. The pressure was growing on what was then known as "Organized Baseball" to desegregate, particularly because soldiers who had come back from putting their lives on the line for the country during World War II found a color bar still preventing them from playing professional baseball other than in the Negro leagues.[11] Boston City Councilor Isadore Muchnick threatened to pull the special permit that the City of Boston accorded the Red Sox which enabled them to play baseball on one of the most lucrative days of the week – Sundays. The Sox wanted to hold onto Sunday baseball and so agreed to hold a tryout for a select three

Negro Leaguers brought to Boston by *Pittsburgh Courier* sportswriter Wendell Smith. Jethroe, Marvin Williams, and Jackie Robinson suited up at Fenway on April 16, 1945 and worked out for coach Hugh Duffy.[12] Red Sox manager Joe Cronin was present as well. Robinson later said of Jethroe, "He looked like a gazelle in the outfield."[13]

Duffy said he was impressed, but none of the three ever heard from the Red Sox again. Rather than becoming the first major-league team to integrate, the Red Sox ending up being the last – in 1959. Jethroe recalled that the Red Sox "said we had all the potential but it wasn't the right time."[14] Cronin later said he told the players that since Boston's top farm club was in Louisville, "we didn't think they'd be interested in going there because of the racial feelings at the time." But he also admitted, "We all thought because of the times, it was good to have separate leagues."[15]

Jackie Robinson was indeed bitter about the incident, at least when he spoke about it later. But as for Jethroe the *Boston Globe*'s Larry Whiteside wrote, "Unlike Robinson, he took life as it came." Though they'd been told that the time wasn't right (Muchnick said he never heard that explanation), Jethroe allowed, "The Sox were nice. I mean they didn't take us to dinner or anything, but they were all right. It was just a workout."[16] He hadn't gotten too upset, he said, because the three figured nothing was going to come of it anyway.[17] As to the idea they might have actually been signed and brought into Organized Baseball, "I don't think it ever dawned on any of us."[18] He also told *Herald* reporter Gerry Callahan that he'd heard no racial slurs on the field that day.

Jethroe may have been a bit more candid shortly afterward with some of his Buckeyes teammates. Willie Grace says that Jethroe told him "…'What a joke that so-called tryout was.' He said you just knew it was a farce" and that Cronin, although he was there, was "up in the stands with his back turned most of the time."[19]

Tryout over, Jethroe reported to Cleveland, put his Buckeyes uniform back on and once more led the league, this time with a .393 batting average. The Buckeyes also won the Negro World Series that year, sweeping the Homestead Grays.

Was Jethroe disappointed, or angry, that the Red Sox had turned him away? "No, I never thought about it," he told Marazzi. "When I played in the Negro Leagues, I enjoyed it. I loved to play ball and baseball was fun then. I played against Don Newcombe, Monte Irvin, Henry Thompson, 'Double Duty' Radcliffe, Gentry Jessup, and many others."[20]

After the 1946 season, Jethroe joined the Satchel Paige All-Stars and barnstormed through 17 games, playing against a team of major leaguers headed by the entrepreneurial Bob Feller. Paige's team won seven of them. Jethroe gave Feller credit for helping Black players into the majors. "He gave us a chance to show what we could do against major leaguers."[21]

Jethroe was courted by Mexican League head honcho Jorge Pasquel to play ball in the Mexican League, but declined. He did go to Venezuela for a while and was there when the news broke that Jackie Robinson had been signed. Jethroe played in the Cuban Winter League in 1947-48 and again in 1948-49. Playing center field for Almendares, Jethroe hit a team-leading .308 and led the league with 53 runs scored and 22 stolen bases.[22] He again led the league in stolen bases (with 32) for the 1948-49 Almendares team, though his 37 strikeouts also led the league. He hit .320 in that year's Caribbean Series.[23]

In his quest for a better Brooklyn team and to desegregate the majors, Dodgers GM Branch Rickey reportedly interviewed Jethroe as well as Robinson. But Jethroe acknowledged that he smoked and drank, and Rickey felt he needed to go with a more clean-cut pioneer. He selected Robinson. "He had everything Mr. Rickey wanted," Jethroe said, "He was a college man who had experienced the white world, and I wasn't."[24]

But Fresco Thompson scouted Jethroe and the Dodgers did purchase Jethroe's contract from the Buckeyes for a reported $5,000, and in July 1948 assigned him to Montreal.[25] He had the two exceptional years noted above, and there were those who called him "the man who made Montreal forget about Jackie Robinson."[26] For instance, in the first 11 games he played against the Buffalo Bisons, Jethroe put together a different sort of streak – he stole at least one base in each game.[27] Buffalo manager Paul Richards, Bob Dolgan wrote, "was so fearful of leadoff man Jethroe's speed, he would intentionally walk the pitcher in front of him, blocking Jethroe's running."[28] When they did pitch to Jethroe in the Negro Leagues, Buck O'Neil recalled, "the infield would have to come in a few steps or you'd never throw him out."[29]

During spring training in 1949, Jethroe was clocked in a 60-yard sprint at 5.9 seconds—two-tenths of a second faster than the world's record at the time. Stunned as to what his stopwatch showed, the Dodgers' Arthur Mann later helped arrange an exhibition 75-yard dash against Olympian Bunny Ewell. Jethroe beat Ewell by a few yards.[30] Another race that spring clocked Jethroe at 6.1 seconds, tying the world record.[31] He could run fast in games, too, of course. Arthur Daley of the New York Times noted the time Jethroe had scored from second – standing up – on an infield dribbler.

Rickey had Duke Snider in center field and really had no place in the big leagues for Jethroe. He may also have decided that Jethroe lacked power in his bat; Jethroe had hit just the one home run for the Royals. During a phone call with Boston Braves GM John Quinn on September 30, Rickey sold Jethroe's contract to the Braves.[32] It was a big deal, said to have been for at least $100,000. New York sportswriter Dan Daniel said the Jethroe sale – one of several Rickey made in a flurry that netted the Dodgers well over half a million dollars – brought Brooklyn $125,000 and Clint Conatser and Don Thompson.[33] The caption for the AP

wirephoto that ran in the October 12, 1949 Boston Herald said Jethroe was "regarded as the greatest base runner since Ty Cobb was in his prime."

It was a big deal in other ways, of course, and it's interesting that more than 10 years earlier, John Quinn's father Bob Quinn, Sr. had talked with Boston journalist Doc Kountze and envisioned the end of segregation in baseball. Quinn felt it only right that the color line should be breached in Boston, which had fashioned itself the "Cradle of Liberty" at the time of the American Revolution. Quinn knew that major-league owners would have voted him down in 1938, but he did predict the change would happen with the National League Braves (they were the Boston Bees in 1938) before it would happen with the Red Sox.[34]

Jethroe wasn't the only Black player in the Braves organization. Announcing the acquisition, the Boston Herald wrote, "He is the first Negro signed to a Braves contract, though there are several Negroes in the organization."[35] There was a rumor a few days later that the Braves had also purchased Jackie Robinson.[36] That was quickly denied, but it was clear that Jethroe, more than the also-acquired Bob Addis, had been the Braves' target in their dealings.[37]

There was some early thought that Rickey had discarded Jethroe; New York writer Joe Williams had dubbed him a "gold-brick…who doesn't seem to be able to throw at all."[38] But Rickey himself said, "It might be the biggest mistake I ever made in baseball."[39]

In any case, come 1950 Sam Jethroe, the first Black ballplayer for the Boston Braves, was indeed a 33-year-old rookie in the major leagues. But he had a resume in professional baseball dating back into the 1930s.

Jethroe felt welcome immediately, although things did not always go smoothly as the season wore on. First, though, there was spring training. The Braves trained in Bradenton, Florida, and while perhaps Bostonians would welcome him – a proposition yet to be tested – this was less likely to be the case in those days in Florida.

A year earlier, Jethroe had trained with the Dodgers at Vero Beach in 1949. Though there were communities that were resistant to "race-mixing" in baseball, the Dodgers had been pleased with Robinson's reception and his being named Rookie of the Year in 1947. The 1948 Dodgers had welcomed future Hall of Famer Roy Campanella, and the Cleveland Indians added Larry Doby, who helped them win the 1948 World Series. In January 1949, several Southern cities that had previously barred Black and White ballplayers from playing in the same games actually reached out with invitations to the Dodgers to come and play in their locales during spring training. They included Miami and West Palm Beach in Florida, Atlanta and Macon in Georgia, Greenville in South Carolina, and Houston and San Antonio in Texas. The Dodgers trained at Vero Beach, although at the Naval Training base that was outside the city limits.

Jethroe played against the Cardinals (March 13) and Yankees (March 21) at St. Petersburg – the first time the color bar had been dropped there -- and "caused no stir whatever…produced no reaction except insofar as a small mention in the local *Independent*."[40] The *St. Petersburg Times* did not even mention that Jethroe was a "Negro." About 300 Negroes were among the 3,157 who came out to the Cardinals game.

There actually had been an incident, but a very quiet one the newspaper apparently had not heard about. Jethroe remembered it years later: "John Quinn met me at the airport and asked me questions about what things might bother me and he told the players about how I felt. One time, at a restaurant in Florida that spring, they refused to serve me and the team said, 'Sam, if they don't serve you, they won't serve us.' I told them to go on in, that I wasn't hungry."[41]

Right from the start, questions were raised about Jethroe's defense. Under the headline "$100,000 Jethroe May Be Flop in Outfield," Bob Ajemian wrote in *The Sporting News* that while there was no doubt whatsoever about his being faster than anyone in the majors, and that he ought to be able to hit major-league pitching from either side of the plate, he "cannot throw with a major league arm" and "cannot field well enough to hold down a vital center field post satisfactorily."[42] He didn't seem to get a good jump on the ball and counted on his speed to enable him to play more deeply than might otherwise be wise; he saw a few balls drop in front of him that a better center fielder may have caught.

Harold Kaese of the *Boston Globe* agreed. He wrote that "he cannot throw or judge a fly well enough to play center field…This Jethroe looks so fast and his arm looks so weak that it's even money he can carry the ball in from center field as fast as he can throw it in."[43]

The Braves brass was worried. Jethroe himself was a little discouraged and said, "Don't know but what I ought to pack up and go home, if they really have quit on me."[44] Bob Holbrook wrote after the 1950 season was over that Jethroe had put together "one of the finest comeback epics in recent years." How could player mount a comeback when he'd never played in the majors before? That's because, Holbrook said, Jethroe had been "washed up before he played a game. Writers took one look at him and gasped. He couldn't throw, he couldn't hit and he couldn't field. Fly balls dropped around him so profusely that people were afraid he'd get hit on the head."[45] Jethroe himself had let one ball drop during a night game, and reportedly joshed, "I lost it in the moon."[46]

He "isn't living up to his pre-training camp raves," wrote Frank Santos of the *Boston Chronicle*, an African-American newspaper, "finding it rather hard to adjust himself to the so-called big league." But Santos added that Jethroe had recently begun to find himself. Manager Billy Southworth stuck with Jethroe, counseling patience. And Santos seemed to have little doubt that Jethroe would get a good reception in Boston, writing, "One thing is certain, that the hometown fans of the Boston Braves will be rooting for him."[47]

Santos was right; Jethroe was quite a hit with fans from the start. Once they saw him run, they were even more convinced. Holbrook wrote, "Jethroe's box-office appeal amazed even the Braves' front office who knew they had acquired a good outfielder but never guessed the staid Boston fans would adopt him as their favorite National League player and murmur with excitement every time he reached base."[48]

Staid, but also racist? Jethroe was eager to play in Boston, "but I was also anxious because I knew when I arrived there, more was required for me to do than a white player," Jethroe told Larry Whiteside.[49] He hadn't been able to board with the team in St. Petersburg, nor in the team hotels in Chicago and St. Louis, and he didn't have a roommate his whole first year with the Braves in Boston.[50] "In Chicago, my first time in," he told Marvin Pave of the *Boston Globe*, "I stayed at a black hotel, but the next time in, our traveling secretary, Duffy Lewis, had me stay in the team hotel with him. Our third time in, I had a room of my own."[51] In Boston, Jethroe stayed at the Kenmore Hotel, not far from Braves Field.

"I was lucky," Jethroe recalled. "Everywhere I went I seemed to have the fans on my side. They kidded me about my fielding but I didn't have rabbit ears. The fans could say what they wanted. The only confrontations I had were on the playing field."[52]

While the Red Sox took more than nine years before they fielded a Black ballplayer, Jethroe seems to have been almost unreservedly welcomed in Boston. And yet, the Braves certainly hadn't signed Jethroe because of his race. In 1950, the "non-White" population of Boston was just 5.3% of the city's overall population. The African-American population itself was an even 5.0%. To be sure, was growing; in 1940 it had been 3.1%, and in 1960 it was 9.1%.[53] Still, this was not in any way a constituency to which either the Braves or Red Sox needed to cater.

Nonetheless, one might think that the signing of a Black ballplayer would have been a major story in Boston at the time. It was not. Instead, the focus on Jethroe over the months through spring training was on his speed. The Boston press made little of his race. An online search of the *Boston Herald*, *Boston Globe*, and *Springfield Union* from October 1, 1949 to April 17, 1950 – the day before Jethroe's debut – turns up 230 stories that mention "Sam Jethroe" but only 30 that mention both "Sam Jethroe" and "Negro," the term used then the way "African American" was used in more recent times. To their credit, more than 86% of the stories made no reference at all to his race, and some of those that did were matter-of-factual, such as the *Globe*'s listing of Jethroe's prior clubs, which included the "Cleveland Buckeyes of the Negro American League."[54]

It could be argued that sportswriters simply shied away from mentioning "social issues" and restricted their coverage to play on the field. However, the online search also included columnists and opinionated men such as Dave

Egan of the *Boston Record*, who had long pushed for desegregation of Boston baseball. Egan had written back in 1945 that Boston was "freedom's holy soil" and that "someday, the bigots of baseball will die, and men of good-will will take their places…on that day, baseball can call itself the national sport."[55]

Boston's African-American newspaper, the *Boston Chronicle*, reported Jethroe's signing, but also with little fanfare. When he signed his Braves contract with GM John Quinn in New York, the *Chronicle* noted that "the speedy Negro outfielder had just played in the Little World Series in Indianapolis before coming to New York." About all Jethroe himself had to say was, "I'll let the records do the talking. I just played in the Little World Series, now I hope to get into the big one."[56]

Before the traditional preseason "City Series" games against the Red Sox, the *Boston Post* – never referring once to his race – wrote, "Jethroe received more press interviews yesterday than all of the other Braves players combined. Sam is easy and natural with all members of the fourth estate."[57]

After the first exhibition game against the Red Sox, Gerry Hern of the *Post* acknowledged race in a single clause. Braves fans, he wrote, "have waited a long time to make a personal appraisal of Sam Jethroe, the first colored player ever to wear a Boston uniform, and Dick Donovan, the 25-year-old Wollaston resident, who earned his letter yesterday. Sam was slightly terrific in his Boston debutante party. There were no flowers, but he slashed a couple of singles that took the strain off the Braves followers, who have not been accustomed to seeing a Braves outfielder who could hit, throw and run."[58] The novelty of Jethroe's darker skin color was apparently on no more than a par with the novelty of a Brave from the nearby Wollaston neighborhood of Quincy, Massachusetts.

The Braves won that first game in the series, 4-1, and the Red Sox came back and won the second, 3-1, at Fenway. It was Jethroe's first time playing in the park he'd tried out in five years earlier. Batting in the bottom of the eighth with the Braves ahead, 1-0, Ted Williams slammed a three-run homer into the right-field bullpen. Jethroe, unfamiliar with the park and anxious to catch the ball, slammed hard into the bullpen wall, in vain. The *Herald* noted he was "courageous and speedy" but didn't see the need to remind readers of his darker hue. He was just another ballplayer – covered exactly the way one might wish. He was "Switching Sammy, getting plenty of encouragement from the 7,049 spectators."[59] But there was no mention of his race.

The *Globe's* game story noted that Jethroe had singled in the first run. It commented on his speed at one point and observed that "Like many another big leaguer, Jethroe is superstitious…He kicks third base to and from the outfield."[60] His similarity to the other players was thus noted; there was nothing in the way of noting his difference.

The next day, in picking both the 1950 Braves and Red Sox to win the pennants in their respective leagues, the *Globe's* Harold Kaese noted race, in passing: "Sam Jethroe, Boston's first Negro player, will display his phenomenal speed of foot by (1) scoring from first on a tap to the pitcher; (2) stealing more bases than the rest of the Braves and Birdie Tebbetts put together; and (3) dashing to the plate in time to catch his own throw from DEEP centerfield."[61]

There was no mention at all of Jethroe's race in Clif Keane's lengthy feature on Jethroe's very first game, which ran the morning of that game in Boston.[62]

The Braves opened the regular season in the Polo Grounds, where they beat the Giants, 11-4. Jethroe went 2-for-4 with an eighth-inning homer in his first game.

When it came time for Jethroe's Braves Field debut, the *Boston Traveler* suggested that "Sam Jethroe's debut in a championship game vies for attention at the Braves opener with the return of Eddie Waitkus to major-league action." It was Waitkus's first day back (he was playing for the Phillies) after being shot by Ruth Steinhagen in Chicago the prior July.

In the home opener, attended by the governor of Massachusetts (who threw out the first ball), the governors of Rhode Island and New Hampshire, and numerous other celebrities, Jethroe singled but his play barely rated mention in the papers. The game wound up a 2-2 tie, called due to rain in the last half of the eighth inning.

A few days later when the Brooklyn Dodgers came to town, Leslie Jones shot a photo for the *Herald* that depicted "five Negroes…advancing the cause of their race in baseball" -- Jethroe with Dodgers Dan Bankhead, Roy Campanella, Don Newcombe, and Jackie Robinson.[63]

Jethroe knocked out nine hits in his first seven games in Boston. On May 6 in Cincinnati, he singled twice batting left-handed and tripled and singled batting righty.

In May, Jethroe was one of the three Boston Braves outfielders invited to a "brotherhood" dinner of the Massachusetts Council of Catholics, Protestants and Jews. Sid Gordon was the Jew, Willard Marshall the Protestant, and Sam Jethroe the Catholic.[64] Sam always wore a St. Christopher's medal.[65]

Almost the only newspaper story that looked at him other than as just another player was a *Boston Globe* feature by Ernie Roberts that ran in July, "Jethroe, Hero of Thousands at Park, Goes Unrecognized on Boston Streets."[66] According to that story, he lived on Columbus Avenue with a young couple who had invited him.

In Boston, Jethroe kept to himself. "I stayed pretty close to home. The High Hat Club on Mass. Avenue was my favorite spot. I didn't go around to many white places – bars, movies, etc. But I met a lot of nice people. One of them was Archbishop Cushing. He would call up to make sure I got to church."[67]

Jethroe had had a little trouble on the road as mentioned earlier, but it was only when visiting his native St. Louis that he could not stay at the team hotel, the Chase. And at St. Louis' segregated ballpark, Sam's father was forced to sit in the "Negro section" of seats.

For the most part, Jethroe roomed alone on the road. Lewis, Luis Olmo, and Earl Torgeson were his closest friends on the team. He did get some razzing at parks around the league, but said it didn't bother him. "I don't have rabbit ears; I don't hear a thing. This is a country of free speech. Why not let the fans get their money's worth?" he smiled.[68]

Jethroe seemed to have been welcomed by Braves fans. "The people in Boston were crazy about me," he remembered later. "Everyone crowded around me for autographs after my first game. There was this woman who wanted to take me to dinner. A white woman. I didn't do it because I figured that was one of the reasons they didn't want us in the majors to begin with."[69] Jethroe had been married since November 11, 1942 to Elsie Allen, whom he had met that year at a dance in Erie, Pennsylvania.[70]

There was no indication that Jethroe received any razzing at Braves Field. In early 2015, there remained a few fans who had seen Jethroe break in with the Braves more than 60 years earlier. None recall racial slurs or even muttering at Braves Field. In fact, the opposite seemed to be true. A young Braves fan named Mort Bloomberg remembered, "A wave of excitement rose from the stands when he stepped to the plate (even noticeable when attendance fell sharply) because he was our hometown answer to Jackie Robinson--a self-assured threat to steal one or more bases each time he reached first...Boos when he came to bat? Never. We just wanted to see Sammy run."[71]

A story in July 1950 showed that the Boston press was picking up on Braves fans' affection for Jethroe. "Fans of Wigwam Sing Sam's Song" was the headline on George C. Carens' article in the *Traveler*. It was his base-stealing ability that captured the imagination. Yes, it was fine that Gordon, Torgeson, and Bob Elliott already had a combined 40 homers, "but the faithful followers are not happy until Sam Jethroe gets aboard. The hum when he comes up to the plate is based on the hope that he will become a base-run-ner...when the subject changes to the Negro center fielder's fancy footwork on the basepaths, everyone switches to su-perlatives. Thousands breathe the hope that Sam can show his stuff...the sensational sorties of Jethroe have Boston all a-quiver."[72]

Jack Barnes worked briefly as a vendor at Braves Field, but went to many more games as a teenage fan. He recalled more than 60 years later, "We never had too many full houses at Braves Field - maybe there'd be 10 or 12,000 of us there - but the racial question, I'm gonna tell you, there was never anybody booing or hissing Sam. We loved him. Everybody would chant, 'Go, Sam, go.' Sam the Jet at Braves Field was a hero. Everybody loved to see Sam run. He brought some life to the ball team. We weren't a very fast team and he was a breath of fresh air to us. I went to a lot of games when Sam was playing and I never

heard anybody...I never heard any racial slurs, or anything but admiration for Sam the Jet. Everybody loved Sam the Jet. I sat in those stands many times. I was a teenager and I was listening, and boy there was nobody booing Sam the Jet. The drunks were there at all the ballgames and they'd be raising their beer and toasting Sam as he was stealing second base. 'Hey, Sam!!!'"[73]

Frank McNulty worked as the visiting team's batboy at Braves Field from 1945 through 1949, with his first year as home batboy being 1950. Had he recalled hearing any negativity from the stands? "I don't remember anything from the general public, anything close to discrimination."

"I loved the Boston fans," Jethroe said nearly 50 years later. "They used to chant, 'go, go, go,' every time I got on base. Never had a problem in Boston."[74]

McNulty noted perceptively that "As far as the club-house was concerned, I didn't detect anything. No group of guys that was ostracizing him or anything like that. I didn't notice anything like that. . . the Braves in those years were somewhat divided into different groups. A number of them had come with Billy Southworth from the Cardinals. So there was that group. Bob Elliott and two or three others had come from Pittsburgh, and there was that group. And then there was Sibbi Sisti and Tommy Holmes and I think Connie Ryan, who had come though the Braves chain, through Hartford, Connecticut, and there was that group." As to Jethroe, "He wasn't part of any of those groups, just because he wasn't part of those, but I don't think that had anything to do with race at all. Jethroe was sort of a loner anyway. He was very quiet."[75]

Future major-leaguer Bill Monbouquette never went to Fenway as a kid; he always went to Braves Field. He was a Knotholer. Monbo, who grew up in the Black sec-tion of West Medford, never recalls any negative reactions in the stands to Jethroe. He joked, mimicking protecting his head against a foul ball, mocking Jethroe's defensive shortcomings, but said every time he got on first, "the fans would say, 'Go, Sam! Go, Sam!' He could fly. He was an exciting guy."[76]

And what about opposing ballplayers? Whatever they might have done to make Jethroe's rookie year in the majors difficult, he didn't seem to be bothered by it. Later in Gerry Hern's lengthy article in the *Post*, Jethroe was asked if he was angry at some pitchers who had thrown at his head as he'd made his way north. Jethroe "chuckled" and said, "Oh no. they're just trying me out. They got to make a living, too. If they can drive me away from the plate, or frighten me, they're going to do it. I don't think there was anything else to it."

On September 15, 1950 the Braves staged a Sam Jethroe Night for him. He'd hurt his foot the night before and had to be helped off the field, but he made it for his night. When it was first announced, he expressed embarrassment. Knowing that gifts were typically presented to those honored with a "day," he asked instead that any money be put into a college scholarship for Negro youths. "That's how the arrangement stands," wrote Arthur Siegel, "and that's why...Jethroe well rates the accolades of Boston sports enthusiasts"[77] Mayor John B. Hynes did present him with a check but also a television, radio, easy chair, matched luggage set, and a week's hunting trip to the Rangeley Lakes in Maine. The *Chronicle* referred to "the overwhelming kindness expressed by many fans" – hardly the sort of fan reaction that would have discouraged the Red Sox from signing a Black ballplayer. Jethroe himself was said by the paper to have been "filled with immense gratitude" and – wanting to express his appreciation with a special performance,[78] – to have tried too hard in the game. He committed two errors and struck out twice in a 1-for-5 night, although he did pull off a double play late in a tight game. His speech was a short one: "Thank you. I appreciate this very much."[79]

Sam Jethroe's rookie season was a clear success. He was named National League Rookie of the Year for 1950. He'd hit for a .273 batting average (.338 on-base percentage), with a league-leading 35 stolen bases. (Jethroe's fleet work on the base paths helped to bring base-stealing back into the game. It had not truly been in fashion at the time. That same season Dom DiMaggio led the American League with 15.) Was he stealing on the pitcher, or stealing on the catcher? "I just runs," he told Bob Holbrook.[80] His steals included an exciting first-inning steal of home on June 6 in Cincinnati. He'd scored an even 100 runs, and driven in 58. He'd hit 18 home runs. He'd committed 12 errors in 384 chances (.969). Jethroe, "weak" arm or not, led the National League in assists as a center fielder both in 1950 and 1951 and ranked second in outfield assists in 1950 and third in 1951. He received more than twice as many points in the Rookie of the Year voting as the second-place finisher, Phillies pitcher Bob Miller.

In January 1951, Jethroe attended the Boston Baseball Writers annual dinner. Howard Bryant reports that Jethroe was seated next to Eddie Collins of the Red Sox, who told the ballplayer that he was pleased to see Sam's success. "Jethroe thanked him and without bitterness replied, 'You had your chance, Mr. Collins. You had your chance.'"[81]

For the 1951 season, Jethroe recorded nearly identical stats: he again led the league in stolen bases, with the same number (35); he hit the same number of homers (18); he scored one more run (101 total); he drove in seven more runs (65); and his batting average was a few points higher (.280 with a .356 on-base percentage).

However, errors were a problem for him; he led league outfielders in errors in 1950, 1951, and 1952. "I'm ashamed I didn't get to the eye-doctor before I did," he told writer John Gillooly in spring training 1952; Gillooly had written that Jethroe "was almost laughed out of the league the early part of last season."[82] Joe Giuliotti is one reporter who said that Jethroe had once been hit on the head by a fly ball.[83] He'd begun wearing eyeglasses in early June 1951.

In 1952, after undergoing intestinal surgery early in the year, Jethroe's performance fell off significantly, pretty much across the board. He struck out quite a bit more and saw his batting average drop to .232 (OBP .318). The Braves finished in seventh place.

Charlie Grimm had taken over as Braves manager early in the 1952 season and he had once called Jethroe "Sambo," which didn't endear him to Jethroe. "Charlie Grimm was a prejudiced man and he didn't like me," he told the *Globe* in 1979.[84]

In 1953, the Boston Braves moved to Milwaukee. Jethroe never played for the Milwaukee Braves. On April 13, he was optioned to Toledo on 24-hour recall, but was never recalled. He hit .309 with 28 homers, but with the emergence of Billy Bruton in their outfield the Braves may have felt they were in good enough shape. On the day after Christmas they traded Jethroe, along with five other players and $100,000, to the Pittsburgh Pirates for infielder Danny O'Connell. Clearly, the Braves wanted O'Connell.

Jethroe had one at-bat for Pittsburgh in 1954. Appearing in two games, he played right field for the final two innings of the April 14 game and he pinch hit the next day, in Brooklyn, grounding into a 4-6 forceout at second base. It was his last major-league appearance.

Jethroe spent his last six seasons (1953 through 1958) in the minors, the last five of them with the Toronto Maple Leafs, averaging .280 for those five years. He also styled a little, notably parking his orchid-colored Lincoln in front of the ballpark.

He also spent one more season back in Cuban winter league baseball, 1954-55 with Cienfuegos. And he played semipro ball into the 1970s.

In his life after his playing career, Sam and Elsie operated Jethroe's Bar and Restaurant, a steakhouse, in Erie, Pennsylvania. The business did well for several years but then in the 1990s the city's redevelopment authority forced him to sell the property. Sportswriter Jim Auchmutey says he took out a loan and bought another place, but it was in a "tougher part of town where drug-dealing and gunplay are commonplace. Once there was a shooting death inside the bar." The business declined rapidly, and Jethroe found himself forced to sell off his Rookie of the Year award for $3,500.[85] By the end of 1994, after he'd lost his home to fire that November, he was living four blocks away in the bar.

Sam Jethroe came back to Boston twice, in 1992 and 1995, to attend player-fan reunions organized by the Boston Braves Historical Association. After the fire, the BBHA was able to raise over $2,100 and present him a check.[86]

At a gathering in Cleveland to honor Larry Doby, Jethroe told his former Montreal roommate Don Newcombe of the difficulties he was having. Sam and Elsie were living in the bar with two grandchildren, aged 10 and 16.

An attorney friend of Newcombe's, John Puttock, was present and felt moved to act. The pension rule at the time was that one had to have served four full years in the majors to qualify. Jethroe had three years and seven days of service time. Arguably, Jethroe and several former Negro Leaguers had been deprived of the opportunity to start sooner than they had. "We were held back because of the color of our skin," said Newcombe.[87]

A class action lawsuit was filed in U. S. District Court for the Western District of Pennsylvania contending that racial discrimination had prevented Jethroe from qualifying and receiving a major-league pension. The major leagues moved to dismiss the suit on the grounds that Jethroe had taken too long to file it, that the statute of limitations had long since expired. The suit was dismissed in October 1996.

Several people appear to have pitched in to help address the problem. One article says that one of Puttock's friends mentioned the problem to U. S. Senator Carol Moseley-Braun (D-Illinois), who talked to Chicago White Sox owner Jerry Reinsdorf. Reinsdorf reportedly persuaded the other owners to create a special fund that was announced in January 1997, providing annual payments of $7,500 to $10,000 to former Negro League players.[88]

Murray Chass of the *New York Times* wrote that National League president Leonard Coleman and former pitcher Joe Black, who like Jethroe played in both the Negro Leagues and the majors, headed up the committee.[89] Noted Negro League historian Larry Lester provided Major League Baseball with the names of qualified players and their mailing addresses.

"I can't tell you how appreciative I am of what (the owners) have done," said Jethroe, who by then had suffered a stroke and had other health issues.[90] It did indeed offer him a little more hope, and a feeling of some validation, in his later years.

Jethroe had always been a forgiving man. Remembering being forced to stay in separate housing from his White teammates back at the beginning, he said, "You get used to it. And you let it go."[91] And after his teenage grandson, known as Sam Jethroe Jr., was killed by a drunk driver, he appeared in court and asked for mercy for the driver. "I don't hold grudges," he said.[92]

On June 16, 2001 Sam Jethroe died of a heart attack in Erie, while he was recovering from pacemaker surgery a couple of weeks earlier.

Elsie Jethroe died on May 17, 2013. She had been preceded in death by their daughter Gloria.

Sam Jethroe's story is that of a solid if not stellar major leaguer whose fate was to have been born the wrong color for his time and his chosen profession. But if he came to the majors late, it was not quite too late; he was one of the handful of African-American players who followed Robinson and, less gifted than he, still proved that Blacks belonged in the middle tier of major leaguers as much as Whites did. *Boston Globe* editor Marty Nolan, in an appreciation of Jethroe written after his death, said it this way: "The lesson in equality Jethroe taught is the civil right to be less than the best."[93]

SOURCES

In addition to the sources noted in this biography, the author also accessed Jethroe's player file and player questionnaire from the National Baseball Hall of Fame, the *Encyclopedia of Minor League Baseball*, Retrosheet.org, Baseball-Reference.com, and the SABR Minor Leagues Database, accessed online at Baseball-Reference.com.

Thanks to Bob Brady and Larry Lester for a careful reading of this manuscript and very useful suggestions that improved it.

NOTES

1   *Boston Globe*, June 21, 2001.

2   On the other hand, the 1950 *National League Green Book* said he "played baseball, basketball, and football for Lincoln High" and had played both as a catcher and third baseman before switching to the outfield.

3   *Boston Chronicle*, March 25, 1950.

4   The team was based in both Cincinnati and Cleveland in 1942, but became the Cleveland Buckeyes exclusively as of 1943.

5   Mike Copper, "Document alters what we know about Sam Jethroe," *Erie Times-News*, April 9, 2010.

6   Rich Marazzi, "Sam JEThroe," *Sports Collectors Digest*, November 11, 1994. In 2010, Jethroe's grand-daughter Rachel Jethroe-Critten discovered a Mississippi birth certificate, notarized in 1987, which provided his birthdate as January 23, 1917.

7   Bob Holbrook, *Complete Baseball*, Fall 1950, 78.

8   Jim Auchmutey, "He's Our Jackie," *Atlanta Constitution*, June 22, 1997.

9   Michael Madden, *Boston Globe*, May 28, 1993.

10 Madden.

11 Larry Lester points out that the National Baseball Hall of Fame no longer uses the words "Organized Baseball" as it implies that the Negro Leagues were "unorganized."

12 Several articles on the subject are gathered in Bill Nowlin, ed., *Pumpsie and Progress: The Red Sox, Race, and Redemption* (Burlington, Massachusetts: Rounder Books, 2010).

13 Jim Auchmutey, *Atlanta Constitution*.

14 Marazzi, *Sports Collectors Digest*.

15 *Boston Globe*, July 22, 1979.

16 *Boston Globe*, July 22, 1979.

17 Bob Dolgan, *Cleveland Plain Dealer*, September 9, 1997.

18 Jethroe to Gerry Callahan, *Boston Herald*, May 28, 1993.

19 David Faulkner, *Great Time Coming: The Life of Jackie Robinson from Baseball to Birmingham* (New York: Simon and Schuster, 1995), 102.

20 Marazzi, *Sports Collectors Digest*. Jessup's name was given as Jim Jessup in the article, but his actual name was Joseph Gentry Jessup.

21 Dolgan.

22 Roberto Gonzalez Echeverria, *The Pride of Havana: A History of Cuban Baseball* (New York: Oxford University Press, 1999), 54, 68. See also Jorge S. Figueredo, *Cuban Baseball: A Statistical History, 1878-1961* (Jefferson, North Carolina: McFarland, 2003), 296.

23 Jorge S. Figueredo, *Who's Who in Cuban Baseball 1878-1961* (Jefferson, North Carolina: McFarland, 2003), 379. The strikeout total is reported in Figueredo's *Cuban Baseball: A Statistical History, 1878-1961* on page 308.

24 Auchmutey.

25 The sum was reported by Dolgan. *The Biographical Encyclopedia of the Negro Leagues* says that Jethroe took a paycut, from $700 a month with the Buckeyes to $400 a month with the Montreal Royals. Thompson scouted Jethroe on the recommendation of Pittsburgh sportswriter Wendell Smith, per Ken Smith of the *New York Daily Mirror*, December 1, 1949. SABR's Scouts Committee credits both Thompson and Branch Rickey Jr. for the signing.

26 Dolgan.

27 *New York Daily Mirror*, December 1, 1949.

28 Dolgan. The story was also told by Arthur Daley in the *New York Times*, September 2, 1949. Years later Richards said it was not true. *Buffalo Courier-Express*, July 13, 1965.

29 Auchmutey.

30 *New York Times*, September 2, 1949.

31 *New York Amsterdam News*, April 9, 1949, 27.

32 *New York Times*, October 2, 1949.

33 *New York World-Telegram*, October 2, 1949. On June 2, the Buckeyes had denied that Jethroe had been sold to the Boston Red Sox. See Associated Press story June 2, 1949. The *New York Times* later reported (November 10, 1950) that the Braves had, perhaps counting the value of the players, paid $137,500 for Jethroe.

34 Mabe "Doc" Kountze, *Fifty Sports Years Along Memory Lane* (Medford, Massachusetts: Mystic Valley Press, 1979), 24. Quinn's ballpark hosted a July 6, 1938 game between the Boston Royal Colored Giants and the traveling House of David team.

35 *Boston Herald*, October 2, 1949.

36 *Washington Times Herald*, October 6, 1949.

37 See Billy Southworth's remarks as in Associated Press dispatches on October 6, 1949.

38 *New York World-Telegram*, April 8, 1950.

39 Gus Steiger, *New York Daily Mirror*, October 4, 1949.

40 Dan Daniel, *The Sporting News*, March 29, 1950.

41 Marvin Pave, *Boston Globe*, August 29, 1997.

42 Bob Ajemian, *The Sporting News*, March 29, 1950.

43 Harold Kaese, *The Sporting News*, March 29, 1950.

44 Dan Daniel, *New York World-Telegram*, April 1, 1950.

45 Bob Holbrook, *Complete Baseball*, Fall 1950, 78.

46 Author interview on January 1, 2015 with John Delmore, recounting a personal memory.

47 *Boston Chronicle*, April 8, 1950.

48 *Boston Chronicle*, April 8, 1950.

49 Larry Whiteside, *Boston Globe*, July 22, 1979.

50 "It wasn't all bad," he told Whiteside. "We actually made money on expenses staying in private homes."

51 Pave, *Boston Globe*, August 29, 1997.

52 Whiteside, *Boston Globe*, July 22, 1979.

53 Campbell Gibson and Kay Jung, "Historical Census Statistics On Population Totals By Race, 1790 to 1990, and By Hispanic Origin, 1970 to 1990, For Large Cities And Other Urban Places In The United States," U.S. Census Bureau Population Division Working Paper No. 76, February 2005, Table 22.

54 *Boston Globe*, October 12, 1949.

55 Dave Egan, "Day of Reckoning Due for Baseball," *Boston Record*, August 10, 1945.

56 *Boston Chronicle*, October 15, 1949.

57 *Boston Post*, April 15, 1950.

58 *Boston Post*, April 16, 1950.

59 Will Cloney, *Boston Herald*, April 16, 1950.

60 *Boston Globe*, April 16, 1950.

61 *Boston Globe*, April 17, 1950.

62 *Boston Globe*, April 21, 1950.

63 *Boston Herald*, April 25, 1950.

64 *Boston Traveler*, May 26, 1950.

65 Marazzi, *Sports Collectors Digest*, 111.

66 *Boston Globe*, July 9, 1950.

67 Whiteside. *Boston Globe*, July 22, 1979.

68 *Boston Globe*, July 9, 1950.

69 Auchmutey, *Atlanta Constitution*, June 22, 1997.

70 *Sentinel*, April 13, 1953.

71 Mort Bloomberg email to author, August 19, 2014.

72 *Boston Traveler*, July 10, 1950.

73 Author interview with Jack Barnes, January 1, 2015.

74 Pave, *Boston Globe*, August 29, 1997.

75 Author interview with Frank McNulty, January 15, 2015. Longtime fan John Delmore said, "Braves fans were very loyal, to a T. We were the second-class citizens in Boston, so to speak. We loved the Braves. Even in the bad times, we hung in there with them. The Red Sox and Yawkey were the spoiled millionaires and we were the lunch-pail crew. All I have is positive memories of Sam Jethroe. I don't remember anybody, anybody at all, ever, bringing up race with Sam Jethroe. None! Robinson took the brunt of it when he broke in. I think by the time Sammy got there with the Braves, a lot of that stuff had dwindled. I'm not sure whether he might have taken some heat in some other ballparks, but he never got any bad vibes in Boston, I can tell you that. If anything, it was just the opposite. They loved the guy." Author interview with John Delmore, January 1, 2015. Delmore added, "By that time, the issue had quieted down. I remember when Jackie Robinson played his first game. It was against the Braves. I was in the eighth grade at St. Theresa's in Somerville. We had a P.A. system in all the classrooms and the head nun brought a radio to school that day. She put the Braves-Dodgers game on because Jackie Robinson was playing his first game, breaking the color barrier." Other longtime Braves fans who concurred with the welcome reception Jethroe had in Boston are Mort Bloomberg (emails to author on January 12 & 13, 2015) and John Quinn (son of Braves GM Bob Quinn) in an interview with the author on January 20, 2015.

76 Author interview with Bill Monbouquette, August 24, 2014.

77 *Boston Traveler*, September 14, 1950.

78 *Boston Chronicle*, September 23, 1950.

79 *Boston Post*, September 16, 1950.

80 Bob Holbrook, *Complete Baseball*, Fall 1950, 78. It may be worthy of note that both rookies of the year in 1950 played for Boston teams; Walt Dropo of the Red Sox was the American League Rookie of the Year. As to the "I just runs" quotation, Bob Brady suggests that "it seems inconsistent with other direct quotes used in [Holbrook's] piece where Jethroe's use of the language does not reflect a 'Stepin Fetchit' dialect." E-mail from Bob Brady, December 16, 2014.

81 Howard Bryant, *Shut Out: A Story of Race and Baseball in Boston* (New York: Routledge, 2002), 33, citing the personal papers of Ann Muchnick. Bryant paints a far-from-benign portrait of Eddie Collins on the subject of race. See pages 28-30 and 43-44.

82   *Boston Record*, April 9, 1952.

83   Author interview with Joe Giuliotti on September 30, 2014. Giuliotti's career started in the 1970s, so this was not something he had personally witnessed.

84   Larry Whiteside, *Boston Globe*, July 22, 1979. Ralph Evans came to know Jethroe through Boston Braves Historical Association gatherings and has had him as a guest in his home. "I do know from talking to Sam that when he arrived at the field, he was talking with Billy Sullivan and Billy Sullivan said, 'I understand that you don't like the nickname Sambo' and he said, 'No, I don't,' and Billy Sullivan said, 'Okay, we won't call you Sambo' – and they made sure that that wasn't done. I don't remember anybody saying anything bad about him." Author interview with Ralph Evans, January 15, 2015. The one negative memory Jethroe had about his time in Boston related to the astigmatism he developed, which led to some embarrassing fielding incidents before he got his eyeglasses. There were jokes about his eyesight, but they were not one which bore an additional burden of race.

85   Auchmutey.

86   *Boston Braves Historical Association Newsletter*, Summer/Fall 1995.

87   Scott Kauffman, "Life among the cinders," *USA Today*, February 22-28, 1997. The old pension rule had been five years, but an agreement reached on February 25, 1969 reduced the pension time to four years. (See *Washington Post*, February 26, 1969.) This still left Jethroe and some others short of the four years required.

88   *Atlanta Journal*, June 22, 1997.

89   Murray Chass, *New York Times*, January 20, 1997.

90   *New York Daily News*, January 20, 1997.

91   *Cleveland Plain Dealer*, July 17, 1995.

92   *Atlanta Journal*, June 22, 1997.

93   Nolan, *Boston Globe*, June 21, 2001.

George Provens

by Richard Bogovich

The title of a Shakespearean play, *All's Well That Ends Well,* seems to fit the life of George Provens. In the midst of some tough years in his 20s fell a genuine bright spot, a brief stint with the Cleveland Buckeyes of the Negro American League in 1945. Though that achievement didn't turn his life in a different direction immediately, his longtime love of baseball eventually took hold so strongly that he was named to two local sporting halls of fame in Ohio.

George Edward Provens was born to Jessie and Herbert Provens on June 1, 1918, in Lexington, Kentucky.[1] However, on Herbert's military registration card a few months later, his address was about 260 miles to the south, in downtown Chattanooga, Tennessee. Despite his urban residence, his job was listed as a self-employed farmer. Perhaps Herbert was transitioning from farm work to a promising job in a big city but wasn't settled in enough for his wife and child to join him there.

The Provens family may not have been counted in the 1920 census anywhere. In early 1924 Herbert was presumably the H.L. Provens living in or near Midvale,

Ohio, a village close to the much larger communities of New Philadelphia and Dover. He was an officer of a newly formed African Masonic lodge.[2]

In the summer of 1925, if not earlier, Herbert likely worked for the Robinson Clay Products Co. at its Royal plant on Midvale's outskirts. Near that plant was the Royal Settlement neighborhood. Herbert lived there, next to a two-story building that included residential space above a combined grocery store/barbershop/poolroom. It's unknown whether his wife and son were living with him when that neighboring building was decimated by fire. The first-floor business's new owner accused Provens of starting the blaze and struck him on the head with a pipe. Though Provens was jailed overnight before his release, it was the attacker who was fined $10 and court costs.[3]

If George Provens was also living at the Royal Settlement that summer, he had opportunities to watch at least two local Black baseball teams nearby. The one that received the most coverage in 1925 was called the Royal Hornets, "comprised of colored athletes residing at the Royal plant, near Midvale," according to a local newspaper.[4] A couple of months later, that paper paid a little attention to a game between a team of White Robinson employees and "a colored team of the same company." The latter lost, 4-1.[5] No Black team drawn from the Robinson workforce received much coverage in subsequent years.[6]

The first mention of George Provens in a local newspaper may have been at the end of 1926. He was listed among students attending the Royal school who had perfect attendance.[7] He was about 8½ years old. One newspaper noted that the school was specifically "maintained for the colored children at the Royal sewer pipe factory."[8]

In the 1930 census, George remained the family's only child. Herbert Provens, who'd been ordained as a deacon of Midvale's Missionary Baptist Church in 1928,[9] continued as a Robinson employee until his death in July 1933 from tuberculosis. He'd been suffering for 19 months. The family was still living at the Royal Settlement.[10] In the spring of 1934, George was listed on the program for an eighth-grade graduation event in Midvale, reciting or singing a piece titled, "The Blue and the Gray," but it wasn't clear if he was one of the graduates.[11]

George Provens was presumably the local athlete with that surname who started showing up in 1937 newspapers as a basketball player. A church league included an African Methodist Episcopal team with a forward named Provens.

Members of Canton Rockets Team

L to R: Billy Goodman, George Provens, and Jim Smith with the 1951 Canton Rockets.

Newark Advocate, August 24, 1951.

George was 18½ at that time. In possibly his first game, his team was clobbered by a Moravian squad by a score of 70-14, with the victors setting a league record for most points.[12]

In the middle of the following year, Provens was mentioned in newspapers for a very different reason: his wedding. He and Willie Belle Houston were married in July 1938 in Wellsburg, West Virginia (about 50 miles from Midvale). She graduated from New Philadelphia's high school and he from Midvale's. Like his late father, he worked for Robinson Clay Products.[13]

The newlyweds lived in or near New Philadelphia into 1945, though in 1940 he reportedly began traveling about 30 miles to play in the City Class-A Baseball League in Canton, primarily as a second baseman and pitcher.[14] Box scores of league games during the early 1940s were quite rare, and thus his sole early baseball team to receive much newspaper coverage may have been the 1939 Dover Lions. For example, on June 11 the Lions had a pitcher named Provens against the Midvale Coals. The latter club featured Frank Baumholtz, a National League outfielder from 1947 to 1957. Dover lost, 7-1.[15]

During the first few months of 1940, the future Cleveland Buckeye was probably amateur boxer "George Proven [sic], 160 [pounds], a tough looking Dennison colored boy." Dennison is five miles from Midvale.[16] In October, Provens completed a military service card identifying the former Willie Houston as his wife and his employer still as Robinson Clay Products. In early 1941 he was among numerous local Selective Service registrants who were required by New Philadelphia's draft board to complete a questionnaire quickly for possible enlistment.[17]

Before June 1941, Black employees of Provens' workplace formed a softball team sponsored by Local 490 of the United Brick & Clay Workers.[18] It's not known whether Provens was among those ballplayers, but very soon he was on Midvale's Dew Drop Inn softball team. He homered twice in their first game in June.[19]

In early 1942, significant cracks in Provens' marriage were publicized when Willie Belle, pregnant with their third child, filed for divorce. She said he was cruel, "threatened to kill her with a shotgun," and squandered their money on gambling and alcohol. Five days later she asked that the suit be dismissed, a request that was granted.[20]

Toward the end of 1943, Provens had to engage with the legal system on another serious matter. On December 18, he faced "a charge of cutting with intent to wound." The victim was his friend Lee Fulp, who died from knife wounds after the two men fought outside the Dew Drop Inn (at the Royal Settlement) on December 3. The two reportedly argued over a woman who left that tavern with Fulp. Provens, his wife, and the Fulps had been close friends dating back to at least 1938, when they belonged to a group that vacationed at the Ohio State Fair.[21]

Within two months of the incident, Provens was found guilty of manslaughter, after he admitted on the stand that he'd cut his friend while trying to disarm him. On February 21, 1944, Provens was placed on probation for five years. He was a father of four at that point.[22]

Later that year Provens was thriving as an infielder and pitcher on the City Merchants team in Canton's City Class-A Baseball League, and on July 16 he was scheduled to try out with the Cleveland Buckeyes of the NAL. He'd recently had a similar opportunity with the Homestead Grays of the Negro National League.[23] The Buckeyes visited the Memphis Red Sox for a doubleheader on July 16, but dominating subsequent coverage was the tragic death early that morning of Memphis pitcher Porter Moss.[24]

If Provens' tryout with Cleveland did occur, apparently nothing much resulted.[25] Regardless, by mid-August he and teammate Marion Motley were both named third basemen on a league all-star team to play in a benefit for the Philomatheon Society for the Blind. Provens was chosen to bat leadoff.[26] In 1968 Motley, a star running back for the NFL's Cleveland Browns, was inducted into the Pro Football Hall of Fame.

In May of 1945, Provens traveled to Cleveland (from his residence at the time, in Dover) for a pre-induction examination by the military, but apparently he wasn't called up as a result.[27] Instead, on July 14 it was announced that Provens had earned another tryout with the Buckeyes. Two other players on the Merchants would join him, fellow pitcher Phelbert Lawson and catcher Tommy Harris.[28]

The trio worked out with the Buckeyes on July 16 and then rejoined the Merchants the following day for a Class-A game. The three teammates were then scheduled to reunite with the Buckeyes on July 22 in Cleveland.[29] Provens' first game with the Buckeyes may have been on July 27, at third base against Brooklyn's longtime semipro team, the Bushwicks. Box scores in two papers showed him as hitless in two at-bats, though with a run scored. Both accounts said he struck out to end the game (one specifying on a full count).[30]

About three decades later, Provens recalled getting two hits against the Bushwicks as his only real highlights during his brief time with Cleveland. The game on July 27 was previewed as the Buckeyes' first trip to the Bushwicks' ballpark that season, and there's no sign of a rematch shortly thereafter.[31] Of course, he may have been incorrect or was thinking of the wrong opponent. On the other hand, the batters listed just before and after him each had two hits, so it's conceivable the box scores could have assigned two hits by him to a teammate.

As of this writing, the Seamheads.com database has stats for two games in which Provens was a Buckeye, both against NNL teams. The first was on July 30 vs. the New York Cubans (at the same ballyard used by the Bushwicks) and the other was on August 1 vs. the Baltimore Elite Giants in Harrisburg, Pennsylvania. He entered the game against the Cubans as a pinch-hitter in the ninth inning and singled, for his only verified hit as a Buckeye. The opposing pitcher was Luis Tiant the elder. His teammates couldn't drive him home and soon lost, 4-3. The other game was a 5-5 tie in which Provens started at third base. He went hitless in four at-bats and recorded one assist on defense.[32]

On or before August 7, Provens was back with the Merchants in Canton's Class-A League, apparently for good. On August 7 he hurled a two-hitter to improve his team's record to 13 wins out of 14 played.[33] Within two weeks, they were crowned the champions.[34]

At some point between May and mid-August, the Provens family moved from Dover to Canton.[35] Before the year was out, George received a less than warm welcome at 3:15 one morning at Beanie's Chicken Shack, when he was hit over the head with a bottle. He was treated at Mercy Hospital for a scalp laceration, but the police didn't identify any suspect in the incident.[36]

Provens had presumably recovered completely by the end of May, by which point he had reteamed with Lawson and Marion Motley in the Class-A Baseball League. That 1946 season they were on a team representing the Wyatt Apex Athletic Club. In late August, Provens and Lawson were named to one of the league's two all-star teams.[37]

Tragically, that offseason Provens was involved in a far more serious incident than at Beanie's Chicken Shack. At the beginning of 1947, Provens and a man named Charles Wilson were involved in an argument at 1:30 one morning, and it escalated. Two newspaper articles about the brawl were short on details, but Wilson apparently shot Provens twice, with a .32 caliber gun, once in the groin and once in the left leg. Wilson had a stab wound to his back. Wilson pleaded guilty to a disorderly-conduct charge and was fined $50 plus costs. Provens, still on probation for Lee Fulp's death, was sentenced to "an indefinite term at Mansfield Reformatory."[38]

By the end of July, Provens was batting leadoff and playing shortstop for the Ohio State Reformatory All-Stars. He continued in 1948 and into mid-September of 1949, if not later.[39] He was back home by the time of the 1950 census, which was conducted on his street on April 19. His job was entered as a "transfer man" in the brick industry. He and his wife, Willie, had six children, five of whom were girls.

At the start of the next month, Provens was back in the City Class-A Baseball League. His new club was the Rockets, sponsored by Dave Towell Inc. Provens finished the season tied for the eighth highest batting average, at .314. On August 15 the Rockets lost the postseason game that determined which Canton team would advance to the Ohio District American Baseball Congress tournament later that week.[40]

In 1951 Provens became a Little League coach, but he continued to play the game with adult friends.[41] That year he was with the Canton Rockets, an independent traveling team that was still considered Class A. In August a

newspaper almost 90 miles away printed a large photo of Provens with two teammates, shortstop Billy Goodman and catcher Jim Smith.[42]

Though Provens played in Canton's Class-A Baseball League in 1952, the 1951 traveling club might've given him his final huge thrill as a player. On September 9, 1951, the Rockets ended their season in Alliance, Ohio (about 20 miles from Canton), with a record reported as 38-7. Provens became the big star by slugging a grand slam.[43] In 1976 Provens reminisced about his final plate appearance in his final baseball game, against an Alliance team. He could've been thinking about the above 1951 game even though some details didn't match (possibly due to an imperfect memory and/or sportswriter error). "I hit a grand slam and drove the ball into the basement window of a house beyond left field," Provens recalled. "They asked me if I wanted to play in the second game that day and I said nope."[44]

As mentioned, Provens played a final year in Canton's Class-A League in 1952, but his team's awful record could've made that entire season forgettable. He continued with the Rockets, though, as a member of Canton's league their fortunes totally reversed with an abysmal last-place finish. The club's batting average was just .179, despite Goodman hitting .344.[45]

For the remainder of the 1950s, Provens' name appeared in local newspapers mainly because he'd become an avid fisherman, whose catches would periodically be reported. For example, "George Provens and son" were among several anglers who reached the local limit for bluegills on a particular day during the summer of 1954.[46] But his love for baseball never subsided, and from 1962 to 1965 he managed teams in Canton's Class-A circuit. As a result, there was speculation in 1968 that he was a candidate to become that league's next commissioner. His dedication was proven when he took "the unenviable job of going door to door to seek money so that players from Canton's southeast sector could have a sponsor in the league."[47]

As a result, it probably came as little surprise when he was elected the next year to the Greater Canton Baseball Old-Timers Association Hall of Fame (later renamed the Greater Stark County Baseball Association Hall of Fame). The keynote speaker during the induction banquet was Bob Feller. In 1976 Provens was also voted into the Canton Negro Old-Timers Athletic Association Hall of Fame, along with his friend Motley.[48]

Provens enlivened the Greater Stark County group's winter banquet in early 1978, when one attendee introduced New York Yankees catcher Thurman Munson to everyone sitting at Provens' table. Munson, a Canton native, probably knew Provens when the latter was managing in the Class-A Baseball League, but nobody could have blamed Munson if he didn't recognize Provens about 15 years later. "Of course, you remember this man, Thurm," said local dentist Irv Felder, gesturing at Provens. But Munson was unsure and simply blinked momentarily. Provens, perceiving Munson's uncertainty, extended his hand and bellowed, "Sure you know me, Thurm. I'm Reggie Jackson!" Everyone at the table, including Munson, reportedly roared with laughter.[49]

George Provens died on May 7, 1982, "after becoming ill at home." His obituary noted that he was a Ford Motor Company retiree and had owned the Provens Family Foods grocery store on Sherrick Road Southeast. In addition to his wife and mother, he was survived by six daughters, three sons, and 18 grandchildren.[50] Another Canton sporting legend, Hymie Williams, who was a columnist for the *Cleveland Plain Dealer* for over 50 years and a familiar voice on radio, said in tribute, "Canton sports, and amateur baseball in particular, lost a good friend when George Provens died at 63."[51]

SOURCES

Except where noted otherwise, information about Provens' personal life is from Ancestry.com (Library Edition) and FamilySearch.org.

NOTES

1   See Kentucky, Vital Record Indexes, 1911-1999, accessible via FamilySearch. org. It specified only the county, not the city. That detail, plus his middle name, were specified on the military registration card he completed in 1940.

2   "African Masonic Lodge in Midvale," *New Philadelphia* (Ohio) *Daily Times*, March 31, 1924: 14. The first officer listed was named Emmet Harris. See Note 4.

3   "Blaze Levels Home; One Is Hurt, 2 Jailed," *New Philadelphia Daily Times*, August 28, 1925: 1. "No Developments in Mystery Blaze," *New Philadelphia Daily Times*, August 29, 1925: 8. According to Herbert Provens' Certificate of Death less than a decade later, he was an employee of the Robinson Clay Products Co. at that time and his family was living at the Royal Settlement.

4   "Colored Baseball Team Seeks Games," *New Philadelphia Daily Times*, April 2, 1925: 8. The manager of the Royal Hornets was E.H. Harris, who could have been the Emmet Harris mentioned in Note 2.

5   "Robinson Clay Co. Teams Play," *New Philadelphia Daily Times*, June 13, 1925: 7.

6   For a rare example of the Royal Hornets making it into a local paper in later years, see "Twin City Club Is Defeated by Royal Hornets," *New Philadelphia Daily Times*, June 16, 1930.

7   "Society," *New Philadelphia Daily Times*, December 28, 1926: 4. He was among 15 students listed. At the end, it was implied that the school had just one teacher (named Maude Peterson).

8   "Goshen Township School Teachers' List Announced," *New Philadelphia Daily Times*, June 2, 1932: 3. This article also implied that the school only had one teacher, the aforementioned Miss Peterson.

9   Irving A. Williamson, "Dayton, Ohio," *Chicago Defender*, March 10, 1928: A9. See the section denoted as having Midvale news.

10   "Tuberculosis Proves Fatal, *New Philadelphia Daily Times,* July 22, 1933: 4. This short article mentioned that, in addition to his wife and son, Herbert Provens was survived by a brother and sister, both Alabama residents. It was his Certificate of Death that noted his employment with Robinson Clay Products. This document also named his parents.

11   "Commencement for Township Schools," *New Philadelphia Daily Times*, May 1, 1934: 5. The "exercises" honored 58 students from multiple schools of Goshen Township.

12   "Gnaden Moravians Score 70 Points in League Tilt," *New Philadelphia Daily Times*, January 20, 1937: 5. Provens was also listed in scoring summaries on February 2 and 9, which saw his team improve somewhat on both defense and offense.

13   "Houston-Prouens [*sic*] Wedding," *New Philadelphia Daily Times*, December 13, 1938: 5; "Dover News," *Cleveland Call and Post*, December 15, 1938: 9. The former reported the date as July 22 but the latter said July 21. A database of West Virginia Marriages, 1780-1970 accessible via the FamilySearch.org genealogical website only reported the year. For no obvious reason, this milestone didn't become public until almost five months after it occurred. The New Philadelphia paper's article concluded that the newlyweds would "reside with Mr. and Mrs. Henry Richards of this city."

14   "Gal All-Star Rosters Set," *Canton* (Ohio) *Repository*, August 18, 1979: 10. The use of "Gal" in the headline referred to Provens' selection as one team's honorary captain for a girls' all-star softball game.

15   "Coals Spank Dover Lions," *New Philadelphia Daily Times*, June 12, 1939: 5. Baumholtz, then attending Ohio University, was the only player mentioned in that paper's brief the day before the game; see "Midvale Coals to meet Dover," *New Philadelphia Daily Times*, June 10, 1939: 5. Neither article mentioned the Dover Lions' race. The Lions had a center fielder named Provens in the box score that accompanied "Sherrodsville Trails Taverns," *New Philadelphia Daily Times*, September 12, 1939: 7.

16   "Small Crowd Sees Good Amateur Program," *Coshocton* (Ohio) *Tribune*, March 14, 1940: 11. See also the mention of "Georgie Provens, Uhrichsville negro boy" in "11 Battles Stir Fans at Legion Boxing Tourney," *New Philadelphia Daily Times*, January 25, 1940: 9. Uhrichsville is within 10 miles of New Philadelphia.

17   "Here Is Latest Draftees' List," *New Philadelphia Daily Times*, January 22, 1941: 2.

18   "Colored Softball Team Seeks Games, *New Philadelphia Daily Times*, May 28, 1941: 10. Many of the players had been with a team called the Evans Ramblers the prior season.

19   "Dew Drop Inns Win First Tilt," *New Philadelphia Daily Times*, June 6, 1941: 7. See also "Dew Drops Defeat Xville Eagles 3-2," *New Philadelphia Daily Times*, August 26, 1941: 5. In the latter game, his two-run homer in the first inning proved to be crucial.

20   "Grant 4 Divorces; New Actions Filed," *New Philadelphia Daily Times*, January 15, 1942: 1; "Strasburg Man Granted Divorce," *New Philadelphia Daily Times*, January 20, 1942: 1.

21   Negro Dies of Knife Wounds," *New Philadelphia Daily Times*, December 18, 1943: 1; Johnnie M. Sherrell, "Midvale, Ohio," *Chicago Defender*, September 17, 1938: 23.

22   "Found Guilty in Fatal Fight," *New Philadelphia Daily Times*, February 5, 1944: 1; "Negro Slayer on Probation," *New Philadelphia Daily Times*, February 21, 1944: 1.

23   "Buckeyes to Give Provens a Tryout," *New Philadelphia Daily Times*, June 22, 1944: 9. At that time, he was leading Canton's league with five straight pitching wins, including a two-hitter. For an example of his early success as a hitter that season, a game in which he collected three hits, see "League Tilts," *Canton Repository*, May 31, 1944: 17.

24   "Ball Player's Killer Held on Bond; Pleads Not Guilty," *Atlanta Daily World*, July 21, 1944: 5.

25   Provens wasn't in the lone box score printed with "Cleveland, Memphis Split Doubleheader," *Pittsburgh Courier*, July 22, 1944: 12. Over the following week, the Buckeyes were scheduled to play in New Orleans, Little Rock, and Oklahoma, but subsequent coverage was meager. He also wasn't among the 13 Buckeyes in a later box score, printed with "Hand Monarchs Beating," *Kansas City Times*, July 25, 1944: 7. He was back in Canton no later than August 1; see "League Tilts," *Canton Repository*, August 2, 1944: 8.

26   "21 Players Named on All-Star Team for Sunday Benefit Game," *Canton Repository*, August 19, 1944: 6; "League Champions Turn Back All-Star Teams In Benefit Bill, *Canton Repository*, August 21, 1944: 8. For information about the the Philomatheon Society for the Blind, see https://philomatheon.com/.

27   "Colored Selectees up for Draft Exams," *New Philadelphia Daily Times*, May 9, 1945: 8. It so happened that Germany had surrendered unconditionally to the Allies the day before, on what's widely known as VE (Victory in Europe) Day.

28   "Sandlot Games," *Canton Repository*, July 14, 1945: 6. This news item incorrectly said the Buckeyes were in the NNL rather than the NAL.

29   "Sandlot Games," *Canton Repository,* July 18, 1945: 10.

30   Wally Croatman, "Veteran Meola Saves Dexters in Hectic Ninth," *Long Island Daily Press* (Jamaica, New York), July 28, 1945: 12; "Bushwicks Notch 13th Straight, Set for 2 Foes," *Brooklyn Daily Eagle*, July 28, 1945: 6. Croatman called the new Buckeyes infielder "Gil" Provens. The two box scores agreed on much, but there were exceptions. For one, the former credited Sam Jethroe with a putout while the latter didn't. Also, they counted the at-bats of the Buckeyes' two catchers differently.

31   Dave Kaminski, "Four Picked to Enter Negro Hall of Fame," *Canton Repository*, April 11, 1976: 54; "Talent-Clogged Buckeyes to Test Dexters Tonight," *Brooklyn Daily Eagle*, July 27, 1945: 11.

32   For complete box scores of both games, see https://www.retrosheet.org/NegroLeagues/boxesetc/P/Pprovu101.htm.

33   "Sandlot Games," *Canton Repository*, August 8, 1945: 10.

34   "Sandlot Games," *Canton Repository*, August 18, 1945: 6.

35   When one of their daughters was born in August, the family's address was identified as 1121 Gary Place Southeast in Canton, where they lived at least through 1962. "Birth Announcements," *Canton Repository*, August 10, 1945: 25. Members of the Provens family were mentioned at that address off and on for years, including when George was fined $5 and costs for his car's defective emergency brake as listed in "Driver Handed Jail Term," *Canton Repository*, January 29, 1963: 7.

36   "Police News in Brief," *Canton Repository*, November 3, 1945: 7.

37   "City Sandlot Leagues," *Canton Repository*, June 5, 1946: 17; "City's All-Star Nines Clash Today," *Canton Repository*, August 28, 1946: 19. Motley might not have been an All-Star simply because he was preparing to make his pro football debut with the Cleveland Browns on September 6 of that year; see https://www.pro-football-reference.com/players/M/MotlMa00/gamelog/1946/.

38   "Two Suffer Wounds in Cherry SE Affray," *Canton Repository*, January 6, 1947: 3; "Canton Man Receives Sentence in New Phila.," *Canton Repository*, January 14, 1947: 8.

39   "OSR All-Stars Top Sandusky, *Mansfield* (Ohio) *News Journal,* July 27, 1947: 24; "OSR Squad Wins, 12 to 11 [*sic*; actually 12-10]," *Mansfield News Journal*, May 30, 1948: 14; "OSR Baseballers Bop Celeryville," *Mansfield News Journal*, September 18, 1949: 18. In the box score for the 1948 example, Provens was the pitcher.

40   "Negro Baseball Talent Returns to Local Scene," *Canton Repository*, May 2, 1950: 47; Chuck Koelble, "On the City Sandlots," *Canton Repository*, August 13, 1950: 49; "Fairmount Tops Towell to Enter Meet," *Canton Repository*, August 16, 1950: 15.

41   "Little League Aspirants to Begin Trials Saturday," *Canton Repository*, April 20, 1951: 31. See Note 14, the 1979 article in which Provens was also called a local pioneer of the Pony League.

42   "Rockets Travel," *Canton Repository*, June 6, 1951: 18; "Members of Canton Rockets Team," *Newark* (Ohio) *Advocate*, August 24, 1951: 15. Beneath the photo it was stated that Provens was "a veteran of three seasons with the Cleveland Buckeyes" but given his years in the reformatory, that seems impossible, even if his 1944 tryout was counted as a stint with the Buckeyes.

43   "Rockets Blast Alliance," *Canton Repository*, September 10, 1951: 20.

44   See Kaminski, the first citation in Note 31. Provens called the team the Merchants rather than the Rockets, but there's a good chance many of the Rockets had played on the Merchants with Provens once upon a time.

45   "Class A Deadlock Continues," *Canton Repository*, July 30, 1952: 13, 15; Germane Swanson, "On the City Sandlots," *Canton Repository*, August 3, 1952: 50. Based on coverage in that paper over the following week, the box score printed on July 30 documented Provens' final Class-A game. A few days earlier, but not quite at the end of the Rockets' 1952 season, they played the same Alliance club as on September 9, 1951; see "Rockets Play Today," *Canton Repository*, July 27, 1952: 45. That could explain why Provens mixed up 1951 and 1952 during his reminiscing in 1976.

46   Monte Cross, "Rod and Gun," *Canton Repository*, August 22, 1954: 58.

47   Art Schrock, "Provens Could Be Next Class A Commissioner," *Canton Repository*, May 12, 1968: 53.

48   Ken Sherer, "Feller Raps Players, Owners," *Canton Repository*, February 21, 1969: 57; "Induct Edwards Sunday," *Massillon* (Ohio) *Evening Independent,* April 24, 1976: 13. Based on the latter article, the Greater Canton Baseball Old-Timers Association Hall of Fame had been renamed the Greater Stark County Baseball Association Hall of Fame before mid-1976.

49   Hymie Williams, "Lefties Lead Claymont, " Cleveland *Sunday Plain Dealer,* January 29, 1978: section 3, 12.

50   "Deaths and Funerals," *Canton Repository*, May 8, 1982: 15.

51   Hymie Williams, "Stark County Amateurs Tee Off Tomorrow," *Cleveland Plain Dealer*, May 15, 1982: 7-C; Todd Porter, "Voice of Canton Sports, Hymie Williams, Dies," *Canton Repository*, January 9, 2002: C-1.

Quincy Trouppe

By Jay Hurd

Quincy Trouppe's passion for baseball led to a long career as player, manager, and scout. An exceptional catcher and switch-hitter, "Big Train" played on Negro League teams including the St. Louis Stars, Kansas City Monarchs, and the Homestead Grays. He also played for and managed the Cleveland Buckeyes, twice leading them to the Negro American League championship; the Buckeyes won the Negro World Series in 1945.

Trouppe competed at a high level across the Americas. His career took him to Mexico, Puerto Rico, Venezuela, Canada, Cuba, and the Dominican Republic. He was also known as "El Roro" ("The Baby") to his Mexican fans, echoing another U.S. nickname, "Baby Face."

At the age of 39, Trouppe signed with the Cleveland Indians, achieving his dream of playing in the major leagues, albeit briefly. Bob Feller of the Indians recalled that "Quincy just came in a little too late because he couldn't get in during his prime. It's a shame because there's no doubt in my mind he would have been a very good major leaguer if blacks had been allowed into the big leagues when he was in his prime."[1] Trouppe later devoted himself to baseball, his teammates, and his fans in yet another role: historian/philosopher, as reflected in his book *20 Years Too Soon: Prelude to Major-League Baseball.*

Quincy Thomas Troupe was born in Dublin, Georgia, on December 25, 1912. When he was born, his family name was spelled with just one 'p'. For the purposes of this story, the spelling Troupe will be used until reference to 1946, when Quincy changed it to Trouppe, as he related in his book.

Troupe's family background lay in slavery. The probate inventory of the estate of George Troup (1780-1856), 32nd governor of the state of Georgia, includes the names of more than 300 slaves. One of them was 21-year-old Obediah Troup, whose identity reflected the common practice of slaves assuming their owner's surname, or being actual offspring. Obediah Troup married Katie (or Caty) and together they had eight children.[2] One was Quincy's father, Charles, who was born in 1867 – four years after the Emancipation Proclamation.

At least as late as 1900, census records still show the family name without an 'e' at the end. Charles and his wife Mary (née Williams) were married in 1891. Quincy was the youngest of their 10 children.

His father, as his grandfather had been, was a sharecropper in a racially divided area. Raised in a loving home, Quincy had for years been unaware of the full nature of tensions and conflicts between Blacks and Whites. However, around the age of 10, a particularly difficult situation involving his brother, Albert ("Buddy"), and the family's White overseer awoke Quincy to the reality of racism. After this incident, Charles and Mary decided it best to leave Dublin for St. Louis, Missouri, where a family friend and an employment opportunity awaited. First, Charles and his sons Albert and George traveled to St. Louis. Within a few months, while the older children moved to northern states (Connecticut and New Jersey), Mary and five children, including young Quincy, moved to St. Louis. This all happened between 1921 and 1922.

In Missouri, Charles had rented a small house near the levee in South St. Louis. Charles promised to find a more comfortable space as soon as he and Albert earned enough through their work at the American Car and Foundry Company (ACF) in St. Charles, Missouri. Their rented

Quincy Trouppe.

home had no running water. Quincy recalled that he and his brothers needed to climb a fence, using a makeshift ladder, to retrieve buckets of water. In time, Charles secured a comfortable three-room home in the Compton Hill area of central St. Louis.

Although the family enjoyed comforts not available in rural Georgia, the all-too-familiar racial divide posed challenges. Later in life, Troupe attributed his abilities, interests, and sensitivities to life experiences – positive and negative. He loved the city and took advantage of its resources and opportunities. To assist his family financially, he took a paper route, which brought him to White neighborhoods and fistfights. He learned not only about support for and from family but also how to box, a talent which would bring him amateur boxing championships.

When time and money permitted, Troupe went to the movies, even though blatant discrimination forced him to sit in the colored section of theaters. The movies, and the technology behind them, thrilled him.

Also, as he wandered the many neighborhoods of St. Louis, he found baseball and the St. Louis Stars of the Negro Leagues. He met players, including James "Cool Papa" Bell, who encouraged Troupe to pursue baseball; in this pursuit, he recalled that he "ate, slept, and breathed baseball."[3] This fed the mentorship of his favorite elementary school teacher, Miss Harmon. It was she who encouraged Quincy to play baseball and to become a catcher.

Troupe attended Vashon High School, the newer of "two high schools for the colored" in St. Louis.[4] Vashon happened to be across the street from the St. Louis Stars' ball park. In his final year at Vashon, 1929, his team faced Sumner High School (the first Black high school in St. Louis) for the city championship. The game was played at the Stars Park and would be umpired by a Negro League umpire, Bill Donaldson. Adding to the excitement, Stars players Cool Papa Bell, Mule Suttles, and Stringbean Trent were in attendance. After the game, which Vashon won, Troupe noticed Bill Donaldson in conversation with Vashon's Coach Sutton. Donaldson coached an American Legion League team named "Peerless" in St. Louis and wondered if Quincy would like to play on that team. Troupe enthusiastically joined as a pitcher/catcher.[5] The "Peerless" team won the American Legion League Colored Division.

Soon thereafter, Donaldson sought a true playoff game with the (White) American Legion League champions. However, he could only schedule an exhibition game between the two teams – the game concluded in a 3-3 tie. This represented another part of Troupe's education around racism; segregated baseball continued.

It was around this time that Quincy's father, Charles, suddenly passed away. He and his family grieved deeply at the loss. However, his loving family and devout Baptist upbringing reminded him that he was not alone and that he could continue his life's journey, which included baseball. He took on duties as batboy for the St. Louis Stars, and soon

started training with the team. His skills improved, and, while visiting his brother in New Jersey, he played briefly with the Newark Browns.

Troupe wanted to be a catcher, but he recognized that he needed to develop his skill, and thus, to find a team that did not already have an established catcher or two. For this reason, he found himself on the mound rather than behind the plate. Although just out of high school, he now competed with Negro League greats, including Josh Gibson. After returning to St. Louis from New Jersey, he had the opportunity to play with the Stars versus the Homestead Grays; here he witnessed the power of Gibson, who sent one of Quincy's fastballs more than 400 feet.[6]

Upon returning to St. Louis, Troupe took a job at a chemical plant. He also played basketball at the local YMCA. At times he felt that professional basketball might be an option for him, but he knew that baseball was his true calling. His life began to revolve around baseball. In 1931, at age 19, Troupe signed his first professional baseball contract with the St. Louis Stars. Many Negro Leaguers played with multiple teams in the course of a season. From 1931 to 1935, Troupe also played with the Pittsburgh Crawfords, the Homestead Grays, and the Kansas City Monarchs, as well as the Posey brothers' short-lived team, the Detroit Wolves.

In 1933 Troupe signed a contract with the Chicago American Giants. He did not report to the team for spring training because at the time he was a student at Lincoln University in Jefferson, Missouri. One of his fondest memories of his time with the Giants was a game versus Satchel Paige in which he hit a triple, single, and a home run off Paige. This began a lifelong friendship between the two men.

Troupe decided not to return to Lincoln University in the fall of 1933. He followed baseball opportunity to North Dakota, where he played for an integrated team, the Bismarck Cubs. Owner-operator Neil Churchill recruited many Negro League stars for this team. It was Troupe who encouraged Paige to try North Dakota as well.

Troupe received pay for some of his play, but on occasion received no pay. One of those games was a postseason match, organized by his brother, in St. Louis before a hometown crowd and his hometown sweetheart Dorothy Smith.[7] Troupe won the game with a home run. At the end of the 1935 season, he returned home to St. Louis, where he played basketball and began to box, as a heavyweight. When full-grown, Troupe was a big man, standing 6-feet-2 and weighing 225 pounds.

Troupe won local championships, including the first Golden Gloves Tournament in St. Louis. At a Midwestern tournament in Chicago he won three fights and lost one. At the National Tournament in Providence, Rhode Island, he had four wins and was presented the heavyweight trophy cup by the state's governor, Theodore Green. In Providence, Quincy met Joe Louis, then an up-and-coming heavyweight contender. Troupe continued his amateur boxing in a tournament in Cleveland; he and future light heavyweight champion Archie Moore reached the semifinals, and Len Franklin won the heavyweight division.

Troupe considered professional boxing as a career, but one evening after he and Archie Moore met with a baseball friend, he realized again his love for baseball. Plus, as Moore said, "Quincy, I don't think you could ever be a fighter. You're just too nice. You're not the mean type…You have the punch. You move faster than the average heavyweight, and you've got a real sharp left jab. But you are not mean."[8]

In 1936, Troupe returned to North Dakota and, through Neil Churchill, played in a tournament in Wichita, Kansas. Troupe and Hilton Smith, the only two men of color on the all-tournament team, attracted attention from major-league scouts. One scout said that had they been White, he would recommend signing each for $100,000.[9] Troupe finished the season with stints on the Kansas City Monarchs roster and played into the postseason versus major-league all-stars.

Troupe did not play baseball in 1937, needing time both to heal his shoulder (a boxing injury) and to settle his relationship with Dorothy Smith. While he worked as a salesman for a milk company, he stayed connected to baseball through weekend amateur games. The following year, Quincy and Dorothy were married, and, although he would be away from his new wife, he signed a contract to play baseball with the Mound Blue team (aka Indianapolis ABC's) for the 1938 season. His fine play earned him a spot in the in the East-West All-Star Game to be played in Chicago.

At the season's conclusion, one of his teammates, Ted Strong, encouraged Troupe to try out for the Harlem Globetrotters. The choice was clear to Quincy, however – his commitments were to Dorothy and baseball. During that offseason, he worked for a steel company, which he called "the hardest job I've ever had."[10] In March, he received a call to report to spring training; he made arrangements with his employer for a leave of absence. Although he "really didn't want to leave [his] wife," he accepted this as "part of baseball."[11]

Soon after arriving for spring training, Troupe received a telegram from the Carta Blanca team of Monterrey, Mexico, which offered him an opportunity on recommendation from Cool Papa Bell. He accepted the team's offer and left for his first of several baseball seasons outside the United States.

During that first season in Mexico, Troupe received word that his son, Quincy Jr., had been born on July 22, 1939. A successful season, an offer to return, and an unwillingness to leave his family led the new father to drive, in 1940, to Monterrey with Dorothy, Quincy Jr. and teammate Theolic Smith. Unfortunately, after reaching Mexico, Dorothy and little Quincy became ill and needed to return to St. Louis. They recovered and the family welcomed a second son, Timothy.

Troupe recalled the 1941 season, his second in the Mexican League, as very competitive – that year Josh Gibson, Ray Dandridge, Willie Wells, Leon Day, and other Black stars were there.[12] When the season was over, Troupe formed and managed (his first managerial post) an all-star team to tour the United States. He extended his 1941-1942 season with winter baseball in Puerto Rico. His baseball play had kept him away from St. Louis and his family for most of that season; unfortunately, it became clear that he and Dorothy were drifting apart.

In 1942, as World War II intensified, Troupe wanted to enlist in the military. He was rejected for being married with dependents, and therefore decided to work in a defense plant, the Curtiss-Wright Aircraft Company. In 1943, while working as an inspector at the aircraft company, he received a letter from Jorge Pasquel of the Mexican League. Sr. Pasquel wanted Troupe to play ball in Mexico, but Quincy's job classification did not permit him to leave the United States. Through negotiations with the draft board, Sr. Pasquel arranged for him to leave the U.S. to play again in the Mexican League.

After the 1943 season, Troupe returned to work in an aircraft plant, and with another baseball season ahead, again received a letter from Pasquel about playing in the Mexican League. This time, evincing his power and influence, Sr. Pasquel arranged a sort of trade – 80,000 Mexican workers, to increase U.S. manpower, for two baseball players, namely Quincy Troupe and Theolic Smith. Quincy noted that "George [sic] Pasquel was a powerful man. It still staggers my mind how he was able to bring about this astounding exchange."[13]

With 1944 came a letter from the owner of the Cleveland Buckeyes of the Negro American League, asking Troupe to join his team as player-manager. He accepted the offer and in his first season, 1945, led the Buckeyes to the Negro World Series, defeating the Homestead Grays four games to none. He remained with the Buckeyes through the 1947 season.

At the conclusion of the 1945 season, Troupe received word from a Venezuelan consulate official about joining a

Quincy Trouppe with Sam Jones.

team to tour that country. He became a member of the American All Stars with other players from the Negro Leagues, including Jackie Robinson, Roy Campanella, and Sam Jethroe. It was also at this time that Troupe and his wife, Dorothy, officially separated – the baseball life had taken its toll.

In 1946, Troupe signed to play winter ball in Venezuela with the Magallanes club. Also in 1946, after having played in Latin America for six seasons, he changed the spelling of his surname to Trouppe, reflecting the pronunciation of his name by his Mexican fans – "Troo-pay."[14] It's noteworthy, though, that American newspapers continued to use the "Troupe" spelling.

In 1947, player-manager Trouppe won a second NAL pennant. Among others, the Cleveland team featured pitcher Sam Jones. However, the Buckeyes lost the Negro World Series to the New York Cubans. For the 1948 season, Trouppe was traded to the Chicago American Giants.

Baseball had been and continued to be a year-round occupation for Trouppe. He played winter ball for teams in Puerto Rico, Venezuela, Cuba, and Colombia. He played spring and summer seasons in the United States, Mexico, and Canada. During offseasons, he played exhibition games with Negro League all-stars versus major-league all-stars. Despite many challenges, including racism, salary constraints, and playing nearly every day, Trouppe recalled his many achievements.

One particularly fond memory came from his time as player-manager of the Caguas Criollos in the Puerto Rican League. Trouppe himself hit a home run in the 10th inning of the seventh game of the playoff finals against Mayagüez to bring Caguas the 1947-48 championship. "This was one of the greatest days of my baseball life. The people made me Honorary Mayor for the day, and because I always loved children, I declared the day a holiday, closing down all the schools in town."[15]

Dorothy finalized her divorce from Trouppe in 1949, the year he was traded from the Chicago American Giants to the New York Cubans. Prior to the start of the season, Trouppe was approached to play for a team in Canada's Provincial League, the Drummondville Cubs. With the decline of the Negro Leagues, many Black players found this league to be a viable alternative. Despite some misgivings, including not speaking French (he did speak Spanish fluently), he decided to play in Canada. Along with star pitcher Sal Maglie and young first baseman Vic Power, Trouppe helped his team to a league championship over the Farnham Pirates.

Trouppe returned to play/manage in the Mexican League for the 1950 and 1951 seasons. In October 1951, he met with Abe Saperstein, the Harlem Globetrotters impresario. Saperstein, who was also involved with baseball, possibly had a position for him in so-called Organized Baseball. Shortly after that meeting, Trouppe traveled to Venezuela to play winter ball, and there he received a call from Hank Greenberg, general manager of the Cleveland Indians.

Greenberg told Trouppe that the Indians were interested in him and offered a minor-league contract with the team's affiliate in Indianapolis. Greenberg reminded Trouppe that it would be "up to you to make the team."[16]

At age 39 – though newspaper reports knocked a full decade off – Trouppe did make the Indians in 1952. He became the first African-American catcher in the American League.[17] To his dissatisfaction and frustration, however, he spent most of his time with the team on the bench behind Jim Hegan and Birdie Tebbetts.

Wearing number 16, Trouppe played in his first big-league game on April 30, 1952. Four days later, at Griffith Stadium in Washington D.C., he replaced Tebbetts behind the plate in the seventh inning. In the middle of that inning, old Buckeyes teammate Sam "Toothpick" Jones came on in relief – they formed the first African-American battery in AL history.

Trouppe got his first start with the Indians the following day. His only other start came on May 10. He had his first hit and scored his first run in the majors; it turned out to be his final game with the Indians and in major-league baseball. In his stint with Cleveland, he had played in six games, and had 11 plate appearances, with one hit.

Trouppe was then demoted to Indianapolis. Reports of the time said that the Indians wanted him to train young pitchers there. According to Trouppe, though, Hank Greenberg told him that he didn't have enough of a record to go on to remain in the majors – which left him incredulous.

Although disappointed, Trouppe played well. He hit six home runs in his first two weeks with the minor-league club. Frustration continued, however, as he learned that catcher Joe Tipton had been bought from the Philadelphia Athletics.[18] Yet, there was joy in his life – this was also the year he married Myralin Donaldson. After their wedding, they traveled to Caracas, Venezuela for winter ball; she soon returned home when they realized she was pregnant.

By the spring of 1953, Trouppe had chosen not to report to Indianapolis. The team's manager – Birdie Tebbetts – suggested that Quincy take time to contemplate his decision. He would not return to the Indians organization. Instead, for the first time in his career, Trouppe traveled to the Dominican Republic, having received an offer to play "that was too good to refuse."[19]

However, after three weeks of spring training, Trouppe received a telegram from the St. Louis Cardinals regarding his application for a scouting position. He returned to St. Louis, met with Cardinals owner August A. Busch and chief scout Joe Mathes, and was offered the job. Trouppe accepted the position, becoming the first African-American scout in the Cardinals organization. As Trouppe assumed his new role in Organized Baseball, he welcomed his new daughter, Stephanie Marie, born May 13, 1953.

Trouppe enjoyed his scouting responsibilities but met disagreement and challenge as he recommended players. He had opportunity to meet and observe talented players, but he was consistently bewildered when some of his recommendations were rejected. They included Ernie Banks (who signed with the Cubs), Roberto Clemente (originally a Brooklyn Dodgers farmhand), and Vic Power (New York Yankees).

Trouppe returned to Puerto Rico for the 1956-57 winter season as manager of the Ponce Leones. In 1957, however, the Cardinals management decided that Trouppe's approach to scouting did not fit with the team's philosophy, and he learned that his services were no longer needed. Despite his disenchantment with the Cardinals organization, Quincy respected some colleagues, in particular Joe Mathes.

At the age of 45, and now out of baseball, Trouppe took a position with the St. Louis Land Clearance Authority, helping to relocate families to "standard housing quarters."[20] All appeared to be going well until he returned home one day and realized that Myralin and little Stephanie were leaving him. He and Myralin divorced and California became his next destination.

In 1963, three years after his arrival in California, he met and married Bessie Cullins. Together they served as proprietors for a senior citizen's home, the Queen Anne Manor, in Los Angeles.[21] They also opened a restaurant which they named Trouppe's Dugout.

Around 1967, hoping to return to baseball, Trouppe contacted George Silvey of the Cardinals (Trouppe had worked with Silvey during his earlier stint with the Cardinals).[22] Within a day, Harrison Wickel, a former player and manager turned scout, met Trouppe in his restaurant — there he signed a contract. He scouted talent in California for the Cardinals until 1970, when he and Bessie left California for Hattiesburg, Mississippi. After Bessie's passing in 1988, Quincy returned to St. Louis.

Quincy Trouppe made "enduring contributions" to baseball and history.[23] They include his 1977 self-published book, *20 Years Too Soon* (which has since been republished by the Missouri Historical Society). He compiled a valuable photograph and motion picture collection – in fact, he supplied almost all of the Negro League footage shown in the Ken Burns documentary *Baseball*.[24]

Trouppe is remembered as much for his character in baseball as he is for his achievements. Riley Stewart, pitcher for the 1948 Chicago American Giants, noted:

"He was one of the few managers that would fit in any era, now or in the past…He was a real gentleman. He was clean-cut, and well dressed. He was a model for the guys on the team. He never cussed. He might say "dawg gone." I never played for a finer gentleman. And he knew the game – very well."[25]

Late in life, Quincy Trouppe suffered from Alzheimer's disease. He died on August 10, 1993, in Creve Coeur, Missouri. He is buried at the Calvary Cemetery and Mausoleum in St. Louis.

SOURCES

In preparing this biography, the author relied primarily on Quincy Trouppe's book *20 Years Too Soon: Prelude to Major-League Integrated Baseball*. Also helpful were newspaper clippings from the National Baseball Hall of Fame Library in Cooperstown, New York; the Laurens County African American History website; and Leslie Heaphy's *The Negro Leagues: 1869-1960*.

NOTES

1   Quincy Trouppe, *20 Years Too Soon: Prelude to Major League Integrated Baseball* (St. Louis, Missouri: Missouri Historical Society Press, 1995), 4.

2   Laurens County African American History, "The Troupes: The Story of a Laurens County Family." http://laurenscountyafricanamericanhistory.blogspot.com/2009/07/troupes.html (last accessed December 23, 2015).

3   Trouppe, 4.

4   Trouppe, 19.

5   Trouppe, 21.

6   Trouppe, 27.

7   Trouppe, 36.

8   Trouppe, 81.

9   Trouppe, 66.

10   Trouppe, 68.

11   Trouppe, 69.

12   Trouppe, 74.

13   Trouppe, 82.

14   Trouppe, 99.

15   Trouppe, 105.

16   Trouppe, 110.

17   Laurens County African American History, "Quincy Trouppe – Dublin's All Star Player." http://laurenscountyafricanamericanhistory.blogspot.com/2009/03/quincy-trouppe-dublins-all-star-player.html (last accessed December 22, 2015)

18   Trouppe, 113.

19   Trouppe, 116.

20   Trouppe, 124.

21   Larry Lester, Introduction to *20 Years Too Soon: Prelude to Major-League Integrated Baseball*, by Quincy Trouppe (St. Louis, Missouri: Missouri Historical Society Press, 1995), 5.

22   Jim Sandoval and Bill Nowlin, ed. *Can He Play: A Look at Baseball Scouts and Their Professin* (Phoenix: Society for American Baseball Research, 2011), 129.

23   Lester, Introduction to *20 Years Too Soon: Prelude to Major-League Integrated Baseball*, 7.

24   Lester, 6.

25   Lester, 4.

Archie Ware

By Alan Cohen

"Couldn't seem to hit, but could field as sweet as you ever saw."
– Connie Johnson, remembering Archie Ware in 1997[1]

Archie Virgil Ware was born on June 19, 1918, in Greenville, Florida. His father was Virgil Ware, and his mother was Sally Emma Simmons. He attended Elder Jordan

Archie Ware.

Elementary School,[2] and his formal education ended after one year at Jonathan Clarkson Gibbs High School in St. Petersburg.[3]

The first evidence of Ware's playing competitively was in semipro ball with the West Indies Royals in 1940. Although the team was based in Port Antonio, Jamaica, it began its season in Florida in April and traveled extensively through the Midwest. The players were as much known for their clowning as for their ballplaying. Their appearances featured a pregame pepper-ball routine, and between innings King Tut, later to gain fame with the Indianapolis Clowns, entertained the fans. And they won most of their games.

The Royals came out on the short end of a 12-2 decision in Des Moines on June 16. Ware homered in the seventh inning. He also doubled in the game.[4] On June 26 they played at Holdredge, Nebraska. Batting leadoff, Ware went 2-for-5 with a pair of triples, scored three runs, and had an RBI as the Royals lost 11-10.[5]

The team did not conclude its season until November, when it returned to Florida for games in West Palm Beach.

In 1941 Ware went to spring training with the Chicago American Giants and then joined the Kansas City Monarchs second squad. The team was managed by Newt Joseph and barnstormed throughout the Western states. Some players from this team, including infielders Herb Souell and Bonnie Serrell and pitcher Booker McDaniel, went on to later play with the Monarchs in the Negro American League. Ware's fielding was highly regarded; in one account, he was called the "Negro Hal Chase."[6]

On July 25, 1941, in Oroville, California, the Monarchs' second team defeated the overmatched Oroville Olives. Ware went 3-for-5 with a double as his team won, 15-5.[7] Earlier that month, on a swing through Oregon, the Monarchs defeated the Eugene Athletics, 14-0, and the Hills Creek Hillbillies, 9-4. In the latter game, on July 23, Ware had three hits and two RBIs.[8] On August 11 the Monarchs went to Washington state and lost to the Bellingham Bells, 5-4, with Ware getting a single and a double.[9]

Ware's full statistics for 1941 are unknown because team stats for the season were not maintained. But toward the end of the season, he was acquired by the Chicago American Giants and played with them on September 3 against the NAL Monarchs. He went 1-for-5 in a 7-5 loss.[10]

In 1942, the 5-foot-9, 160-pound first baseman joined the Buckeyes, who that season split their time between

Cincinnati and Cleveland, and it was with the Buckeyes that the left-handed-throwing and batting player would gain fame.

"Archie Ware, than whom there is none than-whomer at the initial sack"
– *Cleveland Call and Post*, May 30, 1942[11]

The Buckeyes were a new entrant in the league, and in June Ware had a key role in several games. He had three hits and a pair of stolen bases, and handled 18 chances flawlessly at first base in a 5-3 win over Jacksonville at Idora Park in Youngstown, Ohio, on June 2.[12] The next evening, in a game played in Erie, Pennsylvania, he doubled in three runs in the first inning and tripled in a pair in the second inning as the Buckeyes routed Jacksonville, 10-3.[13] On June 14, at Cleveland's League Park, Ware faced Satchel Paige for the first time and had a first-inning single as the Buckeyes won 2-1 in the first game of a doubleheader against the Monarchs. (Cold weather kept the crowd size down to 2,600.)[14]

The Buckeyes played a key series against the Birmingham Black Barons later in June. They won four of the five games, including the last three. In the three games for which there is detailed information, Ware went 6-for-11 including a home run in the series finale at Canton, Ohio, on June 24, won by the Buckeyes, 7-4.[15] By taking this series, the Buckeyes had moved from fifth place to second place, just ahead of the Black Barons, and trailed only the Kansas City Monarchs in the standings. The Buckeyes finished the season in second place.

On August 3 the Buckeyes played against the Newark Eagles in Hartford, Connecticut. Newark's leadoff batter was a player named Walker, who went 1-for-5 with a bunt single during a third-inning three-run rally. Walker is better known these days as Larry Doby. The Eagles beat the Buckeyes, 5-2. Ware went 1-for-3 with a seventh-inning single.[16] Doby was playing under an alias to protect his amateur status. He had completed high school that spring and would enter college that fall.

At 3:30 A.M. on Labor Day, as the team was traveling from Buffalo, New York, to Akron, Ohio, one of the cars in the team caravan was involved in a major collision in Geneva, Ohio. Ware was in another car. Catcher Joe "Buster" Brown and pitcher Raymond "Smoky" Owens were killed, Pitchers Eugene Bremer, Herman "Lefty" Watts, and Alonzo Boone were injured, as was team business manager Wilbur Hayes.[17]

The Buckeyes went 50-27-2 in their inaugural season in the NAL, finishing second to the Kansas City Monarchs. Ware batted .270 with 3 home runs and 41 RBIs.[18]

In 1943 the Buckeyes called Cleveland home for the entire season. They won nine of their first 11 games, and Ware got off to a good start. On May 17 he contributed three hits as the Buckeyes defeated Memphis, 13-6.[19] On May 21, in a game played at Little Rock, he went 6-for-6 in another win against Memphis, this time by a 12-6

margin. At Buffalo on June 2, the Buckeyes defeated the Indianapolis Clowns, 11-0, with Ware adding another three hits to his season's total.[20] In a showdown with the Kansas City Monarchs, Ware's double was the key hit in a three-run ninth-inning rally as the Buckeyes came from behind to win, 6-5.[21] Despite this great early showing, the Buckeyes were caught by the Birmingham Black Barons down the stretch and Birmingham won the first-half championship.

Ware served as team captain during the season, and he filled in as manager when Parnell Woods was not available. In the balloting for the annual East-West Game, Ware was so well regarded by the fans that he finished second to Buck O'Neil.

In the second half of the 1943 season, Ware was managing on August 1 when the Buckeyes swept a doubleheader from the Memphis Red Sox. In the opener, Ware had two doubles as the Buckeyes won, 7-1.[22] However, the remainder of the season was a disappointment, and Cleveland was not in the running as Chicago won the second-half championship. For the season, Ware batted .276 and had 6 doubles.[23]

In 1944, Ware was named to the West team for the annual East-West Game that matched the best players in the Negro American League with their counterparts in the Negro National League. The game took place on August 13, and the West prevailed, 7-4, in front of an estimated 50,000 fans. Five runs in the fifth inning proved decisive. Ware doubled in the inning, scoring Bonnie Serrell with the team's fifth run of the game. Ware scored on a homer by Ted "Double-Duty" Radcliffe. The Buckeyes finished each half of the season in third place and their record was just above .500 (59-56-1 per Seamheads). Ware's offensive numbers were down from the prior season.[24]

In 1945 Ware and the Buckeyes climbed the heights and won the Negro League World Series. Ware batted .280 (according to Seamheads) in 19 games for which they have information. Per contemporary sources, he batted .296, and was among the league leaders in RBIs, posting 39 in 56 games.[25] Ware was not known for his power (he had less than 10 documented Negro League home runs), and extra-base hits were a rarity for him. A timely single drove in the winning run in the 10th inning on May 30 in the second game of a doubleheader at Cleveland's League Park against Memphis.[26]

Ware once again played in the East-West Game, on July 29 in front of 31,714 fans at Comiskey Park in Chicago. He went 2-for-4 with three RBIs. In the second inning, his two-run single put the West in front, 2-0. In the third, as the West broke the game open, Ware drove in Alex Radcliff with a single and then scored his team's seventh run on a single by Jesse Williams. After building up a 9-0 lead, the West hung on to win, 9-6. With two outs in the ninth inning and Willie Wells on second base, Rogelio Linares hit a groundball to shortstop Jackie Robinson, who fielded the ball and threw to Ware for the game's final out.

Cleveland won the NAL championship in each half of the season and went to the Negro World Series without having to win a playoff. Media attention was significant for the Negro World Series as the Buckeyes faced the Homestead Grays, the perennial Negro National League champions, who had won the prior two Series. Like Cleveland, Homestead had topped its league in each half of the 1945 season.

The first three games went to the Buckeyes, with Ware contributing a single during an eighth-inning rally that propelled Cleveland to a 2-1 win in Game One.[27] On September 20, the Buckeyes defeated the Grays, 5-0, to clinch the championship in four straight games. Ware walked and scored in the first inning and singled and was left stranded in the third inning. His fielding was flawless. He had 18 putouts in the game.[28]

Although they had won the Series, the Buckeyes were not finished with the Grays as they played an exhibition doubleheader at Yankee Stadium on September 23. The Grays got a measure of revenge, sweeping Cleveland by identical scores of 7-1.[29]

After the season, Ware participated in the North-South game on October 7, playing for the South team. He went 0-for-4 as the South lost 7-1.

Ware returned to the Buckeyes in 1946 and batted .282.[30] Once again an All-Star, he appeared in the two East-West games played in 1946, going hitless in six at-bats as teams split the two games, one in Washington and the other in Chicago.

The Buckeyes did not fare as well as they had done in the prior season. They finished third with a league record of 37-35-3. In an interleague matchup against the Philadelphia Stars on September 5, Ware had his best game of the season, going 3-for-5 with a pair of doubles in a 10-8 Buckeyes win in the second game of a doubleheader at Shibe Park.

The 1947 season was Ware's best so far at the plate. According to the Howe News Bureau, he batted .349 in 73 games and led the league with 99 hits. The Buckeyes won the NAL pennant and faced the New York Cubans in the

Negro League World Series. In an exhibition on August 31, before the Series, Ware's hitting played a role as the Buckeyes defeated the Cubans, 9-7, at the Polo Grounds. He singled home a pair of runs in the fourth inning, and his sixth-inning solo homer capped a four-run rally.[31] The homer was his third of the season.

The Cubans won the Negro League World Series in six games. The first game was played on September 19 at the Polo Grounds. The game was tied after six innings, and Ware, with Al Smith on first base, came to bat with two out in the top of the seventh. He hit a grounder that went between the legs of shortstop Silvio Garcia. Smith raced around the bases, and the Buckeyes had a 6-5 lead. Unfortunately for the Buckeyes, the rains came, the umpires stopped the game, the score reverted to 5-5, and the game was ruled a tie.[32]

On September 21, at Yankee Stadium, Ware had two hits as the Buckeyes won. He also laid down a sacrifice bunt. With the score tied 7-7 in the ninth inning, he led off with an infield hit. The Buckeyes loaded the bases, but Ware was forced at home. Another out followed, and Al Smith came up with the bases loaded. Smith's single scored two runners, and the Buckeyes added one more to win, 10-7.[33]

On September 23 in Cleveland, the Cubans won, 6-0, and on September 24, in Game Four at Shibe Park, Ware went 1-for-4 with a run scored and two RBIs in a 9-4 Buckeyes loss. Wins in the remaining two games, at Chicago and Cleveland, gave the Cubans the championship. For the Series, Ware batted .263 (5-for-19) with 4 RBIs.

After the Series Ware played winter ball for the first time, for Magallanes in the 1947-48 Caracas Winter League.[34]

In 1948 the Buckeyes finished in third place and Ware again had a good season at the plate. He duplicated his .349 batting average from the prior season, this time with 107 hits in 77 games. He tied for the league lead with 23 doubles. It was a season of streaks for the Buckeyes. They got off to a terrible start and by the end of May had won only five games while losing 17. From May 16 through May 26, they did not win a game, losing 10 and tying one.

Then they turned things around. Ware had several multi-hit games. Against the Monarchs in Youngstown, Ohio, on June 14, he was 2-for-4 with a double and drove in a pair of runs as the Buckeyes won, 9-5 with Eugene Smith getting the win. It was the Buckeyes' 17th win in 18 games. On June 27 against the Monarchs in the first game of a doubleheader, Ware sacrificed in the first, reached base on an error and stole a base in the second, walked in the third, and singled home two runs in the fourth as the Buckeyes won, 14-7 behind Sam Jones. But the early season losses had put the team in too big a hole.

Ware's stats fell off in 1949 as the Buckeyes, in the reconstructed 10-team Negro American League, split the season between Louisville, where they began the season, and Cleveland, to which they returned in early July. Prior to the season, the *Louisville Courier-Journal* referred to

Archie Ware with the Buckeyes.

Ware as "Mr. First."[35] His batting average slipped to .223 in 78 games. Coverage in the media was scant in 1949. In late August, the Buckeyes played the American Giants in Winona, Minnesota. Ware went 2-for-5 with a stolen base and handled 15 chances flawlessly at first base, but the Buckeyes lost, 11-10 in 11 innings.[36]

The regular season ended on Labor Day, September 5, but play continued for the Negro League teams in exhibition series. In one series, between Kansas City and Indianapolis, Ware played with the Indianapolis Clowns. His previously dormant bat came alive shortly after he joined the Clowns. On September 11, in a doubleheader against the Monarchs, he went 3-for-6. The Clowns won the opener but lost the second game.[37] In the offseason, Ware was officially traded to the Clowns for Leonard Pigg, who had led the league in batting in 1949.[38] Ware replaced part-time player and full-time clown Reece "Goose" Tatum, who missed several games at the end of the 1949 season and left baseball to play full-time with the Harlem Globetrotters basketball team.

In October 1949 Ware barnstormed with Satchel Paige and members of the Kansas City Royals. On October 30 at Wrigley Field in Los Angeles, against Bob Lemon's All-Stars, Ware's seventh-inning single was the only hit off Lemon as the Royals lost, 1-0. Mike Garcia finished on the mound for Lemon's team, replacing Lemon in the eighth inning. Pitching for the Royals was National League Rookie of the Year Don Newcombe, who matched Lemon for the game's first seven innings. Gentry Jessup, pitching in relief of Newcombe, yielded an eighth-inning home run to Vern Stephens for the game's only run.[39]

During the winter after the 1949 season, Ware played in the Panama Professional League.[40] He was with the Spur Cola Colonites and was batting .310 (second best in the league) through 31 games.[41] He got off to a great start, getting the team's first hit and scoring their first run on November 15 in a 2-1 win over Chesterfield.[42] After the conclusion of the Panama League season, Ware was named to an all-star team that played a series of games against all-stars from the Canal Zone League.[43]

Ware batted .277 with the 1950 Clowns, who finished the season in first place in the NAL's Eastern Division. Although there was no formal postseason series, the Clowns and the Western Division champion Kansas City Monarchs barnstormed in the weeks after the season ended the day after Labor Day, and Archie Ware played his last Negro League games. In his last official game, he went 1-for-6 and scored a run as the Clowns defeated the Monarchs, 6-2 in 12 innings, at Jefferson City, Missouri, on September 5.[44] Kansas City won most of the games during the postseason barnstorming trip.

Ware once again wintered with the Spur Cola Colonites. Before the 1951 season, his contract was sold to Farnham of the Class-C Provincial League. In his first year of Organized Baseball, he batted .257 with a career-high 6 home runs in 122 games. Farnham was managed by Sam Bankhead, and its lineup included many former Negro League players. The team went 52-71, finishing in seventh place.

Ware returned to Panama once again, but he was batting only .204 for a team that went winless in his first 11 games, and he was sent home.[45] He was 33 years old and played only one more season. In 1952, with Lewiston of the Class-A Western International League, he played in 15 games and batted .286.

Ware's first marriage was to Rebecca Canty on March 24, 1937. He married Fannie L. Lane on March 14, 1949. They had two children, Belinda, born in 1962, and Archie, Jr., born in 1966.

When he completed a questionnaire for the National Baseball Hall of Fame in 1972, Ware noted that he had crossed paths and learned much from great Black players such as Josh Gibson, Buck Leonard, Cool Papa Bell, and Satchel Paige, each of whom was enshrined in the Hall of Fame. Toward the end of his time in baseball, he saw budding stars like Buckeyes teammates Sam Jethroe, Sam Jones, and Al Smith, as well as Birmingham's Willie Mays, Kansas City's Ernie Banks and Jackie Robinson, and Newark's Larry Doby.

Appearing at an old-timers event in Kansas City in 1984, Ware remembered the early days of integration: "After Jackie (Robinson) left for the majors, we all thought about getting in. Everybody could have played in the majors, there was no secret about that."[46] Unfortunately for Ware and most of the other Negro League players, they did not get the richly deserved opportunity to display their talents to the larger audiences.

After his baseball career, Ware worked as a material surface inspector for North American Rockwell Corporation.

He died on December 13, 1990, in Los Angeles and is buried at Inglewood Park Cemetery.

SOURCES

In addition to the sources shown in the Notes, the author used Baseball-Reference.com, Seamheads.com, Retrosheet.org, and the Center for Negro Leagues Baseball Research website.

Seamheads uses statistics only from games for which it has box scores. Howe used more games, but not all of the scorecards and/or box scores it used were from newspaper accounts.

Howe started doing NAL stats in 1944. It stopped doing the stats in 1960 and went out of business not long thereafter. Nobody has been able to track down its records. Its year-end totals for each season (as published in the Black weeklies) are on Leyton Revel's website (Center for Negro League Baseball Research).

NOTES

1   Matthew Schofield, "Holding on to History," *Kansas City Star*, May 29, 1997: S-3.

2   Gwendolyn Reese, "I AM: Black Education in Early St. Pete," *Weekly Challenge* (St. Petersburg, Florida), March 22, 2018. Jordan Elementary School had opened in 1925, and Ware was likely one of the first students at the school.

3 Archie Ware's personal information is included in a questionnaire on file at the National Baseball Museum and Research Center in Cooperstown, New York.

4 "Demons Trip Royals, 12-2," *Des Moines Register*, June 17, 1940: 7.

5 "Holdredge Stops Winning Streak of Colored Boys," *Holdredge* (Nebraska) *Progress*, June 28, 1940: 1.

6 "Fliers on Road: Whiskerinos Play Negro Monarchs Mon.," *Stockton* (California) *Record*, August 2, 1941: 12.

7 "Champ Negro Nine Wallops Locals 15-5," *Oroville* (California) *Mercury Register*, July 26, 1941: 6.

8 "'Billies Lose to Monarchs," *Eugene* (Oregon) *Register-Guard*, July 24, 1941: 2.

9 "Bells Hit Homers to Defeat Negroes," *Bellingham* (Washington) *Herald*, August 12, 1941: 9.

10 "Satchel Paige and Monarchs Defeat Chicago Giants, 7-5," *Illinois State Journal* (Springfield, Illinois), September 4, 1941: 15.

11 G. Porter, "Bucks Trounce Red Caps 13-5, 3-0: Open Here Sunday," *Cleveland Call and Post*, May 30, 1942: 10.

12 "Buckeyes Win, 5-3, in American Loop," *Erie* (Pennsylvania) *Daily Times*, June 3, 1942: 16.

13 Joe Williams, "Buckeyes Cop 10 to 3 Over Jacksonville," *Erie Daily Times*, June 4, 1942: 24.

14 "Only 2600 See Bremer Beat 'Satchel,': Gives Four Hits," *Cleveland Call and Post*, June 20, 1942: 10.

15 "Cincinnati Buckeyes Take Series from Birmingham," *Jackson* (Mississippi) *Advocate*, July 11, 1942: 6.

16 "Newark Eagle Beat Buckeyes by 5-3 Margin," *Hartford Courant*, August 4, 1942: 15.

17 "Buckeyes Players Die in Crash," *Cleveland Call and Post*, September 12, 1942: 1.

18 Batting average per Seamheads. Retrosheet figures, adjusted for Seamheads game log information used for home runs and RBIs.

19 "Buckeyes Win Another," *St. Louis Argus*, May 21, 1943: 10.

20 "Buckeyes' Smith Shuts out Clowns with One Hit, 11-0," *Buffalo News*, June 3, 1943: 26.

21 "Buckeyes' Rally Defeats Negro Champions, 6-5," *Rochester* (New York) *Democrat and Chronicle*, June 9, 1943: 21.

22 "Cleveland in N.A.L. Second Half Title Race," *St. Louis Argus*, August 6, 1943: 10.

23 Statistics from Seamheads. Seamheads had box scores for only 38 games in which Ware played in 1943. The Buckeyes played approximately 95 League games that season. There are no other statistics available for 1943.

24 Negro League statistics are, 80 years after the fact, still in a state of flux. The accepted contemporary source was the Howe News Bureau, which started providing Negro American League statistics in 1943. According to Howe,

Ware batted .267 in 71 games with 7 doubles and 4 triples. Seamheads, which uses statistics only from games for which there are box scores, has Ware with a batting average of .174 in 24 games and is thus incomplete. According to Retrosheet, Ware's only homer in 1944 came at Buffalo on July 12 in an 8-1 win over Memphis.

25 Howe News Bureau.

26 Bob Williams, "Sports Rambler," *Cleveland Call and Post*, June 9, 1945: 6B.

27 "Buckeyes Threaten Rout of Long-Time Champions," *Washington Afro-American*, September 22, 1945: 30.

28 William J. Scheffer, "Buckeyes Blank Grays, Win Title," *Philadelphia Inquirer*, September 21, 1945: 24.

29 "Grays Snatch 2 Games from Clevelanders," *New York Amsterdam News*, September 29, 1945: 22.

30 According to Howe News Bureau statistics in the *Philadelphia Tribune*, September 3, 1946: 11.

31 Haskell Cole, "Cleveland Homers Beat Cubans, 9-7," *Pittsburgh Courier*, September 6, 1947: 13.

32 "Cubans' Rally Ties Buckeyes," *Chicago Defender*, September 27, 1947: 20.

33 "Bucks Stage 3-Run Rally," *Chicago Defender*, September 27, 1947: 20.

34 "Rogovin Beats Jail Rap, Also Rivals," *The Sporting News*, December 3, 1947: 22.

35 "Buckeyes Open Season Today at Parkway," *Louisville Courier-Journal*, May 1, 1949: 2-5.

36 "Giants Nose Buckeyes, 11 to 10," *Winona* (Minnesota) *Republican-Journal*, September 1, 1949: 17.

37 "Goose Again Fails to Show," *Omaha Evening World-Herald*, September 12, 1949: 19.

38 John E. Fuster, "Cleveland Buckeyes Trade Veteran Archie Ware for Batting Champion," *Cleveland Call and Post*, March 25, 1950: 3-B.

39 "Lemon Halts Royal Nine on One Hit, 1-0," *Los Angeles Times*, October 31, 1949: IV-3.

40 "Archie Ware Leads Clowns to NAL First Half Pennant," *Atlanta Daily World*, July 7, 1950: 7.

41 "Panama League Has New Leader," *The Sporting News*, January 25, 1950: 24.

42 L.J. Eberenz, "Overflow Crowd of 13,452 Witnesses Panama Opener," *The Sporting News*, November 23, 1949: 18.

43 "Panama," *The Sporting News*, February 22, 1950: 30.

44 "Four-Run Rally Hands 6-3 Win to Indianapolis," *Jefferson City* (Missouri) *Post-Tribune*, September 6, 1950: 9.

45 Eberenz, "Spur Cola Finds Range After 11 Losses in Row," *The Sporting News*, January 16, 1952: 21.

46 Milton Edwards, "Monarchs Old-Timers Play Ball in Exhibition Game at Paige Stadium," *Kansas City* (Missouri) *Call*, September 14, 1984: 13-14.

Parnell Woods

By Sean Kolodziej

Few people can say that their job made it possible to travel around the entire world. Parnell Woods traversed North and Central America while playing baseball, being selected to eight East-West All-Star Games along the way. After his baseball career, he was able to travel throughout Europe and Asia as the traveling secretary for the Harlem Globetrotters, visiting a total of 87 countries.[1]

Parnell LaPonte Woods was born on February 6, 1912, to Bernard and Bell (Brewton) Woods in Cordova, Alabama, a textile-mill town some 30 miles northwest of Birmingham.

Little is known of Parnell's childhood. He attended Powderly High School in Birmingham, then Alabama State Teachers College (now Alabama State University), a historically Black public university in Montgomery.

In the early 1930s Woods became a teacher in his hometown. He decided to play baseball during the summer to supplement his small teacher's salary.[2] He was "a strong hitter, a successful base stealer, and a good fielder whose only liability was a weak arm."[3]

Records are scarce, but according to James A. Riley, author of *The Biographical Encyclopedia of the Negro Baseball Leagues*, Woods joined the Birmingham Black Barons in 1933 while they were associate members of the Negro National League, and was still with the team when they joined the Negro American League in its inaugural year of 1937.[4] This was the first year that Woods was on a team now considered to be in a "major league,"[5] and his stats show that he was a productive hitter. In 27 games against other Negro major-league teams, he hit .303 with 21 RBIs, 27 runs scored, and an .867 OPS.

In 1938, while still playing with the Black Barons, Woods made his first East-West All-Star Game, grounding out to second in a pinch-hit at-bat for Frank Duncan in the sixth inning. (The Black Barons ended the Negro American League season in last place with a record of 13-44.) On July 19 of that year, Woods married Lessie B. Pinson in Alabama. (His first name is spelled "Pernell" on the marriage license, and in his signature on the document.)

The 1939 season found Woods playing for the Cleveland Bears. The Bears were formed when the Jacksonville Red Caps moved to Cleveland for the 1939 Negro American League season. Woods once again excelled at third base, again being selected by fan vote for the East-West All-Star Game. He pinch-hit again, this time laying down a sacrifice bunt in the seventh inning. The Bears finished in fourth place with a record of 24-29. The most up-to-date

statistics show that Woods batted .262 with 7 stolen bases in 26 games played.

During the winter of 1939-1940, Woods played for the Leones de Ponce (Ponce Lions) in the Puerto Rican League,

Parnell Woods.

Courtesy of Jeffry Woods.

batting .269. This was the first of his many trips south of the border to play baseball.

Woods started the 1940 season playing for the Cleveland Bears, but the team folded by mid-July. He finished the season playing again for the Birmingham Black Barons. Through all this turmoil, Woods for a third year played in the East-West All-Star Game, starting at third base for the West team and hitting a single to center field in the eighth inning.

After failing to finish out the 1940 season, the Bears moved back to Jacksonville and reassumed the Red Caps name for the 1941 Negro American League. Woods played third base for the team and starting in the East-West All-Star Game, his fourth straight year of being voted an all-star. The Red Caps finished fifth in the league with a record of 15-28-2.

After starting the 1942 season with the Red Caps, Woods, by then 30 years old, was traded to the Cincinnati-Cleveland Buckeyes in mid-May. The Red Caps also sent Duke Cleveland to the Buckeyes in exchange for cash and players to be named later.[6] Soon afterward he was named manager of the team. Besides leading the team to a 38-43 record, the well-respected "gentleman manager of baseball"[7] also started both East-West All-Star Games that were played that year.

In mid-August of 1942, John Foster, sports editor of the *Cleveland Call and Post*, asked Alva Bradley, president of the Cleveland Indians, to give Woods, Eugene Bremer, and Sam Jethroe tryouts. The request was written in Woods' name. After promising a tryout for early 1943 (which made national news[8]), Bradley said that based on their performances in the second East-West All-Star Game, none of the three players were major-league worthy. In that All-Star Game, played at Cleveland Stadium, Woods went 0-for-2 with a walk and a run scored. Was his performance in this one game enough to keep him out of the still-segregated major-league baseball?

In 1943 Woods managed the Buckeyes to a second-place finish behind the Kansas City Monarchs. He was voted a starter in the East-West All Star Game but did not play because he had been "bothered by a bad shoulder."[9] Instead, he was a coach.

In March 1944, with World War II raging, Woods was ordered to report for military induction. He had been reclassified as 1-A, available for unrestricted military service.[10] Archie Ware managed the Buckeyes while Woods was gone. But subsequently he was rejected by his draft board.[11] A reason for the rejection was never given. Woods then returned to manage the Buckeyes and play third base.

On Sunday, June 25, 1944, the Buckeyes held Parnell Woods Day at League Park. This occasion was the "result of suggestions arising out of notice of the brilliant playing and strategy of Parnell Woods."[12] Cleveland swept a doubleheader against the Chicago American Giants in front of 6,600 fans.[13]

For the 1944 season, All-Star voting was no longer based on fan votes. The Negro League team managers picked the two teams. W.S. Welch, manager of the Birmingham Black Barons (1943 Negro American league champs), selected Alex Radcliffe to start at third base, with Woods selected as a reserve.

During the winter of 1944-1945, Woods played in the California Winter League for the Kansas City Royals. Teammates included Chet Brewer, Wild Bill Wright, Ray Dandridge, Hilton Smith, Willie Wells, and Sam Jethroe. While there, Woods learned that he would no longer be manager of the Buckeyes. Quincy Trouppe was named the new manager. He had played for Rojos del Mexico in the Mexican League the prior year. Woods was named team captain and kept his same salary.[14] He played third base and hit .273. Under Trouppe, the 1945 Buckeyes won both halves of the Negro American League split season. They met the Homestead Grays in the Negro World Series. The Grays had Hall of Fame players such as Josh Gibson, Buck Leonard, Cool Papa Bell, Ray Brown, and Jud Wilson on their team. Even with such star power, they were swept by the Buckeyes in four games.

After the World Series Woods joined the All-American All Stars, made up of Negro League players, and toured South America. The team included Jackie Robinson playing shortstop.[15] By this time, Robinson had signed with the Dodgers, and would report to the Montreal Royals training camp in February. According to Buck Leonard, Woods hit .419 on the tour.[16] Woods seemed to have a good time; he wrote to the *Pittsburgh Courier*, "I'm the guy who is winning all the money in the card games. Merry Christmas."[17]

Woods, along with Willie Jefferson, failed to report to the Buckeyes for the start of the 1946 season. Wilbur Hayes, owner of the Buckeyes, reported that Woods' and Jefferson's passports were held up by Venezuelan officials. Finding themselves unable to return home, they decided to play for the Caracas team.[18] As a result of this, Woods was suspended by the Negro National League and Negro American League for five years.

On August 10, 1946, the *Cleveland Call and Post* reported that Woods wanted to play for the Buckeyes again, but because of his five-year ban, only a special action by the league could allow him back.[19] No such action was ever performed.

In 1947 Woods again tried to come back to the Buckeyes, but his suspension was upheld. Ernie Wright and Wilbur Hayes tried their hardest to get him reinstated, but to no avail. Woods ultimately played in Venezuela again. He batted .354 and led the league with 21 stolen bases in 36 games. He made that league's all-star team and was awarded an "$800, specially made ring."[20]

Woods enjoyed his time in Venezuela. He went to school there to learn Spanish. He was quoted as saying that "[T]here is no color line. ... The natives like their baseball and they show their appreciation for good players, regardless of color."[21] Woods was invited to sit on a panel sponsored by the newspaper *Ultimas Noticias* that discussed racial discrimination in American baseball. "One only realizes the extent of prejudice when experiencing the fair treatment [in Venezuela]," Woods said.[22]

During the winter of 1947-1948, Woods played in Cuba's Players Federation League. He began with the Santiago club, then joined the Cuba team after Santiago folded in December. Teammates on both of these teams included future Hall of Famer Ray Brown, Sal Maglie (himself in the middle of a five-year ban from the US major leagues for jumping to the Mexican League) and Luis E. Tiant, father of US major-league pitcher Luis Tiant.

The summer of 1948 found Woods, thanks to promoter Abe Saperstein, playing third base for the Harlem Globetrotters baseball team.[23] The team barnstormed against the Hawaiian All-Stars. They played 50 games against each other, including games at Wrigley Field, Shibe Park, Forbes Field, and Yankee Stadium.[24] Saperstein, owner of the Globetrotters, offered Woods a career after baseball, and Woods called Saperstein "the greatest man he'd ever known."[25]

At the start of the 1948-1949 offseason, Woods returned to Venezuela to play with the Caracas team again. On November 24, he witnessed a coup d'etat. Romulo Gallegos, the elected president of Venezuela, was overthrown by a group led by Marcos Perez Jimenez. "We're in the center of all the shooting," Woods told the *Cleveland Call and Post*. "I haven't been out of the hotel for two days and we haven't been able to play ball here for a week."[26] The uprising began while Woods was at practice, he told the newspaper, adding, "All of a sudden people starting running. The hotel was surrounded with tanks and machine guns."[27] Woods was able to return to the United States soon afterward.

Good news was awaiting Woods when he returned home. The Negro Leagues Winter Meeting not only included a merging of the Negro National League and the Negro American League, but the owners also agreed to restore to good standing players who had jumped to other leagues in previous years. Woods was now free to rejoin the Negro leagues.

Woods started 1949 spring training with the Louisville Buckeyes in Panama City, Florida. The Buckeyes had moved from Cleveland to Louisville for the 1949 season. He played with this team until early May, then jumped back to the Globetrotters baseball team. His time with the Globetrotters did not last long, because by July 13, as part of the slow trickle of integration, he was playing for the Oakland Oaks of the Pacific Coast League. The Oaks were looking for an infielder when Wilmer "Red" Fields refused to report to Oakland after they bought his contract from the Homestead Grays.

Woods played 40 games for the Oaks, backing up Cookie Lavagetto at third base. In early August, Woods was beaned by a pitch from Charley Schanz, a right-handed pitcher for the Seattle Rainiers. He was knocked unconscious and played sparingly the rest of the season.

After the 1949 PCL season ended, Woods joined an all-Black all-star team sponsored by Abe Saperstein that scheduled games on the West Coast. Luke Easter headlined the team, which also featured Dan Bankhead, Ted "Double Duty" Radcliffe, and Artie Wilson.[28] In one of the first games, played at San Francisco's Seals Stadium, Woods hit a walk-off double off the left-field fence.[29] In a game against Bob Feller, Woods had three hits, including a three-run homer.[30]

By 1950, at the age of 38, Woods had a new job as traveling secretary for the Globetrotters basketball team. He also found time to play for the Globetrotters baseball team. On October 10, Roy Campanella included him on his barnstorming all-star team that included Don Newcombe, Luke Easter, Monte Irvin, Hank Thompson, and Larry Doby.

In 1951, Winfield Welch bought the Chicago American Giants. Welch had managed teams owned by Abe Saperstein, including the Birmingham Black Barons. Woods played for the American Giants and was also the traveling secretary. Satchel Paige played for the team briefly before signing with the St. Louis Browns. Woods, then 39 years old, was selected for the East-West All-Star Game at Comiskey Park on August 12. For the season, according to the Kansas City *Call*, Woods' batted .375, second to the Monarchs' Willard Brown (.417).[31]

In late October, Roy Campanella's All-Stars, which again featured Newcombe, Irvin, Thompson, Doby, and Easter, in addition to Willie Mays, played against the Negro American League All-Stars. The latter team included Woods at third base.

By 1952, Woods was the full-time business manager of the Harlem Globetrotters. The schedule was very intense. The team played seven nights a week, with doubleheaders on Sundays. "On the long jumps, we sometimes will travel a hundred miles after playing and I have to hustle food and hotel accommodations," he said. "You just cannot play a game, eat and fall into bed."[32] One time, Woods remembered, "we were driving from Rochester [Minnesota] to Minneapolis and it was 20 below zero. The motor fell out of the bus. I told the guys to try to keep warm any way they could and I flagged down a car to ride 25 miles to Rochester for help."[33] True to their name, the Globetrotters, and Woods, traveled the world. In 1959, at the height of the Cold War, the team traveled to Russia and Woods was able to meet Nikita Khrushchev.[34]

In 1962, Woods and Lessie divorced. They were married for 23 years and had two children, Charron (Cox) and Mickey. Soon after, he married Charlotte Williams, a teacher from Fort Wayne, Indiana. They met in her hometown when the Globetrotters played an exhibition game there. They had four children together, Beauford, Brenda, Parnell Jr., and Jeffry.

Charlotte was heavily involved in the Democratic Party and in 1964, was the first Black woman to run for the state legislature in Indiana. In 1965 she hosted the inaugural dinner for President Lyndon B. Johnson. In 1968 she began to work with Pegleg Bates for his country club (Bates Country Club) in Kerhonkson, New York. Parnell worked there as general manager over the summer before heading out on the road with the Globetrotters in the fall. Charlotte also owned Charlotte's Lounge in Wawarsing, New York. Parnell would also help there in the summers.

Woods married Rosa McGivens in 1973. Rosa owned a KFC restaurant in Cleveland and was a member of the Negro Professional and Business Women's organization. She would travel with Woods as he performed public-relations work with the Globetrotters.

Woods continued working with the Globetrotters in some capacity until around 1975. Throughout his time with the team, he saw five Hall of Fame baseball players suit up to play basketball with the Globetrotters: Bob Gibson, Fergie Jenkins, Lou Brock, Ernie Banks, and Satchel Paige.

Woods died of colon cancer on July 23, 1977, in Cleveland. He is buried in Lake View Cemetery, Cleveland.

ACKNOWLEDGMENTS

Gratitude is extended to Brenda Coleman and Jeffry Woods, who took the time to answer my emails about their father.

SOURCES

Unless otherwise indicated, all statistics and team records were taken from Seamheads.com.

NOTES

1 Al DeSantis, "The Happiest Globetrotter Face," *Middletown* (New York) *Times Herald Record*, July 12, 1972: 79.

2 "Parnell Woods Rated Top Third Baseman," *Atlanta Daily World*, September 8, 1942: 5.

3 James A. Riley, *The Biographical Encyclopedia of the Negro Baseball Leagues* (New York: Carroll & Graf Publishers, 1994), 879.

4 Riley, 879.

5 On December 16, 2020, Major League Baseball announced that seven distinct Negro Leagues would be recognized as major leagues.

6 "Buckeyes Lose Pair," *Cincinnati Enquirer*, May 18, 1942: 14.

7 "Parnell Woods Rated Top Third Baseman."

8 Numerous newspapers ran this story, including the *Jackson* (Mississippi) *Advocate*, the *Phoenix Index*, and the *Sioux City Journal*.

9 Fay Young, "Through the Years: Past-Present-Future New Recruit," *Chicago Defender* national edition, August 7, 1943: 11.

10 "Cleveland Pilot Placed in 1-A," *New Pittsburgh Courier*, March 25, 1944: 12.

11 Bob Williams, "Sports Rambler," *Cleveland Call and Post*, April 22, 1944: 9B.

12 Bob Williams, "Expect 15,000 to Witness Chi-Cleveland Contest; Teams Split 2 in Chicago," *Cleveland Call and Post*, June 24, 1944: 6B.

13 "Buckeyes Sweep 2, Play Chicago Again Tonight," *Cleveland Plain Dealer*, June 26, 1944: 14.

14 Bob Williams, "Press Barred from Closed Meeting; Negro Baseball's Joint Meeting at New York," *Cleveland Call and Post*, December 23, 1944: 6B.

15 Wesley Rollo Wilson, "Through the Eyes of W. Rollo Wilson," *Philadelphia Tribune*, October 27, 1945: 12.

16 John Holway, *Voices from the Great Black Baseball Leagues; Revised Edition* (Mineola, New York: Dover Publications Inc., 2010), 267.

17 Wendell Smith, "The Sports Beat – Holiday Greetings from Venezuela," *Pittsburgh Courier*, December 22, 1945: 22.

18 Cleveland Jackson, "3 Buckeye Stars Seek Reinstatement from Baseball Ban: Canizares, Woods, W. Jefferson May Return to Buckeyes; Travel Trouble Kept Stars in S.A.," *Cleveland Call and Post*, February 22, 1947: 8B.

19 "Baseball Notes: Canizares Gripes," *Cleveland Call and Post*, August 10, 1946: 11B.

20 "Parnell Woods Likes Play in South America," *Cleveland Call and Post*, October 4, 1947: 9B.

21 "Parnell Woods Likes Play in South America."

22 "Parnell Woods Likes Play in South America."

23 "Parnell Woods to Play with Harlem Globetrotters Club," *Chicago Defender*, April 3, 1948: 11.

24 Frank Ardolino, "The Hawaiian All-Stars and the Harlem Globetrotters: A 1948 Barnstorming Tour," *Baseball Research Journal* (Cleveland: SABR, 2005).

25 "Trotters Mourn Death of Saperstein," Greensboro (North Carolina) Record, March 16, 1966: 30.

26 "Caracas Uprising No Picnic – Woods," Cleveland Call and Post, December 4, 1948: 13B.

27 "Caracas Uprising No Picnic – Woods."

28 "Luke Easter's Baseball Stars Will Play Here," Fresno (California) Bee October 11, 1949: 26.

29 "Easter's All-Stars Face Fain Nine," Oakland Tribune, October 16, 1949: 34.

30 Art Paymiller, "Luke Easter's All-Stars Put Slug on Valley Nine by 12-8 Margin," Visalia (California) Times Delta, October 20, 1949: 12.

31 "Official Negro American League Statistics for the 1951 Season," Kansas City (Missouri) *Call*, February 1, 1952: 11.

32 "Trotters Attract 9,428 Here," Omaha World-Herald, February 15, 1967: 55.

33 Dwight Chapin, "Trotters' Old Act Still Keeps 'Em Laughing," Los Angeles Times, January 30, 1972: 46.

34 "Harlem Globetrotters Win Friends During Their 12-Day Tour of Russia," Kansas City *Call*, July 24, 1959: 12.

Ernest Wright

By Russ Speiller

In an era when many African Americans lived in poverty and were treated as second-class citizens, Ernest Pearle Wright managed to rise and persevere as a successful businessman.

Born on October 7, 1901, in Zanesville, Ohio, Ernest was the only child to mother Jessie (Forney) Wright and father Luther Wright, who died just a few years after Ernest was born. As a teenager, Ernest had become a good all-around athlete and a well above average pool player. Ernest put his pool-playing skills to use as he traveled throughout numerous cities in New York, Illinois, and Ohio hustling billiards.[1] While in Chicago, Ernest met and married Emma Win in 1927 with whom he had a daughter, Eunice, two years earlier. By 1930, Ernie, Emma, and Eunice had moved to Syracuse, New York, where Ernie was listed in the Syracuse City Directories as selling tobacco and cigars while also running a poolroom.

Sometime over the next five years, Ernie's marriage to Emma went astray as Ernie became involved with a woman named Hannah Gray. The two had a child, Ernest P. Wright Jr., born in Syracuse on August 13, 1935.

With her son Ernest traveling the pool circuit, Jessie moved from West Virginia, where she had been a schoolteacher, to Erie, Pennsylvania, where she married William Pope on July 2, 1918. A few years later, the Popes purchased a piece of real estate at 1318 French Street, initially their residence but soon to become known in Erie as the Pope Hotel.[2]

Jessie Pope was a strong force within the Black community and became a founding officer of the Erie branch of the National Association for the Advancement of Colored People. By 1923 she was the president of the Erie branch. While husband William had many different jobs including railroad conductor, janitor, railroad watchman, and proprietor of the Commerce Street Garage, Jessie was listed as running the 15-room hotel, making her one of the few African American business owners of her era.[3]

Upon the repeal of the Prohibition Act in 1933, Jessie obtained a liquor license for the hotel and asked her son Ernest to move to Erie to help her manage the Pope Hotel. Ernie obliged.[4]

Ernest Wright had an engaging personality and grand vision. He turned the Pope Hotel into a nightclub hotspot for Black culture and music, recruiting top entertainers to perform there, including jazz musicians Duke Ellington, Louis Armstrong and singer/actress Pearl Bailey.[5]

Unlike other clubs in town, the Pope Hotel distinguished itself by employing a live emcee, a regular band, and a female chorus line. And the hotel regularly welcomed both Black and White crowds.[6] The hotel became a place where Whites and Blacks could put their prejudice aside to enjoy great entertainment.

The Pope Hotel wasn't Ernie Wright's only source of business. He was known to be involved in running an illegal gambling racket, which was the subject of police raids in the mid to late 1930s.[7] Playing the numbers was a ubiquitous part of African American life. Popularized in Harlem in the 1920s, the numbers game gave African Americans the chance to supplement low wages and strive for economic security. Thousands of wagers would be placed on a daily number derived from US bank statistics or horse-race betting handles. "Hitting the number" could lead to a very high payout.

While running his various businesses, Wright had an itch he was eager to scratch. He very much wanted to establish a Negro League baseball team. He knew he needed a partner with the skills to scout, recruit, and promote talent. Asking around, Wright was directed to Wilbur Hayes, a successful sports and entertainment promoter in the Cleveland area. Wright drove from Erie to Cleveland to meet Hayes at his shoeshine parlor.

The initial meeting between the two men was described in the *Cleveland Call & Post* by sports editor Bob Williams: "Ernie Wright had driven up in a fine limousine and inquired – 'Are you, Wilbur Hayes?' How'd you like to start up a baseball club with me as a backer?" Hayes replied, "I'm a busy man – if you want the benefit of my baseball

Mr. and Mrs. Wright at a ball game

Hannah and Ernie Wright.

knowledge and experience, you'll have to come back to-morrow." Wright returned the following day and a deal between the pair was consummated.[8] In 1941, with funds from Wright's various business ventures, Wright and Hayes purchased a half-interest in the St Louis Stars, a Negro American League team that played games in Cleveland often enough that some newspapers would refer to the team as the St Louis-Cleveland Stars.[9]

The first season was a trial by fire for Wright. In July the *Call & Post* anointed him with the title of "Gamest Guy of the Year" for attempting to bankroll baseball's comeback in Cleveland, which "has been taking a financial beating."[10]

The first attempt for Wright was a ballgame he financed to be played between the Chicago Giants and Kansas City Monarchs, but it was canceled by rain. Wright then set up a game between the Cleveland White Sox and Kansas City Monarchs. The White Sox were a local semipro team that he took over from business manager Wesley Brooks. Wright purchased uniforms and baseball equipment for the team The matchup failed to draw a lot of fans who instead opted that day to go see famed heavyweight boxer Joe Louis at a horse show.[11]

Wright's third try, a game between the Cleveland White Sox and Indianapolis Indians, was also not to be the charm. Fans were underwhelmed by previous White Sox showings, and few turned out. Wright had paid to bring in six players from the St. Louis Stars to fortify the White Sox. The strategy worked as the White Sox trounced Indianapolis in two games.[12]

At the winter meetings of 1941, 40-year-old Ernest Wright became the Negro League's youngest owner as he was awarded the Cleveland Buckeyes franchise to begin play in the Negro American League in 1942. Wright installed Wilbur Hayes as the team's general manager and William DeHart Hubbard, a former Olympic star and founder of the Cincinnati Tigers baseball team, as its secretary.[13]

For their first season, the Buckeyes split their home games between Cincinnati and Cleveland. Starting in 1943, Cleveland was its only home; the team played home games at League Park.[14]

Between 1922 and 1940, Cleveland had 10 different Negro League teams, only one of which lasted beyond a single season. Cracking the code to winning with the Buckeyes seemed like an impossible task.

The 1942 Cincinnati-Cleveland Buckeyes played to great success. The July 11th edition of the Atlanta Daily World proclaimed, "Cincinnati Buckeyes Hottest Team in Negro Baseball During 1942," finishing in second place during the first half of the season, just behind the Kansas City Monarchs.[15] Though no first- or second-half standings were published, seamheads.com lists their record as 50-27-2 in the Negro American League.

However, the 1942 season also brought the Buckeyes great tragedy. With the team bus broken, players had to carpool between road games. On September 7, 1942, some members of the Buckeyes were involved in a car crash that led to the deaths of catcher Ulysses "Buster" Brown and pitcher Raymond "Smoky" Owens as well as injuries to pitchers Alonzo Boone, Eugene Bremerton, Herman Watts, and general manager Hayes.[16] The team spent the final two weeks of the season engaged in road contests, all of which they lost.

Besides running the Buckeyes, the partnership of Wright and Hayes began a professional basketball team, also named the Cleveland Buckeyes. Hayes leased the Old Elks' Hall to be their home floor.[17]

The basketball squad did not last long. In December of 1944, Hayes released player Louis "Babe" Pressley, who went on to star for the Harlem Globetrotters. Then another pivotal player, Duke Cumberland, left the team. In the end, Wright declared that "Cleveland is not basketball conscious" and ended his financial backing of the team.[18] The team subsequently folded.

With their attention back on enriching the baseball Buckeyes, shrewd player signings and internal growth turned the team around in a positive way, culminating in the Buckeyes' 1945 championship season. By this time, center fielder Sam Jethroe had developed into the league's most valuable player. Wright and Hayes signed former Negro League All-Star catcher Quincy Trouppe to be player-manager. Other players on the 1945 team included pitcher Willie Grace, team captain and third baseman Parnell Woods, and right fielder Lloyd "Ducky" Davenport. According to *Call & Post* sports editor Bob Williams, "With the exception of the World Champion Homestead Grays, the Bucks are reputed to be the highest-paid Negro Club in America."[19]

The Buckeyes finished the 1945 season with a record of 62 wins,17 losses, and one tie. They were led by their pitchers, who had a combined ERA of 2.52. In the Negro League World Series, the Buckeyes clashed with the defending champion Homestead Grays, and did the unthinkable, sweeping the Grays and emerging as World Series champions. The Cleveland City Council passed a resolution commemorating the Buckeyes' championship, and a banquet was held in their honor for the "glory and distinction" they brought to the city.[20]

The Buckeyes followed a middling 1946 season with a terrific 1947 in which they finished with 57 wins and 19 losses, earning themselves another trip to the Negro League World Series. This time, the Buckeyes fell to the New York Cubans in six games with one game being called a tie on account of rain.

It must have been a conflicting feeling for Ernest Wright when in 1947 Jackie Robinson broke the White major leagues' color line. After all, Wright had always believed in the integration of Blacks and Whites, welcoming both into his nightclub at the Pope Hotel. In 1945 Wright became the first lifetime member of the Future Outlook League, a Cleveland-based civil rights organization founded to promote employment, equality, and mobility for young

Blacks.[21] But he was also a man of great business acumen who was becoming victimized by the flow of star Black ballplayers forgoing the Negro Leagues.

In 1947, in his own town of Cleveland, Wright watched as Larry Doby became the first Black player to go directly from the Negro Leagues to the White major leagues, where he helped the Cleveland Indians become World Series champions in 1948. With Doby and superstar former Negro League pitcher Satchel Paige, the Cleveland Indians set a major-league attendance record of 2,620,627 in 1948.[22] Meanwhile Negro League attendance was falling. Wright looked for ways to keep the Buckeyes afloat. At one point he attempted reverse integration, offering a White sandlot pitcher named Eddie Klep a tryout with the Buckeyes. Klep had stifled the Buckeyes hitters in an exhibition game the previous summer. The Buckeyes signed Klep, who became the first White player to train with a Negro League team.[23] Klep's signing, however, appeared to be mostly a publicity stunt as he appeared in just three games before being released.

Wright knew it was the "doom of the (Negro) League when [the major leagues] started dickering for our players," but he tried to hold on as he moved the Buckeyes to Louisville for the 1949-50 season. The Louisville Buckeyes played their home games at Parkway Field, the home field of the Louisville Colonels of the American Association.[24]

Fortunes only got worse as the team went 8-29 in the first half of the season, followed by 7-22 in the second half. Wright lost money, and in 1950 handed over operations of the Buckeyes to Wilbur Hayes.[25] Hayes moved the team back to Cleveland, where he was unable to reverse its fortunes. The Buckeyes were dissolved after the 1950 season.

With the demise of the Buckeyes, Wright's attention focused back on the Pope Hotel, of which he was now the sole owner after the death of his mother in 1942.

In December of 1958, a fire blazed through the main floor of the Pope, destroying its rooms and the bar and grill areas. Though Wright saw this tragedy as an opportunity to renovate the hotel, the insurance covered only 44 percent of the loss; hence, the first floor was never rebuilt and the upstairs never renovated.[26]

By the 1960s, nightspot entertainment was declining, and the Pope Hotel now staged live entertainment only on the weekends. And by the 1970s, attendance at the Pope and in general was in complete free fall. When it came to revenues, it didn't help matters that Wright had a heart of gold. In addition to putting the performers up at the hotel, he would often lend people money and welcome friends like Sam Jethroe to stay there free of charge. In some cases, patrons took advantage of Wright by neglecting to pay their bill.[27]

By the early 1970s, rooms at the Pope Hotel had declined both in quality and as a source of income for Wright. In 1973 the city Bureau of Housing cited the hotel for violations including exposed wires in the bathroom and electrical outlets without faceplates. Doors and windows needed repairs, and the paint was peeling.[28]

Those employed by Ernest Wright spoke highly of him and residents of Erie referred to him as "Boss." Wright was lauded by Mayor Louis J. Tullio for "managing and promoting good will and camaraderie at the Pope Hotel."[29]

Wright was an affable conversationalist whose socialization skills helped make the Pope Hotel a success for a while, but he was also careless when it came to his financial practices which may have been the final straw that broke the back of the hotel. Financial records from the 1960s and '70s indicate certified letters and final notices sent by the Internal Revenue Service demanding payment of taxes. In 1964 a balance of $248.68 was found in arrears, while in 1971 the amount was $1,108.12. In 1974, a federal judgment was entered against Wright for failure to pay $1,483.14 in income tax.[30]

Wright and his wife, Hannah, had three sons, Ernest Pearle Wright Jr., Charles Earl Wright, and William Wright. There were two daughters, Eunice, from his first marriage, and Dorothy. When Wright's health began to decline, he enlisted Ernest Jr. and Charles to help run the hotel. Ernest Jr., who had a degree in in business administration and business management from Howard Univeersity, was unable to prevent the hotel's demise. Profit and loss statements in 1973 showed a deficit in one of every three months. On March 3, 1977, Ernest Wright Sr. turned the Pope Hotel over to his son Charles, who was a bartender and bouncer at the hotel. He loved being around people and never saw his time at the Pope as work. However, the persistent financial problems never ceased and in early 1978 Wright made the tough decision to close the hotel.[31] It was later torn down.

Ernest Pearle Wright died on April 11, 1985, at the age of 84, having accomplished his dream of being a Black owner of a successful Negro League baseball team as well as a husband, a father, and someone fondly regarded by his peers and loved ones, including his children who survived him.[32] Wright is buried at the Erie Cemetery.

SOURCES

In addition to the sources cited in the Notes, the author consulted seamheads.com and Baseball-Reference.com. The author thanks Heber MacWilliams, who shared his research notes on Ernest Pearle Wright, including census records and Wright's World War II registration card, on which he listed his birthday as October 7, 1901, which is in contrast to what is mentioned in his obituary and on the website of the Erie Cemetery, both of which list his birth year as 1900. The author also thanks Steven Mooradian, processing archivist at the Hagen History Center, Erie, Pennsylvania, for providing documentation on Ernest Wright and the Pope Hotel.

NOTES

1   Phillip Nykyforuk, "The Pope Hotel 1928-1978," *Journal of Erie Studies*, Vol 16 Issue 2 (Fall 1987), 23.

2   Nykyforuk, 23.

3   Nykyforuk, 23.

4   Nykyforuk, 23.

5   Nykyforuk, 23.

6   Nykyforuk, 23.

7   "Numbers Sellers Is Fined in Court," *Erie Daily Times*, November 11, 1937.

8   Bob Williams, "Sports Rambler," *Cleveland Call & Post*, September 29, 1945: 7B.

9   Al Sweeny, "Hayes-Wright Purchase Interest in St. Louis Stars," *Cleveland Call & Post*, July 5, 1941: 9A.

10 Al Sweeny, "Gamest Guy of the Year," *Cleveland Call & Post*, July 19, 1941: 9A.

11 Dr. Anastasia Curwood, "From Magazine: A Look at the World War II-Era All-Black Horse Shows," *The Chronicle of the Horse*, https://www.chronofhorse.com/article/from-the-magazine-a-look-back-at-the-world-war-ii-era-all-black-horse-shows/. Accessed August 23, 2024. The appeal of Black horse riding and showmanship increased exponentially when heavyweight champion Joe Louis became a prominent rider and owner. Louis built a combination boxing and equestrian training center in Utica, New York. Tickets to his horse shows were almost as hot a commodity as those for a Detroit Tigers World Series game.

12 Al Sweeny, "Gamest Guy of the Year."

13 "Buckeyes Get Franchise in the Negro American League," *Cleveland Call & Post*, January 3, 1942: 9A.

14 "Buckeye Franchise Moved to Cleveland by N.A.L.," *Cleveland Call & Post*, January 9, 1943: 10.

15 Lucius Jones, "Sports Slants," *Atlanta Daily World*, July 11, 1942: 5.

16 "Buckeye Players Die in Crash," *Cleveland Call & Post*, September 12, 1942: 1.

17 "Buckeyes to Play in Basketball Loop," *Cleveland Call & Post*, October 17, 1942: 10.

18 Bob Williams, "Sports Rambler," *Cleveland Call & Post*, December 16, 1944: 7B.

19 Bob Williams, "Sports Rambler," *Cleveland Call & Post*, January 2, 1945: 6B.

20 Bob Williams, "Posey Nominates Jackson for Negro Baseball Commissioner," *Cleveland Call & Post*, October 6, 1945: 6B.

21 "Ernest Wright Is First 1945 Life Member of F.O.L.," *Cleveland Call & Post*, October 20, 1945: 9A.

22 Japheth Knopp, "Baseball's Integration Spells the End of the Negro Leagues," https://sabr.org/research/article/baseballs-integration-spells-the-end-of-the-negro-leagues/; Accessed August 17, 2024.

23 Cleveland Jackson, "Ernie Wright Does 'Rickey' in Reverse; Gives White Sandlot Pitcher a Tryout," *Cleveland Call & Post*, January 4, 1947: 1B.

24 "Buckeyes Move to Louisville, Ky.," *Cleveland Call & Post*, February 12, 1949: 6B.

25 "Ernie Wright Out, Wilbur Hayes In as Operator of Buckeyes Franchise," *Cleveland Call and Post*, February 18, 1950: 1B.

26 Nykyforuk, 30.

27 Nykyforuk, 26-27.

28 Nykyforuk, 27.

29 Nykyforuk, 29.

30 Nykyforuk, 31.

31 Nykyforuk, 32-33.

32 *Erie Times-News*, November 23, 1986: 5K.

Wilbur Hayes

By Isaac C. Brooks, Jr. and Thomas Kern

There is documented evidence that baseball in Cleveland goes back to the Civil War era. An 1867 article in the *Cleveland Plain Dealer* mentions 22 teams practicing on the ball ground. Two of the teams were composed of African American players.[1]

By 1918, the first professional Black team, the Tate Stars, formed. The Tate Stars joined the Negro National League in 1922. By 1941, nine other professional Negro League teams called Cleveland home – more than any other US city. Those teams all had one thing in common: short-lived with unexceptional, at best, playing records.

That trend of mediocrity began to change at the end of 1941 with the collaboration between Ernest Wright and Wilbur Hayes in the formation of the Buckeyes. There is minimal biographical information on the architects of the most successful of the 11 Cleveland-based Negro League teams. Reliable sources such as Baseball-Reference.com and the Seamheads Negro League Database contain only nominal information primarily focused on the time that the team played in Cleveland. Another site, Blackpast.org, has the following entry:

"The Cleveland Buckeyes were a Negro League baseball team established initially as the Buckeyes Baseball Club, in Cincinnati, Ohio. On the eve of World War II, a white Cleveland sports promoter, Wilbur Hayes, approached Erie, Pennsylvania Black businessman Ernest Wright about financially backing a Cleveland-based black baseball team. The two collaborated and brought together a strong team of professional baseball players who initially played their home games out of Crosley Field, in Cincinnati."[2]

Based on photographs, newspaper accounts, and recollections of those who knew and worked with Wilbur Hayes, this entry is wrong about Hayes' race. He was African American.

Notwithstanding the sparse published biographical information on the key executives, access to heretofore unpublished research compiled by Merl F. Kleinknecht has been invaluable. Kleinknecht's research was gathered during 1994 with the cooperation of the Wilbur Hayes family and research of the *Cleveland Call and Post* and *Pittsburgh Courier* newspapers. This undertaking coincided with activities, programs, and events honoring the 50th anniversary of the Cleveland Buckeyes Negro League World Series championship.

Wilbur Filmore Hayes was born on August 25, 1898, in Owensboro, Kentucky. He was of African American ancestry. His parents were Milford "Doc" Hayes and Ella Mae Daniel Hayes (homemaker). The 1910 US Census identified the Hayes family of five (Hayes, Hayes' mother and father, and two older brothers) as residents of McLean County, near Owensboro, and listed Milford as a farm laborer. Kleinknecht's interviews with the Hayes family confirmed that Hayes attended Orange Elementary and Brownell Junior High Schools in Owensboro into his teenage years.

It is unclear exactly when and why Hayes relocated nearly 400 miles to Cleveland from his home in Kentucky, but in 1919, at the age of 21, Hayes married Gertrude Prinne (born in Buffalo and aged 18 at the time), according to Cuyahoga County, Ohio, records. The marriage license identified Hayes as a chauffeur and living at 2356 Marion Avenue in Cleveland. No record of his divorce from his first wife has yet been found, and 1920 Census records show them living at 2349 East 40th Street. A second marriage was recorded on August 24, 1922, with Beatrice Elizabeth Johnson, with whom Hayes had a daughter, Dorothy. The marriage license listed Hayes as a trucker living at 45 Ridge Street, Akron, Ohio. The license recorded that neither Wilbur nor Beatrice had been married previously, lending an air of intrigue to Hayes' first marriage. Beatrice or Bessie was born in Richmond, Virginia, and was 17 at the time of their marriage. Again, no date of divorce has been

Wilbur Hayes.

found, but Hayes married a third time to Erma Brown (age 25, from Toledo) on May 25, 1925. The marriage license showed Hayes as a driver, residing at 2338 E. 46th Street in Cleveland. Their 32-year marriage ended when Hayes died in 1957. They had two sons (Wilbur, Jr. and Don Leslie) and four daughters (Betty, Garnett, Erma Dee, and Jeannine).[3]

The aforementioned marriage licenses, Cleveland city directories over the years, and census records place Hayes at a number of different addresses. The 1930 Census has Wilbur and Erma at 5812 Thackeray Avenue and the 1940 Census at 2275 E. 70th Street. The 1950 Census and the 1951 City Directory list the family home at 6019 Hawthorne Avenue. At the time of his death, he and Erma were living at 5512 Quimby Avenue. The Quimby Avenue residence is about a half-mile from League Park. Hayes died on February 9, 1957, in Cleveland and was buried in Highland Park Cemetery.[4] Erma lived almost another quarter-century and died on April 14, 1981.

In addition to Hayes' previously cited work as a chauffeur and truck driver for the City of Cleveland Services Department,[5] he also owned a grooming parlor and shoeshine business at East 49th Street and Central Avenue in Cleveland. This appeared to be his base of operations during the 1940s. At the time of his death in 1957, he was reported to have been employed as a factory worker for an unidentified company.

Wilbur Hayes' sports background was varied and impressive. As a young man, he was a star amateur athlete, participating in basketball, baseball, boxing, and football. According to his obituary in the Cleveland Call and Post, "Hayes became interested in sports during the year of 1926, when he managed a Negro team that played its first night baseball at Tate Field, at East 55th Street off Broadway."[6] He has been described as Cleveland's first entertainment promoter catering to the city's Black population. He began promoting events in the city at an early age, including basketball at the Elks Hall, baseball at Hooper Field, beauty pageants at Luna Park, boxing at Marotta's Gym, and football at Kingsbury Run.[7]

During the 1930s, Hayes operated a boxing gym at 49th Street and Central Avenue and he was later involved in the opening of a gym to train young fighters. Hayes was also given credit for forming the Cleveland area's first all-Black football team and operating an undisclosed number of football teams throughout that decade.[8]

In 1941 Hayes assumed operation of the Cleveland White Sox, a semipro baseball team. With that team, he applied for associate membership in the Negro American League. The Cleveland Call and Post included his letter to J.B. Martin, president of the Negro American League, in its March 8, 1941, edition. The letter said, "The Cleveland Fan and Business Men are deeply interested in having a team composed of Cleveland boys as an Associate Member of your League. … We are putting forth every effort to form a first class club."[9] To accomplish this, he forged a partnership with Erie, Pennsylvania, hotel owner Ernest Wright as Wright purchased a half-interest in the Negro American League St. Louis Stars and made Hayes business manager.[10] Arguably, from Wright's perspective, it was his initiative that led to the partnership with Hayes. (See Ernest Wright's SABR biography for this point of view.) The Cleveland Call and Post also captured Hayes' continuing efforts as a promoter to bring top-tier Black baseball to Cleveland: "Encouraged by the interest manifested by Cleveland's baseball lovers in top-flight sepia teams, Wilbur Hayes climbed into the ranks of active promoters this week by grace of a well-heeled backer [Wright], and a contract with League moguls for the use of the Park on the Indians' out-of-town dates."[11]

Hayes did more than reach out to Negro American League officials and organize games by visiting teams to Cleveland. In July 1941 he wrote an open letter to Cleveland's baseball fans. The letter is worth including in its entirety:

> I want to urge all of my friends and all of those persons interested in the perpetuation of Negro Baseball in Cleveland to be on hand, Sunday July 27th, at League Park. My backer and I have spent time and money trying to round out the best baseball talent available to give Cleveland a winning club. I believe that we have finally hit upon a winning combination. Both local boys and the best of the crop in the hinterlands are on this club. So, I'm appealing to, who are interested in seeing Negro baseball in Cleveland to be on hand at League Park this Sunday. I promise that you won't be disappointed.
>
> Wilbur Hayes, Promoter.[12]

These were important foundational steps, but building a successful baseball franchise is not an easy task and Hayes knew that. Over the next few years, he worked tirelessly.

Over the 1941-42 winter months, with his own limited funds and possibly supported by Wright's infusion of capital for the franchise, Hayes traveled throughout the South and Midwest scouting and signing players for the new franchise.

In 1942 the Buckeyes were admitted to the Negro American League with a roster that included a young East St. Louis catcher named Sam Jethroe.[13] Hayes and Wright reached an understanding with the league that the Buckeyes would play home games in Cincinnati and Cleveland to create a statewide appeal for the club and fill the Black-baseball void in both cities. The team's games began in Cincinnati and the May 13, 1942, issue of the Atlanta Daily World seemed to portray the sentiment of many in Cincinnati who were happy to share the Buckeyes with Cleveland:

"After two months of training by the ball players and of watchful waiting by the fans, the 1942 baseball season

THE 1945 CLEVELAND BUCKEYES

will get underway at Crosley Field Sunday afternoon when the Cincinnati Buckeyes cross bats with the famous Jacksonville Red Caps from Florida. This doubleheader will mark the opening of the Negro American League season and signal the return of professional league baseball in Cincinnati. No league teams having represented the Queen City since the old Tigers disbanded in 1938 after blazing a flaming trail across the baseball skies."[14]

A similar storyline appeared in the *Norfolk* (Virginia) *New Journal and Guide* on June 13 when the Jacksonville Red Caps split an Opening Day doubleheader with the Buckeyes at Cleveland's League Park. The team was described as "the first real locally owned team since the boom days of the old Tate Stars," and added, "Mayor Frank J. Lausche threw the first ball to Councilman Augustus G. Parker and Wilbur Hayes, front gate manager of the local Buckeyes."[15]

Further evidence of the commitment to Black baseball in Cleveland came during a meeting of the Negro American and National leagues in Chicago, when Ernest Wright, Cumberland Posey, business manager of the Homestead Grays and Wilbur Hayes were named co-workers of the committee on the benefit game to be played at Cleveland's Municipal Stadium on August 18, 1942.[16] The game was played two days after the annual East-West All-Star Game at Comiskey Park in Chicago. Many of the players from that contest also played in Cleveland. The game drew a crowd of 10,971 and brought in $9,499.04 for the Army-Navy Relief Fund. It was reported that this was the first time such a game for such a purpose had ever been staged in Cleveland. The East dominated the West by a score of 9-2.

During that initial season, the Buckeyes claimed the Negro American League's first-half championship. In September near the end of the season, the team was scheduled to play a four-game series against the New York Black Yankees in Buffalo, New York; Akron, Ohio; and Meadville, Pennsylvania, all in just over 24 hours. Players were traveling in three cars because their bus had broken down. One of the cars was involved in a fatal accident near Geneva, Ohio, that resulted in the death of catcher Buster Brown and pitcher Smoky Owens.[17] Hayes and three other players survived. The Buckeyes chose to finish their season after the accident. All of the games were played on the road and all resulted in losses.

At the beginning of 1943, the league allowed Hayes to drop Cincinnati from the two-city arrangement, and Cleveland became the Buckeyes' full-time home.[18] Also in 1943, while serving in his role as Negro American League sergeant-at-arms, Hayes aided in the ouster of the Consul of Mexico from Forbes Field in Pittsburgh, in response to the consul's pursuit of Negro League players for the Mexican League. (Over the years, Hayes signed at least four players from the Mexican League and lost three players to the league.) A special Wilbur Hayes Day was held on September 12, 1943, as the Buckeyes closed

out a second winning season.[19] At the NAL's December meeting, the Buckeyes were recognized as the league's Most Outstanding Franchise due to a five-fold attendance increase. Sam Jethroe was recognized as the league's "2nd Most Valuable Player."[20]

Despite finishing only three games over .500 in the league in 1944 (45-42), the Hayes-built Buckeyes featured the NAL's best defensive infield, as each infielder led at his position in NAL fielding average as well as having the loop's fastest and hardest-hitting outfield, paced by 1944 batting champion Sam Jethroe. During the December NAL meeting, Hayes traded the rights to Mexican League defector Theolic Smith to the Kansas City Monarchs for the rights to Mexican League catcher Quincy Trouppe.

These initial moves helped set the table for 1945. Hayes named Trouppe the team manager. He told the *Call and Post* that "knowing that catching was our weakest spot last year, we have taken care of that position by signing Quincy Trouppe."[21] He persuaded the previous pilot, all-star third baseman Parnell Woods, to remain with the Buckeyes as team captain. Trouppe brought along far-ranging Mexican League shortstop Avelino Cañizares, a Cuban,[22] to further strengthen an already formidable infield. The Buckeyes' addition of Trouppe as catcher reunited him with former Monterrey batterymate Willie Jefferson. Hayes acquired four former Mexican League players and the Mexican League Raiders had one former Buckeye.

Call and Post columnist Bob Williams wrote, "Spring training is just around the corner, and the Buckeyes do seem really destined to play some real ball this year."[23] The *Call and Post* also declared that the Buckeyes "are now preparing to bring Cleveland that long awaited winning team."[24]

The Buckeyes won 27 of their first 36 league games. Outfielders Jethroe, Buddy Armour, and Ducky Davenport (both acquired by Hayes in 1944) were the league's two, three, and four hitters respectively. With a 31-9 record, the team won the first-half NAL title. Outfielder Davenport defected to the Mexican League before second-half play began.

In July and August Hayes, recognizing the importance of community involvement, sent the Buckeyes into Cleveland's Municipal Stadium for games to benefit the Future Outlook League.[25] The Future Outlook League, founded in Cleveland in 1935, was a civil rights organization focused on promoting employment, mobility, and equality for African American youth and young adults.[26]

On September 2 Hayes was honored in a ceremony at League Park and was presented with a certificate for a new Chevrolet. Wrote the *Call and Post*, "[T]he presentation climaxed an effort to show how much Hayes is appreciated for his years in sports and particularly his outstanding job of building the Buckeyes into a championship ball club."[27] It was reported that his previous car had 250,000 miles on it. The Buckeyes were also crowned second-half NAL champs.[28] Their reward was a slot in the Negro League World Series against the dominant Homestead Grays.

In the run-up to the Series, Hayes received full credit for building the Buckeyes. "Just four years ago Manager Wilbur Hayes began to collect pro and semi-pro ball players from all over the country to begin building today's championship title contenders. The brilliant players who hold down most berths on the Buckeyes' squad were secured only after long and diligent search," wrote the *Call and Post*.[29] The Hayes-built Buckeyes swept the Grays in four straight games in that World Series. The new Negro League world champions were feted on September 30 with a banquet in Cleveland's Majestic Hotel. Hayes "gave credit freely to those who aided in the Buckeyes' progress" and Ernest Wright was "'too overwhelmed to talk' and actually felt like crying, he was so happy."[30]

The team focused on sustaining its championship caliber, but the 1946 season was impacted from the start by a series of offseason occurrences that began when Cañizares signed a contract to return to the Mexican League. Parnell Woods and Willie Jefferson left the team to play in Venezuela and, to top things off, pitcher George Jefferson (Willie's brother) suffered a serious arm injury in winter league play. Nonetheless, "[O]wner Ernie Wright and general manager Wilbur Hayes are leaving no stones unturned in their attempts to strengthen the Forest City Nine for the 1946 diamond campaign."[31]

Hayes signed young prospects Al Smith, Leon Kellman, Tommy Harris, and Vibert Clarke[32] and obtained veteran pitcher Chet Brewer,[33] but the Buckeyes suffered through a so-so campaign, finishing a distant third to pennant winner Kansas City. But the young players gained valuable experience. Willie Grace, who was signed by Hayes late in the 1942 season, emerged as the bright spot of the season and was named the club's most outstanding player.[34] A November scouting trip in the South by Hayes brought in five more prospects including reputed slugger Joe Atkins.[35]

The 1947 season got underway with Hayes trading veteran outfielder Armour for Clyde Nelson and acquiring young right-handed pitcher Sam Jones (who had pitched briefly for the 1946 NNL Homestead Grays). With Smith, Kellman, Harris, Clarke, Atkins, Brewer, Jones, and Nelson all performing at a championship level along with 1945 holdovers Gene Bremer, Quincy Trouppe, Archie Ware, Sam Jethroe, and Grace, Hayes' rebuilt Buckeyes returned to the Negro American League throne with a 57-19 record.

Doc Young in the *Call and Post* reminded readers that Hayes told fans earlier in the year, "Boys, I am going to give Cleveland and the surrounding cities of Ohio another championship team and I don't mean maybe!"[36] In recognition of Hayes' delivering, he was honored for his job as general manager and Trouppe for his job as manager in ceremonies at League Park.[37]

As Negro American League champions, the Buckeyes were set to meet the New York Cubans in the World Series.[38]

A second championship was not to be, however, and the Buckeyes lost 4-1-1 to the Cubans. Deflated but unbowed, Buckeyes fans and the team moved on. And changes were in the works, particularly in light of Jackie Robinson's breaking the color barrier and the slow trickle of Black ballplayers into the American and National leagues. Hayes began in December by naming Alonzo Boone as the team's new manager.[39]

Early in 1948 Quincy Trouppe's contract was sold to the Chicago American Giants, who named him manager. Hayes also sold veteran second baseman Johnnie Cowan to the Memphis Red Sox and sent Atkins to the Kansas City Monarchs for Othello Renfroe, an infielder, and catcher Joe Greene. Renfroe hit .306 as the Buckeyes shortstop and Greene, a veteran, filled in capably for the departed Trouppe behind the plate. Atkins left the NAL to play in Canada's Provincial League. The Buckeyes finished in second place for the NAL's first half. However, the team plummeted in the second half and ended with a record of 47-53-3 as Sam Jethroe, the offensive leader since the team's inception, and Al Smith entered the White major leagues. Jethroe was sold to the Brooklyn Dodgers and Smith to the Cleveland Indians.[40] The Buckeyes received a reported $5,000 for Jethroe; the Dodgers later sold Jethroe to the Boston Braves for over $100,000.[41] As a sign of the times, the *Call and Post* sports pages began covering Black ballplayers in the American and National Leagues, forgoing column-inches in its weekly paper for previously covered Buckeyes in order to focus on the Indians and Dodgers.[42]

The Buckeyes relocated to Louisville for the 1949 NAL season[43] as the Cleveland Indians came to the forefront of integration and drew Buckeyes fans to their games to see former Negro League stars Larry Doby and Satchel Paige perform. The *Call and Post* reported on this development in early 1949:

There will be no Buckeyes to represent this city in the Eastern Division of the Negro American League as previously announced by management last month. ... The franchise was transferred to Louisville by the league directors. ... [I]t is believed that the switch was made to take some of the pressure off the team. It is a certainty that most of the slack in attendance at Buckeyes games last year was due to the tremendous popularity of Larry Doby and the Cleveland Indians. ... Last year, the club was considerably weakened by the loss of Sam Jethroe, who went to the Brooklyn Dodgers and Al Smith, sold to the Cleveland Indians.[44]

Hayes did bring the Buckeyes home to Cleveland for a July twin bill sponsored by the Karamu House, a Cleveland-based center for performing arts and community education. The Karamu Benefit offered Hayes the opportunity to express remorse over the team's move to Louisville and, at least for a day, bring back Black baseball to Cleveland in the form of a Buckeyes-Indianapolis Clowns contest. Hayes "readily admits that he made a serious [mistake] when he took his popular aggregation of Negro stars off to Louisville with the expectations of bigger gates and lusher profits for his boss, Ernie Wright, Erie, PA, sportsman."[45]

The ever-optimistic Hayes hoped that improved business practices would ensure the survival of the Negro American League and Black baseball. In December Sam Jones was sold to the Cleveland Indians for $4,000. At the same time, Hayes announced the Buckeyes' return to Cleveland for the 1950 season.[46]

In 1950 Ernest Wright turned ownership of the Buckeyes over to Wilbur Hayes. The Buckeyes returned to Cleveland.[47] Hayes, cognizant of the competition from the Cleveland Indians with their integrated roster, shared his new business model with the press. "Hayes told the *Call and Post* that he expects to reduce prices for his home games, and that he is trying to arrange a number of night games to be played," the *Call and Post* reported.[48] Hayes' offseason player acquisitions reflected his longstanding commitment to the Hot Stove League. Hayes traded first baseman Archie Ware for Indianapolis Clowns' catcher Leonard Pigg, who was the 1949 NAL batting champion. Joe Caffie from nearby Warren, Ohio, was one of many youngsters that Hayes invited to spring training.[49] Caffie became an American Leaguer, debuting in 1956 with the Indians.

During a preseason interview, Hayes declared that Sam Jethroe was among the best players in baseball.[50] Jethroe became the first Black player for the Boston Braves and was named Rookie of the Year as he led both the American and National Leagues in stolen bases in 1950. Hayes knew the Negro Leagues would no longer be what they once were, given the drain of high-caliber players like Jethroe to the American and National Leagues thanks to integration.

Stubbornly, Hayes vowed that his young Buckeyes would burn the NAL with their blazing youth. With Pigg off to Canada to play, the 1950 Buckeyes went 3-37 and used 50 players as they suffered through a horrendous NAL first-half schedule. In early July, Hayes withdrew the Buckeyes (3-39) from the Negro American League.[51]

Ever the industrious and positive promoter, Wilbur Hayes seemed to recognize from the beginning that for Cleveland to sustain a Negro League franchise, support was necessary from the city's Black community, including its press and civic organizations. Through dedicated effort, he obtained the support of those elements to make the Buckeyes succeed for most of the 1940s.

Hayes masterfully built the Cleveland Buckeyes into a Negro League power. Seven Buckeyes eventually played in the White major leagues with varied degrees of success. Twelve players represented the club in the Negro Leagues' annual East-West All-Star Games, and every one of those players became Buckeyes through the singular efforts of Wilbur Hayes. Eventually Hayes had to recognize that the Cleveland Indians' aggressive role in integration and the success begun in 1947 left little room in the city for his Buckeyes. But for a time, Hayes had marshaled the talent and forces to make the Buckeyes a Cleveland success. In his time with the Buckeyes and the Negro American League, his executive profile was second to none. And at his death in 1957, the Cleveland community expressed their appreciation for his long and industrious career. The *Call and Post* summed it up: "Old sports fans and entertainers will never forget Wilbur Hayes, many of whom he started on their careers. He was loved by all groups for his interest in the sports field."[52]

BUSINESS/GENERAL MANAGEMENT

1942: Cincinnati-Cleveland Buckeyes
[Negro American League – NAL]
1st Half NAL Champions
1943: Cleveland Buckeyes [NAL]
Most Outstanding Franchise
1944: Cleveland Buckeyes [NAL]
1945: Cleveland Buckeyes [NAL]
NAL Champion
Negro League World Series Champion
1946: Cleveland Buckeyes [NAL]
1947: Cleveland Buckeyes [NAL]
NAL Champion
1948: Cleveland Buckeyes [NAL]
1st Half NAL Runner-up
1949: Louisville Buckeyes [NAL]

TEAM OWNERSHIP

1950: Cleveland Buckeyes [NAL]
Withdrew from NAL in early July

NEGRO AMERICAN LEAGUE ADMINISTRATION

Sergeant-at-arms [NAL]

SOURCES

In addition to the sources cited in the Notes, the authors wish to acknowledge the important contributions of Merl Kleinknecht.

Merl joined SABR in 1971.[53] His area of expertise was the Negro Baseball Leagues. Merl cited John Holway as exerting the greatest influence on his research efforts. Merl was a founding member of SABR's Negro Leagues Research Committee and served two terms as committee chair in the 1970s. He authored several articles published in a variety of publications. His research efforts have been recognized by the Ohio Baseball Hall of Fame. According to his son Jon, Kleinknecht is neither active in SABR in 2024 nor in writing and speaking about Negro League baseball. His focus has been on helping residents at an assisted living center. His son granted permission to share the research compiled by his father as SABR salutes the 1945 Cleveland Buckeyes during the 80th anniversary of that historic achievement.[54]

NOTES

1   Extract from a Cleveland Indians (now Guardians) website post from September 2020 regarding the history of Black baseball in Cleveland. As of December 2024, this post appears to be inaccessible.

2   Entry regarding the Cleveland Buckeyes on the website The Cleveland Buckeyes (1941-1950) • (blackpast.org), December 31, 2020.

3   This compilation is based on Federal Census records from 1910, 1920, 1930, 1940, and 1950. Also, Cuyahoga County, Ohio, marriage registries document Hayes' three marriages.

4   Wilbur Hayes (1898-1957) – Find a Grave Memorial.

5   Family members identified his workplace.

6   "Wilbur Hayes, Pioneer Baseball Promoter Dies," *Cleveland Call and Post*, February 16, 1957: 1A.

7   "Wilbur Hayes, Pioneer Baseball Promoter Dies."

8   "Wilbur Hayes, Pioneer Baseball Promoter Dies."

9   "Baseball Hopes Rise as Men Ask for Team Here, Plan to Have More Good Games Here on Sundays," *Cleveland Call and Post*, March 8, 1941: 7.

10   "League Awards Cincy '9' Berth," *Pittsburgh Courier*, January 3, 1942: 16.

11   "Hayes Back in Baseball Picture …with Backer," *Cleveland Call and Post*, May 24, 1941.

12   "Wilbur Hayes Pens an Open Letter to Baseball Fans," *Cleveland Call and Post*, July 26, 1941: 11.

13   "Seven Former 'Ethiopians' Bagged by Cincy Buckeyes," *Atlanta Daily World*, May 9, 1942: 5.

14   "Cincinnati Buckeyes, Jacksonville Reds Pry Lid in Negro American League Sunday," *Atlanta Daily World*, May 13, 1942: 5.

15   "9200 See Red Cap, Buckeyes Split Pair in Cleveland Opener." *Norfolk* (Virginia) *New Journal and Guide*, June 13, 1942: 14.

16   "Ernie Wright Chairman of Fund Game," *Pittsburgh Courier*, July 4, 1942: 16.

17   "Two Ball Players Killed; Four Injured: Pitcher and Catcher Die in Collision," *Chicago Defender*, September 12, 1942: 1-2.

18   "Cincinnati Baseball Club Goes to Cleveland, American League Moguls Plan for '43," *Norfolk New Journal and Guide*, January 9, 1943.

19   "Bucks Whip Cincy," *Pittsburgh Courier*, September 18, 1943: 16.

20   Bob Williams, "Chicago Meeting Gives Unanimous Endorsement; Kills Exhibition Games, *Cleveland Call and Post*, December 25, 1943: 10A.

21   "We Are Ready, Bucks Promise Winning Team, Managers Confer," *Cleveland Call and Post*, March 3, 1945: 18.

22   "Vastly Improved Buckeyes Strong in Every Field, May Bring Out Fans, 10,000 Strong," *Cleveland Call and Post*, May 26, 1945: 7B.

23   Bob Williams, "Sports Rambler," *Cleveland Call and Post*, March 17, 1945: 6B.

24   "We Are Ready: Bucks Promise Winning Team, Managers Confer," *Cleveland Call and Post*, Marcy 3, 1945: 18.

25   "Future Outlook League Night Game to Feature League Leading Bucks," *Cleveland Call and Post*, July 7, 1945: 7B.

26   "Future Outlook League," entry from the *Encyclopedia of Cleveland History*, Case Western Reserve University. https://case.edu/ech/articles/f/future-outlook-league, accessed August 13, 2024.

27   "Fans Give New Car Certificate to Wilbur Hayes … In Appreciation," *Clevland Call and Post*, September 8, 1945: 6B.

28   "Buckeyes Make It Banner 'Hayes Day,'" *Cleveland Plain Dealer*, September 3, 1945: 31.

29   Jimmy Jones, "Buckeyes Aim to Dethrone Homestead Grays, Czars of All Baseball for Six Years, First of Five Games in Stadium Tonight, Expect Record Turnout for Sunday Tilt at League Park," *Cleveland Call and Post*, September15, 1945: 7B.

30   Bob Williams, "Greatest Ball Club Receives Town's Greatest Tributes at Banquet, City Council Fetes," *Cleveland Call and Post*, October 6, 1945: 6B.

31   Cleveland Jackson, "Buckeyes Get Rookies for 1946 Baseball Season," *Cleveland Call and Post*, January 12, 1946: 8B.

32   Jackson.

33   "John Brown Traded for Chet Brewer," *Cleveland Call and Post*, June 22, 1946: 9B.

34   "Willie Grace Wins Seltzer Trophy," *Cleveland Call and Post*, September 7, 1946: 9B.

35   "Acquisition of Prize Rookies Boosts Buckeye's Baseball Hopes for 1947; Joe Atkins at Third," *Cleveland Call and Post*, November 30, 1946: 9B.

36   A.S. "Doc" Young, "Trouppe, Hayes: Winners Again," *Cleveland Call and Post*, September 13, 1947: 9B.

37   "Wilbur Hayes Day on September 7," *Chicago Defender*, September 6, 1947: 11.

38   "Negro League World Series Opens in New York Sept. 19," *Chicago Defender*, September 20, 1947: 20.

39   "Team Names New Manager," *Springfield* (Ohio) *Daily News*, December 27, 1947: 5.

40   "Sell Smith To Indians, Jethroe to Royals," *Cleveland Call and Post*, July 17, 1948: 6B.

41   Bill Nowlin, "Sam Jethroe," Society for American Baseball Research BioProject, https://sabr.org/bioproj/person/sam-jethroe.

42   The September 28, 1948, edition of the *Call and Post* ran separate stories on Jethroe's and Don Newcombe's exploits with the Montreal Royals and one on Dan Bankhead's exploits in the Brooklyn Dodgers' minor-league system. In contrast, it had a brief report on the Monarchs-Barons NAL playoffs and Artie Wilson's batting championship. *Cleveland Call and Post*, September 25, 1948: 6B.

43   "Meeting the Louisville Buckeyes," *Ohio Daily Express* (Dayton, Ohio), March 30, 1949: 1, 4.

44   "Buckeyes Move to Louisville, Ky.," *Cleveland Call and Post*, February 12, 1949: 6B.

45   "Hayes Tells What 'appened to Cleveland Buckeyes, Brings Roster of young, Hustling Players Back Home for Karamu Benefit with Indianapolis Clowns," *Cleveland Call and Post*, July 23, 1949: 6B.

46   "1949 in Sports," *Cleveland Call and Post*, December 31, 1949: 10B.

47   "Play in Stadium," *Massillon* (Ohio) *Evening Independent*, February 3, 1950: 14.

48   "Ernie Wright Out, Wilbur Hayes in as Operator of Buckeye Franchise," *Cleveland Call and Post*, February 18, 1950: 1B.

49   "Youthful Rookies Bring Hope," *Ohio Daily Express*, April 1, 1950: 2

50   "Wilbur Hayes Says Jethroe Will Rate with the Greatest," *Cleveland Call and Post*, March 4, 1950: 1B.

51   "NAL Teams Go into Second Half of Race: Buckeyes Fall by the Wayside in Campaign," *Cleveland Call and Post*, July 22, 1950: 19.

52   "Wilbur Hayes, Pioneer Baseball Promoter Dies," *Cleveland Call and Post*, February 16, 1957: 1A.

53   Society for American Baseball Research, *A History of the Society for American Baseball Research* (Paducah, Kentucky: Turner Publishing Company, 2000), 87.

54   Email from Jon Kleinknecht, September 9, 2023.

League Park (Cleveland)

By Bill Johnson

The 1931 opening of Cleveland Stadium, also known as Cleveland Municipal Stadium, was celebrated by both the team and the entire region as a portent of expansion. Expansion of the commercial hub's national reputation, expansion of the economic opportunity for northeastern Ohio, expansion of the national pastime into an arena that could accommodate more paid customers than any other baseball stadium in the nation, and expansion of the Cleveland Indians to the metropolitan downtown area, also created a scheduling quandary. The new park was enormous, capable of holding more than 70,000 fans, but the historical baseball headquarters of the city stood three miles away, in the shape of League Park, built in 1891 at the

corner of Dunham Street (later East 66th) and Lexington Avenue. (It took its name from National League Park, at Cedar Avenue and East 49th, which had been the home field for the Cleveland Spiders between 1879 and 1884.)

In the 1880s Cleveland was a city on the ascent. Home to luminaries like John D. Rockefeller, and host to a burgeoning port industry on Lake Erie, the expanding metropolis was served by several trolley companies competing for riders in the city's eastern expansion. In 1887, as part of a court settlement resulting from a skirmish among rival rail firms, Frank DeHaas Robison, owner of the Cleveland City Railway Company, was awarded part-ownership of the Cleveland Forest Citys, an American Association team. In

League Park.

1889 Robison's team joined the National League, was re-christened the Spiders, and played in a ballpark at Euclid and Payne Avenues. A gifted businessman and opportunist, Robison and his brother Stanley elected to build a baseball park at their trolley stop at East 66th Street and Lexington Avenue, and move the team from Euclid and Payne, in an attempt to grow both ballpark attendance and trolley ridership.

On May 1, 1891, at just after 4 P.M., Cy Young opened the Cleveland Spiders' National League season against Cincinnati and, in doing so, consecrated the new League Park (now referred to as League Park I, it was actually the third park called "League"). The game was a sellout, and the Spiders won, 12-3. The 9,000-seat facility, a wooden structure largely filled with simple benches, hosted the Spiders for 10 years. Because of a zoning requirement that it fit within the existing neighborhood street geometry (the field was originally built around a saloon and two other houses whose owners refused to sell their land when the park was conceived), League was oddly shaped. It boasted a 353-foot left-field line but a right-field fence that, a mere 290 feet from home plate, seemingly abutted the infield grass. There was also very little foul territory, so the fans were almost in the midst of the action.

After the team's dismal 20-win season (and miserable home attendance of 6,088) in 1899, the franchise was one of four teams removed from the National League, and Robison sold the club to John Kilfoyl and Charles Somers. In 1900, the minor-league Cleveland Lake Shores played at League Park and in 1901 the new Cleveland Blues franchise became one of Ban Johnson's original eight American League teams and moved into the facility.

The Blues opened the 1901 inaugural season on April 29 with a 4-3 win over the Milwaukee Brewers (the following season, 1902, the Brewers relocated relocate to St Louis and renamed themselves the Browns). When Nap Lajoie joined the Blues in the middle of the 1902 season, attendance surged and allowed the franchise and ballpark to become more firmly established.

In 1903 the Indians added bleachers in front of the right-field fence and stands in left field outside the playing field. The right-field bleachers were gone by 1908. The park saw two no-hitters toward the end of that season: by Bob Rhoads against the Boston Red Sox on September 18, and the perfect game tossed by Addie Joss against the White Sox on October 2. In 1909 Cy Young returned to the club and, after drawing an impressive 422,000 spectators, the team, now called the Naps in honor of Lajoie, decided to expand the field after the season.

Osborn Engineering, a noted designer of ballparks, was contracted to make the ballpark safer, more spacious, and generally more accommodating to paying customers. On April 21, 1910, the new and improved League Park (II) reopened, capable of accommodating up to 24,414 fans. The business offices were located upstairs, above the ticket office, and were as cramped as the bullpens, which were wedged between the foul lines and bleachers in right and left fields (the Indians used the first-base side).

The western dimension, the right-field line, was built along East 66th Street, while left field ran along Linwood Avenue. In the outfield, the east face from left field to center field was bordered by East 70th Street. Still only 290 feet down the right-field line (240 feet if roped off for big games), it expanded in a rectangle to a farthest reach of 460 feet just left of straightaway center field (this was shortened to 420 feet in a 1920 renovation). The left-field line extended 375 feet at the pole.

The concrete and steel ballparks that were built starting in the early 20th century to replace the older wooden ones (largely fire hazards like League I) are now collectively referred to as Jewel Box ballparks. Philadelphia was home to the progenitor of the class, Baker Bowl (1895), as well as one of the early, true Jewel Boxes at Shibe Park (1909). With the exceptions of Fenway Park in Boston and Wrigley Field in Chicago, the Jewel Box parks have been consigned to history. Except for Shibe and Comiskey (Chicago), the Jewel Boxes were all built amid the physical limitations of existing city blocks, which resulted in similarly quirky, asymmetrical outfields.

In 1910 baseball suffered the tragic death of Joss at the age of 31. The next year, on July 24, 1911, the team hosted a benefit fundraiser for the family of their deceased pitcher. The all-star contest, featuring players like Ty Cobb and Tris Speaker, raised well over $12,000 for the Joss family, all from admission fees ranging between 25 cents and $1.

The team changed its name to the Indians in 1915, and, from 1916 to 1927, as a perquisite of owning the team, Jim Dunn changed the name of League Park to Dunn Field. It remained so appointed until Alva Bradley bought the team from the Dunn estate in 1927 and restored the name League Park.

During the Dunn era, the Indians brought the city a World Series title (1920). Game Five, at League Park, produced three historic World Series firsts: Bill Wambsganss recorded what remains the only unassisted triple play; Jim Bagby became the first pitcher to hit a home run in a World Series; and Elmer Smith tagged the Brooklyn Robins' Burleigh Grimes for the first grand slam in the major-league postseason.

In 1920 the park underwent a partial renovation as dimensions were changed slightly by the addition of outfield bleachers and a 40-foot wall was erected along the right-field boundary. Prevailing winds tended to carry batted balls to left, but even with strong gusts of wind it was difficult to knock the ball out of the yard.

The right-field fence, if not truly monstrous, was at least odd. The first 20 feet above the ground were solid wall, and on top of that was a 25-foot-tall wire mesh fence with steel stanchions along the border. In all, the fence was 45 feet high, in contrast with Fenway Park's left-field "Green

Monster," which rises 37 feet. In 1934, perhaps because of the proclivities of young left-handed slugger Hal Trosky, the screen was lowered five feet, leaving the barrier an even 40 feet high. A ball hitting the fence at League might have hit the solid wall and bounced predictably; it might have struck the chicken-wire mesh and died; or it might have hit a stanchion and bounced in any direction. There are numerous anecdotes of balls that hit the fence less than a foot apart, one falling limply to the ground after hitting the mesh, and the next bouncing almost all the way back to second base in a ricochet off one of the metal posts.

On July 7, 1923, the Indians scored 27 runs against the Red Sox, setting the American League record for the most runs in a nine-inning game. Also that year, Walter Johnson logged his 3,000th career strikeout, and in 1925 Tris Speaker knocked his 3,000th hit.

The field had no permanent lights, so night games were not an option, but there was one such contest there, on July 27, 1931. Using a portable lighting system borrowed from the Kansas City Monarchs, the Homestead Grays of the Negro National League played the barnstorming House of David in the first (and only) night contest at League.

The final significant event at the ballpark occurred on July 16, 1941, when Joe DiMaggio hit safely in his 56th consecutive game. The streak was broken the next day, at Municipal Stadium.

The 1946 season marked the beginning of the end for League Park. The most notable baseball milestone at the park that year was Ted Williams' only career inside-the-park home run, which gave a pennant-clinching win to the Red Sox. In 1932 the Indians seeking to draw larger crowds, had begun experimenting with their schedule by playing night, holiday, and weekend games at the larger Cleveland Stadium in 1932. That experiment was conducted intermittently throughout the 1930s, until owner Alva Bradley finally settled on a semipredictable split of games between the two stadiums that was used until September 21, 1946. On that date the Indians and the Detroit Tigers closed out both the season and the baseball life of League Park. Tigers pitcher Dizzy Trout defeated Joe Berry and the Indians 5-3 in 11 innings before only 2,772 spectators. The venue had become the smallest ballpark in the American League, and when Bill Veeck bought the Indians in 1946, he shifted the schedule to Municipal Stadium on a full-time basis.

From 1943 to 1949, the park was used by the Negro American League Cleveland Buckeyes. That 1945 Buckeyes season opened with a doubleheader sweep of the Memphis Red Sox, which Cleveland followed with sweeps against the Chicago American Giants and the Kansas City Monarchs. By early September, the Buckeyes sat atop the Negro American League standings, and when league executives chose to cancel the NAL championship series, Cleveland was simply awarded the pennant and a shot at the NNL champion Homestead Grays. Playing, and winning,

two of the four home games of that Negro World Series at League, the Buckeyes went on to capture their only Negro World Series. It marked only the second baseball championship in the city's history.[1]

League Park was also used by the Cleveland Rams of the National Football League between 1936 and 1945, and by the Cleveland Browns of the nascent All-American Football Conference from 1946 to 1950. The Indians eventually sold the park to the city of Cleveland, which demolished most of the facility in 1951. The city left only the structure along the right-field line, including a ticket window, to mark an open city park.

Most of the articles and retrospectives concerning League Park – at least those written between 1960 and 2000 – began with some form of commentary on the state of the neighborhood of Lexington Avenue and East 66th Street. It had become, to be charitable, rough. What was the site of Babe Ruth's 500th home run (off Cleveland's Willis Hudlin in 1929) had become a slum. In 2002, as part of an ongoing effort to revitalize the area, the last of the grandstand structure was demolished in an attempted upgrade, leaving one less tangible trace of the ballpark's existence.

Fortunately, a steward of Cleveland's past and future emerged in the early twenty-first century. In 2014, the Baseball Heritage Museum moved into the old League Park clubhouse, welcoming new fans in to learn about the glory days of the stadium, and helping to save the site in the form of a public recreation facility. Osborn Engineering, the firm that managed the 1910 refurbishment, provided design work for a League Park III. As of 2024, the tiny park at East 66th and Lexington lives again.[2]

SOURCES

Baseball Reference.com (http://www.baseball-reference.com).

Cleveland News (various issues 1933-1941).

Cleveland Plain Dealer (various issues 1933-1941).

Encyclopedia of Cleveland History. Case Western Reserve University. Available online: [http://ech.cwru.edu/ech-cgi/article.pl?id=RFDH]

Jedlick, P. *League Park* (Cleveland, Ohio: Society for American Baseball Research, 1990).

League Park Society, online: [http://www.leaguepark.org]

Lewis, Franklin, *The Cleveland Indians* (New York: Putnam and Sons, 1949).

Lowry, Philip. *Green Cathedrals* (New York: Walker Publishing Company, 2006).

Schneider, Russ. *The Cleveland Indians Encyclopedia,* 3rd ed. (Champaign, Illinois: Sports Publishing LLC, 2004).

NOTES

1   This information, verified in newspapers of the day, was contributed by Ken Krsolovic and Bryan Fritz, authors of *League Park: Historic Home of Cleveland Baseball, 1891-1946* (McFarland & Co., 2013)

2   As of early 2025, the Baseball Heritage Museum may be visited at: https://baseballheritagemuseum.org/

Cleveland Municipal Stadium

By Tom Wancho

Cleveland Municipal Stadium (1931-1996) housed millions of sports fans (boxing, baseball, football), music lovers (the Beatles, the Rolling Stones, Bruce Springsteen), a Shriners convention, the Cleveland Orchestra, religious events, and circuses.

Known by Clevelanders as simply "the Stadium," the steel and concrete behemoth enthused and impaled attendees for parts of seven decades. Its initial sporting event, on July 3, 1931, was a heavyweight championship match between defending champ Max Schmeling of Germany against William "Young" Stribling. The contender stayed on his feet until 14 seconds remained in the 15th round. The Schmeling-Stribling bout mirrored what would become the stadium's history. If the champ was Cleveland's weather, it threw punches at the contender (the Stadium) before reducing it to rubble.

Anyone who went to see the Stadium during the 1970s-1990s saw the wear and tear of standing alongside the windy, icy Lake Erie. Peeling paint, crumbling concrete, inoperable escalators and elevators, uncomfortable seats, flooded restrooms, misnamed luxury boxes, and obstructed views were a recipe for destruction. Thus it wasn't a surprise, after the "original" Cleveland Browns moved to Baltimore following the 1995 NFL season, that the Stadium had outlived its use.

OPEN SESAME

At the first baseball game, a July 31, 1932, Sunday showdown against the Philadelphia Athletics attended by

CLEVELAND STADIUM
Home of the Champs

Cleveland Stadium 1950.

THE 1945 CLEVELAND BUCKEYES

baseball royalty and 80,284 fans, baseball's first commissioner, Judge Kenesaw Mountain Landis, commented, "This stadium is perfect. It is the only baseball park I know where the spectator can see clearly from any seat. Look at those people out there (he said pointing to the crowded center-field bleachers); they can watch every play."[1]

Landis turned around in his box seat near the Indians dugout and swept the grandstands with his hand. "Not a barrier to block anyone's view. Comfortable chairs. This is perfection." Obviously, the Commish never saw a game from beyond the Fat Cats box seats.

John Heydler, the National League's president, said, "Marvelous. It is the last word in baseball parks. A great thing for baseball. And one should not forget to give (Indians President) Mr. (Alva) Bradley credit, either."[2]

And this from Thomas S. Shibe, Athletics president: "This was built for baseball. I wish we had this in Philadelphia for the last three World Series."[3]

BEFORE THE BEGINNING

According to the October 1985 Inventory Nomination form for a listing on the National Register of Historic Places, "Cleveland Municipal Stadium was designed by the progressive city administration as a multipurpose structure to accommodate the great surge in attendance at baseball and football games and other public spectacles that occurred with the rise of the automobile."[4]

The nomination form goes on to read, "Since then, in addition to baseball and football, the range of activities at the stadium has included religious convocations, the Metropolitan Opera, the Beatles, circuses, rodeos, big bands, tractor pulls, and polka festivals."[5]

IF YOU BUILD IT ... WHO WILL COME?

Constructed on a landfill that stretched the lakefront 200 feet farther into Lake Erie, the facility was completed in 370 days at a cost to taxpayers of $3,035,245. Although 21 percent over budget, the cost overruns were attributed to the addition of a scoreboard, sound system, and infrastructure around the facility, including bridges, railroads, and road work.

After their July 31, 1932 "opener" at the Stadium, the Indians played by Lake Erie for the remainder of 1932 and all of the 1933 season. But after attendance dipped in 1933 to 387,936 – nearly 100,000 less than the 483,027 they attracted in 1931 at their last full season at League Park, team owner Alva Bradley moved his club back to the significantly smaller League Park for all but one game during the 1934-36 seasons.

Under pressure from city leaders, unhappy at their 80,000-seat stadium standing vacant, Bradley agreed to play most doubleheaders and other games expected to draw larger crowds at the Stadium. The Tribe did not move downtown full time until 1947, after Bill Veeck purchased the club.

On July 16, 1945, the Cleveland Buckeyes of the Negro American League played their first regular-season game at the Stadium, defeating the Birmingham Black Barons, 6-2, in front of 12,733 fans. The Buckeyes won five regular-season games at the Stadium in 1945 and opened the 1945 Negro World Series against the Negro National League's Homestead Grays on September 13. Cleveland's 2-1 victory ignited a four-game championship sweep. The second game was at League Park and the final two contests were on the road (Washington and Philadelphia).

The Buckeyes' only loss when playing at Cleveland Stadium in 1945 was a 2-0 postseason exhibition loss to the Homestead Grays on October 7.

CLEVELAND BUCKEYES CONTESTS AT CLEVELAND MUNICIPAL STADIUM, 1945

July 16: Cleveland Buckeyes 6, Birmingham Black Barons 2

July 24: Cleveland Buckeyes 3, Kansas City Monarchs 2

August 3: Cleveland Buckeyes 4, Chicago American Giants 1

August 30: Cleveland Buckeyes 1, Memphis Red Sox 0 (first game of doubleheader)

August 30: Cleveland Buckeyes 2, Memphis Red Sox 0 (second game of doubleheader)

September 13: Cleveland Buckeyes 2, Homestead Grays 1 (Negro World Series Game One)

October 13: Homestead Grays 2, Cleveland Buckeyes 0 (exhibition game)[6]

The Buckeyes played occasional other games there as well, in 1945, 1946, and 1947.

NF HELL

The National Football League in the 1930s was not the same league as in the twenty-first century. Major-league baseball was America's national pastime while NFL was an afterthought. It was into this quagmire that the Cleveland Rams were born in 1936. They were initially a member of the American Football League in 1936, and joined the National Football League in 1937. Their first game drew 20,000 fans to Cleveland Stadium on September 10, 1937, a 28-0 loss to the Detroit Lions, Because the Stadium "was too big and the rent too high," the Rams played their home games through 1945 at League Park.[7] With a regular-season record of 9-1, the Rams advanced to the 1945 NFL championship game, hosting the Washington Redskins (8-2). The Rams held the championship game at Cleveland Stadium in anticipation of a larger crowd than League Park could accommodate.

According to Rams public relations director Nate Wallack, "Our season-ticket sale was nothing (in) those days. Maybe 200 at the most. We put the (1945) championship seats on sale and immediately we sold 30,000 and we had another week to go before the game. The weather was beautiful. It looked as though we'd sell out the Stadium. Then a blizzard. I mean an awful one. It ended our sales. Now Bill Johns, our business manager, was worried about the field. He wanted to keep it from freezing. He got in his car and set out toward Sandusky, stopping at every farm to buy hay. He wanted to cover the field with it. He bought over 1,000 bales.

"The day of the game the temperature dropped to zero. I sat in the press box and the windows got so steamed we couldn't see. All the writers had to get out into the stands and freeze. Me too. A water pipe broke in the upper deck and cascading water turned to ice immediately – a frozen waterfall. The fans burned the hay and even the wooden bleacher seats to keep warm. One fan froze his feet and didn't realize it until he started to walk home after the game. An ambulance had to be called. The game was so exciting, though, the fans stayed to the end. We sold about 35,000 tickets and 29,000 showed."[8]

The Rams' 15-14 victory over the Washington Redskins was the team's last game in Cleveland. Mickey McBride, a Cleveland taxicab magnate, purchased a franchise for the new All-America Football Conference, to be named after its head coach, former Massillon and Ohio State head man Paul Brown. McBride signed a long-term lease to play home games at the Stadium. Typical of the doom that would frequent Cleveland professional sports teams, the Rams moved to Los Angeles *after* winning a league championship.

HOME SWEET HOME

The Stadium entered an unprecedented period of success after the Browns and Indians became its chief tenants beginning in 1946 and 1947 respectively. The Browns won every championship during the four-year history of the All America Football Conference, with three of those wins taking place on the Stadium's turf. The Indians set a baseball attendance record in 1948, drawing 2,620,627 fans as they won Cleveland's second – and as of 2024, last – World Series. The Tribe captured Games Three and Four at the Stadium before wrapping up the title at Braves Field in Boston. Noteworthy in the Game Five home loss was a then-World Series-record crowd of 86,288 who had hoped to see the Clevelanders wrap the Series at home.

While the '50s remained kind to the Browns, the Indians began a slow descent that concluded with a remarkable tumble down the American League standings during the latter decades of the twentieth century. Despite posting a then American League best 111-43 record in 1954, the Indians were swept in the World Series by the New York Giants. The last World Series game played at Cleveland Stadium, on October 2, 1954, was witnessed by 78,102 disappointed fans. The final: New York Giants 7, Cleveland 4.

The Browns entered the NFL in 1950 and promptly captured that season's title with a 30-28 Christmas Eve victory over the … Rams, who returned to the Stadium for the first time since leaving for Los Angeles five years before. Cleveland appeared in six of the next seven NFL title tilts (going 2-4), including a 1955 championship at the Stadium. The Browns' 27-0 shutout over the Baltimore Colts at the Stadium on December 27, 1964, remains the last professional championship captured by the Cleveland Browns.

CLEVELAND STADIUM SPECTACLES

Whether it was sports or other events, the Stadium provided a backdrop for a multitude of memorable moments. Ted Williams hit his 500th home run there on June 17, 1960. The Indians' Len Barker pitched the 10th perfect game in major-league history against the Toronto Blue Jays on May 15, 1981. Joe DiMaggio's 56-game hitting streak ended there on July 17, 1941. Bob Feller whiffed a then-record 18 Detroit Tigers on October 2, 1938, from the Stadium's mound. The first Monday Night Football game ever played pitted the Browns against Joe Namath's Jets on September 21, 1970, from the Stadium. Four All-Star Games were played at the Stadium.

Cleveland Stadium was also home to 10¢ Beer Night in 1974 and "The Drive" engineered by John Elway in 1987. During the 1986 AFC Championship game, the Browns had a 20-13 lead over the Denver Broncos with 5:32 left in the contest. Broncos quarterback John Elway drove Denver 98 yards in 15 plays, tying the game with 0:39 remaining. Cleveland lost in overtime on a Denver field goal kick that led the Broncos into the Super Bowl. "The Drive" was born. The Browns again ended up on the wrong end of another playoff game against the Oakland Raiders on January 4, 1981, after quarterback Brian Sipe had a pass intercepted at the east (open) end of the Stadium when a field goal would have won the game. That led to a joke: What do a Billy Graham Crusade and a Cleveland Browns game have in common? Answer: 80,000 fans leaving the Stadium murmuring "Jesus Christ!"

THE END

Stadiums are public gathering places, usually for sporting events. What transpires within their walls brings fans together, be it in victory or defeat. Some fans have fond memories of the Cleveland Municipal Stadium. It represents their youth, possibly the site of their first concert, major league, or NFL game.

Over time, the Cleveland Municipal Stadium became known as the "Mistake by the Lake." After its demolition, the old Stadium's reinforced concrete was dumped in Lake Erie and used as a barrier reef for fishermen. Like Luca Brasi from *The Godfather*, it sleeps with the fishes.

An earlier version of this article is included in the book Pitching to the Pennant: The 1954 Cleveland Indians (Lincoln: University of Nebraska Press, 2014), *edited by Joseph Wancho.*

SOURCES

Box scores for all the Buckeyes games in 1945 are available on Retrosheet.org.

NOTES

6 "Defeat Bucks in Last Game, 2-0," Cleveland Call and P*ost*, October 13, 1945.(Endnotes)

1 Al Silverman, "Landis Lauds Stadium as Perfect for Baseball," *Cleveland Plain Dealer*, August 1, 1932: 17.

2 Silverman.

3 Silverman.

4 National Register of Historic Places Inventory – Nomination Form, October 1985, Accessed from the Cleveland Stadium Clip File at the National Baseball Hall of Fame.

5 Nomination Form.

7 Hal Lebovitz, "Hal Asks: Remember the Cleveland Rams?" *Cleveland Plain Dealer*, January 20, 1980: 3-8.

8 Lebovitz.

Cleveland and the African American Community in 1945

By David J. Goldberg

As World War II came to a conclusion, the African American community in Cleveland looked to the future with a cautious degree of optimism. African Americans had contributed significantly to the Allied victory both by serving in the still-segregated military and by playing a vital role on the home front. "The Double V for Victory" campaign launched by the African American newspaper the *Pittsburgh Courier* had planted the seeds for what would become the modern civil rights movement. The Fair Employment Practices Committee established by executive order in 1941 by President Franklin D. Roosevelt represented the first federal commitment to civil rights since the end of Reconstruction. (FDR issued the executive order to head off a march on Washington planned by the Black leader A. Philip Randolph). Though the FEPC expired with the end of the war, some industrial and retail jobs had opened up to African Americans for the first time. A new union movement, the Committee for Industrial Organization, had welcomed African Americans as members.[1] Many African Americans hoped that the old policy of "last hired and first fired" would be ended.

Cleveland in 1945 was a proud, bustling, self-confident industrial city. Part of the Great Lakes region, which also included Buffalo, Detroit, Toledo, Chicago, and Milwaukee, Cleveland was home to iron and steel, electrical, automotive, machine tools, paint, clothing, and many other types of manufacturing, Cleveland factories had very successfully converted to wartime production. By 1943, tanks and airplanes rather than consumer goods were pouring out of Cleveland factories. Many plants worked around the clock and by 1944 women, often referred to as Rosie the Riveter, moved up the employment ladder to fill industrial jobs that opened for them. Neither Nazi Germany nor Imperial Japan had understood how well the United States would fulfill its role as the "Arsenal of Democracy," as FDR put it.

Most Cleveland industrial workers resided in ethnic neighborhoods like Collinwood, the South Side (today known as Tremont), and Broadway-Fleet in close proximity to their workplaces. These neighborhoods housed the immigrants who had poured into Cleveland from Eastern and Southern Europe between the 1890s and 1924 (the date of a major federal immigration restriction law). Most belonged to Catholic or Orthodox churches and had strong ties to their parish. The women shopped at neighborhood stores and the men drank at neighborhood saloons. Many neighborhoods were badly polluted and run-down because little new housing had been built since the beginning of the Great Depression in 1929.

The residential patterns of African Americans were quite different. During the first Great Migration (1916 to 1918), African Americans had not been able to find housing outside of the Central-Woodland area. The racist housing practices enforced by landlords continued during the 1920s when migration from the Deep South, and especially from Alabama, resumed. And the pattern remained in place between 1941 and 1945 when hundreds of thousands of migrants once again came north seeking a better life. Even if some jobs opened up for them, the new arrivals could not find housing outside of the expanding and densely populated "ghetto" as African American areas of cities had come to be called. Though the new federally sponsored public housing offered an upgrade, it too was segregated.

The rigid segregation actually enhanced African Americans' efforts to establish a separate institutional life. The church was the most important institution. More established African Americans worshipped at large institutional churches like Antioch Baptist Church and Cory United Methodist Church; the poorer, most recent migrants often attended storefront churches. African Americans also owned barber shops which provided places to socialize and exchange news, and residents often purchased insurance from community residents. Most stores in the ghetto remained White-owned through a Cleveland organization known as the Future Outlook League, headed by John O. Holly, had some success in gaining employment for Blacks with "Don't shop where you can't work" campaigns. Big-time racketeers benefited the most from "policy," as the numbers game was known, but many of the numbers runners were local residents. Wartime earnings meant that many workers had money in their pockets for the first time. The House of Wills served as a community center as well as a funeral home. East 55th Street, where the House of Wills was located, served as a community hub and the center of what became known as the "Black downtown." Local jazz clubs and juke joints were often packed on weekends. When established in 1942, the Cleveland Buckeyes provided a point of community pride. All of the community events received extensive publicity in the *Call and Post,* edited by William O. Walker, one of a number of African American newspapers that flourished in the 1940s.

The neighborhood entertainment venues were important because many of Cleveland's hotels and restaurants would not serve African Americans. As evidence of the racist practices at this time, the popular Euclid Beach Park would admit African Americans only on certain days (the park became the target of militant protests in 1946).

Jesse Owens, Chester Himes, and Langston Hughes had all graduated from Cleveland high schools. Owens had embarrassed Adolf Hitler by winning four Gold Medals at the 1936 Berlin Olympic Games. Hines authored a number of cutting-edge novels and Hughes became one of the nation's best-known poets and playwrights. Many of Hughes' plays were performed by the nationally known Gilpin Players at Karamu House, a settlement house that also provided workshop space for a number of talented African American artists and printmakers.

Despite the extent of the segregation, Cleveland had not had a race riot comparable to East St. Louis, Illinois, in 1917, Chicago and many other cities in 1919, Harlem in 1935, and Detroit and New York in 1943. And there had not been the "hate strikes" (protesting the hiring of African American men and women) that occurred in Detroit and Philadelphia in 1943 and 1944.

The Cleveland Cultural Gardens (though lacking an African American garden) symbolized the city's pride in multiculturalism as did the Anisfeld-Wolf book awards, given annually to books promoting ethnic and racial understanding. The Cleveland City Club hosted speakers representing a number of different perspectives. Not surprisingly, Cleveland in 1945 became one of the first American cities to establish a human relations council.

Thus, it seems appropriate that the Cleveland Buckeyes won the 1945 Negro World Series as the industrial powerhouse on Lake Erie reached its peak population of 900,000. Having celebrated the defeats of Germany and Japan, local residents now celebrated achievements on the playing field.

SOURCES

Drake, St. Clair, and Horace R. Cayton, *Black Metropolis: A Study of Life in a Northern City*, (New York: Harper and Row, 1945, 1962).

Duneier, Duneier, *Ghetto, Invention of a Place: The History of an Idea* (New York: Farrar, Straus and Giroux (2016).

Hammock, David C., Diane L. Grabowski, and John J. Grabowski, *Identity, Conflict and Cooperation, Central Europeans in Cleveland, 1850-1930* (Cleveland: The Western Reserve Historical Society (2002).

Kennedy, David, *Freedom From Fear: The American People in Depression and War, 1929-1945* (New York: Oxford University Press, 1999).

Phillips, Kimberly L., *AlabamaNorth: African American Migrants Community and Working Class Activism, 1915-1945* (Urbana: University of Illinois Press, 1999).

Van Tassel, David D., and John G. Grabowski, *Encyclopedia of Cleveland History* (Bloomington: University of Indiana Press, 1996).

Williams, Regennia N., *Cleveland, Ohio* (Chicago: Arcadia Press, 2002).

NOTES

1   The organization became later known as the Congress of Industrial Organizations, and affiliated with the American Federation of Labor

West offense lights up Comiskey Park to break deadlock in series

July 29, 1945: West All-Stars 9, East All-Stars 6, at Comiskey Park, Chicago

By Matt Garvey

The 1945 East-West Game at Comiskey Park in Chicago was the 15th installment of the popular matchup between the best players of the Negro American League and Negro National League. For the first half of the season, however, the possibility of the game was in doubt. World War II was still raging, and even though US Marines had raised the American flag on Mount Suribachi at Iwo Jima in February and Germany had surrendered in May, the United States was faced with the daunting challenge of a possible need to invade the Japanese mainland, and resources and manpower still needed to be rationed.[1] In addition, some team executives, including Homestead Grays owner Cum Posey, were upset with arrangements surrounding previous East-West Games, raising the possibility that the game, which at this point had become an institution in Black society, would not be played.[2] By June 12, however, all grievances and scheduling difficulties were cast aside when the US Office of Defense Transportation gave the Negro Leagues the green light to stage the game.[3]

The next day, team owners gathered at the Grand Hotel in Chicago and set the date of the 1945 East-West classic for Sunday, July 29.[4] Black newspapers began hyping the game with editorials, and also published the ballots that fans used to elect their favorite players to the game. Many of the editorials rattled off the names of the most popular players of the time, enchanting fans with visions of coming baseball grandeur, and the two names most often mentioned were Homestead Grays catcher Josh Gibson and Kansas City Monarchs pitcher Satchel Paige. However, neither of the two superstars would play in the 1945 East-West Game.

It is debatable as to why Paige did not attend. He did not play in the 1944 game either.[5] Two days before the game, the *Kansas City Call* reported that Paige would not pitch in the exhibition because of a sore arm.[6] However, *Pittsburgh Courier* writer Wendell Smith reported on August 4 that Paige had skipped the game "because he could not reach an agreement with the East-West promoters financially."[7] Based on Paige's notorious history of dealings with team owners and promoters, it is likely that he skipped the game because of an inability to negotiate a higher appearance fee.

Josh Gibson did not play in the game after being suspended by Posey for "a steady infraction of training rules," which meant an extended drinking binge.[8] It is possible that the binge was directly related to the illness that would eventually take his life a little more than two years later.[9] Nevertheless, due to the suspension, Gibson was ineligible to play in the game.[10]

In a last-second move, the NAL removed Piper Davis of the Birmingham Black Barons from the team for hitting an umpire, an act that cost him $50.[11] Davis was replaced by Jesse Williams of the Kansas City Monarchs.[12] Additional controversy crept into the game when the FBI and Chicago police arrested several ticket scalpers and ticket counterfeiters who were charging markups in excess of 200 percent over face value. As a result of the markups, scores of tickets were unsold by game time.[13]

EYES OF SPORTS WORLD TO BE FOCUSED ON EAST-WEST ALL-STAR TILT THIS WEEKEND

Atlanta Daily World, July 25, 1945.

Despite the chaos, Chicago was buzzing in anticipation of the game. The Grand Hotel was "running over with baseball people."[14] Celebrities and baseball personalities were spotted inside Comiskey Park, adding to the allure of the event.[15] Congressman William L. Dawson, who represented Illinois' 1st District, threw out the ceremonial first pitch to Cook County Commissioner Mike Sneed, and the game was underway.[16]

Verdell Mathis, a left-hander for the Memphis Red Sox, started the game for the West. He retired Homestead Grays center fielder Jerry Benjamin to start the game, then walked Philadelphia Stars second baseman Frank Austin, who was promptly caught in a rundown on a pickoff play and chased down by Kansas City Monarchs shortstop Jackie Robinson for the first out. Mathis then struck out Newark Eagles left fielder Johnny Davis to end the top of the first. Baltimore Elite Giants left-handed pitcher Tom Glover took the mound for the East in the bottom of the first and retired the West in order. When Mathis retired the East's batters in the top of the second, the game started to look like a pitchers' duel.[17]

The offensive floodgates opened for the West when Memphis's Neil Robinson led off the bottom of the second by beating out an infield hit. Cincinnati-Indianapolis Clowns third baseman Alex Radcliffe then smashed a drive to right field. On this bright July day in Chicago, Baltimore outfielder Wild Bill Wright[18] was not wearing sunglasses, lost the ball in the sun, and it rolled into deep right field. Robinson ended up on third and Radcliffe at second.

The next batter, Cleveland Buckeyes first baseman Archie Ware, lifted a lazy single over Philadelphia Stars second baseman Frank Austin's head to drive in Robinson and Radcliffe for the first two runs of the game. Baltimore catcher Roy Campanella threw out Ware attempting to steal second base, but Cleveland catcher-manager Quincy Trouppe drew a one-out walk, and then was singled to third by Mathis, helping his own cause.

At that point, East manager Vic Harris pulled Gordon from the mound and sent in Philadelphia Stars right-hander Bill Ricks. Jesse Williams, the last-minute replacement for Piper Davis, lifted an 0-and-1 pitch to right field. Incredibly, Wright, still refusing to don sunglasses, lost another ball in the sun. Trouppe and Mathis were able to coast home, and Williams ended up on third with a triple. Ricks then got out of the inning by retiring Jackie Robinson, appearing in his first and only East-West Game.[19] At the end of the second, the West led 4-0.

Mathis cruised through the top of the third without allowing a hit.[20] Cleveland right fielder Lloyd Davenport led off the bottom of the third inning with a groundout, but back-to-back singles by Neil Robinson and Alex Radcliff put runners at the corners. Birmingham Black Barons left fielder Lester Lockett stepped up to the plate and hit a grounder toward shortstop Willie Wells, whose only play was at first. Robinson scored, with Radcliff taking second. Radcliff scored a moment later on Ware's second hit to right, this one a sizzling liner. Trouppe then drew his second walk of the game and Mathis picked up his second hit on a slow roller to Wells that he beat out for an infield hit. Jesse Williams then gave the West a commanding 8-0 lead with a single to left to score Ware and Trouppe. East manager Harris relieved Ricks with New York Cuban Stars multipositional wizard Martin Dihigo, who came in from right field to pitch.[21] The game was effectively decided at this point.

Chicago American Giants right-hander Gentry Jessup took over for Mathis in the fourth and blanked the East for three more innings. The West added a run in the bottom of the fourth inning when Davenport led off with a double, took third on a bunt by Neil Robinson, and scored on Alex Radcliff's groundout.[22] At the end of the fourth inning, the West was leading 9-0.[23]

The East finally got on the scoreboard in the top of the seventh when Kansas City Monarchs right-hander Booker McDaniel relieved Jessup and walked Cuban Stars right fielder Rogelio Linares, who took second on Newark Eagles third baseman Murray Watkins' single. Lennie Pearson pinch-hit for Martin Dihigo and forced Watkins out, putting Linares at third and Pearson at first. Jerry Benjamin then hit into another fielder's choice, forcing Pearson at second and scoring Linares for the first East run of the game. McDaniel gave up a single to Cuban Stars shortstop Horacio Martínez, which drove in Benjamin, before getting Philadelphia Stars left fielder Gene Benson to ground out to retire the side.[24] At the end of the seventh inning, the West led 9-1.

The East team made things interesting in the top of the ninth. Murray Watkins led off with a single and was forced at second when Bill Byrd of the Baltimore Elite Giants, pinch-hitting for Homestead Grays pitcher Roy Welmaker, reached on a grounder. Jerry Benjamin and Horacio Martinez struck back-to-back singles, with Byrd and Benjamin scoring on the second hit to make the score 9-3. Gene Benson hit into a fielder's choice, then took second on a walk to Homestead Grays first baseman Buck Leonard. Roy Campanella then singled in Benson to make it 9-4, prompting East manager Winfield Welch to relieve Booker McDaniel with Buckeyes pitcher Gene Bremer. Bremer immediately gave up a bases-clearing double to Willie Wells, but then got Rogelio Linares to ground out – Jackie Robinson to Archie Ware – to end the game.[25] Roy Glover took the loss, with Mathis earning the win and Gene Bremer picking up the save.[26] The West won, 9-6.

A crowd of 37,714 attended the game.[27] The controversy surrounding ticket scalpers and counterfeiters seemed to have hurt attendance.[28] The absence of Satchel Paige and Josh Gibson most likely affected attendance as well.[29] Two years later, Jackie Robinson would make his debut for the Brooklyn Dodgers, marking the beginning of the end of the Negro Leagues and their beloved summer all-star game.[30]

SOURCES

In addition to the sources cited in the Notes, the author consulted Seamheads.com and Baseball-Reference.com.

NOTES

1   "ODT Ruling Hits East-West Game, Negro Baseball and Pro Sport," *Chicago Defender*, March 3, 1945. The Office of Defense Transportation asked baseball owners to reduce travel by 25 percent, and as a result the White American and National Leagues announced that they would not stage an All-Star Game for the 1945 season

2   "Scalpers take good beating," *Chicago Defender*, August 4, 1945. Homestead Grays owner Cum Posey objected to Chicago American Giants owner Dr. J.B. Martin's influence over the game, especially the flow of the gate receipts. Posey suggested that Martin skimmed money off the top of the gate in order to make up what he lost due to the East-West Game. Despite the game's immense popularity, especially among Chicago residents, Posey

claimed that the game actually caused Wilson to lose money. Posey's theory was that Martin took much higher percentages of the gate receipts on non-all-star weekends, since the gate of the East-West Game was split between every NAL and NNL player and team. (East-West players received $100, coaches received $300, and $300 went to every league team to be divided among players not selected to the game.) He also theorized that the ability for Martin's American Giants to draw fans during the weekends prior to and after the East-West Game were stunted due to the game's popularity, further decreasing his team's earning potential, and giving Martin motivation to skim the gate. NAL President Martin and NNL President and Baltimore Elite Giants owner Tom Wilson had formed a committee consisting of owners Ernie Wright of Cleveland, Tom Baird of Kansas City, Alex Pompez of New York, and Abe Manley of the Newark Eagles, after the previous year's East-West Game, to find ways to improve the exhibition. Posey encouraged the committee to consider their grievances.

3   "No commissioner yet," *Baltimore Afro-American*, June 23, 1945. Originally, the four-man committee decided that due to Office of Defense Transportation travel restrictions, the game would not be staged. Negotiations between the committee and the ODT went back and forth. On May 9 the ODT lifted restrictions on dog and horse racing, eliminated a midnight curfew, and announced an increase in the amount of gasoline that would be available to civilians, giving hope to the committee and baseball fans that the East-West Game would be played. However, when the committee approached the ODT with their plans to organize the game, the ODT "was found to frown on the affair." J.B. Martin had persuaded the ODT to allow the leagues to play the game by claiming that the fans attending the game would be almost exclusively from Chicago. Neil Lanctot, *Negro League Baseball: The Rise and Ruin of a Black Institution* (Philadelphia: University of Pennsylvania Press, 2004), 253.

4   "East-West Game Will Be Played on July 29," *Chicago Defender*, June 23, 1945.

5   Satchel Paige, *Maybe I'll Pitch Forever* (Lincoln: University of Nebraska Press, 1993), 159-167. In Paige's autobiography, he claims that he persuaded Josh Gibson to hold out of the 1943 East-West Game with him for more money. After negotiations with J.B. Martin and Tom Wilson, both players received secret $200 bonuses for playing. When the 1944 game rolled around, Paige came up with the idea to donate the gate receipts from the game to charities for soldiers returning from the war, but was met with the cold shoulder from NAL and NNL owners. Incensed, Paige refused to participate in the game. Russ J. Cowan, "Paige Threatens to Bolt East-West Game," *Michigan Chronicle* (Detroit), August 5, 1944.

6   "Satchel Won't Hurl in Dream Classic in Chicago on Sunday," *Kansas City Call*, July 27, 1945.

7   Wendell Smith, "The Sports Beat," *Pittsburgh Courier*, August 4, 1945.

8   "Through the Eyes of W. Rollo Wilson," *Philadelphia Tribune*, August 11, 1945.

9   William Brashler, *Josh Gibson: A Life in the Negro Leagues* (Chicago: Ivan R. Dee, 2000), 125-136. Despite his monstrous appearance and incredible athletic ability, by 1945 Josh Gibson was suffering immensely both physically and mentally. Gibson lost consciousness and slipped into a coma on New Year's Day 1943. It was soon discovered that he was suffering from a brain tumor. Despite the seriousness of the diagnosis, Josh kept the tumor a secret, refused treatment, and began turning to alcohol and marijuana to ease the pain and the depression that was quickly sinking into his life. He became prone to dizziness and headaches. His increasing substance abuse, along with the growing tumor, began to cause him to have psychotic episodes. He died on January 20, 1947, at the age of 35.

10   "Through the Eyes of W. Rollo Wilson," *Philadelphia Tribune*, August 11, 1945. Cum Posey was a dominant force in Negro Leagues baseball throughout the 1930s, up to his death in 1946. On the morning of the East-West Game, he held court in the Grand Hotel lobby, talking baseball and shopping his suffering catcher, Josh Gibson. He offered to trade Gibson to the Baltimore Elite Giants for Roy Campanella, and club owner Wilson

laughed him right out of the lobby, emphasizing how low Gibson's stock as a player had sunk since he had begun showing signs of a serious mental illness.

11   "NAL player fined for striking umpire," *Baltimore Afro-American, July 28, 1945*. Davis was voted in by fans as the NAL starting second baseman, but had been suspended indefinitely by J.B. Martin and fined $50 for striking umpire Jimmy Thompson with a baseball bat during a heated argument in a game between Birmingham and the Cleveland Buckeyes on July 16.

12   Wendell Smith, "The Sports Beat."

13   "Scalpers Take a Good Beating," *Chicago Defender*, August 4, 1945. "FBI Nabs Ticket Counterfeiters at East-West Game," *New Journal and Guide* (Norfolk, Virginia), August 11, 1945. Rumors had spread before the game that the park had been sold out, when in fact there were thousands of tickets left for sale. The markups by scalpers further depressed attendance. Grandstand tickets with a face value of $2 were being sold by scalpers for $4, and $7.50 box-seat tickets were selling for as high as $10.

14   Wendell Smith, "The Sports Beat."

15   Al Monroe, "Swinging the News," *Chicago Defender*, August 11, 1945. Inside Comiskey Park, celebrities like Lena Horne, Roberta Proctor, and Earl Robinson were spotted in the stands. John R. Williams, a Detroit baseball promoter, walked throughout the stands, engaging team executives and trying to book games at Briggs Stadium. Missing from the assemblage of baseball personalities were Newark Eagles owner, and baseball's only female member of the Hall of Fame, Effa Manley; Kansas City Monarchs owner J.L. Wilkinson; and Gus Greenlee, former Pittsburgh Crawfords owner who had recently partnered with Brooklyn Dodgers President Branch Rickey to start a third Negro League, the United States League. In his column "The Sports Beat," Wendell Smith wrote that Wilkinson felt ill and was resting at his home in Kansas City, and that Greenlee was occupied caring for his sick mother.

16   "Scalpers Take a Good Beating."

17   Wendell Smith, "West Wallops East in Dull 'Dream Game,' 9 to 6," *Pittsburgh Courier*, August 4, 1945; "West Captures Lead in 9-6 Series Win," *Philadelphia Tribune*, August 4, 1945.

18   Radcliffe was the brother of Ted "Double Duty" Radcliffe. Contemporary newspapers dubbed Wright "Big Bill Wright."

19   "West Wallops East in Dull 'Dream Game,' 9 to 6"; Associated Negro Press, "West Defeats East 9-6 Before 32,000 Fans," *New Journal and Guide*, August 4, 1945.

20   "West Wallops East in Dull 'Dream Game,' 9 to 6." Verdell Mathis was lifted after three innings because owners had agreed to a three-inning limit for all pitchers. He struck out four and walked one in three innings.

21   "West Wallops East in Dull 'Dream Game,' 9 to 6." Martin Dihigo is the only baseball player to be elected to Halls of Fame in five countries – the United States, Cuba, Mexico, Venezuela, and the Dominican Republic. He was a multipositional player who earned the nicknames El Inmortal and El Maestro for his mastery of every position, and also for his managing abilities. He was the starting right fielder for the East team in the 1945 East-West Game.

22   "West Captures Annual Diamond Classic, 9-6," *St. Louis Argus*, August 3, 1945.

23   "West Wallops East in Dull 'Dream Game,' 9 to 6."

24   "West Wallops East in Dull 'Dream Game,' 9 to 6."

25   "West Captures Annual Diamond Classic, 9-6."

26   "West Wallops East in Dull 'Dream Game,' 9 to 6."

27   Dan Burley, "Dan Burley's 'Confidentially Yours,'" *New York Amsterdam News*, August 18, 1945. While the reported attendance figure of 37,714 would have been considered a very large crowd for a regular-season NAL or NNL game, for the celebrated East-West Game, the total was a far cry

from previous games. Attendance the two years prior had reached over 50,000 fans. *Pittsburgh Courier* sportswriter Wendell Smith, in his column "The Sports Beat," attributed the drop-off in attendance to several reasons. Traditionally, the East-West game was played in the first week of August, but for the 1945 season owners had voted to move the game up to July. ODT travel restrictions hampered the ability of patrons to travel to Chicago for the game

28 "Scalpers Take Good Beating."

29 Willie Bea Harmon, "Sportorial," *Kansas City Call*, July 27, 1945. Newspapers were promoting the appearances of Paige and Gibson the week of the game. Even the *Kansas City Call*, which was the only paper that reported that Paige would miss the game, ran another article in the same edition promoting Paige in the West lineup.

30 Lawrence D. Hogan, *Shades of Glory* (Washington: National Geographic, 2006), 357-372. The 1945 game was not only Jackie Robinson's only East-West appearance; it was his only season in Negro League baseball. On October 23, 1945, the Brooklyn Dodgers announced that they had signed Robinson to a contract and assigned him to their minor-league affiliate in Montreal for the 1946 season. On April 15, 1947, Robinson made his debut at first base for the Dodgers and broke a color barrier that had existed in major-league baseball since the mid-1880s. The New York Giants, Cleveland Indians and other teams started quickly signing as many Black baseball players as they could. The talent pool in the Negro Leagues depreciated rapidly. By the 1949 season, the level of play had sunk so low that Major League Baseball does not recognize Negro League seasons after 1948 as being major-league caliber. In 1948 the East-West Game drew 31,079 fans, of whom only 26,697 bought a ticket. By 1951, game attendance had fallen to 21,312, of whom 14,161 paid to see the game. Attendance for the 1954 game was estimated at around 10,000. The game moved from Comiskey Park, its home since its inception in 1933, to Yankee Stadium in 1961, the next to last East-West Game. The ageless Satchel Paige, at the time 55 years old (yet still four years away from his final major-league appearance in 1965 at the age of 59 for the Kansas City Athletics) pitched for the West team, giving up only one hit in a 7-1 West win. The attendance at the game was 7,245, a far cry from the era when celebrities and politicians would join the masses to pack into Comiskey Park and root on the cream of the crop of Black baseball talent during the heyday of the Negro Leagues.

The 1945 Negro World Series: Cleveland Buckeyes vs. Homestead Grays

By Richard J. Puerzer

The 1945 Negro World Series, the final one before the desegregation of professional baseball, featured the veteran-led Homestead Grays vs. the upstart Cleveland Buckeyes. The Grays won both the first and second halves of the Negro National League season, with an overall league record of 40-20-2 (.667). Likewise, the Buckeyes won the first and second halves of the Negro American League season, with an overall record of 62-17-1 (.785). Because both teams won the first and second halves of their seasons, they advanced directly to the Negro World Series.

Only one position player under the age of 30, right fielder Dave Hoskins, played in all four games of the Series for the Grays, who had five future Hall of Famers on the team: first baseman Buck Leonard, outfielder Cool Papa Bell, third baseman Jud Wilson, pitcher Ray Brown, and catcher Josh Gibson. They were led by player-manager Vic Harris, arguably one of the greatest managers in baseball history.[1] The Buckeyes, on the other hand, were a relatively young squad, led by player-manager Quincy Trouppe, center fielder Sam "The Jet" Jethroe, and shortstop Avelino Cañizares.

This version of an annual Negro League World Series, played between the Negro National League and Negro American League champions, was initiated in 1942. The Buckeyes, also formed in 1942, were playing in their first World Series. The Homestead Grays were appearing in the Series for the fourth consecutive year, after having won the previous two Series in 1943 and 1944. The Buckeyes and Grays were to play a best-of-seven series to decide the 1945 championship.

Given their success in previous seasons, the Homestead Grays were considered by many to be the favorites going into the Series. "No one thought that we had much of a chance," Trouppe recounted in his autobiography.[2] However, Trouppe had recognized at the onset of the season that the Buckeyes were not a power-hitting team, but instead that his team was fast, and would best embrace the approach of Rube Foster, later to be known as "small ball." The Buckeyes excelled at strategies such as the hit-and-run, sacrifice bunting, and stealing bases,[3] which, along with strong pitching, would serve them well during the season and especially in the Series.

GAME ONE: SEPTEMBER 13, 1945, CLEVELAND BUCKEYES 2, HOMESTEAD GRAYS 1, AT CLEVELAND STADIUM

Game One of the World Series was played at Cleveland Stadium on Thursday night, September 13. Veteran starter Willie Jefferson of the Buckeyes faced off against Grays ace Roy Welmaker. Both pitchers started strongly, as Jefferson retired the first nine Grays batters in order while Welmaker did not allow a Buckeye to reach base in the first two innings. In the bottom of the third, Buckeyes second baseman Johnnie Cowan reached first with a one-out single. Cowan advanced to second on a sacrifice by Willie Jefferson but was left stranded when Buckeyes leadoff hitter Avelino Cañizares grounded out. The Grays mounted their first threat in the fourth when 42-year-old leadoff hitter Cool Papa Bell singled to start off the inning, but he was forced at second when Grays center fielder Jerry Benjamin grounded into a fielder's choice. Benjamin stole second and Dave Hoskins then walked, allowing the heart of the Grays order – Buck Leonard and Josh Gibson – to come to the plate. However, Jefferson pitched out of the situation, retiring both Grays sluggers and leaving the game scoreless. The Grays threatened again in the fifth when Sam Bankhead led off with a single and stole second. However, Grays third sacker Ray Battle struck out, Bankhead was thrown out trying to steal third, and Jelly Jackson grounded out to quell the threat.

The scoring deadlock was finally broken in the bottom of the seventh. Buckeyes catcher-manager Quincy Trouppe led off the inning with a triple. After Buddy Armour struck out, Cowan lofted a ball caught by Cool Papa Bell in the outfield deep enough to allow Trouppe to score. After seven innings, the Buckeyes now held a slim 1-0 lead. In the eighth inning, Grays manager Vic Harris was hoping to create some offense by pinch-hitting two lefty batters against the righty Jefferson. Jud Wilson, 49 years old, batted first but failed to reach base. Harris then inserted himself into the lineup, but also did not reach, and the Grays failed to score in the inning. In the bottom of the eighth, the Buckeyes were able to manufacture another run when Archie Ware singled, moved to second on a walk to Parnell Woods, and scored on a single by Willie Grace. The Grays bats came alive in the ninth, with the Buckeyes clinging to a 2-0 lead. With one out, Dave Hoskins singled and Buck Leonard walked. Josh Gibson then came to the plate and singled, scoring Hoskins and sending Leonard to third. However, Willie Jefferson was able to induce Sam Bankhead to ground into a game-ending double play, killing the rally and preserving the Game One victory for the Buckeyes.

Both Jefferson and Welmaker threw complete games. Welmaker struck out seven, walked three, and gave up six hits in the loss. Jefferson stuck out four, walked two, and gave up six hits, but was able to limit the Grays to one run in earning the victory. Different sources had the attendance at 6,500 to 8,000 fans, and the game was played in one hour and 39 minutes.[4]

Grays	0	0	0	0	0	0	0	0	1		1	6	1
Buckeyes	0	0	0	0	0	0	1	1	x		2	6	0

GAME TWO: SEPTEMBER 16, 1945, CLEVELAND BUCKEYES 4, HOMESTEAD GRAYS 2, AT LEAGUE PARK, CLEVELAND

After playing each other in an exhibition game in Dayton, Ohio, on Friday, September 14 – a 3-1 victory for the Grays – the teams met again on Sunday, September 16. The game was played at 2:30 P.M. at League Park before a crowd of 15,000. Eugene Bremer got the start for the Buckeyes against Johnny Wright for the Grays.

Neither team put together much offense until the top of the fourth, when Buck Leonard led off with a single and advanced to third on a well-struck double by Josh Gibson. Sam Bankhead then rapped into a fielder's choice, resulting in Gibson being forced out at second and Leonard staying at third. Jud Wilson pinch-hit for third baseman Ray Battle and flied out to Sam Jethroe in center deep enough to score Leonard from third. The Grays failed to score again in the inning but now had a 1-0 lead. In the top of the fifth, the Grays manufactured another run when Cool Papa Bell demonstrated that he was still a speedster on the bases. Bell led off the inning with an infield single, advanced to second on a sacrifice by Jerry Benjamin, and to third on a groundout. Bell then scored on a balk by Bremer, giving the Grays a 2-0 lead.

Meanwhile Johnny Wright kept the Buckeye bats quiet until the bottom of the seventh. Willie Grace led off the inning with a home run to right field. Then, after a Trouppe groundout, Buddy Armour doubled. Johnnie Cowan popped out to the infield for the second out. Bremer then reached on an error by Grays second baseman Jelly Jackson that allowed Armour to score to tie the game, 2-2. Neither team scored in the eighth inning, and the Grays were held scoreless in the top of the ninth as well. With the score tied in the bottom of the ninth, Quincy Trouppe led off with a double and quickly advanced to third on a wild pitch. Grays skipper Vic Harris then ordered Wright to intentionally walk both Armour and Cowan to load the bases and bring up the Buckeyes pitcher, Bremer. Once again,

Bremer helped himself at the plate, doubling to right field to drive in the winning run. Although the game ended with Trouppe scoring, two runs were counted as scoring on the final play, thus giving the Buckeyes a 4-2 victory. In addition to driving in the winning run, Eugene Bremer got the win, holding the Grays' offense to two runs on seven hits and two walks while striking out five. Johnny Wright struck out four Buckeyes batters in the loss, giving up three earned runs on eight hits and three walks. In just a few months, Wright was signed by the Brooklyn Dodgers and started the 1946 season, along with teammate Jackie Robinson, on the Dodgers' Triple-A affiliate Montreal Royals. With the victory, the Buckeyes took a two-games-to-none lead in the series.[5]

Grays	0	0	0	1	1	0	0	0	0		2	7	1
Buckeyes	0	2	0	0	0	0	2	0	2		4	8	0

GAME THREE: SEPTEMBER 18, 1945, CLEVELAND BUCKEYES 4, HOMESTEAD GRAYS 0, AT GRIFFITH STADIUM, WASHINGTON

Game Three was originally to be played at Forbes Field in Pittsburgh on Monday, September 17, but was rained out.[6] The teams moved on to Washington, where Game Three was played Tuesday night, September 18, at Griffith Stadium. Roy Welmaker, the Grays' starter in Game One, returned to the mound for the start against Cleveland hurler George Jefferson. Jefferson was the younger brother of Game One starter Willie Jefferson. George was 22 years old in 1945, 19 years younger than his sibling Willie. At least 7,000 fans attended the game, including incoming Baseball Commissioner A.B. "Happy" Chandler.

The Buckeyes threatened in both the first inning, when Sam Jethroe slugged a two-out triple, and the second, when Trouppe and Armour both singled, but failed to score in ether frame. In the third inning, the Buckeyes offense broke through. Leading off the inning, Cañizares hit a foul pop behind home plate that Josh Gibson dropped. Given a second life at the plate, he then walked. Archie Ware laid down a sacrifice bunt, Welmaker muffed the play, and both runners were safe. Next up, Sam Jethroe hit into a fielder's choice, forcing Cañizares out at third. Parnell Woods followed with a single to load the bases. Willie Grace then flied out to right field, deep enough to allow Ware to tag up and score from third. The Buckeyes' hottest hitter, Trouppe, was up next, and was intentionally walked to once again load the bases. Armour followed with a clutch single, scoring Jethroe and Woods. Welmaker got Cowan out to end the inning, but the damage was done and the Buckeyes led, 3-0.

George Jefferson continued to stymie the Grays batters, pitching out of trouble in the third and eighth innings and not allowing a runner to reach third base. In the ninth, the Buckeyes manufactured another run when Armour led off with a single, stole second, advanced to third on an out, and scored on an infield groundout, giving the Buckeyes a 4-0 lead. In the bottom of the ninth, Jefferson got two quick outs before walking Jud Wilson. Vic Harris inserted himself as a pinch-hitter but made an out to end the game. George Jefferson pitched an excellent game, keeping the Grays scoreless while scattering three hits and five walks and striking out three. Welmaker took the loss, his second in the series, despite giving up only one earned run on seven hits, two walks, and five strikeouts. The Buckeyes had now won the first three games in the series and were hoping to sweep the Grays.[7]

Buckeyes	0	0	3	0	0	0	0	0	1	4	7	0
Grays	0	0	0	0	0	0	0	0	0	0	3	2

GAME FOUR: SEPTEMBER 20, 1945, CLEVELAND BUCKEYES 5, HOMESTEAD GRAYS 0, AT SHIBE PARK, PHILADELPHIA

The series shifted to Philadelphia, where Game Four was played at Shibe Park on the night of Thursday, September 20. The previous night the Buckeyes played in Brooklyn in an exhibition against the Bushwicks.[8] With the series on the line, the Grays started 37-year-old veteran and future Hall of Famer Ray Brown. The Buckeyes countered with Frank Carswell, the fourth different starter they used in the Series. A crowd of 9,958 attended the game.

The Buckeyes kept their momentum going, as Avelino Cañizares singled to lead off the game. Archie Ware walked and Sam Jethroe singled to load the bases. Parnell Woods then put the ball in play and Grays second baseman Bozo Jackson muffed it. Cañizares and Ware scored on the play, Jethroe advanced to third, and eventually Woods was put out at second base. Ray Brown was able to pitch out of the inning without further damage, but the Buckeyes had a 2-0 lead. The Grays tried to put together a two-out rally in the third, when Brown walked, Jerry Benjamin singled, and Cool Papa Bell walked to load the bases, but Dave Hoskins batted into an out, ending the threat. The Buckeyes came right back and scored another run in the top of the fourth when Willie Grace singled, advanced to third on a hit and a groundout, and scored on a fly out. The Buckeyes scored again in the top of the seventh. Johnnie Cowan led off with a single. Pitcher Frank Carswell reached on an error, and Cowan advanced to third when Buck Leonard dropped the throw from second baseman Bozo Jackson. Cañizares bunted, moving Carswell to second. After Ware flied out, Jethroe singled, scoring Cowan and Carswell. The inning ended with the Buckeyes leading, 5-0. While the Buckeyes were scoring in multiple innings, Buckeyes hurler Carswell was taking care of business on the mound. The game ended with the Buckeyes victorious, shutting out the Grays for the second game in a row and sweeping the Series with four

straight victories. Carswell scattered four hits and three walks, striking out just one Grays batter in his shutout. Ray Brown, pitching in his final game in the Negro Leagues, gave up 10 hits and one walk, and also struck out just one batter in taking the loss.[9]

Buckeyes	2	0	0	1	0	0	2	0	0	5	10	0
Grays	0	0	0	0	0	0	0	0	0	0	4	2

SERIES POSTSCRIPT

In the series the Buckeyes were led on offense by manager-catcher Quincy Trouppe, who posted a slash line of .400/.438/.600. The Buckeyes used only eight position players, with each player scoring at least one run in the Series. The four Buckeyes starting pitchers were equally impressive, allowing an ERA of just 0.50 and a WHIP of 0.86. Despite featuring five future Hall of Fame players, the Grays' only player performance of note was Roy Welmaker, pitching 17 innings and allowing an ERA of 3.18 and a WHIP of 1.06.

It is interesting that immediately after the decisive game, the Buckeyes played another game, against the Philadelphia Stars, as the scheduled second game of a doubleheader. The Buckeyes prevailed in that game as well, winning 4-1. After the Series, the Buckeyes and Grays continued to play each other in exhibition games. They first played in Wilmington, Delaware, on Saturday, September 22, with the Buckeyes winning 4-1. The two teams then played a doubleheader in Yankee Stadium on Sunday, September 23. The Grays won the first game 7-1, with Jud Wilson slugging a home run, and won the second game by the same score. The Buckeyes eventually returned to Cleveland, where they celebrated their victory with a party at the Majestic Hotel. They were also recognized by the Cleveland City Council, which passed a resolution congratulating them on their championship.[10]

The 1945 World Series was the end of a period of dominance for the Homestead Grays, who had won the previous two Series and eight Negro National League pennants. The Buckeyes remained a strong team in 1946 but took a step back, with the Newark Eagles defeating the Kansas City Monarchs in that year's Negro League World Series.[11] The Buckeyes returned to the Negro League World Series in 1947, losing to the New York Cubans. The 1945 Series victory was the Cleveland Buckeyes' only Negro League championship.

SOURCES

In addition to the sources cited in the Notes, the author consulted Dick Clark and Larry Lester, eds., *The Negro Leagues Book* (Cleveland: SABR, 1994).

Unless otherwise noted, Seamheads.com was used for all Negro League player statistics.

NOTES

1   Per baseball-reference.com, Harris holds a win percentage of .663 (based on 547 wins and 278 losses) as a manager, which is the all-time highest winning percentage for managers who managed more than 500 games. Harris managed in the Negro Leagues for 11 years, winning seven pennants and one World Series.

2   Quincy Trouppe, *20 Years Too Soon* (St. Louis: Missouri Historical Society Press, 1995), 84-86.

3   Trouppe.

4   For Game One, the following references were used: "Buckeyes Top Grays, 2-1, in 1st Game," *Cleveland Plain Dealer*, September 14, 1945: 17; "Cleveland Leads in World Series," *St. Louis Argus*, September 21, 1945: 16.

5   For Game Two, the following references were used: "Buckeyes Win Second in a Row," *Cleveland Plain Dealer*, September 17, 1945, 16; "Cleveland Wins, 3 to 2, In Negro World Series," *St. Louis Star and Times*, September 17, 1945: 15; "Buckeyes Repeat Over Homestead," *Harrisburg* (Pennsylvania) *Evening News*, September 17, 1945: 13; "Cleveland Leads in World Series," *St. Louis Argus*, September 21,1945: 16.

6   "Grays, Buckeyes Game Rained Out," *Pittsburgh Press*, September 17, 1945: 17.

7   For Game Three, the following references were used: "Buckeyes Win Third, 4-0; Need 1 More," *Cleveland Plain Dealer*, September 19, 1945: 14; "Grays Go Three Down as Buckeyes Win, 4-0," *Washington Evening Star*, September 19, 1945: 18.

8   "Jethroe Paces Buckeyes in Bushwick Game," *Brooklyn Eagle*, September 19, 1945: 17.

9   For Game Four, the following references were used: William J. Scheffer, "Buckeyes Blank Grays, Win Title," *Philadelphia Inquirer*, September 21, 1945: 24; "Buckeyes Win Title With 4th In Row, 5-0," *Cleveland Plain Dealer*, September 21, 1945: 14; "Buckeyes Blank Grays to Annex Negro Crown," *Wilmington* (Delaware) *News Journal*, September 21, 1945: 20; "Cleveland Buckeyes Hold Negro Baseball World's Championship," *Monongahela* (Pennsylvania) *Daily Herald*, September 21, 1945: 2; "Buckeyes Beat Grays in Negro World Series," *Dayton* (Ohio) *Daily Bulletin*, September 21, 1945: 1.

10   Stephanie M. Liscio, *Integrating Cleveland Baseball* (Jefferson, North Carolina: McFarland & Company, 2010), 99.

11   Frederick C. Bush and Bill Nowlin, eds., *The Newark Eagles Take Flight: The Story of the 1946 Negro League Champions* (Phoenix: SABR, 2019).

"The 'Cinderella Team' of the Negro Leagues Plays Royal Ball at Griffith Stadium."

September 18, 1945: Cleveland Buckeyes 4, Homestead Grays 0, at Griffith Stadium
Game Three of Negro League World Series

By Bob LeMoine

The 1945 Negro League World Series was taking place in a postwar America. Japan had surrendered, World War II was over, and the famous "kiss" of a sailor and nurse in a celebratory Times Square sparkled on the cover of *Life* magazine. Yet old issues remained. "Jim Crow must go!" African American soldiers demanded, in opposition to the laws in the South that enforced segregation. Wendell Smith of the African-American *Pittsburgh Courier* had recently reported on a mystery meeting between Black star Jackie Robinson and Brooklyn Dodgers President Branch Rickey. Baseball would help guide American society toward the path of desegregation. But we weren't there yet.

"Don't get the idea that baseball was all fun and games for us," George Jefferson said of the Negro Leagues to Dwayne Cheeks of the *Cleveland Plain Dealer* in 1982. "We played a lot of cards and dice to break the monotony of the long bus rides. You saw more trees and bushes than you ever thought existed."[1] There must have been a lot of card playing for Jefferson and the upstart Cleveland Buckeyes as the 1945 Negro League World Series against the champion Homestead Grays was held in Cleveland, Washington, and Philadelphia.

The upstart Buckeyes, winners of the Negro American League pennant, had taken both games in Cleveland: Game One with a tight 2-1 win at Cleveland Stadium, followed by a late-inning comeback to win Game Two, 3-2, at League Park. Both were venues the Buckeyes called "home," although the true home team, the Cleveland Indians, required both teams to use the visitors' locker room.[2] The teams left the wintry weather in Cleveland by train and headed to Pittsburgh for Game Three. Umpire Harry Walker taught rummy to fellow umps Moe Harris and Fred McCleary as they listened to the falling rain as they traveled south. When they reached Forbes Field, one of the Homestead Grays' home parks, they learned the game had been canceled.

They proceeded to their next location, Griffith Stadium in Washington, another home of the Grays. The Washington Senators and Detroit Tigers had just finished an afternoon game in muddy conditions. Game Four would be played at Shibe Park in Philadelphia, and Game Five in New York, if necessary.

The Homestead Grays were a dynasty in Negro League baseball in the 1940s. They had won back-to-back championships in 1943-1944 and seven out of eight consecutive Negro National League pennants. Their roster included several Negro League legends who were getting up in years: Jud Wilson (49 years old), Cool Papa Bell (42), Buck Leonard (37), Ray Brown (37), Jerry Benjamin (35), Bee Jackson (35), Sam Bankhead (34), and a comparatively "young" Josh Gibson (33).

By contrast, the average of the Buckeyes was under 30. They included Sam "The Jet" Jethroe, the speedster who batted .339[3] and would one day be Boston's first Black major-league player. Jethroe had been involved in a "tryout" at Fenway Park with Jackie Robinson earlier in the year. The tryout was more of a publicity stunt, but greater days were ahead when the Boston Braves signed Jethroe.

Baseball Commissioner Kenesaw Mountain Landis, an opponent of integration, had died. Happy Chandler, his successor, who would soon take office following his term as Kentucky senator, arrived at Griffith Stadium to watch Game Three.[4] A supporter of integrating the national pastime, Chandler would later throw that support behind Rickey when he signed Jackie Robinson to a contract. "Some of the things he did for Jackie Robinson, Roy Campanella, and Don Newcombe when he was commissioner of baseball," said Newcombe, who would follow Robinson to the integrated major leagues, "those are the kinds of things we never forget." He remembered Chandler as someone who cared about Blacks in baseball "when it wasn't fashionable.[5]

THE 1945 CLEVELAND BUCKEYES

Chandler was joined by anywhere from 6,000 to 7,500 fans that night, depending on the account. Wilbur Hayes, the Cleveland sports promoter, who with nightclub owner Ernest Wright had built the Buckeyes from scratch just three years prior, received a telegram from Ohio Senator Harold H. Burton, who sent his best wishes. Earlier that day, Burton was nominated by President Harry S. Truman to the United States Supreme Court. Burton would play a crucial role in the landmark *Brown v. Board of Education* ruling which declared that segregating public schools according to race was unconstitutional. The presence of Chandler and Burton foreshadowed changes on the horizon.

"Big" George Jefferson (6-feet-2, 185 pounds) was the Game Three starter for Cleveland. His older brother, Willie, was the Game One winner, while Eugene Bremer won Game Two. "We'd get a few hits and then let the pitchers and the defense do the rest," remembered manager Quincy Trouppe.[6] Jefferson was opposed by the Grays "brilliant southpaw" Roy Welmaker, who "has been the mainstay of the Grays' pitching corps," wrote the *Pittsburgh Courier*.[7]

This would be a game of pitching and defense as well, with very little play-by-play detail provided in the weekly black newspapers. The Buckeyes plated all the runs they needed in the third when errors by catcher Gibson and pitcher Welmaker and singles by Parnell Woods and Buddy Armour gave the Buckeyes a solid 3-0 lead. Armour scored an insurance run in the ninth on a grounder to short by Jefferson. Armour was credited with two RBIs, Jefferson and Willie Grace with one each. Armour, Jethroe (who also tripled), Woods and Archie Ware accounted for all the runs scored. Each pitcher struck out three; Jefferson walked three, Welmaker two.

"They hit and fielded all of them; made the crowd shout for joy," Walker wrote. "The Washington fans almost jumped out of their seats when [Johnnie] Cowan threw a ball on one knee to retire the side, and [shortstop Avelino] Cañizares had them nuts fielding ball after ball that should have been hits," Walker wrote. "The Buckeyes looked like the New York Yankees in their great days."[8]

"Jefferson would turn his body into a windmill and hurl screaming fastballs which broke [a]way from the hitter," Cheeks wrote. "After feeding them a series of fastballs, Jefferson would throw his sneaky curve ball."[9] Jefferson was definitely on his game this day. He allowed only three scattered hits (some accounts gave two or four hits) en route to the victory. His performance was reported as the first shutout of the Grays since Jack Matchett of the Kansas City Monarchs accomplished the feat in 1942.[10] "A pitcher had to get in shape to survive," Jefferson said in 1982. "Teams carried very few relievers, so you knew that most of the time you would be going the distance."[11]

Securing the final out, Jefferson was first greeted by Hayes, the exuberant owner in his "checkered sports shirt which he wore at every game for luck," who ran onto the field to embrace his victorious pitcher.[12]

Smith of the *Pittsburgh Courier* called the Buckeyes a "Cinderella team" who were "fired by determination and youth" and "pulled one of the biggest surprises in baseball history." The legendary Grays, Smith wrote, were "creaking in the joints, in dire need of replacements, and exhausted from that last siege when they had to win nine games in six days to beat out Baltimore and Newark (for the pennant). The Grays just didn't have it in 'em against the inspired, fiery Clevelanders."[13]

The Buckeyes swept the series with a Game Four shut-out, a 5-0 gem by Frank Carswell. It was the only title in the history of the Cleveland Buckeyes.

SOURCES

Cincinnati Enquirer (Associated Press). "Series Game Postponed," September 18, 1945: 12.

Seamheads Negro League Database. seamheads.com/NegroLgs/index.php

NOTES

1   Dwayne Cheeks, "The Cleveland Buckeyes Remembered," *Cleveland Plain Dealer*, January 18, 1982: 7-D.

2   Bob Dolgan, "Championship Memories: The Underdog Cleveland Buckeyes Were Negro League Champs in 1945," *Cleveland Plain Dealer*, February 26, 1996: 1C.

3   According to the Seamheads Negro League Database

4   "Buckeyes Win, 4-0; Need 1 More," *Cleveland Plain Dealer*, September 19, 1945: 14.

5   Robert McG. Thomas Jr., "A.B. (Happy) Chandler, 92, Dies; Led Baseball Integration," *New York Times*, June 16, 1991.

6   Cheeks; "Here's Buckeye Pitching Staff, Rated Peerless," *Cleveland Call & Post*, September 15, 1945. Negro League statistics vary from source to source. Bob Williams called this a "sloppy, slipshod method in which official figures are compiled for the league which calls itself bigtime, intelligent baseball business," "Sports Rambler," *Call & Post*, September 8, 1945.

7   "Grays and Cleveland Set for World Series," *Pittsburgh Courier*, September 15, 1945: 12.

8   Harry Walker, "World Series – Dots and Dashes," *Cleveland Call & Post*, September 29, 1945: 6B.

9   Cheeks.

10   "Cleveland Captures 1945 World Baseball Crown," *Baltimore Afro-American*, September 22, 1945: 26.

11   Cheeks.

12   Walker.

13   Wendell Smith, "The Sports Beat," *Pittsburgh Courier*, September 29, 1945: 12.

Cleveland Buckeyes Dethrone Negro League Champions

September 20, 1945: Cleveland Buckeyes 5. Homestead Grays 0, at Shibe Park, Philadelphia (Game Four of the Negro League World Series)

By Bob LeMoine

The Homestead Grays were a dynasty in Negro League baseball in the 1940s. They had won back-to-back world championships in 1943-1944 and seven Negro National League pennants in eight years. Their roster was full of a who's who of Negro League stars, several of whom would one day be recognized for their greatness in the National Baseball Hall of Fame. In September of 1945, however, the Grays legends were also up in age: Jud Wilson (49), Cool Papa Bell (42), Buck Leonard (37), Ray Brown (37), Jerry Benjamin (35), Jelly Jackson (35), Sam Bankhead (34), and a comparatively "young" Josh Gibson (33). By contrast, the average of the Buckeyes was under 30.

While Negro League records are often incomplete, there was no denying who the Buckeyes hitting star was. Reports listed Sam "The Jet" Jethroe, so-called because of his blazing speed, as batting .393 with 123 total bases, 10 triples, 8 home runs, and 21 stolen bases. Jethroe had been involved in a "tryout" at Fenway Park with Jackie Robinson during the season, as White baseball owners were feeling the pressure to integrate the game. The tryout was more of a publicity stunt, remembered more for a racial slur hurled at them from somebody at the ballpark, but Jethroe became Boston's first Black major leaguer when he suited up for the National League's Braves.

The Buckeyes' strength was their pitching. Brothers George and Willie Jefferson had 16-1 and 14-2 seasons, respectively, while Eugene Bremer was 12-5.

Harry Walker, Mo Harris, Jimmy Thompson, and Fred McCleary were the umpiring crew for the series.

The first two games were held in Cleveland: Game One at Cleveland Stadium and Game Two at League Park. Both ballparks were home to the Cleveland Indians, and both teams were forced to suit up in the visitors locker room. The Buckeyes also relied on discarded Indians uniforms, which were a cherished possession since the name "Cleveland"

was embroidered across the front. In Game One before a crowd of 6,500, the dominant pitching of Willie Jefferson powered the Buckeyes to a 2-1 victory over the Grays. Game Two saw a wild finish akin to a "story-book thriller" (in the *Call & Post's* description).[1] Cleveland rallied from 2-0 down as over 10,000 shivering fans looked on. The Buckeyes tied the score in the seventh, then Bremer sent them home with jubilation with a bases-loaded walk-off hit to secure a 3-2 win.[2]

After Game Two, the teams boarded the bus and headed south to Pittsburgh. A rainout, however, caused Game Three game to be moved to Griffith Stadium in Washington, where George Jefferson shut out the Grays, 4-0, on three hits.

Game Four was played at Philadelphia's Shibe Park and pitted Big Frank Carswell on the hill for the Bucks against Ray Brown for the Grays. The Buckeyes jumped out on top early. Avelino Cañizares, dubbed "the Cuban sensation" by Jimmy Jones of the *Call & Post,* reached on an infield single.[3] Archie Ware walked, then Jethroe beat out a dribbler to the mound that Brown couldn't secure, and the bases were loaded. Parnell Woods, called "one of the greatest clutch hitters in the game" by Jones, scorched a grounder to second too hot to handle for Bee Jackson, and Cañizares and Ware scored. Jackson recovered in time to get Jethroe at second to end the inning.[4]

Only in the third inning did Carswell find trouble. He was helped when Bankhead hit into a double play, erasing Jud Wilson, who had been hit by a pitch. But Ray Brown walked and Benjamin's single put runners at first and third. A walk to Bell loaded the bases, but a grounder by the 19-year-old Dave Hoskins forced Bell at second, and the Grays' best opportunity went by the boards.

The Buckeyes added a run in the fourth when Willie Grace singled and later scored on a long fly ball by Johnnie Cowan, to give the Buckeyes a 3-0 lead.

In the seventh, Cowan singled and Carswell was safe as first baseman Leonard let his roller pass him as he was busy praying for it to spin foul. Cowan snuck all the way to third during the blunder. Cañizares bunted Carswell to second, but Cowan had to hold. Ware flied to Bell in left, not deep enough to score a run, and it looked as if the Grays would get out of the inning unscathed. It was not to be, however, as "the league leading wonder batman" – as Jones described Jethroe – came to the plate. His second hit of the game was punched into center field and the Buckeyes added a pair to grab a 5-0 lead.[5]

Carswell continued for the 5-0 shutout, allowing only four hits to the Grays' superstar lineup.

"Nobody gave us a chance," Willie Grace observed over 50 years later. "But we had a great club ourselves. We were fast and we had good pitchers and fielders. I think we surprised them. They thought they were going to sweep us. If we played them a month later, or a week earlier, we probably wouldn't have beaten them. The timing was right."[6]

Bob Williams, sports editor of the *Call & Post*, recalled the Buckeyes' short history, dating from 1941. Ernie Wright, an Erie, Pennsylvania, businessman, drove up to a shoeshine parlor in Cleveland and made an offer to the man standing there. "Are you Wilbur Hayes?" he asked the local sports promoter. "How'd you like to start up a baseball club, with me as a backer?" The team was born, but its early life wasn't all enjoyable. During its inaugural season, the team had to travel by cars when the team bus broke down. Tragedy struck on September 7, 1942, when one of the cars was in an accident that claimed the lives of two players. The championship was even sweeter considering the Buckeyes' overcoming such sorrow. "At the end of the series," Williams wrote, "we found ourselves staring into the faces of these boys who had been given so little credit as they marched towards their world championship. Yep, we found ourselves staring into the individual faces of these fellows whose united efforts had brought them the highest honor in all Negro baseball."[7]

"They are not individual stars," umpire Harry Walker reflected in his own *Call & Post* column, "but a star team that plays with a lot of team work, and they have taken the East. They are all a nice group of gentlemen."[8]

A "Cinderella team" is how Wendell Smith of the *Pittsburgh Courier* described the Buckeyes, who, "fired by determination and youth … pulled one of the biggest surprises in baseball history." While also acknowledging the greatness of the Grays, Smith also noted the passage of time and the Grays "creaking in the joints, in dire need of replacements, and exhausted from that last siege when they had to win nine games in six days to beat out Baltimore and Newark (for the pennant); the Grays just didn't have it in 'em against the inspired, fiery Clevelanders."[9]

A half-century later, Jethroe mentioned a touch of irony. "We beat them in four straight games. Then we continued playing them (in exhibitions) and never won another game."[10]

But they won the games that mattered, through pitching, defense, and a lot of heart, despite being mostly ignored by the White press. Their legacy still stands, as those gathered at Shibe Park that day saw those traits that supersede the color of one's skin. Later that fall, Jackie Robinson signed with the Montreal Royals, a Brooklyn Dodgers farm team. His next step was the major leagues and a newly integrated American pastime.

SOURCES

The author would like to thank Stephanie Liscio, Rick Bush, and the Cleveland Public Library for research assistance. Readers who would like more information on Negro League baseball in Cleveland are referred to Liscio's book, *Integrating Cleveland Baseball: Media Activism, the Integration of the Indians and the Demise of the Negro League Buckeyes* (Jefferson, North Carolina: McFarland, 2010).

"1945 Negro League World Series," baseball-reference.com/bullpen/1945_Negro_World_Series. Retrieved June 1, 2018.

Baseball-Reference.com

"Cleveland Buckeyes." Encyclopedia of Cleveland History. Case Western Reserve University. case.edu/ech/articles/c/cleveland-buckeyes. Retrieved May 31, 2018.

"Here's Buckeye Pitching Staff, Rated Peerless," *Cleveland Call & Post*, September 15, 1945.

Jones, Jimmy. "Buckeyes Grab First Game of Series, 2-1, Carry On in Fight with Mighty Grays," *Call & Post*, September 22, 1945: 6B.

"Sammy Jethroe Again Bucks' Most Valuable Player, League Leader in Almost Every Batting Honor," *Call & Post*, September 15, 1945.

NOTES

1   *The Call & Post*, founded in the late 1920s and based in Cleveland, covers news of interest to the African-American community.

2   "Second Win for Buckeyes Is Like Story-Book Thriller; Bremer Wins Own Game, 3-2," *Call & Post*, September 22, 1945: 6B.

3   Jimmy Jones, "Series Victor of 4-in-Row, Bucks Stand Out as All-Time Greats, Carswell Wins No. 4," *Call & Post*, September 29, 1945: 6B.

4   Jones.

5   Jones.

6   Bob Dolgan, "Championship Memories: The Underdog Cleveland Buckeyes Were Negro League Champs in 1945," *Cleveland Plain Dealer*, February 26, 1996: 1C.

7   Bob Williams, "Sports Rambler," *Call & Post*, September 29, 1945: 6B

8   Harry Walker, "World Series – Dots and Dashes," *Call & Post*, September 29, 1945: 7B.

9   Wendell Smith, "The Sports Beat," *Pittsburgh Courier*, September 29, 1945: 12.

10   Bill Lammers, "The Cleveland Buckeyes: Champions of a Forgotten League," *Cleveland Plain Dealer*, June 14, 1992: 10.

The Cleveland Buckeyes and the Wider Orbit of Organized Baseball

By Thomas Kern

The Cleveland Buckeyes had their share of decent, even very good players. They were not a juggernaut like the Homestead Grays or Kansas City Monarchs, teams that annually reloaded to maintain their excellence. But they were good, and in that brief time – the mid-1940s – they won two Negro American League pennants and a World Series crown.

BUCKEYES IN THE EAST-WEST ALL-STAR GAMES

One measure of excellence was the number of Buckeyes who played in the East-West All-Star Game. Research identifies 12 who played, including seven starters. Four Buckeyes appeared in more than one All-Star Game: Eugene Bremer, Sam Jethroe, Quincy Trouppe, and Archie Ware. Sam Jethroe, arguably the greatest Buckeye ever, led the way with four appearances.[1]

Player	Year(s)	Position
Alfred Armour	1944	LF (*)
Eugene Bremer	1944, 1945	P
Chet Brewer	1947	P
Lloyd Davenport	1945	RF (*)
Willie Grace	1946	RF (*)
Dave Hoskins	1949	P
Leon Kellman	1949	PH
Sam Jethroe	1942, 1944, 1946, 1947	PH, CF (*)
Theolic Smith	1943	PH
Quincy Trouppe	1945, 1946, 1947	C (*)
Archie Ware	1944, 1945, 1946	1B (*)
Parnell Woods	1942	3B (*)

Only appearances as Buckeyes are listed; (*) = Starter

BUCKEYES IN THE MEXICAN LEAGUE

The Mexican League, founded in 1925, was a viable competitive setting for Negro League ballplayers, motivated by the additional cash and more equitable treatment by Mexican baseball officials and fans alike. According to John Virtue, "Under Mexican League regulations, the [Mexican] teams could have imported any players, but they chose to recruit African Americans."[2]

Player movement to Mexico increased in the 1940s, thanks to businessman Jorge Pasquel investing money to raise the profile of the Mexican League by attracting both White and Black baseball players from north of the border. Researcher Bill Young noted, "[I]n 1946, 22 major leaguers [American and National Leaguers] – 11 of whom were under contract to either the New York Giants or the Brooklyn Dodgers – bolted to Mexico in search of greener (baseball) fields."[3]

In the 1940s, each of the six to eight teams in the league played between 75 and 100 scheduled games per season, beginning early in the calendar year and overlapping with league seasons in the United States. Five Buckeyes took advantage of the league with some making their presence south of the border a fixture. By the early 1950s, movement to the Mexican Leagues by American players diminished, although nowadays the Mexican League has again become a magnet for ballplayers unable to compete at a major-league level.

Player	Buckeyes	Mexican League
Willie Jefferson	1942-1945	1931 -1941
Theolic Smith	1943	1940-1942; 1944-1948
Lloyd Davenport	1944-1945	1940; 1945-1948
Quincy Trouppe	1945-1947	1939-1944; 1950-1951
Avelino Cañizares	1945	1944; 1946-1948; 1954

BUCKEYES IN THE AMERICAN AND NATIONAL LEAGUES

Finally, there are the seven Buckeyes who made it to the American or National League as part of the slow trickle of Black ballplayers welcomed to those circuits. Five of the players, led by Sam Jethroe, who debuted with the Boston Braves on April 18, 1950, and was named Rookie of the Year that season, originated with the team. Information is not currently available regarding any players who might have made it to the previously White minor leagues, whether affiliated with an American or National League team or

THE 1945 CLEVELAND BUCKEYES

not. Sam Jones, who did not play on the Buckeyes' 1945 World Series champion team, had the longest tenure in the American or National League – 12 years.

Player/Buckeyes Tenure	NL and AL team(s)	Debut	Tenure
Sam Jethroe, 1942-48 (*)	Boston (NL), Pittsburgh (NL)	April 18, 1950	1950-52, 1954
Sam Jones, 1946-48 (*)	Cleveland (AL) and other teams	September 22, 1951	1951-52, 1955-64
Quincy Trouppe, 1945-47	Cleveland (AL)	April 30, 1952	1952
Al Smith, 1946-48 (*)	Cleveland (AL)	July 10, 1953	1953-64
Dave Hoskins, 1949	Cleveland (AL)	April 18, 1953	1953-54
Vibert Clarke, 1946-49 (*)	Washington (AL)	September 4, 1955	1955
Joe Caffie, 1950 (*) [4]	Cleveland (AL)	September 13, 1956	1956-57

(*) = Began career with Buckeyes

SOURCES

The author wishes to acknowledge the important contribution of Merl Kleinknecht in assembling these charts. Mr. Kleinknecht originally joined SABR in 1971, was a founding member of SABR's Negro Leagues Research Committee and served two terms as committee chair in the 1970s.

NOTES

1   In 1942, 1946, 1947, and 1948, two Negro League All-Star Games were played.

2   John Virtue, *South of the Color Barrier: How Jorge Pasquel and the Mexican League Pushed Baseball Toward Racial Integration* (Jefferson, North Carolina: McFarland & Company, 2008): 61.

3   Bill Young, "From Mexico to Quebec: Baseball's Forgotten Giants,' *The National Pastime: Baseball in the Big Apple* (Phoenix: SABR, 2017).

4   Joseph L. Reichler, ed., *The Baseball Encyclopedia: The Complete and Official Record of Major League Baseball, 9th Edition* (New York: Macmillan Publishing Company, 1993).

Documenting the Forgotten Champions:

The Making of "I Forgot to Tell You About … The Cleveland Buckeyes"

By Evelyn R. Gregory, Film Director

The story of the 1945 Cleveland Buckeyes represents more than just a championship season. It embodies the resilience, determination, and indomitable spirit of Black America during one of our nation's most challenging periods. As a filmmaker and native Clevelander, discovering this buried chapter of my city's history transformed my understanding of both baseball and the Black experience in midcentury America.

UNEARTHING CLEVELAND'S HIDDEN BASEBALL LEGACY

When I grew up in Cleveland, the narrative of baseball centered almost exclusively on the Cleveland Indians (now Guardians). The city's rich Negro Leagues history remained conspicuously absent from our collective memory. This glaring omission became apparent during my research into Cleveland's African American heritage, undertaken initially to educate my own children about their roots. The discovery of the Cleveland Buckeyes' extraordinary 1945 championship season emerged as a revelation – one that demanded to be shared with a broader audience.

The process of uncovering this history revealed not just a championship team, but a complex web of social relationships, economic structures, and community pride that defined Black Cleveland in the 1940s. Local newspapers of the era, particularly the *Call and Post*, provided invaluable insights into how the team's success resonated throughout the city's African American community.

THE BUCKEYES' JOURNEY: TRIUMPH FROM TRAGEDY

The Cleveland Buckeyes' story begins with profound loss. In 1942 a devastating automobile accident claimed the lives of two players and left four others seriously injured, threatening the team's very existence. This tragedy occurred against the backdrop of World War II, when many Negro League teams struggled to survive due to players serving in the military and wartime travel restrictions.

The team's resurrection from these setbacks makes their subsequent achievement even more remarkable. Operating on a shoestring budget, players drove their own vehicles to games, navigating the dangerous landscape of Jim Crow America. Each road trip required careful planning to find safe places to eat, sleep, and refuel – considerations their White counterparts never faced.

The team's resilience manifested itself in creative solutions to these challenges. Players developed informal networks of safe houses and friendly businesses along their travel routes. Team members often stayed in private homes rather than hotels, creating lasting bonds with Black communities across the country. These connections helped sustain not just the team, but the entire Negro Leagues infrastructure during challenging times.

THE CHAMPIONSHIP SEASON

The 1945 season marked the pinnacle of the Buckeyes' resilience. The team dominated the Negro American League, finishing with an impressive regular-season record and winning both halves of the season. During the regular season, the Buckeyes showcased their exceptional talent through stellar pitching performances and clutch hitting. Their roster included several players who in a more just era might have become major-league stars.

Their World Series sweep of the Homestead Grays, featuring five future Hall of Famers, represented a triumph not just for Cleveland, but for the entire Black community during a pivotal moment in American history. The championship series itself was a master class in competitive baseball, with the Buckeyes demonstrating their skill and determination across several closely contested games.

BEYOND BASEBALL: THE NEGRO LEAGUES' CULTURAL IMPACT

The Negro Leagues served as more than athletic entertainment – they were vital institutions within the Black community. Teams like the Buckeyes provided economic opportunities, created jobs, and established spaces where African Americans could gather with dignity during the Jim Crow era. League games became social events, drawing crowds that crossed racial boundaries and challenging prevailing segregation norms.

THE 1945 CLEVELAND BUCKEYES

Local businesses thrived on game days, with restaurants, hotels, and transportation services all benefiting from the team's presence. The Buckeyes' success helped establish Cleveland as a major center for Black baseball, contributing to the city's reputation as a relatively progressive Northern destination during the Great Migration.

THE INTEGRATION PARADOX

Jackie Robinson's historic integration of major-league baseball in 1947 marked a crucial civil rights milestone. However, this progress came at a cost to Negro League institutions. As top talent moved to the National and American League teams, Negro League attendance declined, leading to the eventual dissolution of these once-thriving organizations. The Cleveland Buckeyes' story exemplifies this bittersweet transition – their championship achievement fading from public memory as integration changed the baseball landscape.

The documentary explores this complex legacy, highlighting how the success of integration paradoxically contributed to the erosion of Black-owned businesses and institutions that had sustained communities through decades of segregation. This perspective adds nuance to the traditional narrative of baseball integration as an unalloyed triumph.

DOCUMENTING HISTORY: THE FILMMAKER'S JOURNEY

Creating this documentary required extensive archival research, combining newspaper accounts, photographs, and oral histories. Interviews with surviving family members of Buckeyes players provided intimate perspectives on the personal sacrifices and triumphs these athletes experienced. The challenge lay in weaving together fragmented historical records to construct a compelling narrative that honors these forgotten heroes.

The research process revealed numerous previously unknown stories and connections. Through painstaking investigation of personal archives, church records, and community newsletters, I uncovered rich details about the players' lives off the field and their connections to Cleveland's Black community.

THE EDUCATIONAL IMPERATIVE

As Director of the Black Film Institute at Simmons College of Kentucky, I recognize this project's educational significance. The documentary serves multiple purposes: preserving vital history, celebrating African American achievement, and illuminating the complex relationship between racial progress and community institutions. By incorporating this story into curriculum materials, we can ensure that future generations understand the full scope of baseball's role in American civil rights history.

TECHNICAL CHALLENGES AND CREATIVE SOLUTIONS

Documenting historical events from an era with limited visual records presented unique challenges. The production team worked closely with historical societies and archives across the country to locate and restore rare footage and photographs. Advanced digital techniques helped bring black-and-white images to life, while careful sound design recreated the atmosphere of 1940s baseball games.

COMMUNITY IMPACT AND CONTEMPORARY RELEVANCE

The documentary's impact extends beyond historical preservation. By highlighting the Buckeyes' triumph over adversity, we draw parallels to contemporary struggles for equality and recognition. The film demonstrates how sports can serve as both a mirror reflecting societal challenges and a catalyst for social change.

Local screenings have sparked important discussions about preserving Black history and recognizing the ongoing impact of historical inequities. The project has also inspired initiatives to commemorate the team's achievements through historical markers and educational programs.

LEGACY AND LESSONS

The Cleveland Buckeyes' championship season offers valuable lessons about perseverance, community solidarity, and the importance of preserving marginalized histories. Their story reminds us that progress often comes at a cost, and that celebrating breakthrough achievements shouldn't overshadow the vibrant institutions that sustained communities through difficult times.

The documentary serves as a catalyst for broader discussions about how we remember and honor Black achievement in American history. It challenges viewers to consider what other important stories might be waiting to be rediscovered and retold.

CONCLUSION

I Forgot to Tell You About ... The Cleveland Buckeyes World Championship represents more than just a sports documentary. It's a crucial piece of American history that illuminates the intersection of race, sports, and social justice. As communities nationwide grapple with questions of representation and historical memory, the Buckeyes' story offers insights into both past struggles and present challenges.

The documentary serves as a testament to the power of resilience and community, while highlighting the ongoing need to preserve and celebrate overlooked achievements in African American history. Through this project, we ensure that the Cleveland Buckeyes' remarkable journey from tragedy to triumph remains a source of inspiration for future generations.

After its showing in March 2025, the documentary received an award for Best Ohio Short -- Audience Choice.

NOTE:

To see the film, please consult www.agvfilms.com and the IMDB website https://www.imdb.com/title/tt29623761/ .

THE CLEVELAND BUCKEYES

OF 1945

![team photo]

MURDERER'S ROW

READING LEFT TO RIGHT

AVELINO CANOZERIS—LLOYD DAVENPORT

SAM JETHROE—PARNELL WOODS—ARCHIE WARE

WILLIE GRACE—JOHNNY COWANS—ALFRED ARMOUR

HEADQUARTERS
4809 Central Avenue
Cleveland, Ohio

WILBUR HAYES, Gen. Mgr.
Tel. No. ENdicott 6328

YEAR BOOK
BEST WISHES TO
CLEVELAND BUCKEYES
CHAMPIONS OF CLEAN SPORTS
JUDGE PERRY B. JACKSON

Meet Your Buckeyes

ALFRED "BUDDY" ARMOUR

30 years old. Born in Jackson, Miss. Started 1936 with "St. Louis Stars" until 1939, then to "New York Black Yankees" (1940). 1941-43 played with "Harrisburg, Pa., Stars". In 1944 signed with "Buckeyes".

•

ARCHIE V. WARE

27 years old. Born in St. Petersburg, Florida. Started in 1940 with "American Giants". Started in 1941 with "Chicago" and ended season with "K. C. Monarchs". Signed by "Buckeyes" in 1942.

•

EUGENE BREMER

29 years old. Born New Orleans, La. Started in 1932 with "Crescent Stars" in Louisiana. In 1935 joined "Shreveport Giants" under W. S. Welch. 1936-37 with "Cinn. Tigers", 1938 "Memphis", 1939 in Mexico, 1940 back with "Memphis". Out in 1941. Signed with "Buckeyes" in 1942.

•

PARNELL WOODS

30 years old. Born in Birmingham, Ala. Started in 1933-37 with "Barons". Went to "Jacksonville Red Caps" in 1938 and winter league in Porto Rico. In 1939-40 "Cleveland Bears". In 1941 signed with "Buckeyes".

•

ROOSEVELT "DURO" DAVIS

40 years old. Born in Bartlesville, Okla. Started in 1924 with "St. Louis Stars" managed by Candy Jim Taylor to 1931. In 1932-33 with "Bismark, N. D." mixed team. In 1934-35 with "Pittsburgh Crawfords". 1936-37-38 with "New York Black Yankees". 1939 in Mexican League. 1940-41-42-43-44 and part of 1945 with "Clowns" and joined "Buckeyes" one month ago.

•

FRANK CARSWELL

27 years old. Born Atlanta, Ga. Moved to Albin, Mich., when young, then to Buffalo and was discovered on sandlots in Buffalo by "Square" Moore and signed by "Buckeyes" in 1944.

Meet Your Buckeyes

LOVELL HARDEN

27 years old. Born in St. Louis, Mo. Started in 1943 off sandlot in Laurel, Miss., and signed by "Buckeyes" and been here since.

●

JOHNNY COWAN

32 years old. Born in Birmingham, Ala. Started in 1934 with "Barons" out in 1935 and 1936 with "Barons", out in 1937 until 1944 and signed with "Buckeyes".

●

JESSE WILLIAMS

28 years old. Opelika, Ala. Picked off sandlot in Dayton, Ohio and signed by "Buckeyes" 1944. Traded to "American Giants" by "Buckeyes" in winter and was released by "Chicago" and signed back by "Buckeyes".

●

SAMUEL JETHROE

28 years old. Born in St. Louis. Started in 1942 with "Buckeyes". Led league in batting in 1944, and now leading so far in 1945.

●

AVELINO CANOZERIS

25 years old. Born in Havana, Cuba. Started with "Cinfugas in 1942. In 1943-44 winter ball with "Almandares", Cuba. In 1945 signed with "Trouppe". In summer of 1944 "Tampica" and 1945 with "Buckeyes".

●

EARL ASBEY

24 years old. Born in Havana, Cuba. Started in 1945 (his first year) (in the states) with "Buckeyes".

●

WILLIE GRACE

28 years old. Born in Memphis, Tenn. Signed off sandlot in Laurel, Miss., by "Buckeyes" in 1942.

Meet Your Buckeyes

I. THOMAS TROUPPE

32 years old. Born in Dublin, Ga. Lincoln U., Jefferson City, Mo., 2 years. Started with "St. Louis Stars" in 1930 while in high school joined "Gray's" and "K. C. Monarchs" in 1932, 1933 with "American Giants". 1934 in "Bismark, N. D." with Satchell Paige on a mixed team until 1936, out in 1937. In 1939 went to Mexico City and played until last year. Played in Cuba and Porto Rico during the winter months and joined "Buckeyes" this year to manage team.

•

GEO. LEO JEFFERSON

23 years old. Born in Baley, Okla. Started with "Oklahoma City Black Indians" in 1937-38. 1939-40-41 with 'Stillwater Tigers". In 1942 with "Jacksonville Red Caps", out in 1943. In 1944-45 signed with "Buckeyes" and now leads league in pitching.

•

JOHN W. BROWN

26 years old. Born in Crossett, Ark. Started with "Greensville Bucks" in 1936 and 1937. In 1938 with "Norfolk, Va. Stars". Out in 1939 and in 1940 with "Oklahoma Indians". In 1941 "Bastrop, La. Blues". In 1942-43 with "St. Louis Giants". Joined "Buckeyes" in 1944-45.

•

WILLIAM JEFFERSON

41 years old. Born in Clearview, Okla. Started in 1928 with "Arkanson City Oilers" with A. C. Beavers in 1929-30. In 1931-32-33-34 with "Sioux City Iowa". In 1935 with "Omaga Packers". In 1936 with "Clay-Brook Tigers" In 1937 with "Cinn. Tigers". In 1938-39 with "Memphis Red Sox". 1940-41 with Mexican League. In 1942 with "Buckeyes" and joined Army and was discharged in March in time for spring training in 1943. In 1944 in Mexican Winter League and joined "Buckeyes" in Summer 1945.

Success Story

By "SCOOPER" COOPER

Mr. Monroe Felton, friend and fellow worker with me at White Motor Co., asked my opinion in writing of the present Cleveland Buckeyes in comparison with other clubs representing our city in organized Negro baseball.

After seeing the "Bucks" trim the Kansas City Monarchs before a crowd of 11,000 cheering fans at the Stadium a couple of weeks ago I can truthfully say, all the glory and success for same victory should be bestowed upon heads of Ernest Wright, owner of the locals and his never tiring business manager Wilbur Hayes. Too much can never be said about these two chaps, for they have traveled a hard road for the past five years to bring to Cleveland, one of the greatest teams ever to play in this city and also in the Negro National League.

All of this brings back memories to 1921 when George Tate, secured the backing of some prominent business men and entered the Tate Stars in the Negro National League and at that time there were some very strong clubs representing Chicago, New York, Washington, Detroit, Pittsburgh, Kansas City and the never to be forgotten Indianapolis A.B.C.'s. The Stars were a group of ambitious young ball players willing to play for peanuts to help the local entrant under the guidance of "Candy" Jim Taylor, now manager of the American Giants. There were no celebrated stars on the club and they finished fourth that year.

At first there were crowds of 2,000, then 4,000 and at the peak of Negro attendance, a good Sunday doubleheader would draw 7,000 and that was something at old Tate Field and later Hooper Field, as Mr. George Hooper, wealthy real estate developer took the park over.

After that, we had many other business men to venture into baseball but they soon got cold feet and pulled out, without profit, but it took Wright, a real go-getter along with the war horse, Hayes, to go along with the game and all its hardships, even disaster when several of their players were mortally injured in an accident while travelling by bus. No friends, that did not stop this winning combination of Wright & Hayes, they went on to victory in two respects—(1) The club is out of the red and (2) they have a championship club this season.

In closing it is merely a suggestion, I believe all Clevelanders should set aside one of the remaining dates the club has here and call it Buckeye Victory Day in honor of Messrs. Ernie Wright and Wilbur Hayes, and fill that Stadium on the Lakefront some evening. There should not be less than 40,000 fans to make it a real appreciative affair. That is all, only to wish the Cleveland Buckeyes the championship of the Negro National League for the season of 1945.

P.S.: Notice there was no mention of the players. Well, first you have to have a good team in the front office to get a team on the field.

Contributors

Richard Bogovich is the author of *Frank Grant: The Life of a Black Baseball Pioneer*, and his prior book profiled another pre-1920 Hall of Famer, Kid Nichols. This is the eighth SABR book on Negro Leaguers to which he has contributed. In 2023 he solved the mysterious disappearance of Negro Leagues superstar Dave Brown a century ago. Richard has degrees from Northern Illinois University and is office manager of the Wendland Utz law firm in Rochester, Minnesota.

Isaac C. Brooks Jr. (Ike) has a keen interest in learning more about and sharing with others the contributions made by African Americans and other people of color to baseball. Since 2006 at the urging of friends, former Negro League players, and their families, he has made numerous presentations regarding this sometimes-forgotten group and their impact and influence on America's pastime. Beginning in 2020, coincidental with the COVID-19 global pandemic, he began a collaboration with the Community Cup Classic Foundation of Northeast Ohio on a series of multigenerational programs showcasing the challenging, historic, and triumphant legacy of baseball's Negro Leagues and the African American experience in baseball. The aim is to strengthen connections among and between people by fostering meaningful conversations about race, equity, and history. Throughout 2025 several monthly "Negro League Soul" series offerings were scheduled to pay tribute to the 80th anniversary of the Cleveland Buckeyes' 1945 World Series championship.

Alan Cohen has been a SABR member since 2011. He chairs the BioProject fact-checking committee, serves as vice president-treasurer of the Connecticut Smoky Joe Wood Chapter, and is a datacaster (MiLB stringer) with the Eastern League Hartford Yard Goats, the Double-A affiliate of the Colorado Rockies. He also works with the Retrosheet Negro Leagues project and serves on SABR's Negro League Committee. His biographies, game stories, and essays have appeared in more than 80 baseball-related publications. He has four children, nine grandchildren, and one great-grandchild, and resides in Connecticut with his wife, Frances, their cats, Zoe and Ava, and their dog, Buddy.

Dominick Denaro inherited his love of baseball and the New York Mets from his grandfather, a Brooklyn Dodgers fan whose first words of English may have been Dolph Camilli, and who was determined that no grandson of his would grow up to be a Yankees fan. He is the former producer and director of *Vermont Expos Weekly*, co-author of an Eastern Colored League card set for the APBA baseball game, and a regular contributor to the *Negro League Soul* series of monthly virtual presentations. Over the years Dominick has created numerous pieces of baseball-related art that have been displayed in local galleries and shared with friends and family.

Jeff Findley has been a member of SABR since 2009. A native of Eastern Iowa, he did the only logical thing growing up in the heart of the Cubs/Cardinals rivalry – he embraced the 1969 Baltimore Orioles and became a lifelong fan. When he's not watching baseball, he works as an information security professional for a Fortune 50 financial services company in central Illinois. He enjoys doing historical research and contributing to both the SABR BioProject and the Games Project.

Matt Garvey is a high-school English teacher in St. Louis. He grew up in St. Louis as a die-hard Cardinals fan from conception and spent some time in the Marines before becoming a teacher. He became interested in Negro Leagues baseball a decade ago, when he discovered *The League of Outsider Baseball* by Gary Cieradkowski in a school library. For the past three years he has been researching and writing his first book, *Cool, Mule, and the Devil: The Story of the St. Louis Giants and Stars*. He has been a SABR member since 2022. This is his first published work.

Darren Gibson spent his Little League and high-school years in Lakewood, California, playing alongside multiple athletes who eventually made "The Show," but his baseball highlight was actually getting a "call-back" during walk-on tryouts at UCLA's Jackie Robinson Stadium in the late 1980s. Darren has been an avid baseball simulation player for decades and he still "bleeds Dodger blue." He has written over 50 SABR baseball player biographies, and is currently a math teacher, coach, and high-school football official in Orange County, California.

David J. Goldberg received his BA from the University of Wisconsin-Madison and his PhD from Columbia University. He is the author of *A Tale of Three Cities: Labor Organization and Protest in Paterson, Passaic and Lawrence* (Rutgers University Press, 1989) and *Discontented America – The United States in the 1920s* (The Johns Hopkins University Press, 1999). He has also written numerous articles related to labor and immigration history. He is currently a professor emeritus at Cleveland State University and is working on a new book dealing with Boston, baseball, and American life in the mid-1950s. He teaches upper-division courses on US history in the twentieth century, US foreign policy, and the history of immigration.

Evelyn R. Gregory is a dynamic director, screenwriter, and film production educator recently appointed as Director of the Black Film Institute at Simmons College of Kentucky. Her work spans collaborations with PBS American Portrait, State Educational Departments, and various organizations, focusing on telling diverse stories that connect generations through multiple media platforms. In her current role, she is creating compelling documentaries that illuminate the college's rich history and its pivotal connections to civil rights and Black advancement, while nurturing the next generation of diverse voices in cinema.

Margaret M. "Peggy" Gripshover retired as a professor of geography at Western Kentucky University in 2024. She earned her PhD in geography at the University of Tennessee and her MS and BS degrees in Geography from Marshall University. She has been a SABR member since 2006 and combines her love of baseball with her geographic research on race, ethnicity, urbanization, horse racing, and cultural landscapes. Peggy has published articles in the *Baseball Research Journal* and contributed a chapter on "Wrigleyville" for *Northsiders: Essays on the History and Culture of the Chicago Cubs*, edited by Gerald R. Wood and Andy Hazucha (McFarland, 2008). She has written numerous biographies for SABR publications including *Bittersweet Goodbye: The Black Barons, the Grays, and the 1948 Negro League World Series* (SABR 2017); *The Newark Eagles Take Flight: The Story of the 1946 Negro League Champions* (SABR 2019); *Pride of Smoketown: The 1935 Pittsburgh Crawfords* (SABR 2020); *When the Monarchs Reigned: Kansas City's 1942 Negro League Champions* (SABR 2021); *The First Negro League Champion: The 1920 Chicago American Giants* (SABR 2022); and *The Stars Shone on Philadelphia: The 1934 Negro National League Champions* (SABR 2023), all edited by Frederick C. Bush and Bill Nowlin; and *The 1939 Baltimore Elite Giants* (SABR 2024), edited by Frederick C. Bush, Thomas Kern, and Bill Nowlin. She is a native of Cincinnati and a lifelong Reds fan. She lives in Bowling Green, Kentucky, with her husband, Thomas L. Bell, and their Australian shepherd, Miss Daisy.

Vince Guerrieri is a journalist and author in the Cleveland area. He's the secretary-treasurer of the Jack Graney SABR Chapter and has contributed to the SABR BioProject, the SABR Games Project, and several SABR anthologies. Additionally, he's written about baseball history for a variety of publications, including *Ohio Magazine*, *Cleveland Magazine*, *Smithsonian*, and *Defector*. He can be reached at vaguerrieri@gmail.com, or found on Twitter @vinceguerrieri.

John V. Haynes II is a paramedic and student at Eastern Kentucky University who resides in Estill County, Kentucky, with his wife and three children. He joined SABR in 2023 but has been a student of baseball history since he was old enough to read the back of a baseball card. A veteran of the United States Navy, he served as a mass communication specialist and contributed to several news articles, photographs, and videos related to military operations published in news outlets around the world. John was born and raised in Cincinnati and is a lifelong Reds fan, but will take in a baseball game anywhere he sees one. He

is passionate about Black baseball history and aside from the occasional guest post on the blog "Home Plate Don't Move," he operates a website that attempts to catalog player uniforms and equipment at nlbuniforms.com.

Leslie Heaphy, associate professor of history at Kent State Stark. Author, researcher, and lifelong Mets fan.

Jay Hurd is a longtime SABR member. He is a librarian, retired from Harvard University, where he worked as the preservation review librarian for Widener Library. He has worked as a museum educator at the Concord Museum, of Concord, Massachusetts. Jay contributes biographies for the SABR Baseball Biography Project, is the co-chair of the SABR Baseball and the Arts Committee, and is co-editor of *Turnstyle,* the SABR journal of baseball and the arts. In 2016 he relocated from Medford, Massachusetts, to Bristol, Rhode Island, where he continues his baseball research and still roots for the Boston Red Sox.

Bill Johnson has contributed nearly 50 essays to SABR's Biography Project and presented papers at the 2011 Cooperstown Symposium on Baseball and American Culture, the 2017 and 2023 Jerry Malloy Negro League Conferences, and the inaugural Southern Negro League Conference (2019). He has published a biography of Hal Trosky (McFarland and Co., 2017) and most recently articles about Negro American League All-Star Art "Superman" Pennington in the journal *Black Ball*, and essays on Josh Gibson and Negro baseball during World War II in the book *Black Baseball in Living Color: The Artwork of Graig Kreindler*. Bill and his wife, Chris, currently reside in the Florida panhandle.

Thomas Kern was born and raised in Southwest Pennsylvania. Listening to the mellifluous voices of Bob Prince and Jim Woods in his youth, how could one not become a lifelong Pirates fan? He now lives in Silver Spring, Maryland, and sees the Pirates, Nationals, and Orioles as often as possible. He is a SABR member dating back to 1984. With a love and appreciation for Negro League Baseball in addition to the Pirates, he has written SABR bios for the 1979 Pirates and Clemente books and has completed bios for Leon Day, John Henry Lloyd, Willie Foster, Judy Johnson, Turkey Stearnes, Hilton Smith, Louis Santop, Andy Cooper, Double Duty Radcliffe, and others.

Sean Kolodziej, a SABR member since 2018, is a lifelong Cubs fan. He was born, raised, and still lives in Joliet, Illinois, with his wife, Amy. His greatest moment at Wrigley Field was watching Glenallen Hill hit a home run onto the rooftop of a building on Waveland Avenue.

Bob LeMoine is a high-school librarian and adjunct professor. He lives in New Hampshire and has contributed to several SABR projects, including two as co-editor. Bob is the author of *When the Babe Went Back to Boston: Babe Ruth, Judge Fuchs, and the Hapless Braves of 1935* (McFarland & Co., 2023).

Len Levin is a longtime newspaper editor in New England, now retired. He lives in Providence with his wife,

Linda, and an overachieving orange cat. He now (Len, not the cat) is the grammarian for the Rhode Island Supreme Court and copy-edits its decisions. He also copy-edits many SABR books, including this one. He is just down the interstate from Fenway Park, where he has spent many happy – and some not-so-happy – hours.

Bill Nowlin was born in 1945 and still remembers his family's drive from Boston to Washington around 1959, and his father refusing to let three hungry kids enter a Maryland restaurant with a small "Whites Only" sign next to the front door. Co-founder of Rounder Records and Down the Road Records and a former political science professor, he has devoted much of the last 20 years to research and writing about baseball, and editing numerous books. He's not gone far in life, living less than eight miles from where he was born in Boston and four miles from Fenway Park.

Tony S. Oliver is a native of Puerto Rico currently living in Sacramento, California, with his wife and daughter. While he works as a Six Sigma professional, his true love is baseball and he cheers for both the Red Sox and whoever happens to be playing the Yankees. He is fascinated by baseball cards and is currently researching the evolution of baseball tickets. He believes there is no prettier color than the vibrant green of freshly mown grass on a baseball field.

Richard J. Puerzer is the chairperson of the Department of Engineering at Hofstra University. His writing on baseball has appeared in numerous SABR books, as well as in *Nine: A Journal of Baseball History and Culture; Black Ball; The National Pastime; The Cooperstown Symposium on Baseball and American Culture proceedings; Zisk;* and *Spitball.*

Carl Riechers retired from United Parcel Service in 2012 after 35 years of service. With more free time, he became a SABR member that same year. Born and raised in the suburbs of St. Louis, he became a big fan of the Cardinals. He and his wife, Janet, have three children and he is the proud grandpa of two.

Kelly Boyer Sagert is a professional writer and editor with 35 years of experience. She is a member of the vetted American Society of Journalists and Authors and the Association of Ghostwriters. She has published dozens of books, bylined (including *Joe Jackson: A Biography*) and ghostwritten, plus thousands of shorter pieces. She is the scriptwriter for the Emmy Award-nominated film *Trail Magic: The Grandma Gatewood Story,* and for *Victoria Woodhull: Shattering Glass Ceilings.* She appeared on an ESPN documentary titled *The Top Five Reasons You Can't Blame the Black Sox.*

Mark Shirk grew up in central Pennsylvania as a Yankees fan. He has a PhD in government and politics from the University of Maryland and has taught international

relations at Stonehill College, the University of Cambridge (UK), and Bucknell University among others. He is currently a consultant living in Catonsville, Maryland. He has been a SABR member since 2020 and is a Yankees fan living in Orioles country with his wife, his dog, and two children. He has developed a research interest in Negro League players who did not have American or National League careers after Negro Leagues fell apart. He has written the SABR bio of Marvin Williams and a story about Bus Clarkson's national league debut for the SABR Games Project.

Russ Speiller lives in Cincinnati with his amazing wife and two children. Russ has been working in research and development for the Procter and Gamble Company for 26 years. A member of SABR since 2023, Russ has contributed to the SABR BioProject, the *Turnstyle* literary journal of baseball & the arts, as well as several SABR books including *Sandy Koufax* and *Dodger Stadium: Blue Heaven on Earth.* He hopes the legacy of the 1945 Cleveland Buckeyes lives on in everyone who hears their story.

Jed Stewart is a lawyer in Birmingham, Alabama, where he has practiced since 1998. He has been a SABR member since 2012 and is co-president of the Rickwood Field SABR Chapter. He is an executive committee member of the board of directors of the Friends of Rickwood Field; and is a regular contributor to the *Rickwood Times.* He has written and edited the Friends' quarterly newsletter, "Rickwood Tales," since its inception in 2019. He has written several biographies for SABR's Biography Project.

Tom Wancho grew up on Cleveland's West Side (Brooklyn) rooting for the Indians. He's a former sports information director at Northwestern State University in Natchitoches, Louisiana. He moved west to Austin, Texas and put in 26-plus years with the State of Texas, including his last 22-plus years as a curator at the Bullock Texas State History Museum. The retired one still follows the Tribe and believes that a self-respecting Clevelander won't ever say or acknowledge the "G" word of the team's current moniker.

Dave Wilkie grew up a third-generation San Francisco Giants fan in Western Canada idolizing Willie McCovey, Vida Blue, and Jack Clark. His obsession with Negro League baseball can be traced to a 1983 mail-order purchase of the book *The All-Time All-Stars of Black Baseball,* by SABR member James A. Riley. He has written SABR biographies on Negro League greats Sam Bankhead, Johnny Davis, Chester Williams, Cool Papa Bell, Frank Duncan, Judy Gans, Rocky Ellis, and Crush Holloway. He also contributed a chapter for the 2023 SABR publication *Nichibei Yakyu: US Tours of Japan* and two chapters for *Black Baseball in Living Color: The Artwork of Graig Kreindler.* Dave lives in Richmond, Virginia, with his son, Monte, and is working on his first book.

Society for American Baseball Research

Become a SABR member today!

If you're interested in baseball — writing about it, reading about it, talking about it — there's a place for you in the Society for American Baseball Research.

SABR members include everyone from academics to professional sportswriters to amateur historians and statisticians to students and casual fans who merely enjoy reading about baseball history and gathering online or in person with other members to talk baseball.

We hope you'll join the most passionate international community of baseball fans!

Check us out online at SABR.org/join

SABR Membership Benefits

- Receive two e-book editions (spring and fall) of the Baseball Research Journal, our flagship publication
- Receive e-book edition of The National Pastime, our annual convention journal
- New e-books published by the SABR Digital Library, FREE to all members
- "This Week in SABR" e-newsletter, sent every Friday
- Regional chapter meetings, which can include guest speakers, presentations, and trips to ballgames
- Participate in research committees and online discussion groups

- Contribute to books, the Baseball Biography Project, and the SABR Games Project
- Collaborate with SABR researchers and experts
- Publish your research in peer-reviewed SABR journals
- Discount on registration to our annual conferences and National Convention
- FREE online access to Historical Black Newspapers Collection via ProQuest, the Newspapers.com World Collection, and The Sporting News via Paper of Record
- Discounts with other partners in the baseball community

SABR MEMBERSHIP FORM

Name _____

Email _____

Address _____

City _____ State _____ Zip _____

Phone _____

If you wish to pay by credit card, please contact the SABR office at (602) 496-1460 or sign up securely online at SABR.org/join.

We accept Visa, Mastercard & Discover.

	Standard	Young Pro.	Student
Annual:	☐$80	☐$55	☐$25
3 Year:	☐$215		
Monthly:	☐$7.95	☐$5.95	

Members who wish to be mailed a printed copy of the Baseball Research Journal should add $7 per issue (U.S.) or $11 per issue (international). Two (2) issues of the BRJ are delivered each year.

SABR memberships are available on an annual, multi-year, or monthly subscription basis. Memberships auto-renew for your convenience. Young Professional memberships are for ages 30 and under. Student memberships are available to currently enrolled middle/high school or full-time college/university students. Monthly subscription members are eligible for SABR event discounts after 12 months.

Mail to: SABR, PO Box 1715, Milwaukee, WI 53201

The SABR Digital Library

Available wherever books are sold

The First Negro League Champion: The 1920 Chicago American Giants

Edited by Frederick C. Bush and Bill Nowlin

Paperback $29.95 244 pages • Ebook $9.99

This book chronicles the team which won the title of champion in the Negro National League's inaugural season. Rube Foster, a Hall of Famer, and his White business partner John Schorling are featured along with biographies of every player on the team include Cristóbal Torriente, a member of both the National Baseball Hall of Fame and the Cuban Baseball Hall of Fame, as well as early Blackball stalwarts Dave "Lefty" Brown, Bingo DeMoss, Judy Gans, Dave Malarcher, Frank Warfield, and Frank Wickware. A comprehensive timeline of the 1920 season and a history of the founding of the Negro National League are included.

We Are, We Can, We Will: The 1992 World Champion Toronto Blue Jays

Edited by Adrian Fung and Bill Nowlin

Forewords by Buck Martinez and Dave Winfield

Paperback US $34.95/Canada $41.95 394 pages • Ebook $9.99

The 1992 Toronto Blue Jays will always be remembered as the first World Series-winning club from Canada. After a near miss in 1991, the 1992 club confidently adopted "We Are, We Can, We Will" as their team motto. This book features biographies of every player who played for the 1992 Toronto Blue Jays including Hall of Famers Dave Winfield, Jack Morris, and Roberto Alomar. Manager Cito Gaston, Hall of Fame general manager Pat Gillick, and radio broadcaster Tom Cheek are also included, as well as a "ballpark biography" of SkyDome. Ten reports describe significant games from the 1992 season illustrating Toronto's championship journey from Opening Day to the last game of the World Series.

From Shibe Park to Connie Mack Stadium: Great Games in Philadelphia's Lost Ballpark

Edited by Gregory H. Wolf
Paperback $39.95 398 pages • Ebook $9.99

This collection evokes memories and the exciting history of the celebrated ballpark through stories of 100 games played there and several feature essays. The games included in this volume reflect every decade in the ballpark's history, from the inaugural game in 1909, to the last in 1970.

Shibe Park was the home of the Philadelphia A's from 1909 until their relocation to Kansas City and the Philadelphia Phillies from 1938 until the ballpark's closure at the end 1970. In 1953 it was renamed Connie Mack Stadium. The ballpark hosted big-league baseball for 62 seasons and more than 6,000 games—over 3,500 games by the A's and 2,500 by the Phillies—and was home to Frank Baker, Del Ennis, Chief Bender, and Robin Roberts.

¡Arriba!: The Heroic Life of Roberto Clemente

edited by Bill Nowlin and Glen Sparks

Paperback $34.95 338 pages • Ebook $9.99

2022 marks the 50th anniversary year of Roberto Clemente's passing. This book celebrates his life and baseball career. Named to 15 All-Star Game squads, Clemente won 12 Gold Gloves, four batting titles, and was the National League's Most Valuable Player in 1966. The first Latino inducted into the National Baseball Hall of Fame, Clemente played 18 seasons for the Pittsburgh Pirates and became the 11th player to reach the 3,000-hit milestone, hitting number 3000 on the season's last day. At the time no one knew he would never play baseball again. Clemente was known for his charitable work. He lost his life on the final day of 1972 while working to provide relief for victims of an earthquake in Nicaragua.

The SABR Digital Library

•••

Print & Ebooks

SABR.ORG
OR
WHEREVER
BOOKS ARE
SOLD

The Stars Shone on Philadelphia: The 1934 Phila. Stars
ISBN 978-1-960819-04-8 $9.99 ebook
ISBN 978-1-960819-05-5 $29.95 paperback
Biographies of Ed Bolden's 1934 Negro National League champions, including Biz Mackie and Jud Wilson.

Yankee Stadium: America's First Modern Ballpark
ISBN 978-1-960819-16-8 $9.99 ebook
ISBN 978-1-960819-21-5 $39.95 paperback
Essays about the history of Yankee Stadium and recaps of over 50 historic games and other events there, including papal visits, football, and more.

Ebbets Field: Great, Historic, and Memorable Games at Brooklyn's Lost Ballpark
ISBN 978-1-960819-16-1 $9.99 ebook
ISBN 978-1-960819-17-8 $39.95 paperback
Relive Jackie Robinson's and Sandy Koufax's debuts, and over 90 other heartbreaks and triumphs in Brooklyn, plus essays on the ballpark.

Nichibei Yakyu: Volume II: 1960-2019
ISBN 978-1-960819-14-7 $9.99 ebook
ISBN 978-1-960819-15-4 $34.95 paperback
Fascinating recaps of the exhibition tours and MLB games by US baseball teams in Japan.

Sox Bid Curse Farewell: The 2004 Boston Red Sox
ISBN 978-1-960819-18-5 $9.99 ebook
ISBN 978-1-960819-19-2 $34.95 paperback
Biographies of every player and coach on the 2004 World Championship team, as well as essays about the season, effects of the win on fans, and more.

Dodger Stadium: Blue Heaven on Earth
ISBN 978-1-960819-20-8 $9.99 ebook
ISBN 978-1-960819-21-5 $29.95 paperback
Essays about the history of Dodger Stadium and recaps of over 50 historic games there, from Fernandomania to Vin Scully's bow.

One-Win Wonders
ISBN 978-1-960819-13-0 $39.95 paperback
ISBN 978-1-960819-12-3 $9.99 ebook
Biographies of 78 players whose entire major league pitching record consisted of just one win, from the tragic, like Nick Adenhart, to the improbable, like catcher Brent Mayne.

Willie Mays: Five Tools
ISBN 978-1-960819-02-4 $9.99 ebook
ISBN 978-1-960819-03-1 $29.95 paperback
Twenty essays on Mays' life and career, plus recaps of 30 historic games.